RATIONALIZING CAPITALIST DEMOCRACY

RATIONALIZING CAPITALIST DEMOCRACY

The Cold War Origins of Rational Choice Liberalism

S. M. AMADAE

The University of Chicago Press
Chicago and London

S. M. Amadae is a research fellow in the Office for History of Science and Technology, University of California, Berkeley.

The University of Chicago Press, Chicago 60637
The University of Chicago Press, Ltd., London
© 2003 by The University of Chicago
All rights reserved. Published 2003
Printed in the United States of America
12 11 10 09 08 07 06 05 04 03   1 2 3 4 5

ISBN: 0-226-01653-6 (cloth)
ISBN: 0-226-01654-4 (paper)

Library of Congress Cataloging-in-Publication Data

Amadae, S. M.
    Rationalizing capitalist democracy : the Cold War origins of rational choice
liberalism / S. M. Amadae.
        p.   cm.
    Includes bibliographical references and index.
    ISBN 0-226-01653-6 (cloth : alk. paper)—ISBN 0-226-01654-4 (pbk. : alk. paper)
    1. Rational choice theory. 2. Liberalism—United States. 3. Capitalism—United
States. I. Title.

    HM495 .A46 2003
    301′.01—dc21

                                                                              2003008901

To Ethan Charles Stock

In memoriam Joseph John Kruzel
1945–1995

Joseph Kruzel dedicated his professional life to the field of national security affairs, both as an academic and as a practitioner. Joe began working at the Pentagon immediately following his graduation from the Air Force Academy in 1967, and he earned his Master of Public Affairs degree from the Kennedy School of Government at Harvard in 1969.

While on active duty for five years, Kruzel served as an intelligence officer in Vietnam and as a briefing officer for the Joint Chiefs of Staff. He also served as a member of the U.S. delegation to the Strategic Arms Limitation Talks (SALT I), where he developed an international reputation as a skilled negotiator and earned the Distinguished Service Award in recognition of his contribution.

Joe earned his Ph.D. from Harvard in 1975 and he taught at both Harvard and Duke before becoming director of the Program on International Security and Military Affairs at the Ohio State University. Wherever he went, Joe inspired and encouraged students as they searched for their personal and professional paths in life, and was selected by students at both Duke and Ohio State as an outstanding teacher. While at Ohio State, he remained a valuable contributor in Washington, serving as a consultant to the State Department, USAID, the Defense Department, and Congress, and as a member of Senator Edward Kennedy's staff.

Joe returned to Washington in 1993 as deputy assistant secretary of defense for European and NATO policy. One of his very first undertakings was to help create the Partnership for Peace, an initiative designed to bring former Warsaw Pact nations closer to NATO. His vision for lasting peace in Europe has been instrumental in bringing greater stability to the region.

In the summer of 1995, reports of ethnic cleansing and mass killings in the former Yugoslavia shocked the world's conscience. Because of his expertise and skillful diplomacy, Kruzel was appointed chief negotiator for the Department of Defense on the U.S. team working to end the conflict. While in Bosnia helping to broker peace, he was killed outside Sarajevo on August 19, 1995. I will never forget receiving that awful news. Just days earlier I had spoken with him on the phone about his becoming my successor as assistant secretary.

Joe's friends and colleagues remember him for his humor, energy, and brilliance, and his dedication to the pursuit of peace. President Clinton said at his memorial service: "The world is a more secure place because of Joe's dedication. May God bless Joe Kruzel, for he was a peacemaker."

—Joseph S. Nye Jr., Harvard University

CONTENTS

ACKNOWLEDGMENTS

I am grateful to many for invaluable conversations, insights, and comments: Amartya Sen, Emma Rothschild, Richard Tuck, Onora O'Neill, Simon Blackburn, Simon Schaffer, Edward McClennen, Robert Sugden, Richard Bradley, Nancy Cartwright, Mary Morgan, David Held, Kenneth Arrow, James Buchanan, Mancur Olson, Thomas Schelling, Kenneth Shepsle, William Niskanen, Steven Medema, Knud Haakonssen, Bruce Bueno de Mesquita, Susan Okin, Robert Bellah, Robert Powell, Shannon Stimson, David Hollinger, Martin Jay, Peter Galison, Robert Cooter, Greg Herken, Bruce Kuklick, John Heilbron, Jill Hargis, Till Grüne, Raja Sengupta, and the two anonymous reviewers of the manuscript. Any miscarriages of understanding are my sole responsibility.

I am indebted to Ethan Stock, who spared no intellectual effort, logistical aid, or emotional support to make this book possible. As well, I would like to thank John Tryneski, Elaine Chandler, Monica Kaufer, Betty Tillman, Diana Wear, Martin White, Leslie Keros, David Bemelmans, Sameer Pabari, Rebecca Hampton, Craig Calcaterra, Noel Stephens, Kate Evans, Brian Coyle, Arthur Bohren, Warrick Taylor, Fiona Steel, Alex Pasteur, Marianne Vizinczey-Lambert, Susan Spath, Márcia Balisciano, Nima Amini, Melissa Kincaid, Aisha Moore, Paul Atwell, and my family for their vital contributions. This book is dedicated in part to Joe Kruzel, honoring him as mentor and friend.

The following provided institutional support during the time of research and writing: the East-West Center, Honolulu, Hawaii; the Centre for Philosophy of Natural and Social Science, London School of Economics; Trinity College, Cambridge University; Office for the History of Science and Technology, University of California, Berkeley; the department of political science, University of Rochester; and the Doreen B. Townsend Center for Humanities, University of California, Berkeley. I appreciate the assistance of Jonathan Green at the Ford Foundation, and Janey Morris at the Rare Book, Manuscripts, and Special Collections Library, Duke University. Finally, I would like to thank the editors of the *Annual Review of Political Science* for permission to use portions of S. M. Amadae and Bruce Bueno de Mesquita, "The Rochester School: The Origins of Positive Political Theory," in *Annual Review of Political Science,* ed. Nelson W. Polsby, vol. 2 (Palo Alto: Annual Reviews, 1999), 269–95.

INTRODUCTION

From George Kennan's admonition in 1946 that communism must be contained, until the fall of the Soviet empire in December 1991, the central organising principle for America and much of the west was the cold war effort to contain the spread of communism. . . . The United States [has been] triumphant in the ideological and quasi-military struggle with communism.
Gary Hart

The great struggles of the twentieth century between liberty and totalitarianism ended with a decisive victory for the forces of freedom—and a single sustainable model for national success: freedom, democracy, and free enterprise. . . . These values of freedom are right and true for every person, in every society.
George W. Bush

DURING the decade since the sudden and dramatic collapse of communism in the Soviet Union and Eastern Europe, two aspects of the West's triumph have been predominant in our understanding. The first of these aspects is the military containment of the Soviet Union, a decades-long struggle of both cold and hot war, played out in many theaters, through proxy states, military aid, and open battle. The second is the economic triumph of the West; in the final analysis, the Soviet Union could no longer afford to both feed and house its people and pursue a global tit-for-tat struggle against the more productive, more efficient, more capable and advanced economies of the West.

Overlooked in this two-part perception is the fundamental and foundational third aspect of victory: the ideological triumph of democratic politics and market economies over the alternative philosophical order proposed by Karl Marx and his adherents. While it is unquestionable that military and economic efforts were the means by which the Cold War victory was delivered, it is less clearly understood that the ideological victory of the West was the motivation behind them. This book is the story of the ideological war against communist and totalitarian forms of economic

1

and political order. A gauntlet was thrown down by an earlier generation of scholars who sought to rescue capitalist democracy from the threat of authoritarian socialism. It was taken up after World War II by a new generation, who fought with tenacity, and won in such absolute terms that it is difficult for a present-day observer to grasp the scope of the victory that was won.

One aspect to our partial understanding of the Cold War struggle is the tendency, particularly in the United States, to think of that struggle as an external one, against a nation-state foe, the Soviet Union. With occasional dramatic exceptions such as the McCarthy hearings, our modern-day perspective is that Marxism was never a serious internal threat to the political or economic order among the nations of the West, particularly the United States. Again, this viewpoint is partial and ahistorical. As I discuss in the prelude, during the 1930s and 1940s there was a pervasive sense of dismay and defeat among the intellectuals of the West over what they took to be the inevitability of the triumph, both internal and external, of fascist or communist alternatives to democratic capitalism. Marxism—forged during the early days of mass production, mass warfare, and mass democracy—appeared to be the inevitable, if not yet victorious, structural principle that eventually would govern world affairs.

Of course, just the opposite occurred. Marxism, communism, and the Soviet Union have all attenuated to nearly nothing, and any proposed alternative to democracy and capitalism in today's world is dismissed as quaint nostalgia, recidivist tribalism, or authoritarian dictatorship, soon to be swept away into the dustbin of history. This state of affairs recently led one observer to note that

> the truly profound consequence is ideological. Marxism is utterly vanquished, if not yet entirely extinct, as an alternative economic system. Capitalism is triumphant. The ideological conflict first joined in the mid-nineteenth century in response to the rise of industrial capitalism, the deep argument that has preoccupied political imagination for 150 years, is ended.[1]

Despite the almost smug perceptions of today, capitalism's victory was not historically inevitable. It was deliberately fought, and actively won, in a story coterminous with the several-centuries-long modern experiment with economic and political liberalism. This philosophic victory over Marx's critique of bourgeoisie political economy is, indeed, a capital accomplishment.

This book recounts the defeat of Marxism by rational choice liberalism: a philosophy of markets and democracy that was developed in part to anchor the foundations of American society during the Cold War. From the closing days of World War II to the mid-1980s, rational choice theory rebuilt the conceptual cornerstones of Western ideals. The effects of that reconstruction, however, transcended the end of the Cold War. The philosophical offensive marshaled by rational choice theorists responded to Marxism and had profound implications for democratic theory heretofore best characterized as an expanding "public sphere" set into motion by Enlightenment printing presses, bourgeoisie social strata, and a quest for individual liberty, culminating in John Dewey's *The Public and Its Problems*.[2] The increasing enfranchisement of the population and the movement toward mass democracy led to tensions within the demos that already had been catalogued by Alexis de Tocqueville and John Stuart Mill.[3]

During the early decades of the twentieth century, American political theorists strove to uphold the republican ideals of the founders in the face of devastating critiques of the meaningfulness of rule "by, of, and for the people." Rousseau's "general will," it was thought, had potentially fascist implications of recognizing a collective entity above and beyond the individuals comprising the state. Walter Lippmann questioned the legitimacy and relevance of public rule in *The Phantom Public*.[4] Joseph Schumpeter and Friedrich Hayek expressed articulate pessimism that public welfare could be surmised from the disparate interests and voices of the people. Yet, despite the worries about the mechanism of creating a viable democracy, no midcentury Western theorist was prepared to give up the democratic ideal for either fascist or totalitarian alternatives. Clearly, democracy needed a new theoretical basis to shore it up against the fearsome tides of organic or group theories that threatened to subsume individuals and their aspirations for freedom.

Thus, a new approach to democracy emerged in Cold War America, one based on the notion of the "rational actor," which was quickly assimilated into the traditions of political and economic liberalism that underlie the modern experiment with democracy and capitalism. The self-interested, strategic rational actor became the central figure around which the reexamination of traditional Enlightenment themes and problems of government was based. The set-theoretic and axiomatic treatment of human rationality came to serve as the new standard for describing the zenith of human consciousness, and could be used as a virtual litmus test to determine if one were a liberal individualist or an irrational collectivist: rational choice theory holds that rational individuals do not cooperate to achieve common goals unless coerced, in direct contradiction to the precepts of Marxism and communism.[5] The methodological assumptions of universal and objective scientific law, individualism, and rational self-interest structure the theory.

Rational choice liberalism, the linchpin of the triumphant West's ideological victory over Soviet communism, initially postulated an implicit and inevitable linkage between free-market economics and democratic politics. However, one profound consequence of the scrupulous individualism of rational choice, echoing latent concerns over postulating a "general will," has been a growing skepticism over the inherent meaningfulness of "the public," "public interest," or "general welfare." This skepticism grows out of the doubt that procedures of collective decisionmaking can achieve rational outcomes, even in the best of circumstances. It is not without historical irony that the ideological front of American society's hard-fought war against communism and the Soviet Union may, inadvertently, have eroded the meaningfulness of the term "American society."

The increasing disrepute of the concept of the public has been accompanied by a significant change in language of sovereignty. It has become commonplace to discuss sovereignty in terms of consumers' choices rather than within the familiar language of citizenship. Recognizing this change of perspective, Eric Hobsbawm points to a recent turn "among politicians and ideologists to an ultra-radical, *laissez-faire* critique of the state. . . . [T]he state tends to rely on private economic mechanisms to replace the active and passive mobilisation of its citizens." Hobsbawm goes on to trace a key transition in the concept of sovereignty over the past quarter century that accompanies the noticeable shift in democratic theory to doubt the *respublica:*

> Market sovereignty is not a complement to liberal democracy: it is an alternative to it. Indeed, it is an alternative to any kind of politics, as it denies the need for *political* decisions, which are precisely decisions about common or group interests as distinct from the sum of choices, rational or otherwise, of individuals pursuing private preferences. Participating in the market replaces participation in politics.[6]

To the point, Hobsbawm observes, "The consumer takes the place of the citizen."[7]

Kenneth Arrow's 1951 *Social Choice and Individual Values,* one of the earliest texts in the post–World War II rational choice canon, mathematically defines "citizens' sovereignty" in terms equivalent to the prevailing economic concept of "consumer sovereignty." The text discusses political decisions specifically as Hobsbawm suggests, "as a sum of choices . . . of individuals pursuing private preferences." No concept of "common or group interests," or of the public, survives Arrow's analysis.

Whereas the mathematics underlying rational choice theory is so rec-
ondite as to require the likes of the recently popularized game theorist and
Nobel laureate John Nash to fully understand its mathematical intricacies, the degree to which it has come to pervade the popular discourse by
the early years of the twenty-first century cannot be overestimated.[8] This
nearly universal presence is driven by the gradual spread, from the 1970s
onward, of the tenets of rational choice theory into leading financial, policy, educational, and legal institutions, which have adopted its language
and approaches to decisionmaking problems. Thus, for example, it has
become a matter of routine economic understanding that all decisions,
from the most banal to the most excruciating, can be made in terms of a
measurable scale of trade-offs. A recent *Economist* article makes this
point with respect to difficult environmental decisions:

> Almost all economists are intellectually committed to the idea that the
> things people want can be valued in dollars and cents. If this is true, and
> things such as clean air, stable sea levels, tropical forests and species diver-
> sity can be valued that way, then environmental issues submit—or so it
> is argued—quite readily to the disciplines of economic analysis. Trade-
> offs can be struck between competing ends, in principle at least, and one
> can begin to think about how the world's consumption of environmental
> goods can be optimised, as economists say, subject to the constraint that
> people cannot have everything they want. . . . [T]he fact remains that
> choices must be made. Even if environmentalists ruled the world, difficult
> choices would have to be confronted—and, working backwards from those
> choices, made according to whatever criteria, it will always be possible to
> calculate economic values that were implicitly attached to different envi-
> ronmental goods. . . . [T]rade-offs, measurable in dollar terms, had in fact
> been struck.[9]

This idea that *all* decisions can be made as rational trade-offs on a com-
mensurate scale of preferences is nonsensical without its basis in rational
choice theory.

Rational choice theory proposes that rational agents have a consistent
set of preferences and act to obtain that which they most prefer. The theory pertains to both parametric environments and strategic environments
with other self-interested rational actors, as well as to uncertain and risky
circumstances. The term "self-interest" encompasses both selfish and altruistic preferences, although most often theorists accept that agents are
self-interested in a narrowly construed, self-oriented manner. For example, Anthony Downs stipulates that "whenever we speak of rational
behavior, we always mean rational behavior directed primarily to selfish
ends."[10] Rational choice is normative, prescriptive, and descriptive in

scope, and it is applied to individuals in varying decisionmaking contexts using highly abstract, mathematically expressed conditions. The theory both defines the conditions to which rational agency must conform, and can be used to explain and predict the actions of agents supposed to be rational. The project of fully exploring the nuances of rational decision-making deserves recognition as a remarkable expression of Western civilization's ongoing fascination with reason.

That the West today is permeated with the precepts of rational choice is clear: the language of that theory is pervasive in articles such as the one quoted above from the *Economist;* rational choice is deployed as an analytical tool by the World Bank and the judicial bench; it tacitly underpinned the emergence of the "Washington Consensus" in development economics in the 1990s.[11] Moreover, in moments of profound stress, when questions of self-identity and values come to the fore, once again rational choice is central. Writing for the *New Yorker* in its response to the September 11, 2001 World Trade Center tragedy, Hendrik Hertzberg stated:

> The calamity, of course, goes well beyond the damage to our city and to its similarly bereaved rival brother Washington. It is national; it is international; it is civilizational. In the decade since the end of the Cold War, the human race has become, with increasing rapidity, a single organism. Every kind of barrier to the free and rapid movement of goods, information, and people has been lowered. The organism relies increasingly on a kind of trust—the unsentimental expectation that people, individually and collectively, will behave more or less in their rational self-interest.[12]

Hertzberg suggests that rational self-interest is the main driver of capitalism, democracy, and civilization. He goes on to suggest that the terrorists involved in the attack on America were irrational. Whether or not the terrorists may be understood as rational within their own set of incentives and rewards is not the primary point of interest. What is key is the extent to which Western theories of economic and political liberalism have come to squarely rest on the concept of self-interested rational action.

The success of rational choice theory in defeating ideological alternatives and in reconstituting Westerners' views of commerce, politics, and scientific inquiry is due to its extraordinary reach and impact within the academic arena. The catalyst for the novel axiomatic approach to human rationality was John von Neumann and Oskar Morgenstern's *Theory of Games and Economic Behavior,* published in 1944. Von Neumann and Morgenstern, a Hungarian mathematical physicist and an Austrian economist, introduced the study of interactions between strategic actors by mathematically defining what it means to be "rational" in all conceivable decision contexts involving payoffs against the actions of other similar actors. Written for economists, their 450-page tome, brimming with equations, failed to stir much interest in the mainstream academic field. Von Neumann was not lacking in options, however. His wide range of scientific researches—including the axiomatic analysis of quantum physics, and his experience as a scientific advisor to the Manhattan Project and to submarine warfare during World War II—led him to explore the possibilities for the strategic significance of the new game theory within the arena of nuclear warfare. There was as yet no standard operating procedure for atomic weapons strategy, and over the next several years the new science of decisionmaking provided by game theory proved to be well suited to the unprecedented bipolar nuclear standoff between the Unites States and the Soviet Union. Both von Neumann and the new theoretical approach soon found a home, the Santa Monica-based RAND Corporation, where game theory was enthusiastically developed during the late 1940s and 1950s.[13]

Game theory developed as one branch of the Cold War rationality project that received its initial funding and prestige, and much of its inspiration, from its promise to best the Soviets by providing a means to arrive at sound tactical and strategic decisions. *Theory of Games and Economic Behavior* contained an appendix on "expected utility theory" that set forth axioms for rational decisionmaking in risky and uncertain circumstances. Within a few years, RAND theorists Duncan Luce and Howard Raiffa published their textbook on the innovative science of decisionmaking in which they discussed both strategic rational action in games and rationality in cases where outcomes were only known probabilistically.[14] Luce and Raiffa stressed how their approach differed from the earlier optimization techniques used by economists. In their view, the new science of rational decision was not limited to constrained optimization problems of scarce resource allocation, but instead addressed all conceivable situations of rational decisionmaking.[15] Their research was at the center of a vortex of activities from which the new axiomatic treatment of human action in strategic and uncertain scenarios would spread to other areas and disciplines.

Over the following decades, many of the keenest minds in America and throughout the world were devoted to further delineating the science of rational choice. This effort was coincident with the forays into linear and dynamic programming, and with the artificial intelligence explorations of von Neumann and Herbert Simon.[16] At the core of these endeavors was the axiomatic treatment of "rationality," whether in the axioms of strategic interactions, of uncertainty, or of individual and collective choice.[17] In the context of this research, the rationality project is better thought of as a normative and prescriptive science of decisionmaking, because it is highly abstract and does not necessarily pertain to the average person's approach to making choices.[18] As the new corpus of ideas developed, especially within the context of military strategy, it was thought of more as a guide to rational action than a matter of empirical description.

The excitement surrounding game theory soon became a catalyst for change in a number of academic and managerial fields. Economics, operations research, and public policy were readily transformed by the new decision techniques. Other American social sciences also responded to the opportunities made possible by this new science of choice: William Riker pioneered positive political theory in political science; James Coleman developed the rational choice approach in sociology; and the psychologists Amos Tversky and Daniel Kahneman undertook experimental tests of the validity of the rational choice axioms in actual decision situations.[19] Beginning in the late 1960s and 1970s, evolutionary biologists began to incorporate the results of game theory in the concept of the "selfish gene" and in biological studies of altruism and cooperation.[20] The rationality project became central in much of American philosophy through the work of Patrick Suppes, Donald Davidson, and David Lewis. Today, its reach extends to the professional programs and daily practice of business, public policy and law, while game-theoretic simulations play a key role in Wall Street portfolio management; it is fair to conclude that by the close of the twentieth century, rational choice theory had become part of the mainstream intellectual endowment of the United States and continues today to have increasing relevance worldwide.

The various branches of the rationality project can be categorized as the study of either individual or collective decisionmaking; game theory is relevant to both branches, because it can be pursued either from the first-person viewpoint of one individual (or nation) seeking to "win" or from the systemic perspective of collective action problems resulting in either unstable social outcomes or in stable "equilibria." Whereas decision theory focuses on individuals' rational attainment of "expected utility," the social sciences that employ rational choice theory concentrate on collective action problems that give rise to complex social phenomena.

The term "rational choice theory" may be used to refer to either the individual or collective branch of study within the encompassing rationality project. Most often, it refers in the social sciences specifically to the study of interactions between two or more individuals resulting in collective outcomes that may be modeled, assuming that the individual agents act in accordance with the rationality axioms. The rational actor formalism offers a precise mathematical means to make predictions about how strategically self-interested agents will interact to produce collective outcomes. Rational choice theorists seek to explain and predict agents' individual and collective actions in political environments such as elections, legislative committees, political party platform formation, constitutional design, as well as individuals' religious affiliations. They have also developed specific tools and concepts for studying collective action problems, thereby bringing such phrases and terms as "tragedy of the commons," "free rider," and "Prisoner's dilemma" into common parlance.

Rational choice theory has provided an innovative means to study the process and efficacy of collective decisionmaking, and has been used to analyze the normative foundations of democratic institutions and public policy. It has offered a fresh approach to what is considered to be a long-standing problem of political action: how individuals' actions can be co-ordinated to achieve effective and legitimate government. Rational choice approaches to politics represent a focused attempt to solve a set of puzzles about upholding individual freedom and achieving a just government reflecting citizens' interests, puzzles that have characterized the discourse of liberal democracy for the past two centuries.

THIS book provides a narrative account of the ascendancy of rational choice theory in the fields of public policy, social choice theory, public choice theory, and positive political theory, and it seeks to understand how and why rational choice has become preeminent. Understanding both the significance of the ideas constituting rational choice and the theory's multiple, interrelated roles is key to this effort: the theory serves as a public policy tool, as a highly abstract approach to social science, and as a philosophic underpinning for American economic and political liberalism. Achieving an adequate sense of the scope and reach of the theory can seem to be an overwhelming project if not approached methodically. This is because the full extent of the rationality project, combined with the tremendous ferment it has generated in social science in addition to its significant impact on democratic theory, could easily fill the pages of multiple volumes.[21] This book focuses exclusively on rational choice theory as it pertains to collective decision problems characteristic of democratic government.

In part 1, my account of the meteoric rise of rational choice theory begins at the RAND Corporation. RAND was not only the nation's first think tank but also was at the center of American Cold War efforts to generate a science of military strategy to aid leaders in making superior decisions. This science, drafted on RAND's drawing boards, was to be relevant to all levels of decisionmaking, from strategy and defense budgets to weapons design. Confidence that policymakers could use decision tools to make rational choices in warfare was soon transferred to the domestic front.

The history of the development and establishment of policy science as an institutionalized and disciplinary norm has all the drama of a Hollywood screenplay involving the missile gap, the Sputniks, John F. Kennedy's presidential election, the overhaul of decisionmaking procedures throughout Robert S. McNamara's Department of Defense, and the introduction of these same policy tools into domestic politics in Lyndon B. Johnson's Great Society program. This set of events gathered a momentum of its own but had crucial intersections with rational choice theory's development in the academy. Two vignettes illustrate the extent of these interconnections. Thomas Schelling, one of the key figures in establishing rational choice theory as mainstay approach to international relations, was one of RAND's alumni who formed McNamara's team of defense analysts in the Pentagon.[22] In a pivotal series of U.S. Senate hearings, Schelling testified on the behalf of the administration about the development and use of rational policy tools throughout the U.S. Department of Defense in 1968. Subsequently he and other RAND alumni, including Howard Raiffa, helped to establish rational choice theory as part of the mainstream American intellectual endowment by virtue of their prominent academic posts at Harvard University's professional school of business. The rational policy analysis approach initiated at RAND would become central to the shift during the 1970s away from the outmoded "public administration" paradigm to one of "public policy," a shift that was evident in the restructuring and renaming of Harvard University's John F. Kennedy School of Government.

Daniel Ellsberg, etched into the nation's memory in 1971 for his controversial and unauthorized release of the so-called Pentagon Papers, was, like Schelling, a RAND alumni ushered into the halls of the defense establishment as part of the McNamara team.[23] Ellsberg, a mathematical prodigy, completed his Harvard undergraduate degree at record speed. At RAND, he contributed to the foundations of decision theory, raising such a significant challenge to one of the fundamental axioms of expected utility theory, referred to as the "sure thing principle," that it has yet to be resolved.[24] Ellsberg proved to be not just a maverick within the rationality project, but also a rebel within McNamara's Department of Defense, similarly posing it with a challenge from which it never recovered. Ellsberg's parallel roles, as a key contributor to the science of rational choice and as a bureaucrat working to reinstitutionalize military decisionmaking, demonstrate the profound overlap between the two worlds of academic rational choice theory and public policy.[25] The rising tide of academic rational choice theory is confluent with the institutional prestige and weight of established practice achieved by practitioners of the new decision sciences. The routinization of social practices around abstract decision tools gave these tools a de facto legitimacy: as Schelling testified, no one knew if the decision tools actually achieved better decisions, but the tools had theoretic legitimacy insofar as they claimed to be based on scientific analysis, and had practical legitimacy sheerly as a consequence of their use. This tendency of the new rational policy tools to attain stature through their widespread use can also be seen in McNamara's eventual departure from the Pentagon and rapid installation as the president of the World Bank, pioneering yet another venue, this time international, for rational policy tools.[26]

It is no exaggeration to say that virtually all the roads to rational choice theory lead from RAND. This observation draws attention to its role as a quintessential American Cold War institution, and in turn to the Cold War motives that underlay much of the impetus propagating rational choice theory. While RAND was one of several foci for the development of decision theory—along with the Chicago-based Cowles Commission, the Public Choice Society, and the University of Rochester's political science department—its members and alumni played an especially pivotal role in making rational choice part of the established American institutional endowment. In the late 1940s and 1950s, there was active sharing of resources and ideas between RAND and the Cowles Commission; in the 1960s many rational choice pioneers from all walks of the academy participated in Public Choice Society meetings; also in the 1960s, University of Rochester political science students benefited from summer workshops on game theory held at RAND.

In the book's second part I demonstrate how, within the university, rational choice theory developed as a series of overlapping, multidisciplinary revolutions. This account replaces two commonly accepted but simplistic views of its generation. Most often, practicing researchers find it helpful to think of the roots of the rational choice tradition as comprising the seven canonical works that by consensus continue to anchor the field: von Neumann and Morgenstern's *Theory of Games and Economic Behavior* (1944); Duncan Black's "On the Rationale of Group Decision Making" (1948); Kenneth J. Arrow's *Social Choice and Individual Values* (1951); Anthony Downs's *An Economic Theory of Democracy* (1957); James M. Buchanan and Gordon Tullock's *The Calculus of Consent*

(1962); William H. Riker's *The Theory of Political Coalitions* (1965); and Mancur Olson Jr.'s *The Logic of Collective Action* (1965). However, understanding this rational choice canon as the exclusive and exhaustive foundation of the movement obscures the fact that in actuality the key texts of the canon in themselves represent the three distinct disciplinary transformations that structure part 2 of this book: social choice, public choice, and positive political theory. Furthermore, representing the rational choice canon as a single, unified trajectory obscures our understanding of how the rational choice canon developed as a "complex of knowledge," characterized by distinct hubs of activity with shared researchers, institutions, ideas, and funding patterns. Concentrating on a canon distracts our attention away from its embodiment in concrete institutions and tangible networks of people. The pathbreaking rational choice scholars all shared two institutional foci crucial to the institutional and professional success of rational choice. Von Neumann, Arrow, Downs, Buchanan, and Olson were affiliated with RAND; and Black, Downs, Riker, Tullock, Buchanan, and Olson were members of the Public Choice Society.

A second frequently held idea about the development of rational choice theory is that it is sufficient to focus on rational choice as a disciplinary revolution in political science or in other social sciences—including economics, sociology, and psychology—to comprehend the essence of the movement. Thus, for example, Gabriel Almond discusses how rational choice theory represents a Kuhnian-style disciplinary revolution in political science.[27] This focus on individual social sciences, or on social science in general, fails to adequately grasp the historical development of rational choice theory, although it is useful to have a sense of disciplinary transformation within disciplinary boundaries. Thus, while articles like the one by Almond are helpful, they are incomplete in not appreciating the manner in which the impetus behind the successful promulgation of rational choice theory had a much broader point of reference than any particular social science or the social sciences as a whole.

The three chapters that address Arrow's social choice theory, Buchanan and Tullock's public choice theory, and Riker's positive political theory explore the significance of the rational choice approach to politics for grounding American capitalist democracy. In its guise as "objective" or "value free" social science, it is difficult to appreciate the full import of social choice, public choice, and positive political theory for reconceptualizing the basic building blocks of political liberalism. In light of the Cold War ideological struggle against the Soviets, this enterprise of securing the philosophical basis of free world institutions was critical. Not surprisingly, Arrow, Buchanan, Tullock, and Riker pitched their newly forged social scientific method as part of the campaign to reassert the tenets of governmental rule legitimized by popular consent, but not susceptible to fascist or authoritarian perversions. The preeminent status attained by rational choice theory throughout American academia is indistinguishable from the vital Cold War activity of reconstituting democratic theory in the wake of Hitler's and Stalin's transgressions against humanity. Appraising the significance of social science methodology for American liberalism requires understanding the nuanced manner in which it refashioned the theoretical cogency and institutional integrity of democracy. Democratic theory itself required revision because its prior reliance on "public opinion," "popular sovereignty," or a "general will" had been severely challenged. Rational choice scholars simultaneously rebuilt the theoretical foundations of American capitalist democracy and defeated idealist, collectivist, and authoritarian social theories. Now that it is apparent that capitalism and democracy have prevailed over Soviet communism and Marxism, it is worth knowing the precise series of arguments through which such a philosophical victory, as important as a military victory, was won. Part 2 tells this story.

Part 3 of the book enlarges the context for assessing the significance of rational choice theory by viewing it against the backdrop of the prior two centuries. This task has been divided into two halves. Granted that rational choice theory is a major contribution to the liberal project of advancing individualism, reason, liberty, and univeralism, it is important to ask precisely how this late-twentieth-century project fits in with the long-abiding tradition of liberalism extending back at least into the Enlightenment. To whittle this question down to manageable proportions, chapter 6 is cast as a comparison of James Buchanan's public choice theory with Adam Smith's system of natural liberty. My goal is to achieve a clear sense of the manner in which rational choice theory stands as a major contribution to Western liberal theory. I find that whereas rational choice theory upholds Smith's project of looking for a just legal framework in which individuals' ends are mutually coordinated, it departs from Smith's approach in resting entirely on the principle of self-interest, as opposed to other human sentiments such as sympathy.

Chapter 7 addresses the relationship between rational choice theory and nineteenth-century marginalist economics, often thought to be its theoretical precursor. This investigation is crucial for determining that rational choice theory and the rationality project are wholly novel theoretical contributions that cannot be understood in terms of marginalist economists' language of "constrained maximization." Whereas the language of "maximizing utility" appears to be coextensive with both marginalism and rational decision theory, in fact the mathematical formalisms underlying the two theories are wholly distinct. In this chapter I further contrast marginalist economics and rational choice theory with instrumental reason, and find greater dissonance than similarity. Finally, marginalist versus rational choice approaches to cost-benefit analysis are discussed to highlight their readily apparent differences. The point of this chapter is to show that rational choice theory is neither a progressive refinement of marginalist economics nor instrumental reason, but instead represents an innovative approach to the study of decisionmaking.

Part 4 places the discussion of rational choice theory in the present context by considering the traditional relationship between American political science and American democracy. Throughout American history the two have been intertwined, and rational choice theory now takes it rightful place within that tradition. Using John Rawls's 1971 *Theory of Justice* as a watershed contribution to American political theory, this chapter articulates the relationship of Rawls's project to that of rational choice theorists. Chapter 8 elaborates the full development of a coherent position of rational choice liberalism in dialogue with Rawls over utilitarianism, social welfare, and liberty as found in the writings of Kenneth Arrow, John Harsanyi, Amartya Sen, and Robert Sugden. Each theorist endorses the characteristic premises grounding rational choice: individualism, universalism, objectivity, and rationality. A second, similarly committed, generation of theorists—Russell Hardin, David Gauthier, Ken Binmore, and Edward McClennen—present their own visions for achieving stable social order. Rational choice liberalism, as the nonnormative, nonideological search for an institutional framework that respects individual liberty and coordinates individuals' self-interested ends, is a vibrant contribution to the two-centuries-long experiment with democracy and capitalism; though not without staunch critics, it has attracted adherents worldwide.

Schumpeter, Hayek, and Popper

If we are to succeed in the war of ideologies and to win over the decent elements in the enemy countries, we must first of all regain the belief in the traditional values [of individual freedom, truth, and democracy].
Friedrich Hayek

Can capitalism survive? No. I do not think it can.
Joseph Schumpeter

THE Cold War has a wholly different appearance when considered from the perspective of 1945 rather than 1991. The victory of the Allies over the Axis powers, culminating in the use of the atomic bomb and erection of the Iron Curtain, brought at least as many uncertainties as it brought triumphs. Sober intellectuals doubted the future of capitalist democracy on a world stage playing host to fascist and totalitarian rivals. Despite the exact correspondence of the phenomenal rise of rational choice theory with the Cold War period, few theorists now appreciate the profound interconnections between the development of that apparently objective social science methodology and the ideological clash between the two superpowers. In order to understand the scope of vision and magnitude of accomplishment that characterize this Cold War rational choice project, we must come to terms with the widely perceived doubts concerning the integrity of Western institutions at the close of World War II. It was this radical questoning, whether prompted by heartfelt concern or opportunism, that generated the movement that would transform American social science and political theory, as it simultaneously impacted public policy and jurisprudence.

The chapters that follow make evident how rational choice theory was structured to sustain a philosophical foundation for American capitalist democracy. The synthesis of rational choice theory, and the closely related "rationality project," had its impetus in the Cold War social drama, and it met America's acute societal challenge of providing social science with

15

a methodological basis negating the organicist or idealist social thought that was feared to support communism. Joseph Schumpeter, Friedrich Hayek, and Karl Popper starkly delineated this palpable threat in their urgent pleas during World War II, pleas that would be heard by the next generation of social scientists. Kenneth Arrow, James Buchanan, and William Riker took up the gauntlet; they developed a theoretical vessel that could navigate the impending perils of organic constructions of statehood, idealist and potentially coercive political philosophy, and conceptions of science vulnerable to relativism. The Austrian trio bemoaned the totalitarian menace threatening "the essential tenets of the liberal faith—individualism, rationalism, political and economic freedom."[1] The emergence during the Cold War generation of rational choice theorists not only rescued these tenets, but used them as a foundation to built a robust and renewed social science capable of sustaining American capitalism and democracy.

Schumpeter's *Capitalism, Socialism, and Democracy* (1943), Hayek's *The Road to Serfdom* (1944), and Popper's *The Open Society and Its Enemies* (1945) convey the tenuous foothold of Western institutions of democracy, capitalism, and science before the rational choice revolution. These three widely read books, each expressing grave apprehension over the future viability of these sacred institutions, outlined the philosophical crises at the heart of Western civilization. Schumpeter and Popper devoted much of their works to analyzing Marx's critique of capitalism; Hayek turned his attention to the ills of socialism and collectivism more generally. Each liberal theorist, to an extent unimaginable from our perspective following the collapse of Soviet communism, readily admitted that capitalism run wholly according to the *laissez faire* ideal did not strike the appropriate balance between social justice and economic freedom and was therefore untenable.[2]

Schumpeter believed that the demise of capitalism was inescapable and that socialism would triumph. Far from presenting the sort of defense of free-market capitalism and democracy confidently assumed today by *Forbes* magazine, his fundamental conviction in *Capitalism, Socialism, and Democracy* is that "a socialist form of society will inevitably emerge from an equally inevitable decomposition of capitalist society."[3] Why would Schumpeter write "so laborious and complex an analysis . . . to establish what is rapidly becoming the general opinion, even among conservatives?"[4] Because he wishes to conclude, contrary to Marx, that "capitalism is being killed by its achievements," not by its failures. Schumpeter finds, as a result of the socialist calculation debate, that socialism presents a viable system. In the final pages of his work, however, he argues that "[a]s a matter of practical necessity, socialist democracy may eventually turn out to be more of a sham than capitalist democracy ever was," and that socialist democracy "will not mean increased personal freedom."[5] Schumpeter's last-ditch argument against socialism rests on his conclusion that ultimately, socialist society cannot support democracy because it does not sustain pluralism.[6] He argues that a capitalist clash of economic interests is necessary for maintaining economic and intellectual pluralism underlying the competition of interests on which democratic society rests.[7]

Schumpeter's defense of capitalism for protecting political freedom may be considered a prelude to Anthony Downs's rational choice classic *An Economic Theory of Democracy*.[8] Certainly, the Cold War juxtaposition of democracy versus communism as alternative political forms organized according to unique principles was evident to Stanley Kelly Jr., who wrote the foreword to Downs's path-breaking text. Kelly observes:

> It is a fact that competitive party systems are a conspicuous feature of virtually all those nations the non-Communist world thinks of as democratic. . . . A theory of democracy that fails to take account of this fact is of little help in giving us an appreciation of the kinds of actions we may expect of democratic government.[9]

In acknowledging the theoretical confluence of Schumpeter's and Downs's approaches, present-day scholars note that both focus on democracy as a "competition in the economic sphere," and both understand that "the democratic method is that institutional arrangement for arriving at political decisions in which individuals acquire the power to decide by means of a competitive struggle for people's vote."[10] For Schumpeter, democracy is sustained by competing economic interests that no longer exist in a monolithic socialist state. Downs, in analyzing democratic politics as a competitive system akin to the marketplace, suggests that democracy draws its vitality and its legitimacy from economic-style competition not possible under communism. Both Schumpeter and Downs, in proposing economic analyses of democracy, place democratic politics and free markets on the same institutional footing governed by competition among diverse interests.

Schumpeter's contemporary, Friedrich Hayek, believed that socialism and democracy are incompatible. Democracy and *laissez faire* capitalism are united in their dependence on individual freedom, all three of which were historically interdependent. For Hayek, individual freedom, upholding "the individual as the ultimate judge of his ends," has been the hallmark of Western and Enlightenment civilization, and provides the motive force of economic, political, and scientific achievement.[11] Hayek counters Marxist historical determinism by stressing that individuals choose their ideas, and that ideas are the determining factor in human civilization. For Hayek, the defense of Western civilization distills to the opposition of two principles: individualism versus collectivism. He argues that it is key to grasp "the full width of the gulf which separates totalitarianism from a liberal regime, the utter difference between the whole moral atmosphere under collectivism and the essentially individualist Western civilisation."[12] In Hayek's analysis, the road to serfdom, socialism, and fascism is joined as soon as any compromise of individual freedom is made. As though infused by the same breath of inspiration, rational choice scholars, too, place a premium on the individual as the ultimate judge of his or her subjectively chosen ends; any compromise of this individualist feature of rational choice theory is regarded as a potential step toward authoritarianism and communism.

Hayek's *Road to Serfdom* sets forth the conundrum at the heart of Kenneth Arrow's Nobel-prize-winning work *Social Choice and Individual Values.*[13] For Hayek, just as it is evident that "individualistic socialism" is an oxymoron, so it is axiomatic that any form of social planning will necessarily be coercive. This is because, in Hayek's view, a society of individuals could never reach an agreement as to ends:

> The "social goal," or "common purpose," for which society is to be organised, is usually vaguely described as the "common good," or the "general welfare," or the "general interest." It does not need much reflection to see that these terms have no sufficiently definite meaning to determine a particular course of action. The welfare and the happiness of millions cannot be measured on a single scale of less and more. The welfare of a people, like the happiness of a man, depends on a great many things that can be provided in an infinite variety of combinations. It cannot be adequately expressed as a single end, but only as a hierarchy of ends, a comprehensive scale of values in which every need of every person is given its place. To direct all our activities according to a single plan presupposes that every one of our needs is given its rank in order of values which must be complete enough to make it possible to decide between all the different courses between which the planner has to choose. It presupposes, in short, the existence of a complete ethical code in which all the different human values are allotted their due place. . . . The essential point for us is that no such complete ethical code exists.[14]

In this discursively argued paragraph, Hayek articulates the social choice problem that Arrow analyzes using set theory in *Social Choice and Individual Values:* how is it possible to determine legitimate social direction from individuals' disparate opinions and concerns? Sharing Hayek's scepticism of a coherent public will formation, Arrow mathematically demonstrates that it is impossible to achieve a comprehensive social goal using individual values and ends as a starting place. Arrow concludes that a consensus on social ends would have to take the form of a Rousseauean "general will," a Kantian "categorical imperative," or Marx's moral precept "from each according to his ability, to each according to his needs." In Hayek's and Arrow's analysis, the difficulty with these political ideals is that they must be imposed on each member of the population, essentially embodying an elitist or coercive corruption of individual freedom.[15]

In rejecting any form of social planning or collectivism as the antithesis of individual freedom and the ideals on which Western civilization rests, Hayek looks hopefully to Adam Smith's political economy as an example of the "unplanned social order" he seeks to establish. This type of social system requires a specific institutional structure that provides a legal framework for commerce without restricting individual freedom to choose ends:

> To create conditions in which competition will be as effective as possible, to supplement it where it cannot be made effective, to provide the services which, in the words of Adam Smith, "though they may be in the highest degree advantageous to a great society, are, however, of such a nature, that the profit could never repay the expense of any individual or small number of individuals," these tasks provide indeed the wide and unquestioned field for state activity.[16]

This remark, though lauding the wisdom of Adam Smith, also betrays just how far the solution to failed markets in the form of economic planning had become accepted in the 1940s. In drawing attention to "[t]he task of creating a suitable framework for the beneficial working of competition," Hayek poses a problem that would become a central concern of rational choice theorists. No one has spent more effort exploring this problem than James Buchanan, who played a key role in articulating public choice theory two decades later. Buchanan belongs to the same canonical tradition as Hayek, drawing insight from Adam Smith as the brilliant inventor of a "system of natural liberty" in which individuals' self-determined efforts are coordinated by a legal framework that respects individual freedom. Also like Hayek, Buchanan is wholly opposed to any social theory that gives priority to the group or collective over the individual; for Buchanan methodological individualism is the founding premise of all legitimate social theory and for any legitimate social institution.

Karl Popper's World War II coda, *The Open Society and Its Enemies,*

opens with the brazen charge that Plato was essentially a totalitarian political theorist who was second only to Karl Marx in locking humans into
the paralyzing script of historical determinism.[17] Popper observes:

> According to Plato, internal strife, class war, fomented by self-interest and
> especially material or economic self-interest, is the main force of "social dy-
> namics." The Marxian formula "The history of all hitherto existing socie-
> ties is a history of class struggle," fits Plato's historicism nearly as well as
> that of Marx.[18]

There is much that can be learned from Marx, according to Popper. Marx
was essentially correct in identifying the problems of social injustice that
resulted from unbridled capitalism; he was also on the right path in adopting methodological individualism.[19] However, Popper assertively parts
company with Marx over what he regards as Marx's unrelenting historical determinism. According to Popper, Marx ultimately reduced all ideas,
whether political or scientific, to material economic relationships governing individuals and interactions among individuals. Therefore, Marx
looked to revolution to undo the current status of economic relationships,
and saw no hope in the gradual achievement of social justice through the
political process. More dangerously, Marx's idea of the material basis of
intellectual pursuits results in a precarious irrationalism, and according to
Popper, the "conflict between rationalism and irrationalism has become
the most important intellectual, and perhaps moral, issue of our time."[20]

In Popper's analysis, the democratic political process has alleviated the
need for social revolution and has achieved the greater part of Marx's
goals. In opposition to economic planning, he advocated a "social technology . . . whose results can be tested by piecemeal social engineering"
(2:222). Popper's dual diagnosis and prescription for the ills of mid-twentieth-century society is summarized as follows:

> Ultimately . . . rationalism is linked up with the recognition of the necessity
> of social institutions to protect freedom of criticism, freedom of thought,
> and thus the freedom of men. And it establishes something like a moral ob-
> ligation towards the support of these institutions. This is why rationalism is
> closely linked up with the political demand for practical social engineer-
> ing—piecemeal engineering, of course—in the humanitarian sense, with
> the demand for the rationalization of society, for planning for freedom, and
> for its control by reason . . . by that Socratic reason which is aware of its
> limitations, and which therefore respects the other man and does not aspire
> to coerce him—not even into happiness. (2:239)

For Popper, rational planning can be resolved with rational individualism
as long as individuals and society do not take the path of social revolu-

tion but instead work within the confines of democratic political institutions. Renouncing the historical determinism used by Marx to study the social relationships among men, Popper states, "'Scientific' Marxism is dead. Its feeling of social responsibility and its love for freedom must survive" (2:216).

In compartmentalizing Marx's ideas neatly into two boxes—one labeled detestable and dangerous, the other humanitarian and worthy—Popper's *Open Society and Its Enemies* brought to the fore those issues that needed to be addressed in order to place civilization on the path to emancipatory and rational individualism, rather than the path to irrational collectivism. This task fell squarely on the shoulders of a new breed of social scientists. The rational choice generation assumed the responsibility for designing a science of social interactions by adopting methodological individualism, and avoiding the pitfalls of historical determinism or of "sociologism," namely, that "doctrine . . . developed recently . . . as a theory of the social determination of scientific knowledge" (2:213). Most important was the need to place social science on a sound epistemological footing that gave it objective purchase through free and open public discussion, as in the case of the natural sciences.

Thus, Popper's petition for a rational and individualist social science was discharged by rational choice theorists. Popper believed that social science should analyze the unintended collective outcomes of individual actions, because to believe that much of what happens in society is intended is to engage in conspiracy theory (2:95). He thought that the key to understanding individuals' rational behavior was to assess it within the context of individual action; "when we speak of 'rational behaviour' or of 'irrational behaviour' then we mean behaviour which is, or which is not, in accordance with the logic of that situation" (2:97). Popper sketched out a view of rational behavior in accordance with methodological individualism (2:98). Like Popper, neither Arrow, Buchanan, nor Riker ever questioned the objectivity of the scientific method relying on deductive logic and empirical facts, and they placed rational choice theory firmly on the path of rationalism, individualism, and piecemeal social engineering envisioned by Popper.

Schumpeter, Hayek, and Popper each sought a new champion to rescue "the basic ideas on which European civilisation has been built," which are best thought of as the liberal creed based on reason, individualism, economic freedom, and secularized sovereignty in accordance with democratic rule.[21] In their view, together and independently these ideas were threatened by state organized planning, organic or ideal social philosophy, and the sociology of knowledge. Capitalism, democracy, and science share the same core commitment to individual freedom and in this respect are a particular product of Western history; socialism, fascism, and totalitarianism, on the other hand, are all perversions of classic Western civilization that arrest personal liberty and crush the open society's access to truth.

Schumpeter, Hayek, and Popper articulated a theoretical puzzle that had to be solved in order to maintain the integrity of the philosophical structure giving shape to democracy, capitalism, and science. The future of these institutions required reasserting the commitment to individualism, to freedom, and to scientific truth in conscious opposition to organic social theory and Marx's critique of knowledge. At the heart of this effort to rescue the foundations of capitalist democracy lay the remnants of democratic theory that, as Schumpeter explains, rested in practical ruin. Classic eighteenth-century democratic theory depended on the ideal expression of "the will of the people," which can never be more than whimsy. Assessing people's will, either as a technical exercise in aggregating individuals' preferences or as an exercise in understanding "public opinion" is doomed to fail as either a constructive or legitimate means to achieve political direction:

> [E]ven if the opinions and desires of individual citizens were perfectly definite and independent data for the democratic process to work with, and if everyone acted on them with ideal rationality and promptitude, it would not necessarily follow that the political decisions produced by that process from the raw material of those individual volition would represent anything that could in any convincing sense be called the will of the people.[22]

Thus, for Schumpeter, as for Hayek, belief in Enlightenment democracy has little more to recommend it than religious faith.

To face this theoretical shortfall, Schumpeter proposed an alternative form of democracy that points in the direction taken by rational choice theorists: that of politics as a competition of interests recognizing a sphere for personal freedom. Rational choice theory is part and parcel of the Western project of modernity that celebrates individual liberty in the pursuits of science, politics, and economics. Understanding rational choice theory as a major contribution to liberalism sets out the significance of its ideas against the backdrop of the prior two centuries, and draws attention to the novelty of its approach. While reasserting the principles of universalism, reason, and individualism, rational choice theorists refashion democratic theory into an individualistic competition that resembles market interactions predicated on self-interest. The early Cold War rational choice protagonists studied the microfoundations of democratic institutions, seeking to offer a palliative for distress in the form of reconstituted knowledge. With their theoretical forays, capitalist democracy rose phoenix-like from the ashes of two decades of destitution and blood-letting. By the end of the twentieth century, Western economic and political liberalism stand victorious on the world stage, resting on a new base fortified by rational choice theory.

PART I

Rational Policy Analysis and the National Security State

CHAPTER I

Managing the National Security State: Decision Technologies and Policy Science

About six or seven years ago there was a "technological breakthrough" at The RAND Corporation in the art of doing Systems Analysis.

Herman Kahn

[I]n the last few years war and defense have immensely stimulated the search for social as well as technological devices of social control, as is illustrated by the work of the RAND Corporation.

Robert Dahl and Charles Lindblom

A particular problem for modern democracies . . . is the predominant response they give to their electoral constituencies. . . . The classical liberal model of the democratic state, therefore, is not particularly reassuring at present technology levels.

Paul Hammond

PART 1 of this book investigates the critical role of the archetypal Cold War institution, the RAND Corporation, in the post–World War II emergence of rational choice. Understanding the forces leading to the development of rational choice theory requires contextualizing its interrelationships with the imperatives of the Cold War national security state. It is not possible to draw a line clearly separating rational policy analysis and rational choice theory. Game theory was rescued from academic oblivion by its active development at RAND for its potential relevance to problems of nuclear strategy. Kenneth Arrow's *Social Choice and Individual Values* was inspired by a research question pertaining to predicting collective outcomes for the Soviet Union.[1] William Riker's ambitious program of positive political theory was partially inspired by two RAND theorists' research into a mathematically defined "power index."

In this first part I tell the story of how systems analysis and rational policy analysis, much of it originating at RAND, became an accepted standard of public decisionmaking, first at the U.S. Department of Defense and then throughout government via Lyndon Johnson's Great Society programs. The incursion of rational decision technologies into the halls of power occurred against the backdrop of the missile gap, the *Sputniks*, and John F. Kennedy's presidential election. The extraordinary impact of these decision technologies on actual government practice is clear in Senator Henry Jackson's 1968–69 congressional hearings into the change in public decision procedures effected by RAND's policy analysis. A decade later, the influence and institutionalization of these tools spread even further as the professional schools of leading universities, such as Harvard's Kennedy School of Government, reorganized their structures and curricula around RAND-style policy analysis.

These new rational decision technologies constitute a "regime of knowledge production." This phrase is used to refer to how the formation of these tools and concepts led to a far-reaching and comprehensive system for defining appropriate beliefs and actions. Participation in this system was controlled by a new policy elite. These leading figures— including Thomas Schelling, Charles Hitch, Howard Raiffa, Henry Rowen, and Alain Enthoven—went from their humble origins as contractors for the U.S. Air Force to controlling enormous budgets, influential departments of government and universities, and key federal initiatives affecting all Americans. It was their ability to redefine "democratic decisionmaking" to suit their agenda, using these analytic tools, that made such a breathtaking rise possible. Once this comprehensive regime came into place, it gained de facto legitimacy through ubiquity rather than proven merit.

Rational choice theory as a social scientific method and rational policy analysis as a decision technology share key theorists, core ideas, institutional venues, and sources of funding. Any attempt to understand the phenomenal success of rational choice theory within the social sciences must acknowledge the interconnections between rational choice as a decision tool for government policy initiatives and as an explanatory device for predicting the outcomes of human action.

SOON after taking office, Secretary of Defense Robert S. McNamara held his first press conference. It was to be one of the shortest on record, consisting of only one question. A reporter asked, "Mr. Secretary, you've been here three or four weeks. The missile gap obviously was an important element in the campaign and a major security issue. What are you doing about it?" McNamara replied, "Well, you're quite right, it was important [and] it is important. I focused on that, and I've determined there wasn't a missile gap, or if there is, it's in our favor." In McNamara's own words, reporters "broke the doors down" running to call their editors. The next day's headlines screamed, "McNamara Denies Missile Gap," and the Republican Senate majority leader called for his resignation.[2] Despite this complete reversal of official U.S. government position and the resulting public outcry, *every* policy idea based on the belief in the (nonexistent) Soviet missile advantage was implemented over the next seven years. This chapter explores the processes of knowledge production and political interaction that manufactured the "gap" in the public mind and public record, initiated a sea change in American national security policy whose rationale originated in the missile gap, and empowered a new policy elite whose authority was grounded in the supposed objectivity of rational policy analysis.

The story of RAND, the Cold War, the missile gap, and McNamara's wholesale reorganization of the Pentagon traditionally has been told as one of decisive response to overwhelming imperative. In the late 1950s, RAND scientists in their Santa Monica ivory tower discover a critical vulnerability in the defensive posture of America. Their findings result in a top secret government report, detailing an unsuspected strength in the Soviet adversary—a missile gap. The unresponsive Eisenhower administration tries to ignore the gap, but the dramatic launch of the Soviet satellite *Sputnik I* forces it into action. The administration begins to improve the U.S. defense in response to this challenge, but it is too hidebound, too traditional, to fully assume the necessary burden. A presidential election brings a dramatic victory for the young, charismatic leader who will take America through these troubled times. He decisively changes the entire structure of the Pentagon and the armed services to respond to the newly perceived Soviet threats, bringing in Robert McNamara to lead a transformed military in the procurement and deployment of the greatest military power the world has ever known. Every effort is justified, and the methodologies and systems that had been designed for the great Cold War struggle are replicated throughout other areas of government, nonprofit organizations, and leading academic institutions.

Even when subsequent intelligence suggested that the substantial military advantage was always on the side of the United States, a fall-back explanation was created: even if subsequent knowledge proved that the United States was not vulnerable to Soviet attack, contemporary intelligence could not *definitively* disprove that the Soviets had a significant military advantage. Thus, again, steps to reform the Pentagon and marshal U.S. power were logically dictated by the necessity of circumstances. Ever since these events were current news, researchers have sought to maintain the reality of the Cold War threat as the rationale for what was then the

U.S. militaristic defense posture.³ Actions on the part of ardent cold warriors were justified by the nature of the palpable threat.

I contend, however, that the Cold War struggle was not so much one of enemy pitted against enemy in a ferocious to-the-death struggle as it was a fight over which *interpretation* of Cold War events would prevail and would serve as the foundation for determining action. Here the drama is recast such that, rather than seeing the United States as a unified actor on a bipolar world stage, it is an internal U.S. struggle among interested parties vying to gain control over defining the Cold War. Those whose interpretation of events were accepted had the power to direct policy. Thus, ironically, the actual Cold War drama lay in the manufacture of the "Cold War" itself, as policymakers sought to convince the American nation of its peril and to orchestrate policy reforms in order to stave off the perceived threat.

Close attention to the historical record discloses a concatenation of actions that demands this alternate narrative. The Cold War drama, though acted out in the Pentagon, executive branch, and the halls of Congress, was scripted and themed within the walls of the RAND Corporation, America's first military think tank. In the first section of this chapter, I consider how RAND developed its unique product, "systems analysis," which McNamara later would use to gain control over the Pentagon. I also sketch out the alliances behind RAND and the Ford Foundation, both of which were built on a steadfast commitment to a rationally managed technocratic society. In such a society, "objective" experts made difficult policy decisions outside the fray of partisan politics characteristic of legislative democracy. In the second section, I relate how President Eisenhower invited H. Rowan Gaither Jr., chairman of the board for both RAND and the Ford Foundation, to head a committee to study the American civil defense program. Gaither's efforts resulted in the top secret "Gaither Report," which was the source behind the fallacious assertion of a missile gap between the United States and the Soviet Union. The Gaither Report also outlined a plan for a tremendous defense buildup and wholesale reform of the department of defense using the tools of rational management. In the third section, I consider how McNamara successfully established control over the U.S. armed forces by using the epistemological leverage afforded by RAND's systems analysis. Then, in the chapter's penultimate section, I trace the implementation of RAND's decision theoretic tools first in the department of defense, and then later throughout the federal government via President Johnson's Great Society programs, resulting in the establishment of a knowledge production regime that would revolutionize government policymaking in the United States. This regime of knowledge production, with McNamara as its chauffeur, shifted governmental decisionmaking from a legislative-democratic platform to a policy sciences model that depended on claims of objectivity and scientific rigor for its authority and legitimacy. A closing section argues that rational policy analysis and rational choice theory in the social sciences both share origins in the toolbox of decision theoretic methods developed at RAND in the 1950s.

The history that emerges is relevant to broader discussions of the tension between the ideal of liberal democracy and the tendency of elites to develop means to control societal decisionmaking processes. Since its inception as a social form predating the French and American Revolutions, and going back to at least the British civil wars, the drama of democratization has in part been about conveying the appearance of inclusion while designing means to retain actual control over decisionmaking in the hands of a social elite. This impetus for elite control has had various guises, from aristocratic resistance to the retrenchment of liberalism on the part of a newly successful bourgeoisie in late-nineteenth-century Britain. But increasingly, as democracy became recognized as the legitimate form of government among Western nation-states and the universal franchise of adult citizens became widespread following World War I, a new form of struggle emerged, evident in the United States, to retake the reins of authority in order to neutralize the unruly potential of mass democratic politics. Guy Alchon makes this argument with respect to the early decades of the twentieth century when American philanthropies and government insiders formed an alliance with "objective" and "impartial" social scientists who were empowered with control over social decisions outside the auspices of democratic politics.[4] This chapter similarly argues that following World War II an alliance was forged between philanthropies (in this case the Ford Foundation), the business community, and scientific policy analysts. This alliance resulted in the development of rational policy analysis, which functioned as a means to relocate the authority for policy decisions from elected officials to a supposedly "objective" technocratic elite.

Systematic Knowledge Production

The story begins at the Santa Monica–based RAND Corporation which, in the 1950s, became the think tank icon of Cold War America. In its halls, nuclear strategists thought the unthinkable as they came to terms with thermonuclear war. RAND physicist Herman Kahn would be memorialized in American folklore as the title character in Stanley Kubrick's

1964 film *Dr. Strangelove,* subtitled *How I Learned to Stop Worrying and Love the Bomb.* To the Soviets, RAND represented "[a]n American Academy of Death and Destruction."[5]

Project RAND (1946–48)

In the wake of World War II, RAND grew out of the joint vision on the parts of General Henry "Hap" Arnold of the U.S. Army Air Force and executive leaders at the Douglas Aircraft Company. General Arnold anticipated that with the conclusion of the war, scientists and technical experts would flock back to universities and industry; he was eager to maintain and perpetuate the symbiosis of scientific talent and defense needs that had been organized to fight the war. Since it seemed doubtful that researchers would give up civilian status, this inventive plan required the creation of a new institutional format conducive to harnessing technical expertise for Air Force ends. Frank Collbohm, assistant to the vice president of engineering at Douglas, whose wartime experience included stints at MIT's Radiation Laboratory and at the Manhattan Project, similarly worried that the exodus of technical competence from the military arena would prove crippling. In his mind, America might have "won the military campaign, [but] we've lost the war."[6] In early 1946 "Project RAND" was hatched: the idea was to fund a autonomous division within Douglas Aircraft that would function quasi-independently from both Douglas and the Air Force, but would be devoted to researching Air Force concerns.

Arnold made available $10 million of Army Air Force funds, Donald Douglas acquiesced to housing the effort, and Collbohm accepted the mantle of leadership. As a pet project of General Arnold's, RAND was structured from the start to have access high in the Air Force chain of command. Collbohm initially reported directly to General Curtis LeMay, future head of the U.S. Strategic Air Command (SAC). The original RAND research team numbered four, and functioned as a separate division within Douglas Aircraft. By 1948, project RAND would grow to have 255 employees and an annual operating budget of $3.5 million. The organization was still funded from Arnold's original allocation, and occupied offices in an old Santa Monica newspaper building. All RAND researchers required security clearances, but in the early days following the war, researchers brought preexisting clearances from previous positions.

According to RAND's charter, "Project RAND is a continuing program of scientific study and research on the broad subject of air warfare with the object of recommending to the Air Force preferred methods, techniques, and instrumentalities for this purpose."[7] Collbohm, an electrical engineer by training, had a solid hardware track record including contributions to aircraft design and radar development. His roving and eclectic assignments during World War II led him to have an expansive vision for RAND. It was from the start envisioned as broadly interdisciplinary, and designed to consider sweeping questions of military strategy through the lens of a hardware orientation. It was also crucial to the RAND mythos that the institution jealously guard its intellectual independence from its patron. Hence RAND was based three thousand miles away from the demanding Washington environment, and RAND researchers took on "voluntary projects" rather than assignments. RAND strove to meet Air Force needs, but did so on its own terms, developing its own strategies for setting up research agendas. From the Air Force's perspective, the arrangement and the objectives underlying it looked different. General LeMay recollected that "[w]e didn't have any of the tools . . . necessary to conduct a program leading to intercontinental missiles and supersonic airplanes . . . [s]o, the gimmick was to contract with a nonprofit organization to accomplish the task, and pay their bills, and let them go out in the open market and hire the talent they needed at the going rate." [8]

RAND's first large-scale study, undertaken at the request of General LeMay, then deputy chief of Air Staff for Research and Development, is telling of the client–patron relationship between RAND and the Air Force. In early 1946, it came to LeMay's attention that the U.S. Navy was drawing up a proposal to the Joint Research and Development Board advocating the potential role of the Navy in space satellite development. Motivated by interservice rivalry, LeMay presented RAND with the task of investigating the technical feasibility of various space satellite systems. When the competing Navy and Air Force proposals were presented to the board in 1947, it favored the Air Force proposal, finding its analysis to be more comprehensive than the Navy's, and subsequently terminated the Navy's foray into satellite development. [9]

RAND had served its patron well: the outcome of the satellite study demonstrated that RAND could provide authoritative clout to Air Force initiatives, enabling them to prevail in policy venues. Attentive to this role, one RAND researcher recounted how Winston Churchill had similarly used "Operational Research" in order to exert his will over military bureaucracies during World War II, using such analysis as an authoritative edge over entrenched leaders. [10] Repeatedly over time, RAND studies would be deemed a success or failure by the simple metric of whether they furthered Air Force weapons procurement and strategic agendas.

Ultimately, and ironically, RAND would outgrow its relationship with the Air Force and take on studies for the Office of the Secretary of Defense in the early 1960s. Then, with the tables reversed, General LeMay would become one of RAND's staunchest critics, since RAND's findings were no longer aligned with Air Force interests. In a second and more penetrating irony, the original 1946 RAND study establishing that satellite technologies were possible within the then-current state of missile and rocketry technologies serves as an anticipatory reminder that the Soviet's launching in 1957 of *Sputniks I* and *II* was not surprising.[11]

In its early days under the auspices of Douglas Aircraft, Project RAND was oriented toward hardware studies, and the RAND team took on a variety of tasks such as the refinement of ductile titanium and the calculation of the trajectories of intercontinental ballistic missiles. RAND's interest was primarily technical, and its professional staff was mostly comprised of engineers, mathematicians, and physicists. Even though Collbohm already harbored the vision of an interdisciplinary and complete research facility dedicated to the science of warfare, this development would only come later, after RAND severed its ties to Douglas.

RAND, H. Rowan Gaither Jr., and the Ford Foundation

In early 1948, Douglas Aircraft leadership grew concerned over the possible conflict of interest inherent in Douglas's personnel contracting directly for the Air Force as "independent and objective" consultants. It seemed probable that the Air Force would exert extra caution in awarding Douglas contracts for fear of evoking the appearance of impropriety. RAND president Frank Collbohm initiated steps to achieve independent corporate status and contacted a wartime acquaintance to aid him in this process. The man he chose was H. Rowan Gaither Jr., who had served as assistant director of MIT's Radiation Laboratory from 1942–44 and was then at the San Francisco law firm Cooley, Crowley, and Supple. Gaither was absolutely discreet, politically sophisticated, had an impressive list of contacts including MIT's former president Karl Compton, and was experienced in serving as an intermediary between scientists, administration, and sources of funding.

Together, Gaither and Collbohm concluded that nonprofit status best suited RAND's aims. Independence required capital and a board of trustees. Gaither took on the responsibilities of drawing up the necessary legal documents and overseeing the reorganization. He also agreed to serve as the chair of the board of trustees, a role he continued to play until his untimely death in 1961. Gaither took on yet another personal stake in RAND's institutional viability when he made available an unsecured loan, and later a mortgage for new buildings, through the bank owned by his family, Pacific National Bank.

Despite Gaither's generosity, more money was required, and a lead was provided by Karl Compton. He and Gaither had built up a friendship while at MIT, and he agreed to serve as a member of RAND's board. Compton was also on good terms with Henry Ford II, son of Henry Ford and chief stockholder of the Ford Motor Company. Gaither assumed the task of approaching Ford to request emergency funding for RAND. At a legendary meeting aboard an East Coast train, Ford and Gaither spoke. The two enjoyed such instant rapport that Ford immediately pledged an initial three hundred thousand dollars to RAND from the Ford Foundation, this at a time when that foundation was $31 million in debt. The initial loan to RAND was increased to $1 million, and then commuted into a grant over the course of the next four years.

In the 1940s, the Ford Foundation had been used primarily to reduce Ford family taxes, and was controlled by Henry Ford II. The foundation had gone into debt consequent to its use as a lien against the tax due on Henry and Edsel's shares of the Ford Motor Company. Thus, although Ford's foundation originally was set up to take its place as the best-endowed American philanthropic organization, in the late 1940s the foundation was only theoretically and potentially well-endowed. When at last the U.S. Treasury and the Ford Foundation trustees reached a legal settlement on the valuation of Ford Motor Company stock in the foundation's holding in 1951, it totaled $417 million. This easily established Ford's foundation as the richest American philanthropy, compared to the Rockefeller Foundation's $122 million and the Carnegie Corporation's $170 million. The relative wealth of these foundations at the time was staggering: for example, Harvard University's 1950 endowment was $191 million, and Yale University's $125 million.[12] This $417 million valuation of the Ford Foundation was further enhanced by bountiful stock dividends earned in the 1950s. It was not until 1976 that the foundation would become fully independent from the Ford family and the Ford Motor Company.[13]

Meanwhile, Gaither had so impressed Ford at their meeting that the auto manufacturer asked him also to produce a policy statement for the Ford Foundation. Thus, while Gaither oversaw the reorganization of RAND, he was additionally responsible for creating a report expressing the Ford Foundation's mission. This statement is telling of Gaither's vision of society as a technocracy governed by an objective elite, and was personally acknowledged by Henry Ford II to have been "the most important step in formulating the policies of the Foundation."[14] Gaither assembled a committee of prominent academicians to draw up the statement. Ford and the trustees, who hoped to determine from the report how the foundation's efforts could best be admired in the public eye, gave the committee so much leeway that after six months members were unable to come to a set of conclusions. Gaither finally wrote the report himself with a small staff.[15] The report—serious, idealistic, and somewhat self-aggrandizing in tone—was regarded by Ford insiders with a mixture of reverence and mirth, but in any case "became a kind of sacred text, scrutinized for many years by those charged with planning or justifying the Foundation's programs."[16] Most crucially, the statement articulated as a plan for philanthropic support specifically what RAND managed to achieve in the 1950s: the development of a professional corps who, due to their superior expertise, could guide the nation through challenging policy decisions. The report describes a society managed by an educated elite outside the public arena and suggests that it is the duty of philanthropies to support this elite.

A quintessential Cold War document, the *Report for the Study of the Ford Foundation on Policy and Program* drew attention to the current "world crisis," and to the seemingly black and white choice between democracy and totalitarianism.[17] According to the foundation's report, a primary goal of philanthropy should be advising "those responsible for the formulation or execution of policy" (54). Policy advice should come in the form of objective analysis or expert consultation. In bestowing charity, the goal is "to replace partisan controversy with objective fact" (114). Unsurprisingly, according to the mission statement, none other than a philanthropy is most qualified to support nonpartisan research, because a philanthropy such as the Ford Foundation, which "has no stockholders and no constituents . . . [and] represents no private, political, or religious interests," is the height of neutral objectivity (22). The report is unequivocal in suggesting that philanthropies and their beneficiaries manifest an objectivity that best entitles them to provide leadership in a democratic society:

> This freedom from entanglements, pressures, restrictive legislation, and private interest endows a foundation with an inherent freedom of action possessed by few other organizations. Further, a great foundation possesses an extraordinary stature in the public mind. By law, as well as by its charter, it is dedicated to human welfare. Its responsibility is to the public as a whole. In political and social issues it cannot be partisan. This very nonpartisanship and objectivity gives to the foundation a great positive force, and enables it to play a unique and effective role in the difficult and sometimes controversial task of helping to realize democracy's goals. (23)

It is striking that as part of the understanding of expert knowledge and politics articulated by Gaither, knowledge and expertise exist on an independent axis from politics and partisanship. Furthermore, it is clear that Gaither's rendering of democratic society is at odds with a model predicated on a communicative and dialogic public sphere. The leadership of both the Ford Foundation and RAND was committed to the view in which difficult and controversial public policy debates are best adjudicated by knowledgeable experts.

In taking on responsibility for the Ford Foundation's mission statement, Gaither's lawyerly instinct had led him to insist that neither he nor any of the report's other authors ever accept any future role in the administration of the foundation.[18] This gesture of nonpartisanship and disinterestedness was reversed when Gaither became part-time associate director of the foundation's program Area V, the behavioral sciences, in 1951. These duties were facilitated by the Ford Foundation's temporary location in Pasadena, California, a stone's throw from RAND's Santa Monica site. Paul Hoffman, appointed in 1950 as the first nonfamily president of the foundation, had accepted the position on the condition that the foundation be located in the health-promoting region of southern California.[19]

Henry Ford II had selected Hoffman for the foundation's presidency because his professional preeminence seemed to guarantee that he could do only good for the foundation. Hoffman, a former president of the Studebaker Corporation, had just successfully completed a term as administrator of the Marshall Plan. However, he soon proved to be a poor choice when his sympathies, operational emphasis, assessment of how the foundation funds might be the most useful, and even his choice of staff clashed with the views of Henry Ford II as well as those of the other board members, including Karl Compton and Donald David. Hoffman downplayed the Cold War, worked in the spirit of international cosmopolitanism, advocated cultural exchange and communication, and looked to the United Nations as providing hope for defusing international tensions. Compton and David grew increasingly concerned that Hoffman was not following the guidelines set down in Gaither's *Report for the Ford Foundation Study for Program and Policy*. Tensions continued to increase following Hoffman's appointment of the controversial Robert Maynard Hutchins to the position of associate director.[20] At the October 4, 1951 board meeting, Compton resigned his trusteeship in protest.[21] Unsettling exchanges occurred at meetings between Ford and Hoffman, with Hoffman allegedly stating that he "was not going to devote his life to educating this young ignoramus [Henry Ford]."[22] In late 1951, Hoffman proudly advertised his allegiance to Dwight D. Eisenhower, and became increasingly involved in the presidential campaign. During this same period, Hoffman and Hutchins chartered the Ford Foundation's Fund for the Republic, which they set up to defend civil liberties and to "attack . . . [the] loyalty investigations . . . [and] the House Un-American Activities Committee."[23] In February of 1953 the antagonism between Hoffman and Ford reached a breaking point, and Ford forced Hoffman to resign. At the trustees' meeting in which Hoffman was ousted, Gaither was elected to the position of president, director, and member-trustee.

The realignment of the Ford Foundation's leadership and philanthropic policies with the conservative political outlook of Gaither, Ford, and David signaled an alliance of old-guard Republican sentiment that opposed the moderate Republicanism espoused by Eisenhower.[24] Under Gaither's direction, the foundation, which by weight of its huge endowment played a crucial role in shaping America's intellectual arena, swung far to the right. A clear and significant shift in the foundation's leadership had occurred, and was evident in its policy changes. This dramatic shift in philanthropic politics was also evident in the contrast between Gaither's and Hoffman's internal foundation directives. Hoffman, for example, was unequivocally opposed to using foundation resources in efforts to destabilize foreign political regimes.[25] Gaither and his close associates Donald G. Marquis and Hans Speier, on the other hand, supported foundation efforts to further political and psychological warfare.[26] Similarly, Gaither's support of the social and behavioral sciences as a tool for an expertly managed society contrasted with Hoffman's interdialogic, democratic cosmopolitanism.[27] Under Gaither's tutelage, the Ford Foundation promoted research oriented toward national security.[28]

The Ford Foundation's swing to the right coincided with the anticommunist sentiment then sweeping the nation and led by Senator Joseph McCarthy. From an internal Ford Foundation point of view, handing over the foundation's leadership to Gaither was an astute and expertly timed decision considering the foundation's pending encounter with the McCarthy investigations. Henry Ford II's assessment of congressional opinion regarding his philanthropic organization revealed serious misgivings about Robert Hutchins on the part of influential congressman. Representative E. E. Cox described Hutchins's outlook as "collectivist," "internationalist," "socialist," and "one-worlder." Cox further stated that, in his opinion, "Dr. Hutchins [and not Paul Hoffman] really runs the [foundation]."[29] Senator Joseph McCarthy formally initiated an investigation of the Ford Foundation in a letter dated March 19, 1953, addressed to Paul Hoffman.[30] It would be Gaither, however, who replied to McCarthy, and who successfully fought charges of communist leanings and of the foundation's infiltration by communists in the ensuing years. During this time, much of the Gaither administration's energies were taken up with fighting the charge of communism, replying to the Reece and Cox committees' requests and subpoenas, and jealously guarding the Ford Foundation's public image by hiring the law firm of Earl Newsom and Company to handle public relations. However, an internal memorandum documenting a conversation between Gaither and former President Herbert Hoover at the elite secret society Bohemian Grove makes clear that while the McCarthy tempest stormed on the public stage, in elite circles the Ford Foundation's standing was secure.[31]

Gaither's professional responsibilities served as a bridge between the RAND Corporation and the Ford Foundation; his views meshed seamlessly with those of Henry Ford II and matched the hawkish sentiment of most RAND researchers.[32] Given his key role in setting the direction for both, it comes as no surprise that the RAND Corporation fit Gaither's bill as the ideal beneficiary of Ford Foundation funds: it supposedly was a neutral and objective body that produced expert policy advice, and claimed to obviate the need for political factions in the policymaking process. RAND would eventually achieve what a concluding section of Gaither's mission statement for the Ford Foundation cited as the ultimate goal, that "[the] foundation's general policy must be to support (a) work that will influence the policies or operations of other institutions on the widest possible scale, or (b) work that will build up a new professional corps or a new system of techniques and operation standards."[33] Indeed, political influence, policies and operations, a new professional corps, and a new system of techniques and operation standards all flowed like water from RAND in the 1950s. Gaither's commitment to a rationally managed society resulted in the development of decision theoretic tools that defined rational policy formation as quantitative and predicated on the authority of scientific expertise, as opposed to the principles of egalitarian democracy.

RAND 1948–57: Systems Analysis

In the late 1940s and early 1950s, RAND grew into one of the keenest sites of intellectual productivity in the United States, with abundant funding, a prestigious board of trustees to lure talent from universities and industry, a flexible work environment catering to idiosyncrasies and eccentricity, and a campus-style site without the presence of students or the burden of teaching responsibilities. RAND also profited from the network of wartime connections that continued to provide strong ties. Much of RAND's talent had formerly belonged to scientific bodies organized to aid the war effort. Included in its ranks were the newly hired division heads Charles Hitch, John Williams, Edward Barlow, and Hans Speier.[34]

In 1948, RAND's orientation toward hardware problems and development was evident in its departmental makeup. Before RAND's reorganization in March of that year, home office sections included evaluation of military worth, rocket vehicles, airborne vehicles, communications, and nuclear physics.[35] In 1949, technical staff including engineers, mathematicians, physicists, and computer scientists comprised 78 percent of the research staff, while political scientists and economists accounted for only 5 percent.[36] In 1950, even though economics and social science had been consolidated under the leadership of Hitch and Speier, ongoing work by the departments of nuclear energy, electronics, missiles, and aircraft continued to evidence RAND's original commitment to hardware analysis. By the end of the 1950s, however, economists had become the dominant professional group at RAND, outnumbering physicists and mathematicians; "systems analysis" was now RAND's unique product.

The phasing out of hardware studies may have been a function of the free-wheeling, voluntary intellectual environment at RAND that, as Edward Barlow surmised, was not conducive to the disciplined team approach to solving problems required to build actual mechanical artifacts such as aircraft.[37] In any event, over time it became quite clear that RAND's research strength was certainly not hardware development. Two problematic hardware studies indicate RAND's lack of aplomb with technical design. In a 1949 study of a nuclear-powered aircraft design, RAND researchers developed a nuclear-powered bomber with two serious design flaws. The reactor of the plane produced sufficient radioactivity to kill the pilot and crew before reaching distant Soviet targets, and when radiation shielding was added, the aircraft became too heavy to fly.[38] Later, in an early 1950s radar study, engineer Edward Barlow and his team investigated the requirements and characteristics of an interlocking radar aircraft detection grid useful for tracking low-altitude planes flying underneath the event horizon of conventional radar tracking stations. Barlow and his group performed the analysis and made preparations to brief the Air Force staff on their findings. But in the final days before the scheduled briefing, the Barlow group labored unsuccessfully in the California desert to set up their tracking system. Saved from the briefing deadline by an attendee's last-minute cancellation, Barlow vowed, "Never again does RAND get into hardware!"[39] Barlow was promoted to head of engineering in 1953.

Whereas the acronym "RAND" had originally been understood as "Research and Development," by the late 1950s it came to signify "Research and No Development," expressing the idea that hands-on technical design was somehow beneath the dignity of the high-powered brain trust collected at RAND, whose duties, responsibilities, and intellectual commitments lay rather in the realm of speculation about the boldest, most unthinkable thoughts regarding nuclear war. And thus it was that RAND's efforts increasingly took on the flavor of abstract studies of strategy, logistics, and warfare, all of which fall under the rubric "systems analysis."

The concept of "systems analysis" naturally worked its way into RAND's idea coffer in the earliest days, when Project RAND existed as an autonomous division of Douglas Aircraft. Systems analysis studies originated as tools used by the aircraft trade to prepare contract bids for the Air Force. They provided quantitative assessments of the superiority and cost efficiency of one aircraft design over other models. Systems analysis was given a central and prominent location on the 1948 RAND organizational chart, graphically showing how its assessments were interdisciplinary efforts utilizing the skills and knowledge bases of researchers throughout the RAND departments.[40] From the early days of the think tank, and in keeping with Frank Collbohm's vision, systems analysis was regarded as an interdisciplinary, quantitative study of a complex problem of weapons design. The original Douglas concept of systems analysis served as a template for a more ambitious scheme of developing a total science of warfare in which any logistical and strategic problem, no matter how complex, could be solved with rigorous, quantitative analysis.

The first ambitious use of systems analysis was the Offensive Bomber Study undertaken by RAND analyst Edwin Paxson from 1947–50.[41] The goal of the study was to decide on the configuration of America's next strategic bomber, and it neglected no aspect of the problem in its analysis. It considered U.S. bomber base location, vulnerability to attack, and target selection as the background information from which to conclude which bomber design and bomb combination would grant the United States optimal strategic advantage. The study incorporated an elaborate modeling procedure to estimate attrition in battle, weapons accuracy, and failure rates. Paxson, an early enthusiast of the application of game theory to problems of warfare, also included game-theoretic calculations of aerial combat routines to estimate battle successes. The study was then augmented to consider projected evolution of U.S. and Soviet technologies and strategies over the following seven-year period. Paxson's assistant estimated that from one-third to one-half of RAND's research staff contributed to the study.[42] The analysis had sufficient component functions and variables to make even the most accomplished equation-crunching mind swirl. A central goal of RAND's in taking on this challenging analysis was to demonstrate that complex problems of military strategy were amenable to scientific solution.

For numerous reasons, when the conclusions were presented to the Air Force's SAC in 1950, the study was considered a failure. From RAND's perspective, the analysis was a disappointment for three reasons. The sheer scope and complexity of the study required that guesswork be used to anchor some of the numbers relied on in the calculation.[43] Second, and this problem would repeatedly arise and would be dubbed "the criteria problem," the study's outcome was inherently a function of the criteria used in setting up the problem. In this case, solutions were ranked by considering the ratio of system cost to damage inflicted, instead of the ratio of the number of air crews lost per damage inflicted. Understandably, Air Force officials did not take kindly to such cavalier treatment of personnel loss when they and their compatriots were the personnel in question.[44] Finally, the study was deemed a failure by RAND because the Air Force, while acknowledging the elegance of the mathematical design, vehemently rejected the RAND finding that the future of the SAC lay in slow, low-flying turbo-prop bombers instead of fast, high-flying jets. The Air Force's prompt repudiation of the Paxson conclusion is telling of the interrelationship among RAND's research initiatives, systems analysis, and their client's interested sponsorship. The Air Force remained committed to their development of the swift B-52 Stratofortress bomber, and responded to RAND with harsh critiques of Paxson's study.[45]

RAND president Frank Collbohm was incensed by the lack of respect the Air Force demonstrated in receiving Paxson's results. The Air Force had not simply disregarded the RAND study, but had even challenged RAND's cost estimates for building the B-52 in comparison to RAND's preferred turbo-prop model. In order to buttress future RAND findings, Collbohm initiated RAND's Cost Analysis section under the direction of economist David Novick.[46] Novick's section became a formidable and necessary component in all future RAND systems analysis studies, because all comparisons of weapons systems based on performance per cost utterly depended on reliable assessments of costs. In determining the cost of a weapons system, Novick's group would estimate the cost of production, including both research and development, and subsequent manning, basing, and maintenance of the system. As Novick's work progressed throughout the 1950s, he increasingly found that estimating costs required evaluating the Air Force budgeting process. Costs were determined somewhere between contractors' bids and defense budgeteers' counterestimates, and in Novick's view, Air Force analysts had no standardized procedure for establishing independent cost evaluations. As the decade wore on, Novick began drawing up a new budgeting system for the Air Force that emphasized budgeting as a strategic planning tool. By late 1958, he contemplated the prospects of implementing the budgeting system in the entire Department of Defense if the incoming administration were favorable.[47]

The second and third ambitious systems analysis studies undertaken by RAND were no less complex, and fared no better, than Paxson's unappreciated bomber analysis. The studies' goals were to determine which radars, fighters, and communications networks were desirable in view of the new Soviet atomic and hydrogen bomb threat. The first phase of the systems analysis had fifty-four component projects, ranging through all RAND departments. However, with the demoralization caused by the negative reception of Paxson's work, the ambitious scope of systems analysis as a total science of warfare was reined in. Project leader Edward Barlow, in a preliminary sketch of his air defense study, reevaluated the systems analysis approach, arguing that "[i]n one sentence this new attitude is that our dominating motive should be to get a correct and convincing set of recommendations on Air Defense for the USAF and that the completion of a quantitative systems analysis be secondary. Our work in the defense field should be recommendation-oriented, not methodology oriented."[48]

Barlow's studies were central to the fading RAND vision of a comprehensive and rigorous science of war. They absorbed significant personnel resources in the early 1950s, but received scant attention.[49] That they were barely recognized was due to the lack of impact the reports had on Air Force policy. The first report presented no recommendations but only comparative analyses, and the second report offended Air Force sensibilities yet again when preliminary conclusions suggested that the future of U.S. air offense lay in missiles rather than manned bombers, which was in direct contrast to the Air Force's predilection for manned flight.

The contrast between the amount of energy expended in producing these unheeded studies and their seeming irrelevance to RAND's history draws attention to two conflicting impulses characterizing the development of systems analysis methodology at RAND. On the one hand, systems analysis as an ambitious science of strategy proved unfeasible, while on the other hand, RAND researchers strove to preserve the label of "systems analysis" to designate a unique product name in order to maintain RAND's edge in the competitive marketplace of ideas.[50] These conflicting impulses are apparent in Edward Quade's development in the early 1950s of a set of lectures to teach systems analysis to staff in the Air Force, Army, Navy, and Department of Defense.[51] This short course served the two-fold goal of initiating military personnel into the rites of systems analysis while simultaneously pointing out the pitfalls of the method.[52] "Systems analysis" was an umbrella term calculated to lend authority to a collection of methods for problem solving ranging from complex quantitative analysis to commonsense logic.[53]

Counterintuitively, just as systems analysis as a complete science of warfare was receding into a dreamlike past, a simplified version of Paxson's strategic bomber study was reformulated under the lead of RAND's Albert Wohlstetter, who took on a strategic bases study at the behest of Charles Hitch in 1951. This reformulation, lacking in complexity and quantification, would gain a reputation of being *the* prototypical RAND systems analysis study. The task of the study was to determine the best configuration of bomber bases in light of three possibilities: utilizing overseas bases as a main staging area during war, using overseas bases only to refuel during war, and operating U.S.-based bombers intercontinentally with midair refueling. The criterion for selection Wohlstetter adopted was cost-effectiveness. By taking the Soviet Union into consideration as a rational adversary, Wohlstetter pondered bomber base vulnerability in time of war, or more frighteningly, in the case of a Soviet preemptive strike. Imagining a scenario like Pearl Harbor but with vastly greater proportions, Wohlstetter conjured up a thought experiment in which all overseas bomber bases were attacked simultaneously, leaving the United States with significantly lessened counterattack capability. It seemed to Wohlstetter that no one in SAC command had taken this possibility into consideration.

Trained in mathematical logic, Wohlstetter did not share his colleagues' predilection for, or facility with, quantitative models. He relied on Paxson's assistant Edward Quade to design his model, which could be calculated with a slide rule or on the back of an envelope. Whereas RANDites were dumbstruck by Wohlstetter's findings at the initial RAND briefing, believing that Wohlstetter had identified the Achilles' heel of American defenses that left the nation open to imminent Soviet invasion, Air Force and SAC officers were less than impressed.[54] Wohlstetter's analysis depended on the assumption that the Russians could mount a total surprise attack on *all* bases, with no prior warning, and it implied that such a preemptive, unprovoked strike was imminent. SAC officers, including General LeMay, dismissed the study for the reason that, if anything, the United States was poised to strike the first blow against the Soviets. Even though a preemptive strike was forbidden by the president, SAC battle tactics called for such action at the slightest sign of a Soviet attempt to marshal a surprise attack.[55] In any case, no one at RAND was privy to these war plans.

Discontent with what he deemed to be a cavalier response on the part of the Air Force to imminent danger, the force of Wohlstetter's personality took over. Even though in later years Wohlstetter, and his conviction of SAC vulnerability, would be celebrated as clinching RAND's historic import, at the time Wohlstetter was held in low repute by many RAND associates. He was seen as pompous and self-aggrandizing—as though his manner was governed more by rhetorical device than by solid content. He was barred from briefing the RAND trustees who were routinely kept abreast of RAND's findings. Wohlstetter was considered to be a lone wolf and worked only with a few trusted colleagues, among them Henry Rowen and Alain Enthoven. He also had a good working relationship with Charles Hitch, who rescued him from professional oblivion when others in RAND leadership had fired him for negligence in handling data.[56] Wohlstetter and his coterie were determined to shake Air Force leaders out of their complacency, and in the summer of 1953 they set up camp in Washington and presented their strategic bomber study over ninety times throughout the chain of Air Force command.

There is a lack of consensus on whether the warnings of peril were heeded, or whether Air Force command duly responded.[57] However, vulnerability became Wohlstetter's obsession. He next applied the Pearl Harbor scenario to U.S.-based bombers, and the Achilles' heel became doubly worrisome. He and Henry Rowen penned the study *Protecting U.S. Power to Strike Back in the 1950s and 1960s* (R-290), which sketched out the ominous scenario of a simultaneous, preemptive Soviet attack on all forty-two SAC bases in the United States. In the event of this bold act, which he did not deem unlikely, Wohlstetter estimated that American forces would be hard-pressed to mount any counterattack at all. Such a lack of response capability was an open invitation to the Soviets to take what they could get while it was available for the taking, and suggested a major breach in U.S. security. Hence came the RAND prescription that in order to maintain an effective defensive posture, America must have a sufficient nuclear arsenal to withstand the most devastating attack imaginable and still maintain a counterforce to act, if not as a deterrent, then to ensure equivalent devastation of Soviet military and industrial facilities. This strategy became known as "second-strike counterforce," in contrast to a minimum deterrent policy postulating that the Soviets rationally would not mount an offensive as long as they were in reasonable danger of sustaining nuclear retaliation.[58]

Wohlstetter and the two strategic base studies formed the nucleus around which RAND's strategic agenda, RAND's strategy cadre, and RAND's mythic history would grow. Wohlstetter's network of associates, which would extend beyond RAND and outlast the decade, came to include Henry Rowen, Fred Hoffman, Alain Enthoven, Steven Enke, and Lawrence Henderson. This group represented a cell of independent action within RAND whose ambitions outstripped the confines of RAND's peripheral think tank status. It would be this cadre's thought that would increasingly define RAND's position on nuclear strategy. By the end of the 1950s, RAND's strategic agenda emphasized SAC vulnerability and second-strike counterforce, which translated into the policy of marshaling an effective counteroffensive despite assuming the inability to protect SAC bases from destruction. RAND's Herman Kahn added to this basic outlook some interest in building passive defenses in the form of nuclear fallout shelters. RAND also advocated building up conventional forces so that Soviet aggression would reap repercussions short of all-out nuclear exchange in the event of smaller-scale incidents.

According to the various assessments of RAND's importance, which all to some extent resemble the original put forth in *The RAND Corporation*,[59] Wohlstetter and his troupe put forth a devastating critique of America's national security, and only by persistent effort throughout the latter half of the 1950s woke the nation out of its complacency in the face of the Soviet threat.[60] Deborah Shapley, in her biography of Robert McNamara, for example, speaks of "the definitive RAND findings."[61] The difficulty with these glorious assessments is that they assume what needs to be explained: that, contrary to all intelligence reports available then or since, the RAND team discovered a fundamental, and heretofore unacknowledged, fact of American vulnerability. The real question is how, despite mounting evidence to the contrary, the RAND defense rationalists managed to convince the nation of its vulnerability and to justify a mind-boggling peace-time arms build up that outstripped the Soviet's armament manufacture pace by a factor of at least 15 to 1. The answer lies in careful political maneuvering, persistence, and through the claims to superior knowledge and objectivity.

By 1957 it seemed clear to RAND researchers and to Air Force officials that RAND's studies were not of much use to the development of Air Force weapons or strategic policy. The mid-1950s were a time of decreased international tension, and military projects were faced with the prospect of funding cutbacks. RAND was no different, and the largest topic of discussion at the spring 1957 board meeting was the impending budget cuts and prospect of staff reduction. RAND's board of trustees, while never entering into the administrative details of RAND, was nevertheless concerned with the institution's overall well-being. H. Rowan Gaither Jr., with his consuming interest in RAND, did not sit idly by as RAND awaited stagnation, even decay, and as RAND's bold national security initiatives faded into obscurity.[62]

The Plan—Radical Reorganization of the Department of Defense through Rational Defense Management

On October 4, 1957, the Soviets launched *Sputnik I*, the first earth-orbiting satellite. Thirty-one days later, H. Rowan Gaither Jr. submitted to President Dwight D. Eisenhower a top secret, fear-mongering report entitled "Deterrence and Survival in the Nuclear Age." Two decades later Senator William Proxmire, vice chairman of the Joint Committee on Defense Production, which first released the top secret report in 1976, acknowledged the report's legacy, stating "few documents have had such a great an influence on American strategic thinking."[63] This report precipitated widespread belief in the fallacious "missile gap" that was to play a crucial role in the 1960 presidential campaign, and led the charge for civilian control of the Pentagon along the lines of rational defense management. Based on extremely hawkish conjectures of Soviet military capabilities and intentions, the report provided a pivotal issue for John F. Kennedy's victorious campaign and launched RAND's strategy cadre into national prominence. The "Gaither Report" continues to be woven into the fabric of American history as an unquestioned source for assessing President Eisenhower's and President Kennedy's national security policies.[64]

On April 4, 1957, President Eisenhower commissioned several studies of the nation's civil defense and nuclear fallout shelter program.[65] Among these was a study to be undertaken by the Security Resources Panel, nominally under the jurisdiction of the Office for Defense Mobilization. The panel, comprised of civilian experts, was modeled on the 1955 Killian Technical Capabilities panel that had benefited from the advice of RAND researchers. H. Rowan Gaither Jr., then chairman of the boards of both RAND and the Ford Foundation, was selected to be the committee chair, and the committee and its report were subsequently named after him. Although Gaither was hospitalized with cancer the following September,[66] which resulted in the committee's leadership being passed on to industrialists Robert Sprague and William C. Foster, Gaither personally oversaw the formation of the committee and presented its findings at the highly classified November 4 meeting of the National Security Council with President Eisenhower attending.

The Gaither committee's roster included sixty-seven project members. Edward P. Oliver of RAND was hired in the fall as a special technical advisor to the steering committee, along with Paul H. Nitze, former assistant secretary of defense. Eisenhower appointed an advisory panel that included retired military officers; Frank Stanton, president of CBS; two prominent Republican financiers, Robert A. Lovett and John J. McCloy; physicists I. I. Rabi and Ernest O. Lawrence; and James R. Killian. Herbert Kahn, who was working on fallout shelters at RAND, was a consultant to the panel.[67] Albert Wohlstetter also worked with the committee contributing his views of SAC vulnerability, which ended up being crucial to the committee's findings on U.S. defensive preparedness.[68] Nitze, author of the important 1950 national security directive "NSC 68," drafted the report.

President Eisenhower had admonished the panel to stay focused on the issue of civil defense. Even so, the committee seized on the opportunity to provide a comprehensive review and critique of the Eisenhower administration's national security policies, both foreign and domestic. The committee members used the fallout shelter program as a springboard to make major policy recommendations. The final report warned of extreme SAC vulnerability, inspired fear of potential Soviet technological superiority, and advocated the expenditure of an additional $19 billion to counter the perceived threat from Soviet intercontinental ballistic missiles (ICBMs), this at a time when the annual budget of the U.S. Department of Defense (DOD) totaled $38 billion. To meet the wildly speculative estimates of existing Soviet weapons capabilities, the report advocated building six hundred ICBMs, rather than the planned 130, in the next several years. Anticipating reasonable concern about footing such a bill, the report went on to express confidence in America's economic capacity to pay for its defense.[69] As monumental as was the military buildup advocated by the Gaither Report, the even more extraordinary aspect of the report was its authors' explicitly stated intent wholly to restructure decisionmaking in the Pentagon. The Gaither Report called for a "radical reorganization of the Department of Defense" to achieve "more effective control and management of our defense resources," regardless of the fact that initially this reordering "might cause such confusion . . . as to weaken our defense."[70] Such a total reorganization of the Pentagon would clearly lead to the opportunity to direct even more extensive appropriations and expenditures. The fallout shelter program also received attention, but was deemed a "lower value" priority and was generally considered to be a losing proposition.

Under the leadership of Gaither, who had chaired the RAND board of trustees for a decade, it was no surprise that the report reflected RAND's strategic agenda: SAC vulnerability was center stage, with the attendant logic of preparedness for nuclear second-strike counterforce capabilities.[71] The Gaither Report's advocacy of rational defense management also resonated with RAND's steadfast emphasis on cost-effectiveness analysis, as well as its "planning–programming" method of budgeting then under development by David Novick. RANDites and the Gaither Report were united in advocating that military strategy and defense planning be based on rational choices.[72] Unsurprisingly as well, the Gaither Report reflected the Air Force's strategic agenda that emphasized second-strike, counterforce capabilities in opposition to the Navy and Army, which adhered to a doctrine of minimum deterrence.[73]

By providing seemingly authoritative documentation, the Gaither Report triggered the 1957 missile gap debate and gave rise to the fear that the United States was lagging behind the Soviet Union in technological war-fighting capabilities. The report grounded speculation that unless drastic measures were taken, rapid Soviet missile production would lead to an 8 to 1 Soviet advantage by 1962.[74] The looming threat of a purported missile gap waxed and waned in the public's mind throughout 1958 and 1959, but eventually took root as a pivotal issue in the 1960 campaign. The strategic logic on which the reality and significance of the missile gap was premised linked the supposed Soviet ICBM advantage, the concept of SAC vulnerability, and the strategic doctrine of second-strike counterforce in a single, mutually dependent logical chain. Any potential Soviet missile advantage was alarming only if the Soviets intended to attempt to knock out all forty-two U.S. bomber bases simultaneously in a preemptive strike; this eventuality assumed that a minimum deterrent threat of retaliation was insufficient to check potential Soviet aggression. Phantasms of such an all-out strike reminiscent of Peal Harbor fueled the commitment to second-strike capabilities that not only could survive such an onslaught but subsequently inflict punitive damage on the order of a preemptive first strike, and in this way function as a deterrent. It would subsequently become evident that the Air Force's repeated doubts about RAND's SAC vulnerability scenario was a function of its offensive plan to strike a preemptive blow at the earliest sign of Soviet aggression, and therefore never to be placed in the position of needing a counterforce.[75]

As the story is often told, the Soviets' launch of the first *Sputnik* on October 4, 1957 galvanized public recognition of the importance of scientific and technological achievement to the Cold War effort, and focused public energy in support of other Cold War policies. However, the immediate press and popular response was one of mixed wonder and enthusiasm for

the Soviets' technological accomplishment, outweighing alarmist, gloomy
views that if the Soviets could launch a 184-pound metallic object into orbit, they would similarly be capable of launching intercontinental ballistic missiles toward the United States.[76] President Eisenhower had received
advanced warning of the launch, and expert opinion as to its significance
and the threat it posed was balanced, suggesting that the launch of *Sputnik* was no real indication of the Soviets' ability to launch missiles and
that, in fact, their missile capability had not changed much from that reported in the 1956 issue of *Missiles and Rockets*.[77]

On November 4, the Soviets launched *Sputnik II*, weighing 1,118
pounds and carrying a live dog. Still, it was recognized that the satellite
launch did not demonstrate the technological facility with reentry and
guidance required for missiles. Before *Sputnik* could assume ominous
proportions, it had to be interpreted as threatening; nurturing a sense of
foreboding was one way to effect such an interpretation, one driven by the
promise of political dividends.[78] *Sputnik* provided Senator Lyndon B.
Johnson, then chairman of the Preparedness Investigating Subcommittee
of the Senate Armed Services Committee, with the opportunity to criticize
the Eisenhower administration's national security posture in his "Inquiry
into Satellite and Missile Programs," initiated on November 25, 1957.
"Sputnik" had to become a processed media event before it could become
a symbol of lagging American technological achievement and then a ral-
lying point for efforts toward a ferocious arms buildup. Much to the disappointment of military hard-liners, in the immediate wake of the satellite's launch, the public's calm response was to trust the assessment of
President Eisenhower, the retired general and World War II hero, that the
satellite signified no real advantage on the part of the Soviet war-fighting
capabilities.[79] As would become evident, *Sputnik* alone was not sufficient
to mobilize public opinion in favor of increased defense spending.[80]

The *Sputniks* did provide an auspicious occasion for the Gaither committee to present its alarmist conclusions.[81] The report was hastily completed a week after the *Sputnik* launch. The report had been circulated
prior to the scheduled National Security Council (NSC) meetings so that
attendees would be primed to respond. At the well-attended November 7
meeting briefed by Robert Sprague, none of the department heads advocated the Gaither proposal; Secretary of State John Foster Dulles spoke
out against it.[82] Republican financiers John J. McCloy and Robert A.
Lovett, on the Gaither committee's advisory panel, advocated the proposal, arguing that the American economy could pay the bill and that
"the people as a whole and the business community in particular would
support the President if he urged increased spending for defense."[83]

President Eisenhower, a career military officer, was singularly unimpressed with the report. Not only did he know it to be based on incomplete Air Force intelligence, he also was not about to concede any national defense weakness. A memorandum of a conversation between Secretary of State John Foster Dulles and the president sums up the administration's view on the Gaither Report:

> On the basis of Mr. Sprague's confidential briefing as to the SAC reaction possibilities under certain extreme circumstances, I expressed to the President the view that I felt that these possibilities were so remote in practice that I doubted whether we would be justified in going to the extremes in the way of cost that alertness would require. The possibility considered was that in a time of relative tranquillity and a reduction of international tension there would be mounted a massive surprise attack against the United States and simultaneously against all our important bases.[84]

As mentioned above, the Gaither Report's dire view of the U.S. strategic situation depended on a scenario in which the Soviet Union launched a successful, preemptive surprise attack on all forty-two U.S. SAC bases simultaneously—a scenario Dulles reasonably regarded as fantastically improbable. Dulles's other reservations included the Gaither committee's lack of consideration for broader issues, such as the effects of their proposal on European allies. The record of an evening meeting between the president and the chiefs and secretaries of the military departments on November 4, 1957 makes it clear that although missile development was a topic of discussion, the joint chiefs were not worried about any looming Soviet military superiority. Eisenhower's major concern was that interservice rivalry detracted from the overall defense preparedness, and this seems to be why he set up the meeting.[85] Normal procedure dictated that the Gaither Report be buried and forgotten soon after the NSC meeting on November 7; Eisenhower's and his staff's comments in the NSC documents make clear that they treated it as just one more report.[86] However, the Gaither committee members refused to let its report be buried and began actively campaigning for their proposal.[87]

In some accounts of the Gaither committee's role in strategic policymaking, leeway is given to their aggressive tone and unsubstantiated assumptions on the basis that committee members were not privy to highly secret data from the U-2 intelligence-gathering flights over the Soviet Union that had begun in June 1956.[88] These missions, which few in the administration knew anything about, eventually allowed the president to be reasonably confident that the Soviet ICBM program was not far advanced.[89] However, the Gaither committee's lack of data does not provide sufficient cause to ground their conjecture of a missile gap. Furthermore, the CIA's Richard M. Bissell, who oversaw the U-2 project, was on the Gaither committee, and thus well-positioned to temper any excess of speculation had he so desired or had committee members been persuaded. [90]

President Eisenhower addressed the nation on the evening of November 7, speaking about science and national security. He announced he was creating the office of Special Assistant to the President for Science and Technology, to be headed by James R. Killian, president of MIT. This announcement anticipated Eisenhower's November 22 transfer of the Science Advisory Committee of the Office of Defense Mobilization to the White House, formally creating the President's Science Advisory Committee.[91] Of all the presidential speeches in the wake of the *Sputniks*, Eisenhower's second radio address on November 14, during which he discussed science and national security, seems most to echo the findings of Gaither Report. Eisenhower stated that SAC vulnerability required additional funds, that deterrent capabilities were needed against a Soviet preemptive attack, and America needed to improve its ability to fight limited war.[92]

The Gaither committee members, who had invested heavily in the urgency of their conclusions, knew that Eisenhower's public speech hardly signified that there would be any quick move to alter SAC alert status, or to accelerate ICBM development. William Foster led the committee's three-pronged strategy that was designed to further their proposal. The committee sought to convince Eisenhower directly, to convince members of relevant executive agencies, and to gain the support of the public and elite groups. The committee members struck out on their first two initiatives; neither the president nor one single executive agency was brought over to their position.[93] One reason that various agencies may not have been enthusiastic about the Gaither program was that all of its recommendations were predicated on there being no budget ceilings; the committee had put forth a plan radically to increase military spending in all of their policy proposals. According to Morton Halperin, hesitancy on the part of agencies may have been due to their fear that increased defense spending meant cuts from other agencies. Halperin, who is the only author to have written an in-depth study of the role of the Gaither committee in the policymaking process, suggests that the committee members acted entirely rationally, and that the president's advisors and Cabinet heads were dragging their feet for their own private reasons. However, Halperin consulted with Paul Nitze and RANDites Thomas Schelling, Henry Rowen, and Paul Hammond in writing his article, and himself was under RAND employment in 1960.[94] Halperin's more speculative conclusions are presented without documentation, and the documents that do exist support the finding that whereas the Gaither group was extreme in its prodefensive posture, those in other executive agencies did not exhibit such a degree of fearfulness or paranoia.

As Halperin describes the politics of the Gaither Report, alliances were broken into two groups. On one side were the president, members of his Cabinet, and some congressional leaders, who at most advocated limited increases in defense spending. On the other side stood the Gaither committee, congressional Democrats, some dissatisfied Republicans, and media moguls, for whom *Sputnik* provided the opportunity to claim that America's very survival was at stake in the face of the Soviets' evil intent and superior military preparedness. The latter alliance sought to awaken a complacent nation to the reality of looming peril. Members of the hawkish element, Halperin acknowledges, had been long-standing proponents of substantially increased defense appropriations.[95] Just how militant the Gaither committee's views were is evident in a conversation personally initiated by Robert Sprague, co-chair of the committee, with the secretary of state and the undersecretary Gerard C. Smith. The printed record of this conversation outlines Sprague's assessment of the four policy options available to the United States:

1. Continue the present policy. Only if the Soviet Union engages in aggression will we attack it.
2. Preventative war. The Soviet long-range striking force is on 27 bases. We could destroy this Soviet striking power, and if "clean" weapons were used we could do this without killing a great many Soviet non-combatants. Since US planes are continually flying around the world, it should be technically easier for us to mount a surprise attack than the Soviets to do the same. After striking out the Russian strategic bombardment capability, we could then dictate disarmament terms.
3. Conduct a "hot" negotiation. This, in effect, would be to threaten the Soviet Union that if it did not settle on US disarmament terms we would change our present policy against preventative war.
4. Place reliance in God to find a solution. Mr. Sprague pointed out that during the course of his work with the Gaither panel his resort to prayer had substantially increased. He wonders what device the Lord could resort to in view of past evil actions of Soviet rulers.

The memorandum of the conversation continues, "Given these alternatives, Mr. Sprague feels that the better opportunities for the survival of freedom lie in alternatives 2 and 3."[96]

Having struck out with the president and the agencies, the Gaither committee members attempted to launch their campaign in the forum of public opinion. This required leaking the results of their top secret document to the press, and pushing for its outright publication. The contents of the report were leaked to the press in late November and December of 1957.[97] Between press leaks and the colorful language of prodefense journalists, the public imagination was fired. Stuart Alsop authoritatively reported:

> There is no doubt at all that strategic missiles will surely replace the manned bombers, as the longbow replaced the knights' swords. The prospect which immediately confronts us is that the Soviets will achieve this replacement before we do. There will then be a gap—in the Pentagon it is known simply and ominously as The Gap—during which we will be in somewhat the position of the mounted French knights at Crécy, sword in hand, facing the skilled British bowmen killing them at will.[98]

"The Gap" had taken on a reality and life of its own.

The battle over retaining the top secret status of the Gaither Report was motivated by the politics entailed in making it public. Eisenhower realized that if the report were published, it would gain an aura of legitimacy that eluded it as long as it remained classified and unavailable. Senator Lyndon B. Johnson, then chairman of the Preparedness Investigating Subcommittee of the Committee on Armed Services, took up the cause of publishing the Gaither Report. Johnson pressed the matter with Secretary of State Dulles. When Dulles spoke of it to the president several days later, their conversation concentrated on how out of hand the Gaither situation had become, with Eisenhower lamenting that "this experience had proved . . . definitively, the unwisdom of calling in outside groups." Dulles concurred, agreeing that, "they seldom took a rounded view of the total situation."[99] The Eisenhower administration had nothing to gain by releasing the report; indeed, if released, it would lend credibility to the report's authors and other critics of the administration's defense policy. Eisenhower was especially concerned to make sure that the Gaither Report's timetable for defense buildups not be entered into the public record as a credible template for guiding U.S. policy.[100] At the January 3, 1958 meeting of the NSC, an exasperated Eisenhower sighed that "before we got done with this Gaither thing we would find ourselves obliged to do things which we normally would never think of doing"—such as releasing a classified, independently commissioned, expert report.[101]

On November 25, 1957, Senator Johnson began hearings, entitled "Inquiry into Satellite and Missile Programs," in which over sixty prominent men inside and outside of government were brought in to testify on the state of U.S. defense preparedness and the implications of the Soviets' recent launchings of the *Sputniks*. Edward Teller and Vannevar Bush led off the testimony, which continued into the next year and filled more than one thousand pages of transcript. Prominent military leaders, including General Maxwell D. Taylor, U.S. Army chief, Admiral Arleigh A. Burke, U.S. Navy chief of naval operations, and General Thomas D. White, U.S. Air Force chief of staff, were called before the committee. Johnson used these hearings to mount pressure on the Republican administration, implying weakness in the face of the Soviet threat symbolized by the its successful satellite program. Johnson's capable leadership kept his senatorial adversary, Republican Stuart Symington, in check and avoided personal attacks on the president, while casting doubt on the administration's ability to carry out effective national security policy. Throughout the questioning, references were made to the elusive Gaither Report, which Johnson insisted he was constantly putting pressure on the Eisenhower administration to release.[102]

In making their case, the network of individuals in favor of the Gaither committee's conclusions did not limit themselves to direct and secret means of support. Donald K. David, chairman of the executive committee of the Ford Foundation, headed an organization that represented a consortium of business interests: the aptly named Committee for Economic Development, or CED. This committee, which had been founded by the Ford Foundation's Paul Hoffman and Theodore O. Yntma of Ford Motor Company during World War II, claimed to provide objective, expert advice in the form of national policy statements.[103] In 1957 the CED was significant both for its overlap of membership with the Gaither committee and its inclusion of representatives from the top management of over one hundred of America's leading industrial corporations. The Gaither committee's co-director, William C. Foster, served on the CED's Subcommittee on Economic Policies for National Security. Gaither committee advisory panel member and Republican financier Robert A. Lovett served as an honorary trustee of the organization. Richard M. Bissell Jr. served as an advisor, along with RAND's head of economics, Charles Hitch. Other members of interest with prominent CED roles include Don K. Price, vice president of the Ford Foundation; W. Allen Wallis, dean of the University of Chicago's school of business and future president of the University of Rochester; and Ralph W. Tyler, director of the Center for the Advanced Study in the Behavioral Sciences, which had been established at Stanford University with Ford Foundation money in 1955.

In July 1958, the CED publicly issued a report entitled "The Problem of National Security: Some Economic and Administrative Aspects," which echoed the findings of the Gaither Report. The clear intent of the tract was to convince its readers of the necessity of increased military spending in view of the Soviet's growing technological superiority, which it claimed to be demonstrated by the *Sputniks* and their presumed ICBM lead. The statement also sought to persuade its readers of America's economic ability to "afford what we have to afford." [104] The report pointedly argued for the role of "civilian economizers" in defense planning, and for the need to reorganize decisionmaking within the Department of Defense along the lines of "rational and efficient" defense management. [105] Taking a leaf from RAND's economics chief Charles Hitch's studies of defense economics, the report emphasized the need for rational decisions and rational choices in defense management; promoted "maximiz[ing] our military capability to achieve national objectives"; advocated "rational techniques for making good choices of defense strategy and management"; and anticipated the planning–programming method of budgeting. [106] Thus, in addition to a massive defense buildup, the CED policy statement called for a wholesale restructuring of decisionmaking practices within DOD on the premise that civilian defense experts could rationally manage defense resources better than military commanders.

There was a lull in public interest in the missile gap for much of 1958. [107] In May 1958, RAND strategist Albert Wohlstetter was invited to speak at the Council of Foreign Relations in New York. [108] In September he was selected to serve as deputy chief scientist in charge of a delegation of 105 scientists and strategy experts to Geneva negotiations on reducing the dangers of surprise attack. While not notable for their success, these meetings helped further Wohlstetter's career and those of other RAND defense rationalists who managed to place themselves in the national spotlight. [109] In January 1959, Wohlstetter published his well-known article "The Delicate Balance of Terror" in *Foreign Affairs*, reigniting concern over the missile gap and U.S. vulnerability to surprise Soviet attack. Presidential contender John F. Kennedy, who had earlier made speeches capitalizing on Eisenhower's national security weakness, ignored the gap in the late-spring Democratic primary election. In August, however, he geared up his campaign by touting Republican weakness in the face of the Soviet threat and missile gap. Wohlstetter and fellow RANDites participated eagerly as Kennedy speechwriter Theodore Sorenson worked their views in campaign speeches. [110] Republican candidate and vice president Richard Nixon was unable to respond effectively because President Eisenhower refused to let him reveal the secret intelligence that formed the basis of his confidence in America's military preparedness. Kennedy's successful exploitation of the missile gap theme in the election is consistently cited as a crucial factor in his victory.[111]

Despite the exposure of the U-2 spy flights, Eisenhower's secret source, in May of 1960 when the Soviets shot down a plane, Eisenhower had decided to remain silent about his knowledge of Soviet military capabilities at the peril of his own reputation, and a Democratic election victory, most likely because the veil of uncertainty over Soviet capabilities reassured the Russians.[112] As he stepped down from office and bade farewell to the American people, he pointedly warned of the encroachment on public decisionmaking procedures by a "military-industrial complex," etching his famous phrase into public consciousness. He further warned that "public policy could itself become captive of a scientific technological elite." In this remark, Eisenhower was likely referring to the Gaither committee, which had gained a life of its own in American strategic history.[113] Indeed, whereas Eisenhower had been alarmed at the steady increases in estimation of the potential damages of nuclear weaponry that could be delivered and sustained by both sides during his years in office, and had committed his administration to a policy of disarmament and to reducing the chances of fighting a nuclear war, the legacy of the Gaither Report's "Deterrence and Survival in a Nuclear Age," and of RAND's strategic agenda was to render nuclear war as thinkable, fightable, and survivable. A second legacy was about to rock the Pentagon, as Kennedy's victory landed key RANDites powerful positions in DOD. These RAND alumni carried the firm commitment to reorganizing decisionmaking procedures within the Pentagon along the lines of rational defense management strategies developed at RAND and ushered into the high councils of government a new science of policy analysis.

Implementation—Rational Defense Management

President-elect Kennedy's choice of Robert S. McNamara to serve as his secretary of defense, after McNamara had assumed the presidency of Ford Motor Company one day following the election, completed the network of connections initiated by the early alliance of RAND and Henry Ford's foundation. The alliance of Henry Ford II, his philanthropic organization and its chairman H. Rowan Gaither Jr., Gaither's RAND compatriots, as well as a business constituency represented by Robert A. Lovett, John J. McCloy, and the Committee for Economic Development, were united in their objectives. They promoted massive defense expenditures and a plan wholly to reorganize decisionmaking procedures within the Department of Defense by vesting a new policy elite whose authority would derive from the supposed objectivity of rational policy analysis.

McNamara, a protégé of both Henry Ford II and Robert Lovett, served as the point man to implement the set of strategic policies and management methods that had been under development at RAND for a decade.

McNamara's style and résumé appealed to Kennedy for a number of reasons: He was a Republican, which would help reduce partisan criticism of Kennedy's foreign and defense policies; he was Ivy League and enjoyed rapport with academics; he bristled with quantitative reasoning and economic efficiency, which fit Kennedy's image; and he was imbued with youthful vitality and vigor. Most important, he came to Kennedy on the recommendation of Robert A. Lovett, the prominent financier on the Gaither panel, who had followed McNamara's career ever since his fledgling steps with the Army Air Force's Statistical Control during World War II.[114]

McNamara's condition for accepting office was to have complete autonomy and control over all decisions affecting DOD. As a mid-level executive at Ford, McNamara had subscribed to Henry Ford II's modern, rational management program and had implemented centralized financial planning and control. Two tenets encapsulated McNamara's management philosophy. He believed that "[m]anagement is the gate through which social, political and economic and technological change . . . is rationally and effectively spread through society," and that "running the Department of Defense is no different from running Ford Motor Company or the Catholic Church."[115]

Shortly after taking office, at his first press conference, reporters asked the new secretary about the missile gap. McNamara admitted that "if there was a gap, it's in our favor." When McNamara's easy tongue came to Kennedy's attention, the president was quite displeased, suggesting that the continued public belief in the gap was important. At subsequent press conferences, McNamara would contradict his initial statement, maintaining the existence of a fallacious gap.[116] As 1961 wore on, the believability of the gap grew increasingly difficult to sustain, and by the year's end the gap had evaporated into the annals of history.[117] By 1963 it was out in the open that as of September 1961, the Soviets had only produced one-thirtieth of the missiles they had been forecast to have in 1959.[118]

The missile gap, while ultimately having all the substance of the Cheshire Cat, nonetheless left as its legacy an indelible toothy grin. Whereas the purported gap gradually disappeared between 1957 and 1963, the manufactured fear of Soviet military superiority served as the rationale to initiate an unprecedented peacetime armaments buildup. The ironic legacy of the "gap," once the U.S. weapons program got underway, was an American ICBM advantage of at least 15 to 1. The Kennedy administration, on McNamara's initiative, presided over the largest peace-time build up of the armed forces in American history, with the annual military budget rising from $41 billion in 1961 to $49 billion in 1962 and $54.3 billion in 1963.[119] Despite the initial American advantage in missiles, within his first year of office McNamara increased the number of Polaris submarines from Eisenhower's six to a force of forty-one carrying 656 missiles. Since submarines could move about the ocean undetected, and provided a guarantee of a surviving deterrent in the eventuality of a Soviet first strike, a small Polaris force had satisfied those in favor of a policy of minimum deterrent. But McNamara took his advice from RAND strategists who advocated a devastating second-strike counterforce policy that depended on the more accurately guided, land-based ICBMs. Thus, McNamara also doubled the production of intercontinental Minuteman missiles. Whereas Eisenhower had planned to have only forty Atlas missiles in addition to the six Polaris subs, by the end of their first year in office, McNamara and Kennedy were building the U.S. arsenal up to 1,856 missiles, at a time when most contemporary intelligence reported that the Soviets had at most fifty to one hundred missiles. Counting manned bombers, by 1967 McNamara planned to have 3,455 nuclear warheads aimed at the Soviet Union.[120] This massive arms build up continued throughout the 1960s, resulting in the doubling of the defense budget between 1961 and 1968, with a staggering 56 percent of the funds in the 1969 federal budget—10 percent of America's gross national product—going to the military.[121]

McNamara assumed the position of secretary of defense with the vision of cutting through bureaucratic red tape and streamlining traditional military modus operandi. His determination to apply rational management techniques was matched only by his ambition for total control. During McNamara's tenure in the Pentagon, rational management and absolute central control went hand in hand. McNamara's changes in procedure had the effect of radically shifting the locus of authority from officers ranging the chain of command throughout the services to the single figure of the secretary of defense himself, a man with no prior military experience who had contempt for military traditions. This de facto shift in power paralleled a shift in the principle grounding legitimate authority: instead of relying on the experience and judgment of seasoned military officers who had been tested in the crucible of battle, the new principle of authority was anchored in claims of scientific rigor and objective calculation. McNamara's takeover of the defense establishment was all or nothing; he did not deign to share decisionmaking power with military men, but rather sought to dictate decisions to them. Samuel

Huntington captured the essence of the McNamara revolution in military management as it unfurled. Looking ahead to McNamara's success, Huntington observed that "strategic programs, like other major policies, are not [yet] the product of expert planners, who rationally determine the actions necessary to achieve desired goals. They are the result of controversy, negotiation, and bargaining among officials and groups with different interests and perspectives."[122]

As appealing as it is to credit McNamara and his zeal for power with the rational management takeover of the Department of Defense, which "sparked an intellectual revolution that changed American policy making and public life," this attribution shifts attention away from a more pervasive and interesting pattern of operational forces that underlay the implementation of a top-down, centralized decision procedure of "managerial . . . control and command" within the Pentagon.[123] Although it was McNamara who facilitated the total restructuring of DOD, he did so by acting as a gatekeeper for the wholesale importation of a defense management infrastructure that had been under design for more than a decade at RAND. One can only marvel that the rational defense strategists installed under McNamara brought to Washington precisely what H. Rowan Gaither had first envisioned as the goal of philanthropy: a professional elite, with its own set of practices and standards, that would objectively decide difficult questions of policy affecting the nation.

McNamara, who knew nothing of military matters, studied up in the few days before taking office. He was introduced to RANDites Charles Hitch's and Roland McKean's *The Economics of Defense in the Nuclear Age*,[124] whose plan for rational defense management struck a chord with the new secretary. McNamara met with Hitch in December and immediately proposed that Hitch serve as DOD comptroller. Hitch was the first of an influx of RAND appointments under McNamara. The incoming secretary, who was not studied in military matters such as weapons systems or strategy, found in RAND researchers like-minded individuals, similarly committed to rational analysis, who could provide him with the counsel and methods he required to run the defense establishment. The list of RAND appointments would grow to include Alain Enthoven, Henry Rowen, Thomas Schelling, William Niskanen, Daniel Ellsberg, James R. Schlesinger, Bruno Augenstein, and Frank Trinkl. Many other RANDites would work with the secretary of defense in contracts set up through his office. William Kaufmann advised McNamara and wrote speeches for him. In short, RAND alumni suited McNamara's style of quantitative analysis and became his closest associates in a world of military men whom he held in contempt.[125] McNamara also worked closely with the Gaither Report's author, Paul Nitze, whom he appointed as assistant secretary of defense for International Security Affairs.

Alain Enthoven, who had risen to prominence on the wings of Albert Wohlstetter's SAC vulnerability conjecture, became one of McNamara's most trusted appointees. McNamara was captivated by RAND's promise of decision theoretic tools and management techniques, and he created the Office of Systems Analysis, which Enthoven directed as an assistant secretary.[126] In an action that would end up forever changing U.S. governmental policymaking practices and that prepared the way for the dawning of a new era of policy analysis, RAND's "systems analysis" became an official designation. Although in practice no more clearly defined than during its RAND days, this new status signified the de facto acceptance of RAND's notion of "systems analysis" as a credible method for reaching decisions in complex matters of logistics, weapons procurement and military strategy.[127] However, as was always the case with RAND's decision technologies, their use proved to be inseparable from the politics of control. In the years ahead, Enthoven's office would oversee all of DOD's systems analysis studies. As one example of the range of authority this office carried under McNamara, Enthoven headed a team of eighteen analysts who were charged by the secretary with the task of rethinking all of the Army's standard operating procedures, even down to the level of two-man well-digging detachments.[128] Just as workers, foremen, and engineers had been shut out of decisionmaking at the Ford Motor Company, so frontline military personnel lost autonomy over local decisions in accord with the rationale that analysts with equations could make large- and small-scale decisions better than men in the field. McNamara's consistent pattern was to place civilian defense analysts in positions of authority over high-ranking military officers. For example, he put the former RAND economist William Gorham in charge of a military pay schedule study, making as Gorham's subordinates several senior generals. Even though Gorham's study resulted in the largest pay increases in the history of the armed services, McNamara's management procedures continually alienated the military.[129]

McNamara's takeover of the Pentagon was made possible by the set of decision-theoretic and management tools supplied to him by RAND staff. He brought with him the commitment to, and experience with, rational management techniques he used at Ford. However, managing the defense establishment required more specialized tools, such as those that RAND researchers had been contributing to throughout the 1950s.[130] Thus, the core of McNamara's management tools were developed by RAND, including systems analysis, cost-effectiveness (or cost-benefit) analysis, and

Planning-Programming-Budgeting.[131] The Planning-Programming-Budgeting System, which was foreshadowed in both the secret Gaither Report and the public Committee for Economic Development policy statements, was the centerpiece of McNamara's summary transfer of authority from uniformed officers to himself and his cadre of civilian defense rationalists. McNamara in effect functioned as point man for a plan to place the forty-plus billion dollar defense establishment into the hands of civilian leadership, tied more closely to the business community's interests than to military imperatives.

At the Senate hearings to confirm McNamara's nomination of Charles Hitch to the powerful position of DOD comptroller, legislators expressed incredulity at placing the DOD into the hands of men with little military experience and, in the case of Charles Hitch, no prior budgeting experience. This concern was best articulated by Senator Bridges, who remarked: "[I]t seems to me very peculiar that this new administration should pick out a man like yourself, with no experience and background, for this job. . . . [O]ne of the things that has troubled me and many other people is that you were selected for this particular spot." [132] Despite such concerns, Hitch was confirmed, and by the spring of 1961 Secretary McNamara assigned him the task of installing RAND's Planning-Programming-Budgeting System throughout the DOD within four months. This was a challenging order for which Hitch required the help of David Novick. Thus one of three contracts to RAND from the office of the secretary of defense was for Novick and a sizeable RAND team to implement the new budgeting system.[133]

That system, officially designated as "PPBS," was characterized by three interlocking features. One was an emphasis on "planning," or associating the budgeting function with the planning function such that budget formation became a decisionmaker's tool for creating policy. Achieving this association required changing the categories according to which the defense budget was traditionally prepared, so that instead of being ordered according to broad categories such as manpower and construction, the budget was organized by program functions that the military fulfilled, such as "Strategic Retaliatory Forces," and "General Purpose Forces." [134] The recategorization of budget items permitted the associating of "inputs" with "outputs," so that programs would be amenable to cost-effectiveness studies. This direct linkage of strategy and budgeting represented a major change in military organization, effectively shifting the jurisdiction for strategy and operations from military officers to civilian policy analysts.[135]

The use of systems analysis represents the second significant feature of

PPBS. Alain Enthoven's Systems Analysis Office, which would grow to have a staff of 130, had the responsibility for preparing cost-effectiveness studies on all potential budget items so that Secretary McNamara could base his decisions on objective, quantitative assessments of the military worth of various proposals. Instead of year-to-year budgets, costs and potential financial outlays were estimated for longer periods of five years.

Finally, as the Gaither and CED policy statements strongly urged, budget ceilings were removed so that defense planners could stipulate their perception of national security needs without the annoying constraint of working within the guidelines of appropriations decreed by Congress. The Gaither Report, the CED policy statement, Hitch's and McKean's *The Economics of Defense,* and McNamara were agreed on inverting the policy process: instead of fiscal appropriations being handed down from Congress to meet operational needs, defense planners would articulate their needs using presumptively objective and thus incontrovertible cost-effectiveness studies. Instead of Congress' determining how much national security the nation could afford, national defense imperatives should determine defense allocations on the principle that "there . . . [be] no presumption that the defense budget is now, or should be, near any immovable upper limit." Hitch and McKean further authoritatively observed that "[a]s far as physical and economic feasibility is concerned, national security expenditures could be raised . . . by, say, $30 billion per year." [136]

The authority for this bold restructuring came from the supposed scientific rigor promised by such a budgetary process. Enthoven, in his capacity as assistant secretary of defense for systems analysis, frequently lectured at the nation's war colleges on the new PPBS and systems analysis approach to defense planning. As part of his presentation, he would make the following points:

(1) Systems Analysis is a reasoned approach to problems of decision, accurately described as "quantitative common sense."
(2) Systems Analysis is an application of scientific method, using that term in its broadest sense.
(3) There are limitations in the application of Systems Analysis, although these have often been overstated.[137]

"Systems analysis," while in practice no less vague than during its RAND days, was constantly promoted by advocates as a "scientific" means of reaching difficult policy judgments. Charles Hitch also spoke publicly on the advantages of the new "management techniques" that aided decisionmakers in "achieving realistic, balanced, rational plans." [138] For analysts and some policymakers, PPBS and systems analysis offered the promise that "[m]any significant decisions on resource allocation . . . [could] be rational, objective, quantitative, depersonalized, de-bureaucratized, [and] de-politicized." [139] McNamara's management device carried authority precisely because its practitioners wielded an epistemic edge afforded them by their claims to scientific method.

Whereas even Comptroller Hitch was quick to acknowledge that the "whole [PPBS–systems analysis] systems seems to be singularly plagued by terminological confusion," consensus on the impact of PPBS by critics and proponents alike was unequivocal: it dramatically centralized decisionmaking in DOD, squarely placing authority for decisions in the hands of Secretary McNamara. [140] Thomas Schelling, a high-profile RAND alumni who worked under the secretary, told the Senate that "budgetary processes are a means of control. Secretary McNamara surely did not use PPBS . . . merely to cut waste and to improve efficiency or to save money. He took advantage of his central role in the defense-budgeting process to exercise what he believed to be his authority over military policy." [141] PPBS worked to centralize and consolidate authority by eliminating discussion over policies and procurement decisions, and by presenting budgetary information to McNamara in such a form that he could rapidly make decisions about any financial outlay of more than $20 million.

In the turf battle for control over the U.S. armed forces, the civilian defense rationalists won a decisive victory. Power for strategic weapons procurement decisions was shifted from the joint chiefs to the DOD secretary and his "whiz kids" administrators. Outside observers were clear that the centralization of power into the hands of the civilian administrators had been both the intention behind and the result of the RAND-inspired budgeting system. [142] Furthermore, it was also clear that the means by which authority was shifted was through the epistemic leverage afforded by supposedly scientific cost-effectiveness analysis. One observer noted how the new decisionmaking methods shifted power not just to civilians, but to a particularly trained policy elite:

> [T]he more distinctive features of PPBS . . . [such as] the application of cost-benefit studies to budgetary decision, the analysis of alternative programs, and the consideration of tradeoffs . . . relied upon esoteric knowledge and techniques not immediately familiar military officers or "traditional" budgeteers. Thus PPBS in Defense had the effect of shifting influence and power not alone upward from the military services to the Secretary of Defense but also to different kinds of specialists, i.e., particular kinds of economic analysts. [143]

PBBS worked to establish a hierarchical and centralized decision procedure of "managerial . . . control and command" within the Pentagon. It functioned by establishing the parameters of all discussions through the oversight of Enthoven's Office of Systems Analysis, and by presenting budgetary proposals in such a fashion that McNamara had unitary authority over all decisions.

Whereas it is easy as to be distracted with the appearance that McNamara and the defense rationalists were proponents of *civilian* control over the U.S. armed forces, it is necessary to recall that arguments for such authority are based on the premise that legitimate military authority be granted to serve the ends of representative government and to uphold the Constitution. The new policy elite were altering the rules such that authority over military procurement, strategy, and operations would be in the hands of "objective" policy analysts, removed from democratic politics.

McNamara initiated the most dramatic and forceful showdown with military leaders within his first months of taking office. He launched his campaign for greater efficiency in the military with his proposal to build one kind of tactical fighter to satisfy divergent Air Force and Navy specifications, promising that this move to "commonality" would save the nation $1 billion. Military commanders were aghast when McNamara, who had no engineering training or mechanical background, overruled expert engineering judgment and concluded that having one aircraft design serve two conflicting functions was technically feasible and pragmatically wise. The Air Force required a highly maneuverable, high-bomb-yield plane capable of intercontinental flight and supersonic low-altitude dashes to evade Soviet radar detectors on bombing raids. The Navy had little interest in the TFX tactical fighter because it required a slower, lighter, lower-performance aircraft to loiter around, land on, and be stored on aircraft carriers. An unprecedented four-stage bidding process ensued, with the field narrowed to Seattle-based Boeing and Forth Worth's General Dynamics after the first round. Finally, on November 22, 1962, the largest procurement contract in American history, valued initially at $6 billion dollars, was handed to the beleaguered Texas company. McNamara had forced the outcome, despite the fact that the military had selected the Boeing model at each stage of the bidding process and despite the unanimous opposition of the joint chiefs, including General LeMay, chief of staff of the Air Force; ten assorted generals and admirals of the Air Council; General Walter C. Sweeney of the Tactical Air Command; General Mark E. Bradley of Logistics Command; Lieutenant General Bernard Schriever of Systems Command; Admiral Anderson, chief of naval operations; Admiral William E. Ellis, assistant chief of naval operations for Air; Rear Admiral Kleber S. Masterson, Bureau of Weapons; and five general and flag officers representing the Source Selection Board. McNamara's sole authority in his showdown with the military's top brass was conferred by his use of presumptively scientific cost-effectiveness studies. It was widely reported that the TFX project was "the showcase of . . . [McNamara's] cost-effectiveness program," and that the TFX decision represented McNamara's "way to drive home his concept of 'value engineering' in the tradition-encrusted procurement system of the U.S. armed services." [144]

However, McNamara's flagship for cost-effectiveness and efficiency in the nation's military establishment left many questions unanswered—most significantly, what analysis did the secretary use to reach his TFX decision? Congressman John L. McClelland's subcommittee of the Government Operations Committee of the U.S. Senate launched an investigation on February 26, 1963 that continued until President Kennedy's assassination. In testimony that filled over twenty-five hundred pages of transcript, legislators labored to get to the bottom of the TFX decision.

At first Secretary McNamara and his civilian secretaries Eugene M. Zuckert and Fred Korth of the Air Force and Navy relied on a memorandum they had prepared after reaching the decision to explain their rationale. This document, which not only contained numerical errors but also claimed to have relied on a decision procedure that senators could only conclude was "a little ridiculous," was soon repudiated by the secretaries as they scrambled to construct a more credible, ex post facto account of their decisionmaking. [145] They began arguing their case afresh, offering new explanations and submitting new documents not relevant to the original decision.

After months of questioning and painstaking concentration on countless details regarding airplane construction and the contracting process, the senators learned that Secretary Zuckert had reviewed the military's Source Selection Board recommendation and evaluation and had determined that the board had rested its decision on criteria that he deemed to be of only secondary significance. Whereas the military had concentrated on performance attributes of the plane designs to gain a winning edge in battle, Zuckert, at McNamara's behest, emphasized commonality of the Air Force and Navy versions of the TFX, less demanding technological innovation, and cost-realism. In reviewing the Air Force's assessment of the costs of the two fighters, Zuckert felt that the General Dynamic's proposed bid of $5,803,500,000 was more "realistic" than Boeing's $5,387,500,000. [146]

Zuckert had first briefly met with Navy Secretary Korth. Korth, it became evident in testimony, was utterly ignorant about aircraft design and the details on which the decision had hinged; he had deferred to Zuckert's judgment.[147] It was subsequently revealed that Secretary Korth was from Forth Worth, Texas, and when it was disclosed in the hearings that he had engaged in active dialogue with the Forth Worth business community as secretary, and that his bank had loaned General Dynamics' Fort Worth plant four hundred thousand dollars, he was forced to resign in fall of 1963.[148] Zuckert had next presented his case to McNamara. Jointly, they dismissed the Air Force's internal cost analyses of the General Dynamics and Boeing bids, without so much as a back-of-an-envelope calculation of their own. This dismissal, on which the contract seemed to hinge, became the object of intense scrutiny, since the Air Force cost analysts had put in twenty-seven thousand man hours devising their estimates.[149] Ultimately the investigating committee was led to conclude, as McNamara himself admitted, that the TFX decision rested on "rough judgments." [150] In 1963 Congressmen could only suspect what history would confirm. The Navy later canceled its contract with General Dynamics in 1968, and the Air Force ultimately obtained only six hundred of the originally contracted twenty-four hundred planes, at a cost of $22 million each instead of the initially proposed $2.8 million.

Obviously, despite the fancy footwork and claims of superior analytic techniques, the TFX decision was more about cutting the military out of decisions than it was about careful and rigorous analysis.[151] Documents from August of 1962, prior to the final contract bidding round, indicate McNamara's intent to change the established Source Selection Board evaluation process so that his office would carry full and unquestionable authority over decisions.[152] The established procedure was highly decentralized, with officers from all levels of the chain of command voicing input into the evaluations. McNamara objected to the tendency of the top command to, in his mind, "rubber stamp" the Source Board recommendations without performing independent analysis. However, in changing the role of the Source Selection Board to a nominal advisory function, McNamara indicated that he was not interested in reaching decisions through fuller discussions aimed at eliciting varying opinions. After all, he had not held one single meeting with the Joint Chiefs of Staff to question their reasoning; McNamara simply wanted to alter the decision procedure so that the secretary's office alone had authority. This meant that in major decisions affecting the U.S. armed services, the experience and judgment of military officers was inconsequential. Once again, McNamara acknowledged a business constituency first: instead of holding discussions with military leaders, he established the Defense Industry Alliance Counsel (DIAC) through which executives of contracting firms helped the DOD secretary redraft the procurement process so that it would be amenable to the business community's interests.[153]

In later Senate hearings, Alain Enthoven would testify that the PPBS system had little, even nothing, to do with the TFX decision.[154] However, in other decisions in which the PPBS procedure was used, such as Skybolt and "the purchase of a $277 million oil-fueled aircraft carrier [the John F. Kennedy] that was obsolete before it was launched,"[155] the pattern was the same: McNamara and his civilian defense rationalists would reach conclusions without holding discussions with the various parties involved, and consistently touted their rigorous cost-effectiveness analysis as providing them with rationale for their decisions. The PPBS and systems analysis process altered the rules, permitting the analysts to set the terms of discussion, maintain control over the forum, and impose decisions. Thus, when Admiral Hyman G. Rickover attempted to challenge McNamara's rejection of the Navy's proposal to build nuclear-powered aircraft carriers, he was forced to first challenge the cost-effectiveness method itself.[156] Just as with the TFX decision, senators ultimately concluded that McNamara's choice had rested on unsubstantiated judgment. However, in each case the decision had already been accorded authority, and lives and budgets both were already affected.

In August of 1965, President Lyndon B. Johnson would mandate that PPBS become standard operating procedure in all federal agencies. This sweeping institutional success of RAND's budgeting system, designed to facilitate top-down management, triggered public debate over the goals and efficacy of the system. Just as H. Rowan Gaither Jr.'s original vision for "eliminating politics from decision making" seemed on the verge of becoming government status quo nationwide, senators found themselves asking, "Does PPBS provide a wholly rational basis for decision-making? Have we arrived at a technocratic utopia where judgment is a machine product?"[157] As Congress was keen to emphasize, a vital characteristic of democracy is that a people be governed by reasoned argumentation in which citizens participate, directly or through elected representatives. But the new technologies of social management filtering into federal agencies from the Pentagon had an entirely different logic and looked to the claims of science, objectivity, and expertise to obviate the legislative, democratic process. In Senate hearings investigating the budgeting procedure in 1968 it was apparent that "[s]ome advocates of PPB[S] express regret that the results of this budgetary approach must be subject to legislative review and decision, on the ground that such review introduces what they regard as elements of 'politics' in what would otherwise be a 'rational process' of decision-making." [158] Frederick C. Mosher, a political scientist at the University of California, Berkeley, also was concerned by "the ignoring of, or less generously, contempt for, democratic values and processes." He found that virtually all the proponents of PPBS disregarded "the executive and legislative processes of review and decision," and regarded "[t]he President and Congress . . . as enemies of rationality." He lambasted the "technocratic and authoritarian language" espoused by PPBS supporters, and concluded:

> At no point does one gain the impression that the budget process is a "due process" of administration wherein the facts, the analyses, the interests, the politics and the prejudices of people enter. Much of the literature of PPBS resembles that of the technocrats of the thirties; its aim seems to be to eliminate *politics* from decisionmaking. [159]

The new decision techniques replaced the traditional approach in which persons of equal status reached decisions in open discussion with the idea that trained analysts should provide leaders with studies of how efficacious various policy proposals would be in meeting "objective" national goals. [160] Senators were not reassured by the great secrecy that PPBS advocates thought mandatory for the "Program Memorandum," the analytically prepared budget proposals on which agency executives acted. PPBS proponents argued that secrecy and anonymity were essential to maintaining the impartiality of the cost-effectiveness studies. [161] Furthermore, senators were skeptical of the zeal with which PPBS was presented as the panacea for all of society's ills and complexities. President Johnson introduced PPBS to Americans with the promise that it could "[i]dentify our national goals with precision," and that it would enable "us . . . [to] [c]hoose among those goals the ones that are the most urgent." [162] The president also proposed that the new system could aid in understanding "how . . . we [can] best help an underprivileged child break out of poverty and become a productive citizen." [163] Alain Enthoven stressed that "Systems Analysis can be applied to the problems of State and local government, including programs for social welfare." [164] In a compilation of articles assembled by RAND's David Novick, the architect of PPBS, authors advanced the idea that "the program budget is a neutral tool. It has no politics." [165] Other authors refer to the political process as comprised of "haphazard acts . . . unresponsive to a planned analysis of the needs of efficient decision design," which obstruct "future planning for a rationally ordered program budget." [166]

Congressmen and scholars shared in the optimism that the new decision techniques could aid policymakers in reaching conclusions. [167] Critics did not contend that quantitative analysis evaluating policy alternatives was inherently bad or useless. Instead, they were wary of the proponents' either naive or self-serving view that these procedures did not in themselves represent a reconstitution of political power, effectively concentrating it into the hands of analysts and agency executives seeking centralized control. Mosher observes that "the potential effects of PPBS on power distribution within the government are surely as important as the technical improvement which are hoped for." [168] Aaron Wildavsky, another astute observer, noted that "[p]rogram budgeting is a form of systems analysis that attempts to break out of the confines . . . [of] existing governmental policies . . . [and] the general decision-making machinery of the political system." He also found that "[n]ot everyone would go along with the most far-reaching implications of program budgeting . . . but the RAND Corporation version, presumably exported from the Defense Department, definitely does include 'institutional reorganization to bring relevant administrative functions under the jurisdiction of the authority making the final program decision.'" [169]

PPBS, conceived at RAND, realized H. Rowan Gaither Jr.'s original vision of a nonpolitical decision apparatus, handled by experts, to advise executives' policy formation. Secretary of Defense Robert S. McNamara, a former midlevel manager at the Ford Motor Company swept into power with the momentum of John F. Kennedy's successful exploitation of a fictitious missile gap, brought to the Pentagon the budgeting system and its practitioners. After helping McNamara achieve control over America's defense establishment, PPBS gained currency throughout American society when instituted as part of President Lyndon B. Johnson's Great Society programs; the promise of top-down control appealed to Johnson's sense of how to govern. By the end of the 1960s, the blueprint for a rationally managed society was at odds with America's democratic foundations of legislative politics. Two positions were starkly delineated. The defense rationalists cum policy analysts staunchly advocated a "rational" means for reaching public decisions based on scientific rigor and objective analysis, claiming that PPBS would identify national priorities and the best policies to achieve them.[170] Opposed to this confidence in the power of rational analysis alone to remove politics from judgment, congressmen and academics countered that whereas systematic study might yield helpful information to decisionmakers, the PPBS system as described and instituted by its advocates contradicted the democratic political process and led to a centralization of executive judgments. This critique on the part of some congressional leaders and scholars faded, however, as the force behind the rational analysts established the new decision technologies as part of the nation's intellectual and institutional endowment.

Stabilization of a Knowledge Production Regime

PPBS required tremendous institutional infrastructure. This was especially the case after 1965, when President Johnson mandated that PPBS become the standard operating procedure in all federal agencies. The same techniques used in the Pentagon were advocated for the smooth operation of civil society. Johnson's programs of the Great Society and War on Poverty proved to be fertile ground for proliferating the burgeoning field of policy analysis. David Jardini convincingly argues that as social unrest simmered to the boiling point in the 1960s, Cold War decision technologies that had been developed and harnessed to fight an external adversary were turned inward, as the real threat to democracy was seen to be discontented citizens.[171] And the management techniques developed at RAND to stand off a nuclear-armed opponent could similarly be deployed to fight a war on poverty. As the 1960s wore on, and as perceived threats on the national security front tapered off, consulting in the field of domestic social welfare policy became a high-growth sector. RAND, which would have faced cut backs and institutional stagnation, led the way toward honing the tools of rational policy analysis for the challenges of domestic policy. "Systems analysis" underwent a face-lift and reassumed its identity under the more vogue term "policy analysis."[172] The basic set of decision-theoretic tools developed at RAND in the 1950s would serve as the new conceptual foundation for what would become the new field of "public policy," applicable to both domestic and foreign venues.[173]

By the time PPBS was officially discontinued in federal bureaucracies in 1969 due to the lack of compatibility between its tendency to centralize authority as part of a top-down hierarchy and civilian agencies' being unaccustomed to military-style regimentation, the RAND-style cost-effectiveness analysis had become central to numerous institutional practices. A disciplinary revolution was already well underway: The new field of policy analysis had a specially trained elite corps of practitioners. Training programs were created for government staffers, and curriculum at leading business schools was transformed to create marketable graduates with the appropriate decision-theoretic tools. These tools were the hallmark of the proliferating think tanks and consulting agencies. "Public Administration" schools were transformed into "Public Policy" programs as the new curricula and practices became entrenched. The new field of policy analysis was anchored by a conceptual foundation that would ground future thinking about legitimate policymaking practices and standards of fairness.

The key to success of the dual conceptual and institutional revolution was that the new methods gained a de facto legitimacy before they had been tried and debated in any public forum. The decision technologies did not filter into mainstream practice from the world of academia, but were designed in a hands-on manner to revolutionize national security decisionmaking and to integrate budgeting with strategic planning in order to centralize control. Subsequently, as officials such as Secretary of Defense McNamara employed the RAND-PPBS system in order to exercise top-down control, and as practitioners were appointed to prestigious, influential posts, the new decision tools that frontally challenged democratic legislative processes gained widespread currency. One example of this institutionalization of RAND's decision technologies is the DOD's internal publication "Systems Analysis Southeast Asian Analysis Report," which was established and maintained during the Vietnam war.[174]

The de facto legitimacy acquired by systems analysis and RAND's program budgeting is contrary to the common understanding that acceptance presupposes that legitimacy has already been established. With "scientific knowledge," or at the intersection of politics and processes of knowledge production, it is often believed that superior explanatory power is the criterion for successful promulgation. For example, in *The Structural Transformation of the Public Sphere,* Jürgen Habermas argues that growing belief in the right and capability of all men to participate in governance fueled the momentum behind the increasing franchise in nineteenth-century Europe: an abstract theory of legitimate social practice served as a rationale that brought about its manifestation in material culture.[175] A concept of legitimate governance served as the rationale anchoring the evolving practice of public sphere democracy.

With the institutionalization of systems analysis and PPBS, and the subsequent development of the new discipline of policy analysis, the interplay of theoretical validity and successful promulgation were reversed: rational decision technologies gained legitimacy not on paper or in intellectual debate, but *because* they became institutionalized in practice and played the role of transferring authority, rationalizing ponderous decisions, and shaping the material reality of people's lives. McNamara's showdown with the Joint Chiefs of Staff hinged on his claim to superior judgment and normalized untested decision practices that in turn empowered a new policy elite and shifted the basis of authority from multi-layered discussion throughout the military chain of command to his own office and person. As the new decision technologies propagated in the programs of Johnson's Great Society, "policy analysis" became an accepted manner of making foreign and domestic policy judgments. Congressional leaders could only question the legitimacy of the role the new policy tools had come to play after the fact; questions were raised after the decision technologies had already become normalized procedures with institutional capital and socially empowered advocates.

This broad de facto legitimacy, which rational policy analysis maintains to this day by virtue of its widespread institutional currency, cannot be isolated from the high academic standing it has come to achieve. Planning-Programming-Budgeting and cost-effectiveness analysis became confirmed as decisionmaking methods not because they demonstrated their credibility and worth, but because they became institutionalized as social practices carrying the weight of social decision.[176] When senators asked whether there had been any attempts to assess how effectively PPBS and systems analysis made decisions, Alain Enthoven, assistant secretary of defense who oversaw the Office of Systems Analysis, replied that this had never been attempted because it would cost too much and because the officers in question would be unable to attain the necessary objectivity. As contemporary observers noted, the new analytic policy methods were popular because they carried weight in policy discussions.[177] Their authority seemed distinct from the voluminous studies themselves, which, most likely, few people ever read.

The establishment of rational policy analysis as a knowledge production regime followed a straightforward pattern. In a single stroke, PPBS and systems analysis gained an impressive institutional footing in the Pentagon. Because it was such a large organization, commanding more than half of the nation's federal budget and 10 percent of it gross national product by the end of the 1960s, and controlling the lives of 4 million civilian and uniformed personnel, the RAND-incubated decision technologies rapidly achieved authority over many lives and resources.

The myriad and weighty decisions funneled through PPBS, especially when it was instituted in the Bureau of the Budget, required echelons of trained analysts. By 1968 the number of federal employees whose jobs were devoted to PPBS had risen to over eight hundred. Senate hearings during the late 1960s made apparent the extreme shortages of such appropriately trained staffers. According to Kenneth Mulligan of the U.S. Civil Service Commission, the government was short by more than ten thousand people in the administrative-analysis area. Government training programs were held for staff working with PPBS. Thousands of employees took courses ranging from two-day seminars to nine-month courses of university study. Economists with the appropriate background took leading roles. As Mosher observed, "[t]he new leadership in federal budgeting consisted of a . . . special breed of economists . . . equipped with experience and training in the analysis of governmental programs . . . gained in the RAND Corporation."[178] Alain Enthoven found that graduates from business administration programs were more suited to analysis than were economics majors. In order to find qualified people, Comptroller General Elmer B. Staats worked with the deans of leading schools so that curriculum and training could meet the government's needs. Comptroller Staats testified in Senate hearings:

> We have made a very major effort to recruit good people. We have an educator consultant panel which meets with us two or three times a year. This panel includes several deans of business schools. It also includes the dean of engineering at Johns Hopkins, a representative of the field of public administration, and so on. These people can help us relate our training programs to the changing curricula of the colleges and universities. They can help acquaint their own students with opportunities that would be presented if they came with out organization. They can also help us on our own internal training program.[179]

Thus, the institutionalization of PPBS and systems analysis directly affected the curriculum of professional graduate programs. Harvard University's School of Business Administration was also caught up in the excitement of the new decision technologies. Before assuming responsibility at the Ford Motor Company, Robert McNamara had been on the faculty of Harvard's business school. During his tenure as secretary of defense, he inspired colloquiums at Harvard in which the new policy ideas were discussed.

The pattern of interlocking RAND alumni careers weaving in and out of government, consulting organizations, and universities was another powerful factor in establishing a knowledge production regime. The most highly visible of these career paths were those of key alumni who helped to bring about the disciplinary shift from "public administration" of the 1940s and 1950s to "public policy," which had recognizably replaced it by the mid-1970s.[180] At Harvard, RAND alumnus Thomas Schelling, who had a joint appointment at Harvard's schools of government and business, along with his rational-choice oriented student Richard Zeckhauser, led the movement for core curriculum reform and the reconstitution of the old Graduate School of Public Administration under the new name of the Kennedy School of Government. At the University of California, Berkeley, RAND and DOD alumnus William Niskanen presided over the establishment of the curriculum for the new Public Policy Program. After assuming the presidency of RAND in 1964, and pursuing the newly established high growth area of domestic policy analysis, Henry S. Rowen joined Stanford's business school faculty and served as director of the Urban Management Program.[181] Alain Enthoven similarly joined the business school faculty at Stanford. This set of career paths is only the most visible and easiest to articulate in the wider network of connections that established rational decision technologies as a basic part of the American intellectual endowment, and as the core idea set of the newly emergent field of public policy.

The institutionalization of the rational decision technologies into the practices of government, the birth of the discipline of public policy with cost-effectiveness modes of analysis as its core conceptual apparatus, and the professionalization of a new policy elite realized Gaither's original vision that philanthropies such as the Ford Foundation must support "(a) work that will influence the policies or operations of other institutions on the widest possible scale, or (b) work that will build up a new professional corps or a new system of techniques and operating standards."[182] The network of contacts with whom Gaither worked and supported in his dual capacities as chair of RAND's board of trustees and first president and later chair of the Ford Foundation, ended up bringing about not just Gaither's dream of far-reaching policy impact, but also establishing rational management techniques as part of the intellectual and institutional endowment of the United States.

One final indication of the establishment of a regime of knowledge production results from the fact that despite the clear failure of rational defense planning to prosecute the war in Vietnam, rational policy analysis would go on to colonize a venue of global proportions. When, in 1968, a teary and emotionally embattled McNamara seemed incapable of enduring the pressures of his office, his aides searched for a position of sufficient prestige to which the secretary of defense could retreat without humiliation. Thus, upon his ignominious exit from DOD, McNamara immediately assumed the presidency of the World Bank, where over time the RAND-style, objective, cost-benefit strategy of policy formation would become the universal status quo in development economics—a position it still holds today.[183]

Virtually All Roads to Rational Choice Lead from RAND

The rise of rational choice theory in the social sciences, especially economics and political science, cannot be considered independently from the world of military strategy of the defense rationalists. In the 1950s, the phrase "rational choice" was used in reference to the policy environment in which RAND researchers attempted to base policy decisions on rational and objective calculation.[184] The cadre of RAND defense economists proceeded on to Washington under the designation of "defense rationalists." Leading figures in developing rational choice theory in the social sciences were also key contributors in the world of rational defense strategy, including Thomas Schelling, Howard Raiffa, Duncan Luce, William Niskanen, Henry Rowen, Alain Enthoven, Herbert Simon, and Mancur Olson—all of whom spent time at RAND. Other crucial theoreticians in the rational choice world who were less focused on national security concerns but were also associated with RAND include Kenneth Arrow, James Buchanan, Paul Samuelson, and Robert Solow.

With the overlap of theoreticians who were both concerned with national security and advocated rational choice theory, it is not surprising that the conceptual toolbox for rational choice theory was developed predominantly at RAND in the 1950s. This toolbox contained rational decision analysis considering risk and uncertainty, and more important, game theory. In the late 1940s and early 1950s, John Williams, head of RAND's mathematics division, avidly supported research into game theory because he and others, incorrectly, thought it promised great dividends for warfare.[185] RAND researchers hoped to apply game theory to situations of nuclear strategy. Von Neumann and Morgenstern's *Theory of Games and Economic Behavior,* which gained no supporters among economists in the 1940s, served as a fruitful point of origin for a research community that emerged at RAND.[186] The innovation of game theory was its dependence on an axiomatically defined concept of human rationality and a context in which two parties select strategies that enable them to maximize their expected utilities. It differs from neoclassical economic theory insofar as it models actors who strategically interact with each other instead of simply maximizing diminishing marginal utility per dollar spent without the presence of rational competitors. Von Neumann and Morgenstern developed the rational rules of engagement for a situation with two players and a zero-sum outcome, which seemed exploitable for the new challenges posed by atomic bombs in a bipolar Cold War.[187] While economists were slow to recognize the potential of strategic actors vying with one another for outcomes to model a marketplace by, the logic of "rational action" was exploited to study the two superpowers caught up in a nuclear showdown.

Locating the development of the conceptual apparatus for rational choice theory within the national security environment counters a basic myth frequently perpetuated about the origin of rational choice theory.

First, that the "rational actor" has always been at the heart of, if not all economic thought since Adam Smith, then at least neoclassical economic thought of the marginalists: the rational actor seeks to maximize his pleasure per dollar spent. Second, that rational actor theory, which was originally developed in the domain of economics, was subsequently exported to other disciplines including political science, sociology, and psychology.

In acknowledging RAND of the late 1940s and 1950s as crucial to the development of rational choice theory's conceptual apparatus, some of the peculiar tensions characterizing rational choice theory seem less puzzling. In the popular account, rational actor formalism developed in economic theory and anchored the neoclassical paradigm. It was natural that other disciplines would seek to capitalize on the explanatory power offered by neoclassical microeconomic theory: other fields sought the payoff of regarding humans as utility maximizers. But this account assumes theoretical continuity within economics that cannot be substantiated. The tools of economic theory were changing in the late-twentieth-century synthesis, just as rational choice theory was gaining currency in the other social sciences. Thus, the toolbox of decision theoretic methods developed at RAND in the late 1940s and 1950s, including game theory, decision theory, and Herbert Simon's "satisficing," served as a point of origin for rational choice scholarship that coalesced in various fields.[188]

With this shift in understanding, the role RAND intellectual leadership played in articulating and promulgating rational choice theory can be grasped directly, without the distraction of a supposedly parallel historical trajectory of rational choice theory already serving as the status quo in economics. This lineage reveals two crucial facts that are otherwise hopelessly obscured. The conceptual framework for rational choice theory was initially developed to solve strategic, military problems and not problems of economic modeling, even though its potential usefulness in economics and other social sciences was later recognized. Furthermore, this idea set was developed to inform policy decisions, not merely retrospectively to analyze behavior as the social sciences often claim of their own methodology. Thus, the first strategic "rational actor" as conceptualized in game theory and the decision sciences was a nation-state locked in the icy and treacherous grip of the Cold War.[189] The theory of rational action had interlocking descriptive, normative, and prescriptive components, and was developed to inform action respecting nuclear strategy and complex questions of weapons procurement. This set of conditions inspiring the early development of the rational choice toolbox helps to explain why the theory typically carries the self-referential presumption of intentional rational calculation on the part of actors, which must resemble something analogous to the theory itself. It also explains how the academic world of rational choice theory in the U.S. social sciences seems only a breath away from the world of policy analysis: the two began in one motion, with one set of theoreticians defining, supporting, and championing the same basic idea set in two contexts.

Four of the six canonical works of rational choice are linked directly to RAND research and alumni. Kenneth Arrow formulated the ideas structuring *Social Choice and Individual Values* while he was at RAND, surrounded by the fervor of game theory, in the summer of 1948. In the 1950s, Arrow continued contracting for RAND even as he assumed a professorship at Stanford University. His student Anthony Downs wrote the second canonical text, *An Economic Theory of Democracy,* before leaving academia to both consult for RAND and found a consulting firm. James Buchanan, another founder of the rational choice approach to politics, wrote *The Calculus of Consent* with Gordon Tullock in 1962. Buchanan had spent the summer of 1954 at RAND. His work emphasizes the implications of rational choice analysis to the world of public finance and policy. Mancur Olson, who consulted for RAND in the early 1960s, received copious notes on his manuscript for *The Logic of Collective Action* from prominent RANDite Thomas Schelling.

Only three key contributors to the early history of rational choice theory did not set foot at RAND: Duncan Black, Vincent Ostrom, and William H. Riker. Black worked outside the context of America national security and public policy, and in taking the road less traveled each remained largely marginalized from the dynamic forces shaping the new discipline. Nonetheless, Ostrom and Riker benefited from the same patronage afforded by RAND's original chairman of the board, H. Rowan Gaither Jr. Gaither, who since the 1940s had been committed to developing the social sciences as a means to solve various problems facing humanity, was inspired to establish a center for the study of the behavioral and social sciences in the early 1950s. This idea reflected his abiding interest in Program Area V of the Ford Foundation, devoted to studying human behavior. When Gaither assumed the presidency of the foundation, he was unflagging in his efforts to establish such an institution. His vision for the center was that it have independent grounds and buildings for scholars working on research interests furthering the understanding of human nature and society. One stumbling block was finding a university to allocate the buildings and grounds. Gaither and his associates had little success at Harvard and other East Coast schools. In conversation with Clark Kerr, then president of the University of California, the idea emerged of building this center at Stanford University. Stanford, with its spacious campus, accepted the Ford Foundation's proposal, and in 1956 the Center for the Advanced Study of the Behavioral Sciences (CASBS) was established on a hill overlooking the campus. Like RAND, the center was off the beaten track, and permitted its researchers the luxury of concentrated work balanced with stimulating conversation. Fitting even more closely with Gaither's vision, the center was remote from the world of mass culture. Its experts enjoyed the environment of a think tank far above the fray of everyday social politics. Nor were its thinkers accountable to mass society. Gaither's Ford Foundation staffer who was investigating the public perception of the foundation concluded, "People seem willing to grant us special areas of competence which they don't presume to judge; the Center, for instance, is referred to as 'the Monastery' and 'the think factory,' both of which emphasize that it's outside plain folks' orbit."[190]

Vincent Ostrom, who would become a path-breaking rational choice theorist working at the intersection of rational-choice-oriented social science and policymaking, resided at CASBS its first year, in the company of the RAND decision theorists Howard Raiffa and Duncan Luce. William Riker, who was rescued from a year of teaching responsibilities at Lawrence University by a Ford Foundation grant in the 1950s, also profited from the center. Riker spent his crucial year of 1961–62 there, before taking up his position on the faculty of the department of political science at the University of Rochester. It was during this year, spent in the company of Kenneth Arrow, that Riker wrote his first rational choice–based theoretical account of the workings of American democracy, *The Theory of Political Coalitions.*

H. Rowan Gaither Jr.'s steadfast support of the social sciences as tools for social management and rational defense management had a two-fold impact on the emergence of the rational choice framework. Both at RAND and through the Ford Foundation's establishment of the CASBS, theorists had the freedom to generate a body of ideas. Furthermore, the empowerment of the defense rationalists helped to gain currency for their ideas of rational and objective policy analysis. As these theorists found their way back to academia after stints of service in Washington, they returned with the prestige helpful to making their idea set part of the mainstream intellectual endowment of American society. William Riker's establishment of a public policy program within the department of political science at the University of Rochester in 1975 is consistent with this general pattern of the inseparability of rational choice theory as an empirical social science from rational policy analysis.

A final twist helps keep perspective on the aim versus the outcome of philanthropic beneficence. Despite the seeming complete triumph of his original vision, a generational gap existed between Gaither and the next wave of hard-hitting rationalists who he helped to establish. Gaither, though elitist and promoting a concept of enlightened social management at odds with public sphere democracy, believed spiritual fulfillment and mental and emotional well-being to be essential attributes of human life.[191] Gaither's world was still one in which the idea of public service offset the narrowness of self-interested rational action.[192] Gaither took a dim view of "schools of economic thought [that] have from time to time constructed over-all 'systems' through the use of convenient and unrealist abstractions, such as . . . the fiction of the 'economic man.' "[193] One can only marvel at what Gaither may have made of the self-interested rational actor epitomizing the new breed of cold warrior and consumer of politics.

PART II

Rational Choice Theory in American Social Science

CHAPTER 2

Kenneth J. Arrow's *Social Choice and Individual Values*

In a capitalist democracy there are essentially two methods by which social choices can be made: voting, typically used to make "political" decisions, and the market mechanism, typically used to make "economic" decisions. . . . In the following discussion of the consistency of various value judgments as to the mode of social choice, the distinction between voting and the market mechanism will be disregarded, both being regarded as special cases of the more general category of collective social choice.
Kenneth J. Arrow

KENNETH J. Arrow's text *Social Choice and Individual Values* (1951) is among the most captivating a political theorist could hope to engage. It is epochal in its account of the fiercely contested debates over social welfare that dominated economics of the 1930s and 1940s, pitting social planning against *laissez faire* capitalism. Arrow asked whether it is possible to derive collectively rational social decisions from individual preferences, and demonstrated that collectively rational group decisions are logically impossible. Although trained in economics and statistics, Arrow claimed that his arresting result applies with equal validity to democratic voting, the market, and social welfare; his result rules out *any* means of assaying individual preferences into a legitimately representative social outcome. Arrow formulated his proof using the language of set theory, unfamiliar to economists who had formerly cast their analyses in terms of calculus and algebra. He generalized the definition of "rational action," distancing himself from the marginalist economists' fixation with "maximization of utility under a budget constraint," and introducing the more general concept of a well-ordered set of transitive preferences. Arrow's "impossibility theorem," as his result came to be called, struck a deathblow to the tradition of welfare economics in the United States, and initiated the field of social choice theory in its place. It defined the underlying tenets for "capitalist democracy" while simultaneously excluding any philosophical principles derived from Marxism,

Kantian moral philosophy, Rousseau's general will, or classical utilitarianism. Through its widespread acceptance, Arrow's theorem made four philosophical commitments part of the mainstream economic currency of his day, commitments that, not coincidentally, were precisely those that had been at the center of the controversies characterizing economics in the decades preceding Arrow's text. Arrow's four assumptions are that science is objective; that it yields universal laws; that reason is not culturally relative; and that individuals' preferences are both inviolable and incomparable.

The sweeping success of Arrow's *Social Choice and Individual Values* poses a historical quandary insofar as the substance of its finding was itself hardly surprising to contemporary theorists. Arrow proved that collective expressions of public interest or social welfare based on individuals' preferences are a logical impossibility when two or more individuals are making joint decisions over three or more alternatives. Two theoretical results, one extending back to the Enlightenment research of the Marquis de Condorcet and the other growing out of the 1940s-era welfare economics tradition, both contain a diminutive version of Arrow's negative result. Condorcet showed that three voters selecting from three alternatives can easily result in a deadlock. Welfare economists had all but determined that the goal of their field, arriving at objective statements of collective welfare, was impossible. In light of Condorcet's and the welfare economists' findings, there was already sufficient reason to doubt that individual preferences could be analyzed as a collective decision legitimately representing individual choices.

The brilliance and elegance of Arrow's formal proof demonstrating the logical impossibility of achieving collectively rational outcomes is unimpeachable. It remains to be understood, however, how a result of small intellectual wonder can be elevated to greatness, no matter how dazzling the form in which it is presented. Commenting in 1964, the economist E. J. Mishan observed, "While the formal layout of Arrow's argument was impressive, it would not be unfair to suggest that the conclusion was hardly surprising." [1] The reason for Arrow's greatness, I argue, is to be found in the philosophical work his theorem achieves in grounding democratic and economic liberalism. The outlines of this story are not difficult to make out. It is widely acknowledged in the post-Soviet era that "[f]rom George Kennan's admonition in 1946 that communism must be contained, until the fall of the Soviet empire in December 1991, the central organising principle for America and much of the west was the cold war effort to contain the spread of communism." [2] It is also widely acknowledged that the United States has been "triumphant in the ideological and

quasi-military struggle with communism."[3] What is not so well understood is the step-by-step manner in which this ideological victory of capitalist democracy over communism was waged and won. Arrow's set-theoretic defense of the ordering principles of capitalist democracy in
opposition to Marxism, idealist democracy, and totalitarianism was at
the center of the ideological struggle on the part of *laissez faire* individualism to overcome all that is implied in the dictum "from each according
to his ability, to each according to his needs." The brilliance of Arrow's
work is its masterful but imperceptible resolution of this controversy and
its creation of the philosophical infrastructure upholding American economic and democratic liberalism. As it happens, the text also anchors the
philosophical commitments basic to rational choice theory, making it
possible to propose that the theory's development is inseparable from the
defense of democratic and free market institutions that came to define
America's cultural heritage in stark opposition Soviet collectivism.

Kenneth Arrow was a consummate defense intellectual whose career as
a key contributor to the neoclassical synthesis in economics is inseparable from his Cold War policy role. It was at the RAND Corporation as a
summer intern in 1948 that he was charged with determining a mathematical expression for the Soviet Union's collective utility function that
would be useful for game theoretic strategy computations of nuclear
brinkmanship. This puzzle led to Arrow's initial formulation of his impossibility theorem, titled "Social Choice and Individual Values," RAND
report RM-291, 28 July 1949, during his second summer at RAND. Immediately thereafter, Arrow received a "top secret" level security clearance, which he retained from 1949 to 1971.[4] Most of the documentary
evidence for this period in Arrow's life remains unavailable, either because it is covered by the secrecy blanket of secured information or because Arrow's personal papers are available only selectively from Duke
University's archive of the work of twentieth-century economists. Though
not directly involved with military strategy or weapons development, Arrow's career could not have passed closer to the drumbeat of the Cold War
fervor against the Soviets.[5]

Not only was Arrow a high-level participant in the Cold War defense
establishment, he was also one of the key creators of the intellectual tradition that would give shape to orthodox American economics during the
Cold War period. His professional trajectory was defined by top-rank institutional affiliations: the Cowles Commission, RAND, Stanford University, and Harvard University. Within economics he contributed to four
fields: "social choice and justice," "general equilibrium theory," "decision theory," and "economics of information."[6] Arrow's research served

to establish the disciplinary standard within economics; some papers, such as the widely influential "Behavior under Uncertainty and its Implications for Policy," informed U.S. government policy.[7]

With John R. Hicks, Arrow received the 1972 Nobel prize in economics, only the fourth ever awarded, for "their pioneering contributions to general economic equilibrium theory and welfare theory."[8] In its announcement of the prize, the Royal Swedish Academy observed that Arrow's "possibility theorem" published in *Social Choice and Individual Values* is "perhaps the most important of Arrow's many contributions to welfare theory."[9] The combination of the broad impact of the monograph, the acclaim it won Arrow, and the enigma over how a "hardly surprising" result could produce such a response make Arrow's impossibility theorem ripe for exegesis. An investigation into the political theoretic significance of Arrow's logical proof must start with identifying the discussions to which it directly responded. The litany of cited sources in *Social Choice and Individual Values* make it a literary accomplishment as much as one of economics. It is precisely this well-documented record of source material to which Arrow responded that enables a historically accurate assessment of the issues in play in the formulation of Arrow's logically unassailable proof.

The first section of this chapter brings to life the debates prefiguring Arrow's impossibility theorem by revisiting the contested issues preoccupying economists in the 1940s. The lack of consensus about basic issues preceding Arrow's impossibility theorem, and their relevance to social order, dramatically highlight the scope of his resolution. For example, throughout the 1940s the two socialist economists Maurice Dobb and A. P. Lerner argued over whether economic science is objective and produces universal laws of general applicability, or whether there is a particular "socialist" economics of special relevance to socialist societies. Another point of contention concerned whether individuals' desires could form the legitimate basis of social ends, or whether they are too subjective and whimsical to make a sound basis for social policy. In addition to debating these issues, the economists Oscar Lange and K. W. Rothschild disagreed over the definition of "rationality" at the core of economic analysis, giving voice to the possibility that there is one type of "reason" characteristic of capitalistic societies and another type characteristic of communist societies. These discussions overlapped those asking whether there is any objective, interpersonally comparable measure of social welfare, on either an individual or a collective level. Lionel Robbins and J. R. Hicks argued against such objective measures, while A. C. Pigou and Alfred Marshall argued in favor. In crucial passages of *Social Choice and*

Individual Values, Arrow directly quotes the work of these economists, making clear that his theorem was informed by these various debates over the fundamentals of economic theory and method.

The second section of this chapter is divided into two discussions, the first focusing on Arrow's resolution of the widespread disagreement over economic method. Arrow's resolution of these debates is remarkable for building the philosophical basis for a new consensus by weaving firm stands on the contested issues into his theorem without ever acknowledging their contested nature. Thereafter, economists accepted Arrow's authoritative stance that economic science is objective, that it yields universal laws not particular to capitalist or socialist economies, that reason is not culturally relative, and that individuals' preferences must be the basis of any legitimate social choice. After introducing the philosophical underpinnings of Arrow's theorem, I explore how it triumphed over Marxism, Kantian moral philosophy, Rousseau's political theory, and classical utilitarianism. Arrow's impossibility theorem is a theoretical masterpiece precisely because it covers extensive philosophical ground in an apparently incontestable fashion, both providing a basis for American political and economic liberalism while simultaneously undermining the alternative social philosophies of communism, idealist democracy, and totalitarianism.

In the third section of this chapter, following the detailed discussion of the philosophical structure and significance of Arrow's theorem, I discuss its impact on the tradition of American welfare economics. Welfare economists were wholly unimpressed with Arrow's theorem, finding it irrelevant to their concerns. Yet their tradition floundered as it failed to attract a new generation of adherents, while scholars adopting the methods of Arrow's social choice theory were able to built up a new disciplinary standard. With Amartya Sen's being awarded the 1998 Nobel prize in economics, social choice theory can be seen to have achieved the status of a global standard for addressing questions of social welfare and justice.

The fourth section of this chapter examines the hard-fought priority dispute between Arrow and the British economist Duncan Black over the fundamental insight underlying Arrow's impossibility theorem. The details of this dispute remain little known beyond those directly involved, yet its substance brightly illuminates what scholars found irresistible about Arrow's research and less compelling about Black's. I propose that, though the two scholars' work occupies the same disciplinary niche, Arrow's *Social Choice and Individual Values* met with more scholarly attention specifically because it tackled the difficult issues at the heart of the ideological battle with the Soviets over which economic and social system was legitimate and scientifically sound.

A concluding section considers Arrow's philosophical *tour de force* from the perspective of the change of intellectual leadership from such wartime public intellectuals as John Dewey and Robert Merton to those of Arrow's generation, characterized as "defense intellectuals." I follow here a lead provided by David Hollinger, who argues that Dewey and Merton, among others, held the light of civilization during the dark hours of the struggle against fascism and totalitarianism by embracing the partnership of science and democracy based on the Enlightenment values of "universalism," "disinterestedness," "communalism," and "organized skepticism." [10] I suggest that it is not difficult to see in Arrow's defense of the principles underlying capitalist democracy another set of "Enlightenment values," those of objectivity, universalism, reason, and individual liberty.

The Planned Economy and Social Welfare Debates

There are two ways to set into relief the rampant debate over the economics of capitalist versus socialist economies, and over the appropriate methodology for economic science. One is to recount the arguments as set forth in the copious literature cited by Arrow in *Social Choice and Individual Values*. The other is to attempt to convey a sense of the *Zeitgeist* of American economics leading to the publication of Arrow's epochal work. The first method is likely to be more relevant to understanding the historical significance of Arrow's theorem, because it provides direct insight into the issues he faced. It is nevertheless worth pausing for a moment to get a sense of the general turmoil characterizing economic thought as it grew out of the worldwide depression, Roosevelt's New Deal, and wartime economic planning. One does not need to examine many economics texts to appreciate the widespread doubts over the merits of capitalism in the wake of the 1929 American stock market crash and ensuing worldwide economic depression. In 1933, none other than the famed "Chicago school" economist Frank Knight announced:

> The dualistic social order of nineteenth century liberalism, made up of economic laissez-faire and political democracy, that is of economics and politics alike based on competitive, mass selling-talk, is bankrupt, and it is only a question of a successor to bid in the effects of the defunct at a nominal figure.[11]

Knight proposed that this successor might best be communism, and made his statement "From the Standpoint of an Ex-liberal." [12] At this point in history, Knight suggested, what the world needs is "vastly more political control," and he argued that communism, as essentially a government by elites, could best supply this control.[13] Lionel Robbins and Henry Simons, who would become arch-supporters of economic liberalism, also wrote articles doubting the efficacy of *laissez faire,* unless contained within a "system of impersonal rules . . . at least as ambitious . . . as the conception of prescribing positively each action or each type of action by a central planning authority," and run by a state "with heavy responsibilities and large 'control' functions."[14]

Despite the doubt cast on free trade economics by the upheaval of the depression and by the countervailing policies of planning, the rise of National Socialism and the European experiment with fascism, violating every covenant of civilization, generated a new choir of voices skeptical of collectivism and philosophical ideals violating individualism. This choral assembly is best represented by those well-known soloists Friedrich Hayek, Joseph Schumpeter, and Karl Popper.[15] These virtuosos sang a different tune, one troubled by the rise of socialism and communism. They understood these social philosophies to violate the sanctity of the individual, to signify the replacement of freedom by the bondage of serfdom, and to represent the retrenchment of the continual progress of civilization since the Enlightenment celebration of reason, democracy, and individualism. Still, the widespread lack of confidence in capitalism, and the parallel belief in the wisdom and necessity of social planning, meant that Hayek, Schumpeter, and Popper were voices in the wilderness, crying out against what then seemed a likely outcome: the victory of socialist planning over capitalist democracy.

What is now obvious in considering the doubts shared by Knight, Robbins, and Simons about unregulated, *laissez faire* markets, on the one hand, and on the other the misgivings of Hayek, Schumpeter, and Popper about socialism, is that in the late 1940s it was not clear that capitalist democracy was superior to socialism; nor was it clear that capitalist democracy would eventually triumph over socialism. What is clear, however, is the extent of debate and uncertainty underlying discussions about the two systems. These discussions boiled down to a specific set of issues. Popper was concerned lest the Marxist critique of science mire civilization in a malaise of paralyzing relativism. Hayek worried that the sanctity of individual freedom would be violated by coercive and smothering collectivism. Schumpeter, while seeing no way out of the eventuality of socialism, maintained his suspicion that socialist society would be unable to hold in balance the pluralism required for a healthy democratic polity.

While the outlook of this trio of pessimists certainly sets into relief the backdrop for Arrow's defense of the basic principles of economic and political liberalism, we see it with the benefit of historical hindsight that nevertheless does not help us appreciate how Arrow's *Social Choice and Individual Values* resolved concrete disputes argued in the pages of the *Economic Journal*, the *Review of Economic Studies*, *Econometrica*, and the *American Economic Review*. It is these debates over scientific objectivity, universal law, reason, and individuals' preferences, while intersecting with the landmark texts of Hayek, Schumpeter and Popper, that provide a "footnote" view of this history in which issues are contested by the "foot soldiers" of economics: those numerous individuals comprising the profession, though one day to be forgotten. It is in those pages, recording the vivid present for a future distracted by a Cold War struggle in which membership in a communist party signaled automatic ostracism from American society, that the contentious debates culminating in Arrow's impossibility theorem come alive. Arrow resolved the issues of dispute with such surgical precision that the healed body politic of capitalistic democracy emerged from the contentious 1940s apparently unscathed, no longer stigmatized by impolitic ideological wrangling.

In providing the details of this historical narrative, I rely exclusively on the texts Arrow himself cites in developing his arguments. The 1933 article by Maurice Dobb, "Economic Theory and the Problems of a Socialist Economy," which is not only one of the very few articles Arrow quotes from but is also referred to in the crucial passage in which Arrow denounces Rousseauian, Kantian, and Marxist social philosophies, places many of the issues on the table.[16] These issues concern the nature of scientific method, economic law, and individual freedom. In the 1930s, as characterized by Dobb's article, it was debated whether communist or socialist societies run according to unique economic laws, or whether a single set of economic laws apply universally, regardless of a society's institutional makeup. Dobb identifies two groups of economists, the first of which, represented by Ludwig von Mises, "declares . . . that a socialist economy must fail because the absence of a free market and price system would preclude the application of any economic criteria." The second school of thought, represented by H. D. Dickenson, believed it possible to combine a socialist economy with a price system. In Dobb's assessment, "[b]oth [schools] assume that categories of economic theory are equally valid in a socialist as in an individualist [capitalist] order" (589). Thus, these two schools of economics both adhere to the idea of the universal validity of economic law, regardless of the socialist or individualist composition of society.

Dobb further explains that consistent with this claim to universality, these theorists uphold the "purely formal character of economic theory."

According to Lionel Robbins, for example, "Economics . . . is unconcerned with norms and ends: it is concerned strictly with constructing patterns for the appropriation of scarce means to given purposes." Dobb notes that "[t]he more formal, of course, that Economics is made, the more universal become its propositions." Dobb is dissatisfied with this fate for economic analysis because "[i]t is powerless to *prescribe* a maximum [that is, a social state best utilizing scarce resources among economic agents] for us." Economic theory, viewed in this way, could not aid a social planner's attempt to select from "*n* possible alternative equilibria." Therefore, construed as such, "[e]conomic theory reduced to these dimensions provides no criteria of judgment at all" (589–90).

However, Dobb distances himself from the idea that economic science can be value neutral and suggests that economists, N. Kaldor and J. R. Hicks for example, tacitly assume the utility-based hedonistic approach that makes possible "the scientific dignity of an ethical neutrality." Dobb explains:

> The crucial assumption is as simple as it is questionable: it amounts to the sacredness of consumers' preferences. . . . The virtues of "economic democracy" which it confers on a free market rest on a similar sacredness of individual choice to the virtues of Parliamentary democracy. Both operate through a convenient franchise system: in the one votes are cast by offers on a market, in the other by crosses at a polling both. The highest economic good consists in giving the consumer what he thinks he wants, as political good consists in giving the people the government it thinks it deserves. (591)

Dobb is highly skeptical of the emphasis on "consumers' preferences" because he does not believe they can accomplish the work they are intended to in a value-free economic theory. Borrowing from "a similar sacredness of individual choice to the virtues of Parliamentary democracy," it became conventional for economists to respect individual choice by privileging individual preferences in economic analysis. Just as parliamentary democracy gains legitimacy from its reliance on individual expression of opinion, so the market gains legitimacy by responding to individuals' preferences. For Dobb, "[b]oth conceptions are part of our bourgeois heritage of the nineteenth century" (ibid.). He is skeptical that this respect of individual preferences can legitimate free market society because in his opinion it has been soundly demonstrated that individual preferences are not autonomous, but instead are dependent on advertising, or the press magnate. Also, Dobb points out that individuals are not respected equally in this scheme because "in the economic sphere there is not even an approach to universal suffrage"; in selecting commodities, individuals are ultimately limited by their incomes (ibid.). Therefore Dobb suggests that sanguine acceptance of the free market system as supplying the pricing system most useful to a socialist economy must be in error. Moreover, he finds that relying on the "judgment of the future[,] the 'natural' individual is notoriously unreliable" (592–93).

Dobb challenges the facile assumption that economics of Robbins's stripe is in fact value free. He believes different economic laws apply to capitalist and socialist economies respectively because they function differently. He does not trust the authenticity of individual choice in free market systems and believes that planned economies have a superior chance of using resources effectively (597). In a conclusion quoted by Arrow, Dobb states:

> I am conscious that what I have said has been mainly of a negative order. But, as Kant observed, negative may be as significant as positive conclusions in setting thought on new paths. Yet I do not wish to follow Kant and "limit knowledge in order to make way for faith." Planned economy will have its economic laws, as has *laissez-faire* economy; it will have its economic accounting and calculation. (Ibid.)

Dobb believes that the distinct laws of a planned economy will not be faith-based, but will follow from rigorous analysis (598).

A decade later, in 1943, also in an article quoted by Arrow, the socialist economist A. P. Lerner challenged Dobb's position in "Economic Theory and Socialist Economy." [17] In Lerner's article the issues addressed by Dobb grow in complexity, but remain central to the enterprise of economic theory. Lerner maps out two mutually exclusive positions, one held by the pro-*laissez faire* economist Ludwig von Mises and the other represented by Dobb. Lerner writes that, according to Mises, "[i]n the absence of the unhampered markets of a competitive capitalist economy, there can be no possibility of maintaining that rational economic calculus which is essential to the efficient organisation of production" (51). According to this view, rejecting the principle of "rational economic calculus" will doom socialist economies to failure. Calling into question the scientific objectivity of capitalist economics, Dobb, among others, counters by denouncing Mises's arguments

> as meaningless anti-socialist propaganda, produced by reactionary professors sacrificing their interest in scientific truth at the altar of class interest. They might be the victims of a class ideology which made it impossible for them to envisage a society in which their class had lost its place or they might be mercenarily selling their theories to the Capitalist for cash. (Ibid.)

In Lerner's analysis, Dobb and other socialist economists insist on two sets of economic laws—one for socialist societies, another for capitalist societies. Lerner recognizes that Dobb and other socialist economists doubted the nonideological value neutrality of economic science.

After identifying these two positions, a *laissez faire* economics based on objective laws and a socialist economics based on localized laws, Lerner recognizes a third position. This position, upheld by a group of socialist economists, proposes "a synthesis between the economists' and the socialists' points of view," suggesting that "[t]he demands for *Wirtschaftsrechnung*, prices and markets are no longer considered as anti-socialist tricks or even as bourgeois illusions" (ibid.). According to this alternative socialist argument, both socialist and capitalist economies can sing the tune of efficiency, which exists as an objective standard. However, as Lerner recounts, this acceptance of markets, prices, and efficiency was viewed by many socialists as a Trojan horse:

> Socialists are suspicious in the extreme of such new-found allies coming from the "ideological" centre of the enemy's camp. The attempt to base the socialist economy on a rationally worked-out system of prices and markets may be a subtle scheme of sabotage for building the socialist society on rotten foundations. (52)

Rejecting the idea of universal law applicable to all economies, many socialist thinkers attempted to eradicate the heresy of capitalist economics, upholding the slogan "The categories of capitalist economy are inapplicable to the socialist society" (ibid.).

Lerner outlined three camps: the proponents of capitalist economics (Mises), the socialist economists who denounced the scientific neutrality of "bourgeois economics" (Dobb), and a third group represented by H. D. Dickenson who believed that the criterion of "efficiency" is beyond ideology and can serve as an objective criterion for organizing a planned economy. Lerner defends the third position, rejecting Dobb's claim that consumer preferences are easily manipulated, and accepting that searching for "maxima" consistent with consumer preferences make eminent sense: "As a human being and a sympathiser with socialist ends, it seems to me that a maximisation on such lines is completely in the spirit of all socialist ideals and particularly sympathetic to the slogan of 'scientific socialism'—'. . . to each according to his needs'" (53–54). Lerner goes on to explain why he believes it to be important to uphold the "sacredness of consumers' preferences":

> A superior contempt for the tastes and judgment of the "masses," and a paternal solicitude in choosing for the people what is good for them, does not seem to me to be the avoidance of an unscientific major premise about "sacredness." It consists rather in supplanting the democratic assumption that—in the absence of vitiating factors—people try to get what they like,

by the much more suspect proposition that somebody else (the Government, Mr. Dobb?) knows better than the people themselves what is really good for them. (54)

Considering the Soviet example, Lerner expresses concern over the supression of the "Dictatorship of the Proletariat" by the bureaucratic class. In his estimation, the sanctity of consumers' preferences is all that wards off "a contempt for the masses" and dictatorship. Lerner believes the Soviet example shows how

> [t]he people become more and more a somewhat recalcitrant material for the weaving of social patterns pleasing to bureaucratic aesthetics; and the usurpation of the individual's freedom to choose his own way of life is justified by minor variants of the ancient plea of apologetic tyrants: "It's for their own good!" (54)

Therefore, upholding individuals' preferences is crucial for obviating Robbins's scathing rebuke, "[S]cratch a would-be planner and you usually find a would-be dictator!" [18]

Against Dobb, Lerner consistently maintains that "the competitive price system has to be *adapted* to a socialist society." He envisions a middle ground between "authoritarianism" on the one hand and "Intransigent Liberalism" on the other (55–56). Having rejected consumer preferences as being of any help to a planner, Lerner argues that Dobb requires "some transcendental optimum other than that shown by a free market." This question of deriving a transcendental optimum is "quite distinct from the freedom of consumers' preferences" and leads to the bureaucracy's freeing itself "from the direct democratic control of the masses" (58). Lerner quotes Trotsky to make his point: "In truth, the bureaucracy often conceives that just such a mind is at its disposal; that is why it so easily frees itself from the control of the market and of Soviet democracy." [19] He summarizes his appraisal of Dobb's socialism, whose "arguments which, while professing to guard socialism from 'counter-revolutionary elements' and 'Bourgeois Economics,' really plead for the safeguarding of bureaucratic irresponsibility" (59).

Challenging Dobb, Lerner argues that economic science can be value free; that, therefore, it can apply equally to capitalist and socialist economies, without the necessity of deriving two exclusive sets of principles. Lerner believes that "scarcity is common to both kinds of society." He concludes that whether or not one trusts consumers' preferences, and no matter whether they choose their goods or a "single dictator chooses," a price mechanism based on universally valid economic principles is necessary (60).

The entanglement of the three issues—the value neutrality of economic science, the ability to deduce universal economic law equally applicable to socialist and *laissez faire* economies, and the significance of consumers' preferences—is made more clear by Dobb's reply to Lerner.[20] As will become evident, Arrow's *Social Choice and Individual Values* addresses each of these points, siding more with Lerner than with Dobb.

Dobb strictly maintains that he sees "no sufficient necessity for a competitive pricing system":

> As Mr. Lerner's own argument shows, the "necessity" of a pricing system does not follow as a corollary of any "universal economic principle," but of some imported postulate such as his *dictum* that it is desirable "to give people what they want"—which I have suggested is by no means an unambiguous conception. That we should be so obsessed with enquiries of this kind in terms of *optima*, and impotent to avoid them even when we would, is, I think, part of the pernicious heritage of subjective economics. (149)

In Dobb's analysis, Lerner's attempt to use the pricing system relying on individuals' preferences, combined with the achievement of a maxima, is no more than "subjective economics." Instead of an economic science's having increasing recourse to abstract, formal, mathematical relations, Dobb pins his hopes on economic laws expressing objective relations that obtain in the social world. He concludes, "The economic laws which rule a socialist economy, whatever they be, will have this resemblance to those of classical Political Economy: they will be objective relations between events, which determine the actions of man and to which an effective plan will have to be adapted" (ibid.). Dobb puts forth an alternative vision of a socialist economy to the one suggested by Lerner. In Dobb's socialist society, humans reflexively grasp economic law and regulate their own activities accordingly: "Economic activity would be ruled by conscious recognition of the objective laws which bound it; and collective man, being conscious of his limitations, would suit his purposes to the objectively possible." From this interpersonal acknowledgment of objective economic laws a group plan would emerge: "[H]uman action . . . [would now be] subordinated to a collective plan, in place of unco-ordinated individual wills" (150).

Lerner's 1943 rejoinder emphasizes that "individuals should have the maximum of freedom to conduct their lives," and that it is unclear how "well-meaning regulation" respects individual freedom; most likely it will do "more harm than good."[21] He doubts that "technical knowledge," or a "universal mind" can stand in place of individuals' preferences. He upholds the "maximum . . . [that is obtained] when people get what they want," which requires a pricing mechanism.[22]

It is important to recognize that in this dispute between the two socialist theorists, which Arrow adjudicates, the key issues of contention boil down to what constitutes appropriate scientific method in economics: Is economic law universally applicable, and what should be the role of individual preferences in determining legitimate collective outcomes? As we shall see, Arrow reaches definitive conclusions on all of these points. In his *Social Choice and Individual Values,* he fashions a consistent approach to these questions that becomes the basis for the "rational choice" analysis of collective decisionmaking procedures, and the basis for the consensus on American economic and political liberalism among rational choice theorists.

A second duo of articles, Oscar Lange's "Scope and Method of Economics" and K. W. Rothschild's response "The Meaning of Rationality: A Note on Professor Lange's Article," both also prominently showcased in *Social Choice and Individual Values,* serves to further indicate key points of contention in mid-1940s economics.[23] Like Lerner, Lange upholds a socialist economics based on the same economic principles governing capitalist societies. He is keenly interested in the nature of scientific method in economics and the attainability of universal law. He, like others, wrangles with the question of whether there is a unique "bourgeois" or "socialist" economics while simultaneously acknowledging that "all scientific production contains an ideological element."[24] Of course "a special discipline[,] the *sociology of knowledge*" is widely recognized as growing out of the Marxist critique.[25] Lange believed, however, that regardless of this development, "the validity of scientific statements can be ascertained with impersonal objectivity through an appeal to facts."[26] Thus facts have "interpersonal validity" because they are "interpersonally objective . . . [and] can be observed by everyone" (22). Similarly, "the rules of logic," applied to empirically verified facts, are "interpersonally objective." Moreover, "the ideological element in scientific inquiry need not always be a handicap in reaching interpersonally valid results. . . . Most important contributions of the social sciences are due to passion for social justice and betterment" (24).

For Lange, economics "tries to discern general patterns of uniformity in the administration of scarce resources" (20). Economic analysis, relying on theories that describe regularities in economic institutions, can be used to evaluate the administration of scarce resources for the purpose of achieving such social goals as the satisfaction of personal preferences, industrialization, prosecution of war, or the attainment of social justice. In each of these cases "ideal use" refers to the most effective achievement of the postulated social goal. Welfare economics is one branch of economic science that tells us how to best achieve the goal of social welfare by utilizing economic laws. Given his carefully constructed case for the objectivity of economic science, Lange does not believe different economic laws pertain to different societies. In a section titled "Capitalism and Other Forms of Economic Organisation," Lange identifies the pursuit of money profit as characterizing the activities of firms but that social economies, by contrast, must be "operated for the satisfaction of the wants of the whole community" (28). He points to Great Britain's Labour Party, the Co-operative Commonwealth Federation in Canada, socialist and communist movements in various parts of Europe, and the Soviet Union as political entities that have this socialist objective.

Lange introduces a new key element into his discussion of scientific method and universal law: "the postulate of rationality." This postulate is of paramount importance to economists because it enables them to build models of consumer and producer behavior using mathematical analysis. Even though such deductive analysis is not a substitute for "painstaking empirical study," "the postulate of rationality is a short-cut to the discovery of laws governing the decisions of units and to the prediction of their actions under given circumstances." The postulate can be used to predict behavior and ultimately "must be treated as an empirical hypothesis." In capitalist economies, rational action implies "the objective of maximizing money profit" (30). According to Lange, the pursuit of this "single objective, expressed as a magnitude" is a habit referred to by some authors as the "capitalist spirit." He explains that "[u]nder the influence of the mental habit mentioned, households are encouraged to order their preferences along a scale, i.e., to maximise utility" (31). "[T]herefore," Lange concludes, "[i]n capitalist society . . . the decisions of households are more likely to conform to the deductions derived from the postulate of rationality than in societies which preceded the rise of modern capitalism" (ibid.). Whereas Lange proposes that scientific method can achieve universality across cultures by overcoming biases, he implies that "rationality" may embody different principles in different societies.

After discussing the cases of the firm and the household, Lange turns the discussion to public services and to welfare economics. He explains, "Public services act rationally when the social objective they aim at can be expressed as a single magnitude to be maximised. The magnitude is then called *public welfare*" (31). Significantly, "the decisions of public services in any given situation can be derived by the rules of logic from the postulate of rationality" (ibid.). Lange's discussion of the postulate serves as an overture to Arrow's more ambitious and broader accomplishment in *Social Choice and Individual Values*. He observes that "the community seldom has such definite and ordered preferences." Hence, "the study of the operation of public services has to be based on the observations of institutional economics and economic history rather than on logical deductions of the postulate of rationality" (ibid.). But Lange goes on to suggest that "we can consider the conformity of public services with the postulate of rationality as a social objective." He carefully explains, "[W]e can set up a chosen set of ordered preferences, i.e., some concept of public welfare, as our own (that is, the student's) social objective and require that all public services be guided by this objective as a norm" (ibid.). For Lange, the "postulate of rationality becomes then the basis of a theory of welfare economics" because, based on a criterion of efficiency, it can provide an objective standard as a social goal.

At this point, Lange had brought to the fore all the issues that Arrow's theorem would adroitly address: the scope and method of economics, the attainability of universal economic law, the role of individuals' preferences in economic science, and the assumption of rationality. Lange believed in interpersonally valid economic science based on interpersonally valid facts and laws of logic. Hence, economists are able to derive universal laws and test them against empirical findings. Both the postulate of rationality and individual preferences are crucial to economists: the postulate enables economists to build predictive models of human behavior and individuals' preferences ordered in such a way as to "maximize utility." Lange implies that only capitalist societies evince the mental habit, or "capitalist spirit," captured by the postulate of rationality's norm of "maximizing utility;" precapitalist households acted differently. However, to secure the universally valid postulate of rationality beyond the bounds of capitalist society, Lange argues that public services can also be ordered according to the principle of rationality. This requires maximizing the quantity of "public welfare." Ideally, maximizing public welfare would be a function of the maximum utility of the individuals comprising a society; however, Lange worries that it is difficult to find an objective expression of public welfare to maximize. Not giving up on his theory of welfare economics, he suggests that the postulate of rationality necessary to scientific economics can be upheld if a concept of social welfare is put forward as the social objective. In another article, Lange constructed a case for how this measure of social welfare could be achieved scientifically.[27] Thus Lange, like Dobb, doubts the reliability of individual preferences and seeks a measure of social welfare derived in another way, for example, through the adoption of "an equalitarian social ideal, i.e., the marginal social significance of each individual is the same. . . . Each individual has to get the same income."[28] However, unlike Dobb, Lange seeks to build on the platform of interpersonally valid economic science informed by the postulate of rationality applied equally in cases of planning or *laissez faire*.

Capturing the gist of these crucial methodological debates at the core of 1940s economic science is necessary for fully appreciating the role Arrow's *Social Choice and Individual Values* would play in settling these debates and in providing a platform for American capitalist democracy. Arrow's succinct text obviates a series of potential liabilities. He avoids the pitfalls of asserting that there are different economic laws for socialist and liberal societies respectively; of acknowledging an ideological component in economic science; of permitting planning bureaucrats to have superior knowledge of individuals' preferences; and of permitting the possibility that "rationality" defined as "maximization" uniquely pertains to capitalist society.

The economist K. W. Rothschild was troubled by Lange's treatment of rationality. Rothschild agreed with Lange that capitalist societies evince a particular form of rationality but he went on to emphasize that the rejection of this particular form of rationality is not equivalent to no rationality; there are other forms of rationality:

> For the modern economic theory of the consumer, just as the classical theory, depends to a large extent on a very special kind of rationality: the rationality of *homo economicus*. This consists above all in fixing preferences along a scale in an order, which is decisively influenced by market prices.[29]

Rothschild agrees with Lange that "[t]his is indeed the 'capitalist spirit' which is fostered by a capitalist environment, and which gives the present economic theory of the consumer a high degree of relevance in our society." [30] However, Rothschild argues that there may be other forms of rationality that order preferences according to different criteria, such as according to the "taboos" in "primitive man's society." Similarly, "the true Christian will cease to desire a thing if his possession of it will hurt the feelings of those who have to do without it." Thorstein Veblen's conspicuous consumer provides another possibility. Pointedly, Rothschild concludes:

> And if the Soviet Union tries to replace the "capitalist spirit" by the principle "From each according to his ability, to each according to his need," then they do not do it in order to kill rational behaviour, but in order to substitute a new kind of rationality for a traditional one.[31]

Rothschild promotes the possibility that "rationality" may operate according to different principles in capitalist, primitive, Christian, or Soviet society. "Rationality" itself may be culturally relative, hence in due course giving rise to different social patterns and to distinct economic laws. Rothschild's rejection of the notion that a "deviation from the 'capitalist spirit'" signifies irrationality[32] was critical for Arrow in articulating his definition of "rational choice."[33] At stake was the construction of the most general and universally valid economic theory that neutralizes the legitimacy of Soviet or communist economics.

Many economists were concerned to preserve the normative neutrality and universal validity of economic laws. S. Moos of Oxford University traced the increasing disrepute into which welfare economics had fallen into in its attempt to strip normative elements from economic analysis.[34] Providing an overview of economics derived from Oxford and Cambridge University economics exams, and using trends in economic thought from Adam Smith to Henry Sidgwick, A. C. Pigou, and J. N. Keynes, Moos recounts how welfare considerations in economics were especially denounced by Lionel Robbins and J. R. Hicks. Moos challenges these economists' homage to the "God of efficiency,"[35] thus helping identify the tradition of economic thought to which Arrow would later contribute. Before writing *Social Choice and Individual Values,* Arrow had planned to write his dissertation on Hicks's *Value and Capital.*[36] Hicks was adamant that economics be nonnormative, and that it apply equally to all people. In Hicks's view, "[p]ositive economics can be, and ought to be, the same for all men; one's welfare economics will inevitably be different according as one is a liberal or a socialist, a nationalist or an internationalist, a christian or a pagan."[37] He rejected any attempt to achieve a welfare economics that would not be "acceptable universally" (697).

In the 1940s, the debate over finding a scientific basis to welfare economics amounted to determining whether it is scientifically possible to compare degrees of satisfaction as a function of consumption across individuals.[38] Robbins and Hicks strictly argued that no interpersonal comparisons of utility or preference satisfaction is possible. This prohibition of comparing utilities across individuals challenged the entire enterprise of scientific welfare economics, because it made it virtually impossible to define objective states of individual welfare. In these economists' opinion, it is not scientifically valid to compare the social welfare involved in the two cases of giving water to a man dying of thirst and to a socialite buying diamonds. All satisfaction is subjective, and hence is not objectively comparable. Hicks believed that the only objective measure of economic performance is to be found in mathematically defined problems of economic efficiency that leave aside value-laden questions of distribution. He builds what he takes to be a "*positive* theory of economics," which solely relies on the criterion of efficiency,[39] and concludes that "[t]here are general conditions for optimum organisation; they are universally valid, being applicable to every conceivable type of society" (706).

Given this fundamental presumption as a starting point, Hicks attempts "to put welfare economics on a secure basis, and to render it immune from positivist criticism."[40] He develops a scheme measuring the compensation necessary to pay losers for their losses based on monetary measures that need not necessarily be paid out: if the total added welfare exceeds the loss to a particular party, then *regardless of whether compensation is actually paid,* in Hick's analysis social welfare is augmented.[41] Arrow devotes an entire chapter of *Social Choice and Individual Values* to this scheme for compensation, once more indicating his intimate engagement with the 1940s economic debates over scientific method and social welfare. Again, a core issue, recognized by Hicks's respondent William J. Baumol, is whether "[o]ne's welfare economics will inevitably be different according as one is a liberal or a socialist, a nationalist or an internationalist, a christian or a pagan."[42]

A more recent article by Robert Cooter and Peter Rappoport—asking "Were the Ordinalists Wrong about Welfare Economics?"—recounts the debate over the scientific validity of interpersonal comparison of utility and identifies two schools of thought.[43] One school, represented by Robbins and Hicks, rejected the scientific status of interpersonal comparison of utility, and instead turned to Nicholas Kaldor's compensation principle combined with Paul Samuelson's serious doubts about the efficacy of welfare economics. On the other side of this debate were Pigou and Marshall, joined by others such as Lange and Lerner, who insisted that individuals' welfare can be objectively measured. They believed that objective claims about an individual's well-being based on such criteria as health and poverty can be made. At the core of this discussion was a disagreement over standards of scientific theory. As Cooter and Rappoport point out, it was not that the "material welfare economists," as they refer to them, had lesser standards than did the ordinalists; they had different standards. The ordinalists adhered to the philosophy of logical positivism, and on that basis advanced a "positive theory of economics." However, the material welfare economists, too, believed they upheld rigorous standards of scientific analysis because according to them, study of material well being is more objective than is study of the "efficient distribution of scarce resources"; "efficiency" is itself a normative standard.

Cooter and Rappoport argue that in the debate between the ordinalist welfare economists and the material welfare economists, the first side emerged as the victor by circumstance, and not as a consequence of having successfully out-argued their opponents. Thus, they contend that the prohibition of interpersonal comparisons of welfare characterizing the positivist economics of Robbins and Hicks is not itself based on unimpeachable scientific reasoning. Although falling just outside the time period considered by Cooter and Rappoport, as will become obvious below, it was Arrow's *Social Choice and Individual Values* that normalized the standards of scientific research that would become central to rational choice theory following the leads presented by Robbins and Hicks.

In this section, I have discussed three sets of debates among specific economists comprising key subject matter that Arrow incorporates and responds to in his epochal text of 1951: Dobb versus Lerner, arguing over the cultural specificity of economic laws; Lange and Rothschild, questioning the intercultural validity of "capitalist reason"; and Robbins and Hicks's "positivist economics" versus material welfare economists upholding interpersonal comparability of utility. Each of these brought to the fore contentious issues that had to be resolved in order for a unified school of economic thought to emerge, one that could concentrate its energies on research instead of methodological debates. The central issues were over scientific objectivity, universal economic law, definitions of rationality, and whether preferences are an authentic expression of personal freedom and are interpersonally comparable. The brilliance of *Social Choice and Individual Values* in part results from the manner in which it molds each of these issues into a coherent theoretical foundation grounding "capitalist democracy" without raising suspicions of ideological bias, an authoritarian or socialist impulse, or assumption of the cultural relativity of economic laws.[44] It is part of the genius of Arrow's classic work that it represents a threshold moment in the history of economic thought, dispelling the many points of contention among economists of the day and consigning them to the annals of history. *Social Choice and Individual Values* so effectively closed the resounding debates of 1940 economics that Arrow's arresting philosophical system has become the unquestioned status quo, even while its historical significance has faded and its philosophical adversaries have been forgotten.

Arrow's Impossibility Theorem

Kenneth Arrow created his impossibility theorem while firmly ensconced within the context of America's Cold War with the Soviet Union. In the early days of this conflict, America defined its destiny to be in stark opposition to that of its former ally, which was apparently well-positioned to challenge the American way of life both philosophically and materially. It was no accident that Arrow's inspiration for his famous theorem came during a summer internship at the quintessential Cold War institution, the RAND Corporation. Prior to the war, Arrow had studied statistics as a graduate student in mathematics at Columbia University. After a wartime stint in the U.S. Army Air Corps as a captain at the Headquarters Weather Division and a dissatisfying year back at Columbia, Arrow became a research associate at the mathematically oriented Cowles Commission in Chicago from April 1947 to July 1949. While there, he was invited to spend a summer at RAND. It was during the summer of 1948, having been granted a "confidential" level security clearance, that Arrow was assigned the task by Olaf Helmer of defining a collective "utility function" for the entire Soviet Union. This task fit in with RAND's overall mission to reduce warfare and military strategy to objective science, and RAND researchers' efforts to harness John von Neumann and Oskar Morgenstern's game theory for the purpose of making predictions in complex scenarios of nuclear brinkmanship. In order to carry out this large-scale project, it was necessary to define a utility function for the Soviet Union that could be used by game theorists to predict its actions in a zero-sum nuclear conflict against the United States.

Receiving the full attention of Arrow's intellect, this task quickly became highly abstract. Arrow first considered the social welfare of Abram Bergson, who strove to define a function of collective welfare for a society based on individuals' desires. It was while working on this problem, as Arrow recounts his intellectual development, that he came upon the "transitivity problem" reminiscent of Condorcet's voting paradox— namely, the impossibility of guaranteeing a collectively rational preference profile derived from individuals' preferences.[45] Using set theory, Arrow demonstrated that starting with the premise of individual rationality and several other minimalist assumptions, "collective rationality," or rational expression of ends, is unachievable; Arrow proves that for three or more people choosing from three or more alternatives, it is impossible to guarantee a "collectively rational" outcome accurately representing individuals' preferences.

Understanding the significance of Arrow's accomplishment requires both grasping the substance of his result and recognizing its meaning with respect to economics of the late 1940s. Two interpretive puzzles plague the attempt to convey that understanding. First, as I argue below, in light of the findings of welfare economics preceding Arrow's theorem, its result surprised no one. This lack of surprise is also logically consistent with the existence of the eighteenth-century Condorcet paradox; the earlier result called into question efforts to achieve collective expressions of individuals' preferences. It is thus possible to argue that Arrow's impossibility theorem was theoretically anticipated in both the new welfare economics and by Condorcet's analysis of voting. Second, it seems perverse that a result that impugns the legitimacy of social welfare economics, democracy, *and* the market as means to achieve valid social decisions from individual preferences could stand at the heart of the new orthodoxy characterizing the rational choice approach to democratic capitalism.

The core of Arrow's theorem can be introduced in simpler terms by focusing first on a society comprised of two individuals choosing from three alternative resource allocations, and next on a society of three individuals selecting from three or more alternatives. This is the same way Arrow himself presents his proof.[46] As Arrow designed the first scenario, it can be represented by a Edgeworth box, with the left and bottom axis representing the resource distribution allotted to person 1, and the right and top axis representing the resource allocation allotted to person 2.[47] In this problem, Arrow assumes that standard indifference curves obtain for each individual, upholding the standard economic premise that individuals prefer more to less; hence each individual necessarily prefers a distribution of (5,1) to (4,1), with each number referring to units of distinct commodities. Using preference rankings among these three potential distributions of (5,1) and (5,9) units of two commodities to each person respectively; (4,2) and (6,8) respectively; and (3,3) and (7,7) respectively, Arrow proves that it is not mathematically possible to achieve a collectively coherent preference profile for the two individuals across the three alternatives.[48]

In order to achieve this result, Arrow assumes that the two individuals are *rational,* by which it is understood that (1) they have consistent preferences ordered in accordance with the principle of transitivity. In addition his proof requires that (2) preferences must count as the data to be assayed into the collective outcome, (3) individuals' preferences are unrestricted,[49] (4) neither person can be a "dictator," and (5) individuals' preferences cannot be interpersonally compared. Given that Arrow assumes no initial distribution of resources, his conclusion, that no coherent preference order is guaranteed, is wholly consistent with the contemporary findings of the new welfare economics. This tradition, strictly upholding the noncomparability of utility among individuals, and represented by Hicks and Samuelson, concluded that whereas some distribution points may be considered by both individuals to be preferable to others, it is not possible to define any specifically optimal point. Samuelson's pessimistic conclusion is that

> [a]n infinity of such [optimal] positions exists ranging from a situation in which all of the advantage is enjoyed by one individual, through the sort of compromise position, to one in which another individual has all the ad-

vantage. Without a well defined W[elfare] function, i.e., without assumptions concerning interpersonal comparisons of utility, it is impossible to decide which of these points is best.[50]

Samuelson's comments about the new welfare economic tradition makes it clear that its goals are less ambitious than Arrow's theorem because it only sets out to select one superior resource allocation, not a logically consistent ordering of all possible resource allocations. Based on the same restriction of interpersonal comparisons of utility, then, Arrow's result is neither out of line nor surprising given the well-worn discussion leading up to the development of his theorem.[51] Indeed, it is an elementary result of the two-person Edgeworth box that there are numerous optimal points; that the set of possibly selected outcomes among the two individuals achieved through trade is a function of their initial resource endowments; and that the lack of a specified initial resource endowment would make it impossible to define any optimum. As Samuelson suggests, this final point follows as a consequence of refusing to take into consideration interpersonal comparisons of utility. Hence, the varying resource allocations of (9,9) for person 1 and (1,1) for person 2, the inverse, or an equitable distribution, cannot be discriminated between. It is hopeless to attempt to achieve a collectively "rational" resource allocation of goods among two individuals when no initial resource endowments, or interpersonal comparisons of utility, are considered.

Arrow's two-person, two-commodity example is a familiar economic case useful either for deriving principles of exchange or grounding discussions of social welfare. However, his three or more person proof is more reminiscent of voting problems, relying on the language of "decisive sets," and does not correlate with market exchange scenarios, but is familiar in the situation of majority rule wherein some individuals "win" and others "lose." Arrow introduces his result in a straightforward, almost facile, way by referring to Condorcet's paradox of three voters whose preference rankings are as follows:

person one prefers X > Y > Z;
person two prefers Y > Z > X;
and person three prefers Z > X > Y.[52]

Obviously, in this case of democratic voting an irreconcilable deadlock is achieved: two people prefer X to Y; two people prefer Y to Z; and two people prefer Z to X, resulting in the intransitive relationship X > Y > Z > X. This problem of "intransitivity" in the collective preference expression is fundamental to Arrow's proof. While the latter pertains to the general case of three or more individuals, and three or more alternatives, the three-person case subsists as an embryonic form of the n-person proof that Arrow subsequently elaborated.[53] Again, the general result is not astonishing given the problems of guaranteeing a collectively consistent group preference in a society of three.

Yet despite these theoretical precursors to Arrow's theorem, his "general possibility theorem," holding for three or more individuals selecting from three or more alternatives, became fundamental to democratic political theory, terminated the American tradition of social welfare economics, and initiated the economic subfield of social choice theory. In order to understand these dramatic shifts in research practices, it is necessary to fully grasp not just the logical content, but also the philosophical work achieved by Arrow's theorem. It is this, I argue, that is at least as fundamental as the logical result of the proof; and it is this that explains the crucial role the theorem played in establishing the Cold War orthodoxy of rational choice liberalism.

The first aspect of Arrow's theorem that should be noticed is its unproblematic *assumption* of the intersubjective validity of empirical matters of fact and the rules of logic. Economic relations derived from mathematical reasoning, and tested against the empirical world, have objective interpersonal validity for Arrow.[54] His formal method for analyzing collective decision processes has universal validity; it applies equally to any group decisionmaking procedure. Hence he claims that his theorem applies equally to the market, to democratic voting, and to social welfare economics. His theorem is relevant to capitalist or socialist societies attempting to achieve group decisions reflecting individuals' preferences; it is universal. The assumption of universality is crucial for rendering any social context accessible to a single mode of scientific analysis, and for postulating that the resulting "universal laws" are applicable to all peoples. Furthermore, the possibility that any "ideological element" could intercede in scientific analysis is not only anathema to Arrow, it is also theoretically infeasible. This conclusion, though hotly debated in economics in the 1940s, was henceforth standardized within the rational choice approach to economics and politics. The propositions that economic analysis yields universal laws and that scientific knowledge is objective represent two key elements of Arrow's watershed accomplishment within the field. They counter socialist theorists such as Dobb who insisted that socialist economies run according to different laws than do capitalist economies; and they also counter Marx's claim that scientific knowledge is produced by culturally relative material conditions.[55]

Arrow is part of the school of thought upholding individuals' preferences as the only possible legitimate measure of individual or collective well-being. Thus Arrow incorporates a premise of individualism into his theorem via his stipulation of "citizens' sovereignty," and he continues the convention of using the phrase "consumers' sovereignty" to refer to the inviolability of consumers' preferences in economic theory. Arrow builds into his theorem the conviction that the individual is the absolute and final arbiter of his own preferences. He is here consistent with earlier work in economics, which first borrowed the "sovereignty" metaphor from political theory as a way of describing consumer choice. Now, under Arrow, the metaphor was exported back to the domain of political decisionmaking in democratic regimes. In defending the notion of consumers' sovereignty, Arrow is content that it convey the idea that individuals' preferences are the basic information out of which legitimate collective decisions must be built; he leaves aside additional questions characteristic of 1940s debates among economists over the sanctity and meaningfulness of consumers' preferences.[56] In formulating his definition of "citizens' sovereignty," Arrow endorses the assumption of a thoroughgoing individualism that leaves it entirely up to the individual to decide what suits him, whether that individual acts as a Veblenesque conspicuous consumer or not.[57] Arrow's definition of "citizens' sovereignty," upholding the individual as the final arbiter of his preferences, ends and values is a third element in Arrow's watershed.

Without fanfare or acknowledgment, Arrow incorporated three additional assumptions into his theory of social choice that were similarly implicit in the definition of consumer sovereignty. Writing in 1939, L. M. Fraser points to the additional elements often unconsciously incorporated into this definition:

([U]nder capitalism) consumers' preferences are in some sense independent and "autonomous" factors in the total situation; that they are of greater ultimate significance than other manifestations of economic choice; and that their maximum realisation represents an ideal or norm of economic policy.[58]

Fraser adds, "None of these further propositions can be allowed to pass unchallenged." The wide acceptance of Arrow's theorem left unanswered many such troubling questions as to the scientific and philosophical significance of "consumers' sovereignty." It is not an unfair conclusion that Arrow's set-theoretic definition of citizens' sovereignty is one of the least philosophically examined concepts of sovereignty in the history of political theory.

Arrow defines his concept of citizens' sovereignty to capture the idea that the "social welfare function is not to be imposed," and specifies that

[a] social welfare function will be said to be imposed *if, for some pair of distinct alternatives x and y, x R y* [denoting that *x* is collectively preferred or
indifferent to *y*] *for any set of individual orderings $R_1, \ldots, R_n$, where R is
the social ordering corresponding to $R_1, \ldots, R_n$.*[59]

Arrow's definition of imposition signifies a social choice rule that may dictate an outcome independently from individuals' preferences. Just as
Dobb and Fraser avidly contested the meaningfulness of consumers' sovereignty, Arrow's construct of citizens' sovereignty is open to attack on
the basis that such preference-altering considerations as advertising,
propaganda, and deliberation are left entirely out of his analysis. For Arrow, legitimate collective decisions must be derived from individual preferences. Supporting the line of argument offered by A. P. Lerner, Arrow
insists on the sanctity of individuals' preferences as the bulwark against
coercive totalitarianism.[60]

Having established the concept of citizens' sovereignty by set-theoretic
definition rather than argument, Arrow defines that "individuals are rational"[61] if they order their preferences of social outcomes in accordance
with two set-theoretic axioms:

Axiom I: *For all x and y, either x R y or y R x.*
Axiom II: *For all x, y, and z, x R y and y R z imply x R z.*[62]

In layman's language, this means that to be rational, individuals must
know either what they prefer among choices or be indifferent to them in a
consistent fashion, eliminating the possibility, for example, that someone
prefer coffee to orange juice, orange juice to tea, and tea to coffee. Such a
"preference ordering," in Arrow's terms, would be logically impossible.

Seldom is it appreciated how dramatic a shift Arrow made by defining
rationality in terms of these two axioms upholding the logical relation of
transitivity, instead of defining rationality in accordance with the preference fields characteristic of marginalist economics. Surely the language
seems the same, in both cases "preferences can be ordered along a
scale."[63] Arrow himself notes that "the concept of rationality used
throughout this study is at the heart of modern economic analysis."[64] In
uttering this great truth, however, Arrow can be seen to emphasize his
continuity with the tradition of economic thought as passed on through
the marginalists, instead of drawing attention to the differences from that
tradition that he introduces.[65] Arrow implies that he continues "the traditional identification of rationality with maximization of some sort," but
what is being altered in Arrow's set-theoretic treatment of rationality is
precisely the role that the "maximization of a magnitude" typical of marginalist economics plays.[66]

In marginalist economics the ideal rational consumer acts in accordance with economists' calculus-based demand equations, which use an individual's diminishing marginal utility for two or more commodities, combined with a budget constraint, to predict consumer spending. In this calculus-based system, it is crucial that consumers' preference fields obey certain mathematical relations: they must be continuous and convex. Because the mathematics is so complex, it was not assumed by economists that consumers actually had demand functions in their heads. Samuelson goes some lengths to explain this:

> *The utility analysis rests on the fundamental assumption that the individual confronted with given prices and confined to a given total expenditure selects that combination of goods which is highest on his preference scale.* This does not require (a) that the individual behave rationally in any other sense; (b) that he be deliberate and self-conscious in his purchasing; (c) that there exist any *intensive* magnitude which he feels or consults.[67]

It is sufficient that the demand functions accurately predict consumer's behavior.

By contrast, Arrow's two axioms of rationality only demand that between any two potential social states, an individual is able to specify that one outcome is either equivalent or superior to another outcome, in such a fashion that no logical inconsistencies result when all the potential outcomes are aligned in a single ordering. Gone are the complex demand functions and, in their place, is the comparatively simple requirement that individuals know what they like and dislike; gone are the references to ratios of commodities and equivalent satisfaction derived from each final unit purchased, and instead there are simple pair-wise comparisons between potential end states in the world. In Arrow's new formulation, the individual need only know what she prefers among two outcomes, without engaging in activity entailed by the more laborious calculation of "maximizing utility given a budget constraint." Whereas Samuelson is abundantly clear in not attributing the laws of "rational economics" to anything occurring in a consumer's head, Arrow has a different take on the proposition of rationality. He deems mathematics to be the "acme of consciousness," and suggests that a rational individual reasons in accordance with the rules of logic.[68]

One consequence of Arrow's reformulation of "rational action" in terms of set theory, instead of the calculus-based demand functions capturing the economics of constrained maximization, is that he generalized the principles of reason so that consumer economics mandating that more is always better to less may be considered a special case. Arrow observes

that the "representation of the choice mechanism by ordering relations . . . has certain advantages . . . over the more conventional repre-
sentations in terms of indifference maps or utility functions."[69] One advantage is that Arrow's method accommodates more dimensions than is
possible in graphically illustrated "indifference maps." The usual assumption of continuity required for indifference maps is rendered superfluous. In addition to these important differences between marginalist
economists' "rational consumer" and Arrow's "rational choice" theory,[70]
the logical relations among preferences implied by the set-theoretic formulation of rationality differ from the relations implied by the mathematical relations structuring marginalist economics. The specific relation
between the two systems is discussed in chapter 7.

Arrow's simplification and generalization of the principles of rational
choice obviated the controversies then embroiling the attempt to define rational behavior in a way particular to a capitalist society. Arrow's theorem
accommodates the preferences of individuals ranging from narrow self-interest to altruism. He devotes more than a paragraph to refuting Rothschild's dual challenge that some individuals' choice patterns may not be
orderable "in the sense of a one-dimensional ordering of all possible alternatives," and hence may counter the possibility of deductive economic
theorizing. Although Arrow does not specifically address the case of
whether any meaningful economic theory could reflect patterns in which
consumers defied the logical relation of transitivity, he does insist that
"choice functions" can be built into many cases of behavior, even possibly those that Rothschild regarded as situations embodying "real irrationality." In effect, Arrow's theory of rational choice, extrapolating individuals' orderings out of pair-wise comparisons, can accommodate a
number of situations, and need not be limited to one in which a specific
magnitude is maximized, as in the paradigmatic case of "capitalist rationality."[71] This, then, is another significant element of Arrow's intellectual
achievement: he fashions a set-theoretic definition of rationality by permitting the spirit of marginalists' commercially inspired "maximization
under a budget constraint" as a special case, thereby rejecting the possibility that reason, as he defines it, it is a culturally relative phenomenon.

Arrow resolves many of the controversies among economists in the
1940s by weaving firm positions on those contentious issues into the fabric of his impossibility theorem. His assumption of the objectivity of logic
and facts combined with the subjectivity of preferences, values, and ends
made his theorem apparently applicable to all societies, regardless of their
modes of organization. Arrow requires that legitimate collective decisions
be based on individuals' preferences and, by virtue of his commitment to

the notion of citizens' sovereignty, upholds the individual as the final arbiter of his own preferences. He defines rationality in set-theoretic terms
such that it can be construed as consistent with traditional marginalist
economic analysis, but at the same time not be limited by this special case
of consumer rationality. In sum, Arrow incorporates methodological individualism into this principle of citizen's sovereignty, he constructs his
science to be objective and to yield universal law, and he defines rationality in a way not limited to the demand functions potentially characteristic of a "capitalist spirit."

The general acceptance of Arrow's theorem and the replacement of the
welfare economics tradition with social choice theory implied acceptance
of the basic premises structuring his theorem. If this was not a sufficient
accomplishment, Arrow's impossibility theorem also effectively rejected
Rousseauian, Kantian, Marxist, and classical utilitarian political philosophies as untenable. Thus, his theorem serves both as a platform for the
acceptance of scientific objectivity, universal law, individual freedom to
determine ends, and "rational choice" defined by the logical relation of
transitivity while simultaneously undermining idealistic democracy,
Marxism, totalitarianism, and classical utilitarianism.

I next consider how Arrow achieves this victory over these alternative
social philosophies in his set-theoretic analysis of group decisionmaking.
To do so requires that we have some idea of the logical structure of Arrow's theorem, that is, how Arrow derives "collective rationality" from
"individual rationality." Again, what is key here is not so much Arrow's
negative result—his indictment that neither democratic voting, a social
welfare function, or the "market mechanism" can "create a rational social choice"—but rather the scope of the philosophical assumptions
structuring the theorem.[72] Arrow reiterates his fundamental conclusion
that "[i]f consumers' values can be represented by a wide range of individual orderings, the doctrine of voters' sovereignty is incompatible with
that of collective rationality" (60). He achieves this "impossibility" result
by identifying five minimalist assumptions or "conditions" delimiting the
logical structure of the procedure that derives a collective preference ordering from the preference orderings of individuals. First, Arrow maintains that there can be no restrictions on preferences expressed by an
individual, save that they obey the logical relation of transitivity. This
condition is referred to as "universal domain." Arrow's second condition
is that the resulting social ordering must positively reflect individuals'
preferences. His concern here is to eliminate the possibility of moving
from individuals' preferences to a group preference ordering in such a
way as to inversely reflect individuals' desires. The third condition is

referred to as the "independence of irrelevant alternatives," which stipulates that all individual and collective preferences must be consistent with
simple pair-wise comparisons between all potential outcomes. This condition is discussed in greater detail below. Arrow's fourth assumption is
of citizens' sovereignty, already discussed above; it requires that "all social choices are determined by individual desires," and are not "imposed"
by considerations external to individuals' preferences.[73] The final condition enunciated by Arrow is the "condition of nondictatorship," specifying that it is not permissible to have a single person's preferences dictate
the group's preferences over any pair of choices.

Acknowledging that each of these conditions plays a fundamental role
in his impossibility theorem, Arrow restates his theorem:

> *If we exclude the possibility of interpersonal comparisons of utility* [hence
> upholding condition 3], *then the only methods of passing from individual
> tastes to social preferences which will be satisfactory* [that is, not in viola-
> tion of condition 2] *and which will be defined for a wide range of sets of in-
> dividual orderings* [condition 1's universal domain] *are either imposed* [vi-
> olating condition 4's citizens' sovereignty] *or dictatorial* [in violation of the
> nondictatorship of condition 5].[74]

Each of these five conditions thus plays a crucial role in Arrow's theorem;
if any of them is relaxed, the theorem becomes a "possibility theorem,"
instead of an "impossibility theorem." As his argument is structured,
these normative conditions define the *only* legitimate means by which a
"collectively rational" social preference ordering is made; Arrow's five assumptions, then, specify the principles that either welfare economics,
democratic voting, or the market must uphold in order to be valid. The
conditions on which Arrow's theorem hinges have received endless, laborious, and microscopic attention by scholars intent on breaking free from
the logical impasse in which Arrow mires the market, democracy, and social welfare economics.[75] However, comparatively less attention has been
paid to understanding the manner in which each of these five conditions
also plays a central role in defining the Cold War consensus on the philosophical foundations of economic and political liberalism. In effect,
whereas Arrow's result appears to be a crushing indictment of the ability
of capitalist democracy to achieve collectively rational and therefore legitimate social outcomes, what is more important is that the acceptance
of this negative result requires adopting the conditions on which it is
based, which in turn repudiates a philosophical system sustaining Marxism or totalitarianism. Arrow's five conditions are normative desiderata
that are supposedly so minimally demanding as to serve as the basis of an
uncontested consensus.

Again, what is most interesting about these assumptions underlying the impossibility theorem is how they emerged as the philosophical foundation for American liberalism during the Cold War. Rational choice theory, as initiated by *Social Choice and Individual Values*, became a mainstream disciplinary standard within economics and political science, and increasingly in public policy and jurisprudence, while incorporating specific philosophical commitments inseparable from a staunch defense of capitalist democracy. The conditions of nondictatorship and of the positive association of individual and collective preferences are in a way trivial, because they are necessary assumptions for any group decision-making process, be it the market, voting, or social welfare economics. However, Arrow's other three conditions of universal domain, independence of irrelevant alternatives, and citizens' sovereignty are not trivial. I earlier emphasized the condition of citizens' sovereignty specifically because the meaningfulness of individuals' preferences as a basis for building a social order had been a matter of contention in the 1940s. It is this condition that Arrow uses to defeat the "idealist position" that he associates with the political philosophies of Rousseau, Kant, and Marx.[76] The combination of individuals' status as the final arbiter of personal preferences with the logical requirement that individuals' preferences should be permitted any range of expression save that violating transitivity is opposed to the type of restriction on preferences Arrow's deems to be characteristic of these political theories. Rousseau postulates a "general will" that transcends individual desires to achieve a consensual agreement of ends; Kant orders his society in accordance with the "categorical imperative," which similarly restricts the expression of individual preferences to achieve a societal consensus on ends; Marx's dictum "from each according to his ability, to each according to his needs" replaces individuals' unfiltered preferences with "objective needs" that presumably are determined by a source external to subjective desire, thereby violating citizens' sovereignty.

In his effort to defeat what he takes to be the philosophical idealism of Rousseau, Kant, and Marx in the spirit of the "liberal heritage," Arrow refers to "the debate a few years back between Mr. Dobb and Professor Lerner."[77] In raising doubts as to the reliability of individuals' tastes as a guide for sound public policy, Dobb had suggested that there be a superior standard for policy. Reviewing the debate at some length, Arrow concludes that Lerner was just in his assessment that Dobb "implies some transcendental optimum other than that shown 'by a free market or in any other way.'"[78] In Arrow's view, Dobb represents "the rationalist tradition common to utilitarianism and Marxism," and comes up against the difficulty of erecting an absolute moral standard that transgresses liberalism and the sanctity of the individual to select his own ends and preferences. In grouping together Rousseau, Kant, and Marx as theorists looking to absolute philosophical ideals to enforce standards of behavior beyond the discretion of individuals' subjective desires, Arrow argues that moral relativism is more consistent with liberalism. His theorem rejects the possibility that a social consensus on ends could emerge as a result of a philosophical ideal transcending individuals' desires as a guide to collective decisionmaking. Since, as Arrow presents it, Marxism requires such an ideal, it is incompatible with the liberal tradition to which *Social Choice and Individual Values* contributes.

What is noteworthy in Arrow's discussion of these three philosophers is the manner in which his set-theoretic proof undermines their philosophical systems: he insists on a thorough-going individualism that is incompatible with any standard for collective social norms or self-legislation that may impinge on an individual's right to have *any* (transitive) set of desires, and he defines collective rationality in accordance with this priority granted to individual desire. Here Arrow's philosophical position clearly reflects the attempt to erect a basis for American economic and political liberalism that cannot be thwarted by authoritarianism. As the debates over consumer sovereignty discussed above indicate, there was a niggling suspicion that any attempt to censor individuals' "raw" preferences necessarily entails the erection of an elite figure or idealist philosophy that determines what is best for individuals and society. Whereas Arrow's insistence on citizens' sovereignty is understandable given the Cold War fear of fascism or totalitarianism, the significance of the broad acceptance of this principle derived from consumer economics and transposed to serve as the legitimating criterion for democratic sovereignty cannot be overstated. Arrow's proof pertains to a society in which there is no principle for achieving collective decisions save amalgamating individuals' preferences, no matter what they may be or how they are formed, to achieve a mathematically derived collective expression that is consistent with a few minimalist criteria. It also requires the bifurcation of the world into facts and logical principles that are interpersonally and objectively valid, and the subjective domain of values and preferences.

The combination of Arrow's conditions of universal domain and citizens' sovereignty preserve the capacity of individuals' preference to take any form and to serve as the basis of the collective decisionmaking procedure. In the burgeoning literature following Arrow's epochal work, various restrictions on individuals' preferences, such as "single-peaked preferences," received copious attention, whereas the foundational condition of citizens' sovereignty was accepted as basic.

Among all of Arrow's conditions, however, the one that received the greatest attention is "the independence of irrelevant alternatives." Even in Arrow's first expression of it in *Social Choice and Individual Values*, the example he uses to illustrate its significance, and its logical expression, seem to suggest two different ideas.[79] An anecdotally irreverent and likely apocryphal incident perhaps best illustrates the spirit of Arrow's third condition. The story is told that, prior to formulating his proof, Arrow was up for consideration to receive a prestigious award that was to be decided by majority vote among committee members. It was clear that Arrow would be awarded the prize insofar as he held a majority of the votes. Unfortunately, as the results were being tallied, one of the other candidates for the award unexpectedly died, and her death altered the possible social states in such a fashion that another of the candidates ended up winning. It is specifically this sort of outcome that Arrow's "condition of irrelevant alternatives" is formulated to exclude.

Arrow's condition is controversial because it assumes that a collectively rational outcome must remain stable even when the set of possible outcomes directly under consideration changes. It is also controversial because it strictly maintains that any collective expression of preferences must be potentially constructed from pair-wise comparisons. This alternative means of reading Arrow's condition is logically related to the stipulation that individuals' preferences cannot be interpersonally compared. If interpersonal comparison of preferences were permitted in voting situations, then votes would be weighted in accordance with the intensity of individuals' preferences—for example, "I want my choice more than you want yours." A mathematical mapping from individual to collective preferences would then be forced to consider the intensity with which individuals' register or report their preferences, which in turn would lead to the violation of the one-person, one-vote principle characterizing most democratic decision procedures.

As controversial as Arrow's third condition has been, it is possible to state that the condition of the independence of irrelevant alternatives is a logical consequence of the prohibition of comparing individuals' utility.[80] For Arrow this had the important outcome of undermining classical utilitarianism, and with it the material welfare tradition of A. C. Pigou and Alfred Marshall. Arrow's adroit elimination of the interpersonal comparison of utility at the heart of his theorem again served to build a new consensus on what had earlier been issues of marked debate. In maintaining this tenet as fundamental to welfare economics, Arrow continued in the tradition of Lionel Robbins and J. R. Hicks, additionally insisting that it should be upheld in any legitimate collective decisionmaking procedure.

In the early 1950s, this contradicted accepted disciplinary standards governing economics. In his 1954 Brookings Institution lecture, Arthur Smithies observed in a discussion of social welfare economics that "[a]ny economist today who proposed that public policy be based on the view that utilities are not comparable would scarcely get a political hearing."[81] The broad acceptance of Arrow's theorem, as attested to by his being awarded Nobel prize, demonstrates that a completely new disciplinary consensus regarding the normative conditions structuring his impossibility theorem had emerged.

The five conditions upholding the sacredness of individual choice, combined with Arrow's commitment to objective scientific knowledge, universal law, and reason, are the foundation stones of the emerging Cold War consensus anchoring the rational choice approach to democracy and capitalism. Arrow's theorem demonstrating the logical impossibility of achieving a collective preference ordering from individuals' desires was not surprising in view of Condorcet's earlier voting impasse reached by only three voters' expressing preferences over three alternatives, and given the large number of "socially optimal" points characterizing "Edgeworth box" welfare economics analyses. Moreover, the great theoretical elegance of the impossibility theorem distracts attention from the brilliance with which Arrow created a philosophical system that serves to ground a universal science of economics. This system put forward a particular view of individual freedom, it defines rationality as transitive preference orderings, and it embraces capitalistic democracy while undermining idealist democracy, Marxism, and classical utilitarianism.

Arrow's condition of citizens' sovereignty is presented as the philosophical alternative to elite rule by an authoritarian government that claims to know what is best for the people. Arrow insists that the liberal tradition rejected philosophical idealism and accepted instead moral relativism consistent with permitting individuals' total freedom to choose values and outcomes. The far-reaching acceptance of the impossibility theorem therefore supplanted the socialist tradition as represented by Maurice Dobb. A second type of mid-twentieth-century socialist philosophy was maintained by Oscar Lange and A. P. Lerner. Their tradition is better thought of as "scientific Marxism" rather than the "idealist Marxism" espoused by Dobb; it is also consistent with the "material welfare" economics tradition represented by Pigou and Marshall. Just as Arrow undermined idealist Marxism by steadfastly stressing individualism and moral relativism in the spirit of the liberal tradition, so he overcame the philosophical viability claimed for scientific Marxism by prohibiting the comparison of personal utilities on the basis that it is unscientific.

The Demise of American Social Welfare Economics

The reception of Arrow's *Social Choice and Individual Values* falls into three categories: the text's impact on the tradition of social welfare economics, its implications for political theory, and the scant attention it received for its critique of the marketplace. As for economists' interests in its ramifications for the ability of the marketplace to yield collectively rational preferences, the literature in the 1950s is nonexistent. Apparently it did not trouble economists that the market cannot deliver collectively rational decisions because, following James Buchanan, they deemed that "the market does not call upon individuals to make a decision collectively at all." [82] Yet despite this conventional and convenient belief, Buchanan's 1954 observation continues to hold: "So far as I know, the differences between the market and political voting as choice processes have never been clearly and precisely analyzed.[83] By contrast, in the 1950s and 1960s, scholars in the fields of social welfare economics and political theory were led by Arrow's work to reevaluate their fundamental assumptions. This uneven reception accorded Arrow's impossibility theorem provides further evidence for the text's use in building a foundation for economic and political liberalism. The mere fact that whereas Arrow indicts social welfare economics, democracy, and the market equally, but that only the tradition of welfare economics was unseated, demonstrates how the work's basic principles were widely taken to support democratic capitalism and to undermine social planning. In this section I focus exclusively on the impossibility theorem's impact on social welfare economics.

Social Choice and Individual Values received immediate attention from a wide-ranging array of academic journals, including the *Journal of Political Economy*, the *American Sociological Review*, the *American Catholic Sociological Review*, and *Ethics*. These reviews commented on Arrow's unprecedented use of symbolic logic to construct his argument, which was presaged only by von Neumann and Morgenstern's *Theory of Games and Economic Behavior*.[84] Respondents explained Arrow's theorem as a generalization of the well-known Condorcet paradox of voting that obtains among three individuals and three choices.[85] The *Journal of Political Economy* provided a helpful synopsis Arrow's proof, explaining the five conditions required of a legitimate social welfare function and his conclusion that the move from an individual to a group preference ordering cannot be made unless unpalatable, restrictive conditions are applied to individuals' preferences. The *American Sociological Review* pointed out that Arrow's proof requires the exclusion of the possibility of interpersonal comparisons of utility.[86] *Ethics* found that Arrow's theorem has fundamental and far-reaching relevance for "social scientists in general, and to ethical and social philosophers as well." This is because Arrow tackles a foundational problem of society, that of deriving legitimate collective decisions from individuals' preferences. Arrow's theoretical breakthrough was described as presenting a familiar problem of the paradox of voting in a "highly perspicuous form," drawing on "the logic of relations," and setting the apparatus in motion to analytically study the relationship between individuals' desires and collective outcomes in social welfare economics and democratic government.[87] *The Journal of Political Economy* concluded that "this is a challenging and disturbing book that demands the attention of everyone concerned with economic policy," because any selection of public policy requires a rationale of somehow serving the public.[88] The *American Catholic Sociological Review* was alone in noting further that *Social Choice and Individual Values* "gives small comfort to those who advocate using the market mechanism as the social welfare function."[89]

Three authors from within the social welfare economics tradition did not review Arrow's text so much as present articles challenging the impossibility theorem's relevance to welfare economics. Two of these scholars, I. M. D. Little and Abram Bergson, were leading figures in social welfare economics. Throughout the first half of the twentieth century, the problem of social welfare—namely, how to guarantee that an economic system yields maximum benefit to all participants—was a focal question for economists. Much of this interest in social welfare stemmed from the concern with demonstrating that free competition results in beneficial social states.[90] At the core of welfare economics was the attempt to construct mathematical functions that would enable the theorist to evaluate how various policies, such as lump-sum taxes or bounties, would effect a community's overall welfare. Discussions did not shy from adopting the perspective of a social planner, which was not inconsistent with the economics of the New Deal or with the planned economy of wartime.[91] It was recognized that social welfare economists played a role in evaluating the impact of public policies, such as the British Corn Laws, and their goal was to build scientific models that would demonstrate how various policy initiatives effect constituents' interests.[92]

In the 1940s, the new school of welfare economics crystallized around the assumptions that welfare economics must only take into consideration ordinal preferences and that cardinal preferences cannot be measured and are therefore unscientific.[93] Abram Bergson was considered the leading theorist of this school, and one of the leading social welfare theorists of the 1940s. A goal of the new welfare economics was to maintain the relevance of welfare considerations to economic theory by arguing that normative judgment is inescapably related to decisions over economic policy. It was already suspected in 1948 that discussions of social welfare barring any ethical assumptions were void of much content, and it was questioned whether a meaningful social welfare function that could differentiate objectively between the collective desirability of various social states could be derived. According to Samuelson, the ordinalist welfare economics program of the 1940s was little further in its ability to draw conclusions than Pareto's ordinalist welfare economics of optimality: In both cases, it is possible to identify a set of points representing individuals' social welfare socially preferable to a larger set of points, but not possible to further narrow the field of points.[94] The welfare economists recognized the inherent impossibility in attempting to derive objective measures of social welfare from scientific analysis, and recognized the inescapable role of normative judgments in selecting economic policies.[95]

In constructing his "possibility theorem,"[96] Arrow synthesized his knowledge of the Bergsonian social welfare function constructed as a constrained maximization problem considering wages, productivity, and consumption, with the aggregative logic leading to the intransitivity paradox with voting over three outcomes. Arrow combined two formerly distinct approaches to social welfare and voting by considering under one approach.[97] Using "transitivity" as the key concept characterizing individual and collective rationality, Arrow proved that collectively rational group decisions achieved through the marketplace, voting, or the social welfare function were all logically impossible, granted the acceptance of his conditions. For the welfare economists, discussion had centered on how individuals' welfare was affected through normative judgments such as equalizing the distribution of resources.[98] Arrow's proof shifted the focus from an ethical evaluation of ends achieved through manipulating economic policies to a demonstration of the impossibility of achieving a rationally consistent statement of collective ends, given the starting point of rational self-interest and mild assumptions about preferences and methods of aggregation.

The response of welfare economists to Arrow's theorem was overwhelmingly negative. Little wrote, "Arrow's work has no relevance to the traditional theory of welfare economics," and Murray C. Kemp argued that "Arrow's conditions are unreasonable and . . . the conclusion is uninteresting."[99] Bergson, too, was in agreement: "Arrow's theorem is quite different from, and has little relevance to traditional welfare economics."[100] Writing with more hindsight, the welfare economist E. J. Mishan found the theorem trite, given the state of welfare economics.[101] This sentiment was not driven by an imperative to "save welfare economics," since these theorists had developed their own independent critiques of the welfare economics tradition. Rather, their criticism of Arrow's impossibility theorem and its relevance to their field was constructed on three different levels.[102] First, they found that the conditions on which Arrow based his proof were not essential to social welfare economics. Second, they argued that Arrow's theorem applies to social decisionmaking processes, but not to the discipline of social welfare, which only attempts to assess the consequences of varying economic arrangements for participating individuals *without making a grand statement about the social welfare function representing individuals' choices*; thus Arrow's theorem applies to problems of designing collective decisionmaking procedures, but not to questions of social welfare.[103] Third, they contended that Arrow's design of the social choice problem formulates as relevant the wrong questions and misapprehends the relationship between ethical judgment over ends and collective social choices; Arrow attempts to derive collectively rational ends *from* the social choice function while the welfare economists sought to determine how normative judgments affected social outcomes.[104]

It is remarkable that the welfare economists, to whom Arrow most explicitly directed his argument in *Social Choice and Individual Values*, were united in finding the theorem uninteresting and irrelevant to their field of study. And yet Arrow's theorem would over time initiate the tradition of social choice theory, would be one of the most cited classic texts in the social sciences, and would come to represent a common point of departure for the conceptual foundations of public policy analysis and for political theory. It might seem that the welfare economists had a rather bad case of sour grapes, and were mounting an intellectual battle to save their field from demolition. However, the welfare economists had already established a powerful internal critique of their own field and were not critical of Arrow's theorem simply out of fear that it made any legitimate discussion of social welfare impossible.[105] Instead the debate was over retaining control over which set of terms was crucial to the practice of social welfare economics. Arrow's theorem adopted as standard fare precisely those considerations that the welfare economists already recognized as rendering their field powerless to make positive statements about social welfare, such as ordinal utility and the Pareto condition, but posed a different question. Insisting that collective social ends be selected as a direct product of his social choice function, Arrow demonstrated that a function upholding even the most minimally desirable conditions cannot guarantee a collective rational agreement on ends. Thus, his proof ruled out the even more stringent conditions common to the discussion of the social welfare economists, such as investigating the condition of egalitarian distribution. The welfare economists were aware that these minimalist conditions failed to produce a meaningful statement of social welfare, and they held that normative judgments were unavoidable. [106] In their estimation, individuals are affected by economic principles along with economic policies. It is economists' job to show how these various normative policy goals such as Pareto optimality or equitable distribution affected individuals. Usually they took each individual as interchangeable, each seeking a likable job with good wages, with strong consumption related to strong productivity.[107] Arrow turned the tables on this discussion by insisting that any selection of social ends must be the product of the social choice function, and he proved that the social choice function itself is an impossibility.

Arrow's theorem, then, was fatal to the new school of welfare economics because it introduced a new conceptual apparatus for addressing issues of "social choice" that undermined the possibility of speaking meaningfully about social welfare. Arrow's theorem altered the relationship between scientific analysis and normative judgment by making the latter subject to the former. The welfare economists created economic models to show how individual welfare was affected by varying policy initiatives; Arrow's theorem forbad the very discussion of "social welfare" because it could not stand up to the rigors of logical analysis. Although publications in the new welfare economics tradition continued throughout the 1950s,[108] by the 1960s the language of *Social Choice and Individual Values* had become the intellectual standard for addressing questions formerly its domain.

The indications of the rise of the social choice approach as standard to the discipline are now everywhere apparent. Looking back, Amartya Sen, the 1998 Nobel laureate in economics who spent his life working within the social choice framework, observed in 1985 that

> [w]ithin a comparatively short time, the new subject of social choice theory was firmly established as a discipline with immediate and extensive implications for economics, philosophy, politics, and the other social sciences. . . . Welfare economics, in particular, was quite transformed.[109]

Supporting his conclusion, Sen cited the establishment of the specialist journal *Social Choice and Welfare,* and the fact that nonspecialist journals such as the *Journal of Mathematical Economics, Theory and Decision,* and *Mathematical Social Sciences* also published social choice articles. In addition, editors of *Econometrica, Journal of Economic Theory,* and *Review of Economic Studies* began to actively discourage social choice submissions due to their overrepresentation. Sen estimated that by 1985 the number of papers and books addressing social choice theory exceeded one thousand.[110] Another indication of how dramatic and clear cut was the rise of social choice as a subdiscipline is found in Charles K. Rowley's three-volume, fifteen-hundred-page collected set of papers representing core research developments within social choice theory.[111] These collected papers clearly delineate the literature and core research questions structuring social choice scholarship.

In acknowledging the burgeoning development of social choice around Arrow's text, it is necessary to confront the following questions: What is unprecedented in Arrow's theorem? In what ways does it represent an advance over previous work in welfare economics and political theory? Does Arrow's social choice present an original analysis that affords formerly unattainable results? Arrow's most significant conclusion is that it is impossible to achieve collectively rational decisions that respect individuals' freedom to determine personal ends. His novelty lies in formally proving this result; the conceptual content embedded in the formal proof resembles that of the Condorcet paradox, welfare economics, and Schumpeter's and Hayek's doubts over meaningfully defining "public interest."

Arrow's theorem breaks new ground in providing a set-theoretic proof that expands on and formalizes these earlier findings. However, it is the philosophical structure of the proof that is key to understanding the creative genius of the theorem as much as it is the proof's deductive logic. It is here that Arrow introduces a new sweeping definition of human rationality as a consistent preference ordering that nullifies the possibility that other societies either can enact different reasoning practices or can achieve collectively rational decisions without violating the presuppositions of the theorem. It is also here that Arrow relies on methodological individualism to serve as the bulwark against claims that authoritarian or totalitarian political systems could be legitimate. Arrow's theorem is not new in questioning the potential of groups to achieve collectively rational decisions. It is new in establishing that rationality, objective and universal law, and individual freedom over subjective choices represent the bases of capitalist democracy. Recognizing the interconnection between rational choice theory and economic and political liberalism is crucial for fully grasping the historical significance of Arrow's *Social Choice and Individual Values*.

Kenneth Arrow versus Duncan Black

Arrow's timely ingenuity in securing the foundations of American liberalism is perhaps best viewed against the backdrop of a lurking priority dispute with Duncan Black (1908–91) over the crucial insight that linked Cordorcet's voting paradox with collective decisionmaking characterizing a firm or nation. Black developed a pioneering branch of economic analysis that studied committee decision problems as analogous to the manner in which "price is fixed by demand and supply." [112] Black studied these committee voting problems using a method of comparative statics in which an equilibrium is attained when voters select an outcome presenting their individual preferences without exhibiting intransitivities. Whereas Arrow focuses on proving the impossibility of achieving collectively rational outcomes, Black is interested in analyzing cases in which collective choices are legitimately representative. Hence, in his first publication in the field of economic analysis of political decisions, Black argued that if voters' preferences all have the structure of "single-peakedness," then the difficulty of intransitive collective outcomes is negated; hence, a legitimate result obtains. [113]

Black's account of the means by which he arrived at his "pure science of politics," as he came to refer to his research initiative, is expressed in detail in several essays. Like his friend and conversational partner, economist and future Nobel laureate Ronald Coase, he was fascinated by the puzzle surrounding a firm's decisionmaking process given that a firm is necessarily constituted of individuals with disparate interests. At Warrick Castle in February of 1942, "firewatching" in case of air raids, Black's key insight was to recognize that collective decision problems had an equilibrium solution if members' preferences "could be represented by a set of single-peaked curves." [114] For Black, the "political problem [of committee decisionmaking] had been transformed into a mathematical problem." [115]

The priority dispute between Black and Arrow over the mathematical analysis of election problems was bitter and unresolved. With his 1948 publication of "On the Rationale of Group Decision Making," it would seem that Black's prior understanding of collective decision problems was securely established. However, the dispute only intensified when Black's second article, co-authored with R. A. Newing, slowly proceeded through what turned out to be a lengthy review process at the journal *Econometrica*. This paper was submitted in November 1949. A year and a half later, after badgering the managing editor William B. Simpson for some idea of the article's status, Black was informed that it would be accepted on the condition that the authors thoroughly revise it in consideration of Arrow's recently published *Social Choice and Individual Values*. Black's outrage was complete when he learned that Simpson played another professional role as assistant director of research at the Cowles Commission in Chicago, where Arrow worked. [116] It took the better part of a decade for

Black to regroup, finally publishing his book *The Theory of Committees and Elections* in 1958. [117]

In Black's defense, his autobiographical recounting of the skirmish with Arrow and the detailed chronology of his intellectual trajectory leading to his mathematical analysis of committee decisionmaking are as complete as they are sincere. Arrow's account of the dispute, by contrast, is anecdotal and vague. He explains that he first came across the problem of collective decisionmaking while deciding whether to write his dissertation on J. R. Hicks' *Value and Capital,* in 1946. Arrow asked how firm members, all of whom had different interests, could reconcile those interests into a joint decision. Assuming the decision would be reached by majority voting, he notes that "[i]n economic analysis we usually have many (in fact, infinitely many) alternative possible plans, so that transitivity [of the group decision ordering] quickly became a significant question. It was immediately clear that majority voting did not necessarily lead to an ordering." [118] Arrow at first believed this negative consequence was a "nuisance" that could be overcome. He then reports: "Besides, I was convinced that what we presently call the Condorcet paradox was not new. I am at a loss to identify the source of my belief, since I could not possibly have seen any of this obscure material prior to 1946." [119]

The paper trail documenting Arrow's intellectual development in this regard remains incomplete because no version of his social choice theorem exists prior to his 1950 paper "A Difficulty in the Concept of Social Welfare." [120] Unfortunately, his original statement of the theorem in a 1949 RAND publication appears to have been "systematically purged" from RAND's archive. [121]

While Arrow and Black both worked on the problem of collective decision results obtained by voting, their orientations to the issue were diametrically opposed. Arrow's theory of social choice was entirely normative. Despite his claim that economic science must ultimately be empirical, in setting up the conditions for a legitimate democratic decision process Arrow's theorem articulates the properties a voting system *should* exhibit. Black, on the other hand, turned his attention to practical decision procedures as social events whose rules and results should be assessed from the standpoint of empirical investigation coupled with mathematical analysis. For Black, voting rules themselves constitute part of the empirical data; for Arrow the decision rules are axiomatically defined ideals. Black investigated the actual procedures groups of individuals used to achieve collective decisions; Arrow concerned himself with esoteric proofs so removed from social reality that few were competent to assess their relevance or validity.

Black's original article "On the Rationale of Group Decision Making" and his subsequent book *The Theory of Committees and Elections* are widely acknowledged to stand alongside Arrow's *Social Choice and Individual Values* in the canon of rational choice literature. However, despite the fact that Black thoroughly understood the practical significance of the new vein of research he and Arrow had opened up, his career was one of isolation and instability while Arrow became a Nobel laureate and his work central to the mainstream intellectual establishment structuring American economics and public policy. Before the full significance of Black's work would be recognized, Arrow's *Social Choice and Individual Values* received numerous citations, transformed social welfare economics, had a profound effect on political theory, and initiated the subfield of social choice theory.

The question looms: Why did Arrow's approach to collective decisionmaking inspire a vast intellectual legacy while Black's writings and reputation have to a significant degree been secured only posthumously? This question is telling for bringing to the fore facets of their respective work that have largely been overlooked. Of course, part of the answer is to be found in Arrow's close affiliations with such powerful institutions as RAND, the Cowles Commission, and Stanford University. However, this cannot be the full story. In 1948, Joseph Goldman of RAND wrote to Black asking for articles to be studied by RAND researchers. Black, a British subject, learned from the British consulate in San Francisco that RAND's research was highly classified and oriented toward matters of military strategy; he ignored the request, deliberately choosing not to become a cold warrior.[122]

It is this distinction between Arrow and Black, one man's fate and fortune inextricably linked to Cold War America and the other's scholarly work standing outside the blistering antagonism over the future of America's democracy and free markets, that sets the two apart. Over and above its mathematical sophistication, Arrow's *Social Choice and Individual Values* achieves its status as a classic economics text of the twentieth century by facing the challenges to American freedom as posed by Joseph Schumpeter, Karl Popper, and Friedrich Hayek, and by the visceral threat of the palpable social alternative offered by Soviet Russia. Black, on the other hand, resided at the margins of the Cold War both geographically and intellectually; he was absorbed in constructing a pure science of politics as an inquiry sufficient unto itself, apparently oblivious that the intellectual dimensions of his age intersected with a pitched battle over the basic characteristics of capitalist democracy versus communism.

Whereas on a field of social scientific inquiry Black's contributions stand equal to Arrow's, the greater fame enjoyed by Arrow results from the role he played, with others, in securing a steady foundation for Western liberalism at a time when this philosophical project had the same magnitude and significance as did that of ensuring military supremacy over the Soviets. As Black himself acknowledged, Arrow ignited enthusiasm for social choice theory because of the elegant axiomatized system he presented. However, the roots of Arrow's intellectual achievement go deeper than facility with mathematical formalism; Arrow's mathematical axioms, definitions, and conditions represent the tenets that secured the rational choice approach to Western liberalism. Writing about the crucial importance of mathematical formalism for building a science of politics, Black once observed that "language permeates thinking to its innermost core in all the recesses," adding that "the degree of success achieved in presenting the system of thought will largely depend on the adequacy of the technical terms involved." [123] However, subsequently, when confronted by the "new factor" that "Arrow's technical-mathematical skills" introduce into the theory of collective decisionmaking, Black promotes the idea that ultimately it must be possible to state any mathematical argument in discursive terms. Black remarks that "[a]lthough very different in appearance, the mathematical treatment and literary treatment of this type of problem are isomorphic" (402). In effect, Arrow adds nothing in his "Symbolic Logic and set theory" expression of voting that cannot be made manifest in an alternative discursive articulation. Black's change of heart over the significance of formal language leads him to admit he is "poorly equipped to [contribute to the formal discussion initiated by Arrow] and excuse . . . [myself] from any attempt to expound the matter," and points us back in the direction of the content of Arrow's theoretical achievement to look for clues to its bountiful recognition (ibid.).

Arrow believed that *Social Choice and Individual Values* was the logical consequence of both Western liberalism and of the minimalist assumptions we find basic to Western democracy.[124] It is obvious he wrote in a Cold War context because his agents make decisions over such end states as "disarmament, cold war, or hot war" (2). Also, betraying his close proximity to the tradition of social welfare and the planned economy debate, Arrow explained that individuals make choices among social states that are most appropriately defined as

> a complete description of the amount of each type of commodity in the hands of each individual, the amount of labor to be supplied by each individual, the amount of each productive resource invested in each type of productive activity, and the amounts of various types of collective activity, such as municipal services, diplomacy and its continuation by other means, and the erection of statues to famous men. (17)

Arrow's *Social Choice and Individual Values* by its very conceptual structure tackles the key issue facing his generation: that of resolving his predecessors' open-ended debate on the merits of social welfare economics and planning versus spontaneous democratic control predicated on the primacy of the individual consumer or voter. To achieve this theoretical milestone, Arrow effectively wove a discursively interpretive strand throughout his set-theoretic tapestry. His recourse to literary meaning over and above pure logical analysis is evident in his discussion of "rationality and choice." Arrow believed that "the concept of rationality used throughout . . . [his] study is at the heart of modern economic analysis" (19). For Arrow, defining "rationality," individually and collectively, is central to his enterprise of exploring the normative foundations of collective decision in either the voting, market, or social welfare economics. Rationality, both as the zenith of human consciousness and as the principle governing predictable human action, lies at the heart of his project to generalize his abstract theory of social choice so as to have universal applicability. By "rational choice making" Arrow means that individuals are rational in the sense of obeying his two axioms upholding transitive relations among agents' preferences.[125]

Black, who was not thinking in terms of putting forth a minimalist set of normative tenets consistent with Western liberalism, found Arrow's use of the term "rationality" to be emotive and misplaced.[126] To Black, all Arrow means by "rationality," as indicated by his formal language, is the concept of "transitivity." In this regard, Black was correct, because Arrow's impossibility theorem could not otherwise have so easily captured the imagination of numerous scholars interested in exploring the conceptual foundations of Western liberalism. Arrow himself christened his set-theoretic account of individual preferences and collective decision-making as a theory of "rational choice." The term "rational" is laden with significance that the term "transitivity," or "transitive choice," does not convey. One finds in Arrow's text a discursive, interpretive layer apart from the dry formality of its analysis that serves to translate desiccated mathematical symbols into a manifesto for the ideals he deemed basic to American democracy and free market institutions. Arrow's treatise securely links the rationales for both free-market liberalism and democratic liberalism, suggesting that both decision procedures share the commitment to objectivity, universalism, rationality, and individualism. Moreover, this rationale subverted the theoretical basis of idealistic democracy, Marxism, or classical utilitarianism. Whereas Black analyzed the practical outcomes of actual decision rules in real situations, Arrow offered a purely formal blueprint of the conditions necessary to sustain Western liberalism in opposition to competitors violating its founding assumptions.

Black is properly recognized as an important founder of positive political theory. Arrow is more appropriately regarded as the founding architect of what would become the establishment understanding of the obvious and inviolable partnership between free markets and democracy, both relying on the same axioms and conditions.

Conclusion

A final illuminating method of appreciating the consensus forming among American social scientists about the significance of Arrow's theorem is by tracing its uneven impact on social welfare economics, democratic theory, and the market mechanism, respectively. As discussed above, the American welfare economics tradition did not recover from the blow dealt by Arrow's theorem; the theory died out with its adherents, who failed to win over another generation of students. The field of social choice theory that replaced it was indebted to *Social Choice and Individual Values* as its founding text. Democratic theory, at least insofar as theorists became aware of Arrow's theorem, would likewise never be the same. As a result of the rational choice approach to political decisionmaking pioneered by Arrow, theorists worried about the meaningfulness of democratic elections, and struggled over the question of whether voting itself is a rational activity. Quite by contrast, however, economists and other social scientists largely ignored Arrow's insistence that the impossibility theorem applied equally to the marketplace. For example, Charles Rowley, a scholar wholly committed to rational choice theory, concludes:

> It is important to note that, although the impossibility theorem itself offers a negative result, Arrow's contribution should not be viewed as a negative contribution. . . . For . . . the author, who do[es] not share the general optimism concerning collective choice processes, *Arrow's contribution provides incontrovertible support for market process* and encouragement for those who seek to constrain the range of collective choice to the limited functions of the minimal state.[127]

Whereas little effort has been made to understand in what sense the marketplace represents an Arrovian social choice mechanism, with many theorists thinking it preposterous to believe Arrow's social choice theory indicts the market, Arrow himself is the truest and most steadfast reader of his theorem. He consistently asserts that his impossibility theorem indicts the market just as it does welfare economics and democratic voting. Thus, even though building his theorem out of principles consistent with liberal capitalist democracy, Arrow himself has no more or less faith in the market than he does in social planning.[128] He does, however, consistently abhor and reject any social theory that does not uphold individuals' sovereignty over their own and society's preferences, for the reason that such a theory could be subverted to support an authoritarian or coercive regime. It cannot be overemphasized that Arrow's commitment to the ideals of objective science, universal law, human rationality, and individual freedom defined as sovereignty over personal ends provide both the structure for his impossibility theorem and the basis of the mainstream American Cold War consensus on social philosophy characterizing rational choice liberalism.

Assessing Arrow's theoretical achievement in the context of the entire twentieth century, it is insightful to appreciate the generational shift from the cohort of public intellectuals maintaining the alliance of science and democracy against the evils of fascism and totalitarianism in 1930s and 1940s America, to the Cold War defense intellectuals responsible for defending the West against communism. In assuming this bird's eye view of the past century, I take a lead from David Hollinger, who examines the work of John Dewey and Robert Merton with the goal of "discovering and analyzing the function these same ideas performed in the cultural wars of the era of World War II." [129] Hollinger's two essays, "The Defense of Democracy and Robert K. Merton's Formulation of the Scientific Ethos," and "Science as a Weapon in *Kulturkämpfe* in the United States during and after World War II," illuminate the rich cultural significance of this generation of American public intellectuals who viewed their professional contributions as part of their personal commitments to science, democracy, and cosmopolitanism. Merton believed that science and scientific communities prosper because they embody the four norms of "universalism," "disinterestedness," "communalism," and "organized skepticism." [130] These norms were absent in Nazi society, according to Merton, and America and its allies stood apart in their unified commitment to science and democracy in accordance with the spirit of these four ideals.

Whereas the World War II struggle was against the external threat of fascism, Merton and other midcentury academics waged a second battle against those at home whom they deemed to be narrow-minded, parochial, and superstitious. As Hollinger describes it, midcentury American academics were keen to preserve the freedom of scientific inquiry and the norms underlying it as a public standard of America's values in opposition to those who favored Christian doctrine to pave the way for America's postwar order. In Hollinger's analysis, tackling concerns both at home and abroad, these intellectual leaders represented "the continuum of Enlightenment purpose stretching back to the seventeenth century." [131]

Their efforts embodied Enlightenment enthusiasm for science over superstition and authoritarianism, and for cosmopolitanism based on universal law.

It is striking how similar and yet how distinct the theoretical commitments giving shape to Arrow's *Social Choice and Individual Values* are compared with John Dewey's and Robert Merton's faith in science and democracy as partners against the perverse social forms of fascism and totalitarianism. Arrow's four tenets of objective science based on deductive logic and empirical facts, universal law, rationality, and individual freedom are not worlds apart from Merton's four norms. And yet, the views of science and democracy put forward by Dewey and Arrow are overtly different. Perhaps the greatest agreement among the two generations is to be found in their commitment to universalism as a necessary element of both science and social order. For both, the basic principle underlying both scientific laws and social laws is that they should have universal validity, pertaining equally to all social and natural phenomena and to all individuals, regardless of their cultural specificity. However, Arrow's positivist version of science, assuming the unproblematic objectivity of logic and facts contrasts with Dewey's and Merton's view that impartiality and disinterestedness are personal attributes of the scientist or citizen that are vital to either scientific inquiry or to democratic deliberation. For Dewey and Merton, science itself is a social practice governed by norms ensuring its efficacy and validity. By contrast, for Arrow, logic and facts speak for themselves and they are by nature objective and interpersonally valid.

Merton's value of organized skepticism, too, stresses that science is a social practice embedded in a community of individuals. Here the stress is on an indomitable spirit of inquiry that parallels Dewey's sense of the relationship between the scientific search for truth and the democratic goal to achieve a consensus on ends.[132] In both cases, antidogmatic and antiauthoritarian sentiment guarantees a search for truth unhindered by superstition, propaganda, or absolutist rule. Arrow's defense of democracy adopts a different strategy. Instead of looking to a social process of open-minded collective deliberation to dismantle coercive authority, he looks to upholding individual freedom over personal preferences as the basis of legitimate rule. Here the premium is placed on individuals' subjective freedom, and not a socially based process of antidogmatic deliberation.

Similarly, while for Dewey and Merton both democracy and science are social activities inseparable from the communities in which they are enacted, Arrow's defense of democracy based on the premise of individualism takes a distinct turn. Hence, Dewey's value of "communalism" means that both scientific inquiry and democratic decisionmaking are communally based. In contrast, Arrow's theorem, pertaining to collective decisionmaking in social welfare economics, democracy, or the market, embodies a view of society constituted by independent agents whose collective decisions are solely a function of a mathematical aggregation of subjective desires. Agents share a world of objective logic and fact, but privately determine values and ends. Arrow's social world is one in which individuals have personal preferences, and the world of things and other individuals serves as the background in which individuals realize their private ends. The entire role of language in Arrow's world is that of communicating information among rational agents so that they may more effectively achieve personal goals.[133] Arrow does not so much envision a shared social world as he does a collection of individuals whose identities are defined by their well-ordered sets of preferences, and who strive to achieve their most preferred outcomes.

Rational choice theory as it was articulated in *Social Choice and Individual Values* is both a social scientific method and the basic set of ordering principles structuring a liberal society. In contrast to Merton's four values underlying both scientific and democratic practices, Arrow's philosophical system rests on objective scientific knowledge, universal law, rationality defined as a well-ordered set of transitive preferences as opposed to deliberation, and individual freedom to determine ends and values. In building his philosophical system to be consistent with traditional liberalism as he understood it, Arrow not only repudiates the alternative political philosophies of Rousseau, Kant, and Marx, but he also rejects Dewey's political theory. For Dewey, citizens who embody a public deliberate over social ends much like scientists debate research findings.[134] It is this process of rational deliberation that validates both public decisionmaking and scientific research. It is the most dramatic result of Arrow's rational choice theory of politics that the concepts of "public," "public interest," and "social welfare" are rendered meaningless by the impossibility theorem.

It may seem that there is a danger underlying Arrow's theorem as a defense of American liberalism given that the proof mires capitalist democracy in logical inconsistency. It seems implausible that Arrow's social choice classic can meet the challenge posed by Schumpeter, Hayek, and Popper when his theorem appears to drive a final stake through the heart of free markets and democracy. While ensuing social choice researchers have focused on the negative impact of the theorem in their attempts to obviate the impossibility result, the key aspect of their endeavors has been the full acceptance of the constructive philosophical work achieved by the theorem. Arrow's concept of citizens' sovereignty was unproblematically accepted, his definition of rationality replaced marginalist economists' focus on problems of efficiency and scarcity, and the assumption that social science is objective and yields universal laws appealed to many economists and political scientists. Standing across the growing divide that would come to distinguish rational choice theory from postmodern critiques of science and objectivity, it would be these specific postulates that informed approaches to social science crystallizing around the character of the self-interested rational actor. The rational actor, as he grew to maturity, was inseparable from Cold War efforts to anchor the supports of a revitalized liberalism upholding individual liberty to determine personal ends.

As rational choice theory developed in social choice, public choice, and positive political theory, several strategies were adopted to obviate the intransigency of Arrow's devastating logic from undermining democracy and capitalism. The public choice approach, taken up in the next chapter, focused its efforts entirely on individual freedom to trade goods or political favors and altogether renounced the concept of the public without nostalgia or conscious dissonance. Hence, for public choice theorists, the market survives Arrow's impossibility theorem simply because it has no pretensions to serving the "public good." Positive political theorists, discussed in chapter 4, were more apt to follow Duncan Black's lead, and to notice that many areas of actual democratic decisionmaking do not demonstrate the instabilities predicted by Arrow's proof.[135] Arrow himself, perhaps due to his close associations with the defense and public policy communities, came to accept a modification of methodological individualism that allows identifying the preferences of a prototypical individual through the assumptions of anonymity and impartiality: Arrow agrees that a prototypical preference profile may be drawn up as long as it is required that each individual not know who's identity she will have in the selected social outcome, thus enabling the formation of legitimate public policy. In each of these cases, the uncomfortable indictment of capitalist democracy is reversed and American liberalism stands intact, although in a recognizably different form from the versions characterizing earlier eras.

CHAPTER 3

James M. Buchanan and Gordon Tullock's Public Choice Theory

IN 1993 James M. Buchanan presented a lecture in which he announced, with reference to Nietzsche's statement "God is dead," its twentieth-century equivalent: "socialism is dead." It was Buchanan's perception that the intellectual movement he had fostered over the past decades, public choice, had helped bring reality home to citizens and politicians alike. It revealed the "normative delusion, stemming from Hegelian idealism: the state was, somehow, a benevolent entity and those who made decisions on behalf of the state were guided by consideration of the general or public interest."[1] From the earliest ruminations that came to comprise public choice as a cogent school of thought, a thorough-going individualism opposed to any stripe of collectivist theory had characterized the movement.

This chapter, which spans the period from Buchanan's earliest published essay in 1949 to his 1997 collection *Post-Socialist Political Economy,* presents a story of epic proportions in which Buchanan and Gordon Tullock's incubation of public choice coincides with the demise, in theory and practice, of socialism and communism. One goal in chronicling these events is to uncover the philosophical principles responsible for the defeat of socialism and its replacement with rational choice liberalism. The ensuing theoretical debate, growing out of the challenges sounded by Joseph Schumpeter, Friedrich Hayek, and Karl Popper, accompanied the gradual defeat of Soviet communism culminating on the world stage with the collapse of the Berlin Wall and the implosion of the Soviet Union. It may be difficult, or even impossible, to credit public choice scholars with a share of the responsibility for the material fall of communism. However, it is certain that public choice theory was from its earliest days staunchly opposed to socialism and therefore now appears to be a victor in the hard fought ideological strife over the fundamental principles of government.

Today, a decade later, the victorious partnership of democracy and free markets seems almost inevitable; but fifty years earlier, when Buchanan, Gordon Tullock, and other rational choice theorists toiled mid-twentieth century, this triumph could only have been prognosticated from as- trologers' charts. In the 1940s the most able social theorists had predicted the inevitable defeat of democracy and capitalism . . . unless their warn- ings were heeded and Western individualistic liberalism be unhesitatingly supported. Buchanan, Tullock, and other rational choice scholars in the public choice camp made it their mission to articulate and promulgate Western liberalism. From the discipline's earliest inception, public choice scholars combined scientific method with individualism to construct the foundations for American constitutional democracy in opposition to any philosophical principle that could be construed to support communism or collectivism. One casualty in this effort was any concept of "the pub- lic" or "public interest," which could be interpreted as supporting an "or- ganismic state" comprised of interests transcending those of the individ- uals constituting it.

"Public choice" has two connotations, one referring to a specific school of economic and political thought and the second being broadly synonymous with the encompassing disciplinary designation "rational choice." Under either connotation Buchanan and Tullock were leading figures who not only formed that school of thought but were also the founding members of the interdisciplinary Public Choice Society. Unlike Arrow's *Social Choice and Individual Values,* which initiated a school of thought unrelated to any specific institution, Buchanan and Tullock's public choice theory has been furthered by the earnest institutional-based efforts of the two founders and like-minded colleagues. Instead of pro- viding an exhaustive catalogue of the theoretical contributions made by public choice scholars, this chapter focuses on the work of Buchanan and Tullock, and their establishment of the Public Choice Society.[2] Their im- portant text, *The Calculus of Consent,* is explored and its innovative find- ings discussed. I also use John Rawls's early presentation to the Public Choice Society of his emerging theory of justice as a way to tease out the structure of the public choice version of liberalism. In focusing on Buchanan and Tullock's contributions to the theory of constitutional design, this chapter articulates how public choice theory was designed to oppose collectivism—be it communist, socialist, or Keynesian—by stressing the significance of the individual over the group, thereby under- mining any concept of "the public." I also argue that the early days of ra- tional choice theory were characterized by interdisciplinary ferment at the peripheries of many established academic fields, including economics. A concluding section appraises the relationship between the abolition of communist regimes and the philosophy of public choice theory.

Buchanan's Early Writings:
The "Organismic" versus "Individualistic" State

James Buchanan graduated from the University of Chicago with his doctorate in economics in 1948, and throughout his career he would adhere to the creed of free trade, limited government, and fiscal conservatism that characterizes the so-called Chicago school of economic theory. Buchanan's first published essay, "The Pure Theory of Government Finance," demonstrates his interest in differentiating between two approaches to understanding and constructing the state: "organismic" and "individualistic."[3] While not indicting the organismic approach to fiscal policy as would become characteristic of Buchanan's public choice writings, this early essay touches on several themes that would be prominent in Buchanan's subsequent analysis. Organismic theory sees the state as a unified entity that arrives at fiscal policy by specifying public expenditure in accordance with the "general welfare" of society.[4] Policymakers seek "to maximize some conceptually quantifiable magnitude" in determining how tax revenues should be spent."[5] While not deeming this system inappropriate for being normatively laden, Buchanan's major reservation pertains to its "vague and general terms," that it offers "little or no direct guidance to governmental fiscal authorities."[6]

In explaining the individualistic approach to fiscal policy, Buchanan observes that "redistribution is one goal of responsible social policy," an assertion that contrasts with his subsequent public choice research presenting government taxation and expenditure as a constitutional question best conservatively adjudicated. Notwithstanding this eventual shift in perspective, however, Buchanan's early essay identifies crucial points on which his later research would pivot: the sharp distinction between organismic and individualistic views of the state; the inherent vagueness of defining "general welfare," and the suggestion that the best means of evaluating fiscal policy is strictly by the *quid pro quo* approach in which an individual's input into government tax coffers are weighed against their output. This early essay, while not condemning organismic theory outright, establishes a theoretical framework that would be used to build a calculus of individuals' interests in joining with others within a framework of constitutional democracy.

Buchanan's next two essays were prompted by Kenneth Arrow's *Social Choice and Individual Values* and shed light on the manner in which social choice and public choice scholarship are simultaneously cast in the same mold and yet diametrically opposed in their goals.[7] Buchanan profited from Arrow's axiomatic treatment of the impossibility of defining "social welfare," which gave him a clarity lacking in this first essay. Whereas Buchanan had previously thought that the concept of social welfare is vague, he was now able to conclude that it is meaningless. Buchanan takes a further step than Arrow did in claiming that the central project of the impossibility theorem, that of satisfactorily defining "collective rationality," is itself misguided: "Rationality or irrationality as an attribute of the social group implies the imputation to the group of an organic existence apart from that of its individual components."[8] In the ensuing years, scholars attracted to Arrow's approach to collective decisionmaking processes formulated their thoughts in the axiomatic deductive style characterizing *Social Choice and Individual Values* and continually strove to provide a cogent theoretical means to discuss collective social welfare obviating Arrow's impossibility theorem. By contrast, Buchanan and his collaborators relied less on formal language and strictly upheld the premise that *any* discussion of public interest or social welfare violated their commitment to individualistic philosophy.

Buchanan's 1958 book *Public Principles of Public Debt: A Defense and Restatement* more resembles his first publication of a decade earlier than his critique of Arrow's impossibility theorem.[9] Although he rejects the "'social welfare function' approach to fiscal theory," the book is structured in accordance with contemporary discussions of public debt with no hint of Buchanan's future fruitful collaboration with Gordon Tullock.[10] It makes all the more noticeable the later transition in Buchanan's own thinking when he joined his efforts with Tullock in rethinking the interrelationship between political economy and constitutional democracy.[11]

Buchanan and Tullock's Collaboration: *The Calculus of Consent*

Buchanan became acquainted with Gordon Tullock when Tullock spent a year at Buchanan's Thomas Jefferson Center for the Study of Political Philosophy at the University of Virginia in 1958–59. Tullock had worked for nine years in the U.S. Foreign Service and had experienced firsthand the role that self-interest plays in bureaucracy. *The Calculus of Consent*, published in 1962, was the product of a quickly forming collaboration by correspondence in the year following Tullock's visit at Virginia.[12]

Buchanan and Tullock's *The Calculus of Consent*, subtitled *Logical Foundations of Constitutional Democracy*, may be regarded as a new analysis in the rapidly forming study of politics that had been articulated by John von Neumann and Oskar Morgenstern, Duncan Black, Arrow, and Arrow's student Anthony Downs.[13] Arrow and Black had considered the properties of collective decisionmaking procedures characteristic of elections, and in his *Economic Theory of Democracy,* Downs applied the concept of self-interested rational action to political parties' attempts to win office and hold power. Downs's novel approach was to focus his analyis on individuals' decisionmaking and to explain individual action in terms of the narrowly construed rational self-interest using transitive orderings and utility schedules. According to Downs's estimation, a political party's primary goal is to win elections and not, as was generally supposed, to enact specific policy initiatives. From this hypothesis, and using quantitative analysis, Downs concluded that political parties will "converge upon the center" in the attempt to gain the most votes.[14] Buchanan and Tullock followed Downs in maintaining the theoretical possibility of evaluating political outcomes as a direct consequence of politicians' self-interested calculations.[15]

The Calculus of Consent was reviewed by numerous journals representing the fields of economics, political science, sociology, and law.[16] As the authors had predicted, their book was extremely timely and was generally accepted as an important contribution both to political theory and to the newly burgeoning field of political economy. One reviewer observed, "*The Calculus of Consent* is . . . a closely reasoned and major contribution to systematic political theory."[17] Buchanan and Tullock's rapid collaboration was fueled by the sense that being the first to get precedent-setting ideas in print was more important than getting all the details right the first time around.[18] Unlike Arrow, who delineated a new language of social choice in precisely defined terms and reached definitive conclusions using symbolic logic, Buchanan and Tullock's new approach was much more one of an unremitting commitment to methodological individualism and politics as trade, combined with analytic tools drawn from game theory and the welfare economics tradition.[19] They reach conclusions from discursively presented analyses instead of by formal proof.[20] Despite the lack of formal proof, they quantitatively assess the premise that individuals' personal calculation of costs and benefits must provide the foundational rationale for the practice of constitutional design. Buchanan and Tullock conclude that the principle of majority rule cannot be rationally motivated, and propose that unanimous consent is necessary to legitimize constitutional rule.

Buchanan and Tullock set about the task of explaining the constitutional foundations of democracy based on the premise of methodological individualism and self-interested rational action. Their interest in government is at two levels: the decisionmaking that goes into designing a constitution, and the subsequent collective outcomes of decisionmaking following the adoption of laws. First, Buchanan and Tullock attempt to model the sort of constitutional structure self-interested rational actors would create given that they will only agree to a constitution that is in their self-interest. Second, having adduced a constitutional structure built on individuals' calculated self-interest, Buchanan and Tullock proceed to analyze the results of self-interested rational action within the confines of these rationally motivated constitutions. They study both the initial adoption of a constitution and the consequences of the constitutional rules once adopted.

Buchanan and Tullock's analytic structure and new way of conceptualizing the problem of constitutional design were responsible for the book's being accorded classic status more so than were its models, which are somewhat ad hoc demonstrations of the principles on which the book was founded. In couching their analyses in terms of self-interested, rational acceptance of constitutional rules, Buchanan and Tullock considered themselves to be working squarely within the contractarian tradition of political theory, which holds that at its root the formation of a constitutional state depends on the social contract between the individual, who agrees to obey the constitutionally mandated sovereign, and the state, which guarantees individual rights under the law.

Tullock and Buchanan's contribution to this contractarian tradition was to use their idiosyncratic logic of market relations to refashion political liberalism.[21] They provided a new interpretation of American political liberalism that could be read in such fundamental documents as the U.S. Constitution and the Federalist Papers, and suggested that their analyses upholding methodological individualism and self-interested rational action grasped the fundamental elements of the process of constitution building expressed in these documents. This interest in the foundations of American democracy had been evident already in Buchanan's fashioning of the Thomas Jefferson Center for Studies in Political Economy and Social Philosophy at the University of Virginia with Warren Nutter in the 1957.[22] Buchanan and Tullock believed their work to be in the spirit of James Madison and the other Founding Fathers who respected the impact of political factions in shaping constitutional design. Commenting on Madison's Federalist No. 10 they observe:

> A careful reading of this paper suggests that Madison clearly recognized that individuals and groups would try to use the processes of government to further their own differential or partisan interests. His numerous examples of legislation concerns debtor-creditor relations, commercial policy, and taxation suggest that perhaps a better understanding of Madison's own concep-

tion of democratic process may be achieved by examining carefully the implications of the economic approach to human behavior in collective choice.[23]

As I discuss more fully in chapter 6, Buchanan and Tullock believe they unite Adam Smith's classical political economy with the interest-based politics of James Madison to derive the underlying ordering principles of their reunification of political economy. There is a strong sense in which the *Calculus of Consent* draws its appeal from its claims to revitalize fundamental insights animating Enlightenment predecessors: "With the philosophers of the Enlightenment we share the faith that man can rationally organize his society."[24]

Despite their attempts to find commonality with Madison's federalism, Buchanan and Tullock's *Calculus of Consent* is an unprecedented contribution to political theory that reinvents the logical foundations of constitutional democracy so that it resembles the logic of the marketplace. In markets, individuals participate if they stand to gain, and theoretically, in all voluntary market exchanges, all parties gain. Buchanan and Tullock similarly find politics to be a process of exchange in which individuals accede to the power of the state because in promising obedience, they stand to gain from the rule of law. For Tullock and Buchanan, the puzzle of legitimate constitutional design lies in determining how much coercive power to invest in government, which can either enhance or hinder individuals' strictly measured interests. In agreeing to the terms of a constitution, each person balances the negative impact of decision rules that may yield outcomes based on less than unanimous consent against the negative costs of decisionmaking if strict unanimity were to be required for every policy decision. Decision rules requiring less than unanimity may impose costs on an individual because he cannot veto policies he does not agree to; on the other hand, requiring unanimous agreement in all cases adds a procedural cost of time and resources devoted to obtaining collective decisions.

Methodologically speaking, the authors incorporate individualism and the assumption of self-interested calculation into mathematical models of three forms: gains versus losses, Pareto optimality, and game theory. They adopt simple net gains and losses calculations of the various aspects of participating in collective decisionmaking both at the level of constitutional design and of daily practice within accepted constitutional rules. These cost–benefit considerations include an individual's expected net inputs to and payments from collective actions, and the individual's calculation of whether he will gain more through collectivized versus voluntary action (43–62).

The authors introduce a two-person bargaining model, based on an "Edgeworth box" diagram, to incorporate the hallmark of methodological individualism—namely, Pareto optimality:

> The underlying premise of the modern Paretian construction is the purely individualistic one. The individual himself is assumed to be the only one who is able to measure or to quantify his own utility. No external observer is presumed able to make comparisons of utility among separate individuals. (171–72)

Thus, they join Arrow in endorsing both the ideas of citizens' sovereignty over personal ends and the infeasibility of interpersonal comparisons of well-being. On the basis of these two, the Pareto condition is defined as:

> The "welfare" of the whole group of individuals is said to be increased if (1) every individual in the group is made better off, or (2) if at least one member in the group is made better off without anyone being made worse off. (171)

This criterion of "welfare" is based on each individual's achieving a superior outcome, or at least not an inferior outcome, solely on the basis of her own preferences over outcomes. The criterion of Pareto optimality is used to compare collective decision results between voluntary outcomes to which each unanimously agrees and decisions reached by majority rule that result in coercing the minority (83–116).

Ever mindful that agents may have reasons to engage in strategic expression of their preferences over outcomes to better achieve personal ends, Buchanan and Tullock also use a game theoretic model of bargaining among two or more individuals. This analysis demonstrates the likelihood for coalitions to form with the result of an inequitable distribution favoring the majority and depriving the minority (147–88). All such examples are used to throw doubt on the legitimacy of achieving collection decisions through the process of majority rule.

In *The Calculus of Consent*, Buchanan and Tullock's political theory and science of political economy boils down to one basic principle with far-reaching implications. Their assumption of self-interested rational action, although a normative hypothesis subject to empirical testing, permits them to draw a line between moral philosophy and political science: moral philosophy pertains to discussions of how individuals *should* act given such concepts as responsibility, obligation, and duty, while political science is concerned only with the minimalist assumption that agents will be rationally self-serving in their actions. Public choice analysis involves a tricky equipoise between accepting people "as they are"—angelic or otherwise—and hedging bets on narrowly self-interested behavior in the view that government must not assume altruistic behavior (27–36). This division of labor between moral philosophy as judging human action and political science as accepting humans as they are enables Buchanan and Tullock to create analytic, value-free models of how self-interested agents act given their need both to design a constitution and to act within a system of law once a constitution has been adopted. These latter considerations fall squarely within the province of a science of politics and political economy for Tullock and Buchanan. Their system of political economy is not normative insofar as it makes no assumptions concerning ethical standards for behavior, but tacitly accepts rational self-interest as the norm of human conduct.

Tullock and Buchanan are concerned with some normative questions, however, namely those that relate to constitutional design; but under their system they maintain that such questions can be approached scientifically. In fact, for Tullock and Buchanan, the entire enterprise of political science should be oriented toward having practical, hence prescriptive, impact. Tullock and Buchanan argue that they have traced out the logical consequences of self-interested rational behavior in both arenas of constitutional design and operational rule-following, and that a normative approach to politics can be objectively built on this platform. Buchanan states:

> Normative theory must be erected upon and must draw its strength from the propositions of positive science, but it is only when this extension of normative theory is made that "reform" in existing institutions can be expected to emerge from specialized scholarship. Indeed the only purpose of science is its ultimate assistance in the development of normative propositions.[25]

Given the assumption of self-interested rational action, it is possible to strive for a more effective constitution by analyzing the consequences of constitutional design on the lives of those individuals who agreed to live in accordance with it. As Arrow maintained in *Social Choice and Individual Value,* normative standards can be evaluated and possibly validated through scientific analysis. It is a hallmark of the rational choice approach to politics to insist that normative judgments can be derived from positive, objective, scientific analysis.

Buchanan and Tullock believe that their recasting of constitutional design in the language of narrowly construed rational self-interest creates a new strand of political liberalism that resonates with Adam Smith's political economy.[26] In Buchanan and Tullock's calculated version of political

consent, the political destiny of individual self-oriented utility maximizers can only ever be the unintended by-product of individuals' efforts toward self-gain. Despite their agreement with Smith's system of political
economy, Buchanan and Tullock's foray into political theory put forward
a clearly articulated version of political liberalism, adding to the contractarian tradition of political philosophy and setting forth a new precedent
for understanding the foundations of a constitutional state.[27] In an appendix, Buchanan places *The Calculus of Consent* within the long-standing traditions of both political realism and contractarianism, mentioning
such thinkers as Plato, Hobbes, Spinoza, and Locke. The puzzle for theorists working within this nonidealist, nonorganic tradition is whether
"the existing organization of the State [can] be 'explained' as an out-
growth of a rational calculation made by individual human beings"
(316). Although finding much to admire in Spinoza's *Tractatus Politicus*,
Buchanan believes that his and Tullock's new approach to political science and political economy surpass all of the earlier efforts.

Within the contractarian tradition, the authors believe that they have
made three main theoretical advances over their predecessors. First, they
draw a clear distinction between moral philosophy and positive political
theory, and argue that normative conclusions can be built on positive
analysis. Second, they are not concerned with the origins of the social
contract; rather they are interested in providing an analysis of the implications of contemporary constitutional design for current collective action problems. It is their hope that the basic legal structure can be altered
to best serve individuals' interests according to the familiar efficiency criterion of Pareto optimality consistent with unanimous consent. Third,
they use the Pareto efficiency condition to reach the iconoclastic conclusion that the principle of majority rule has no more theoretical basis than
would a rule of 49 percent or 51 percent. Majority rule potentially incurs
too much cost for a rational agent who seeks to avoid the negative repercussions of unfavorable policies. Instead, Buchanan and Tullock advocate
near unanimity in collective decisionmaking at the level of constitutional
design to best serve individuals' interests. They also conclude that the
principle of majority rule is of limited value even within the routine decisions made under the auspices of the constitution.

In exploring the question of whether individuals will select to adopt a
social insurance policy at the level of constitutional design, thus enter-
taining the possibility of some level of income redistribution, the authors
suggest that self-interested rational actors will rely on a constitution
aimed "toward an equalization of opportunities rather than an equalization of rewards" (196). Although only tentatively suggesting that rational

individuals in the position of ignorance as to their fates within the constitutional system will opt for a minimal social insurance system, they are adamant that adopting procedures of majority rule to decide on income redistribution questions necessarily results in too much redistribution if honestly assessed "on the basis of long-run utility maximizing considerations" (194-96).

In addition to these findings, Buchanan and Tullock's analysis in *The Calculus of Consent* has one more important implication for political theory: it obliterates the concept of "the public" as a meaningful category for analysis (316). It is a fundamental result of all rational choice theory that the notion of the public cannot meaningfully be sustained in a theoretical system upholding individuals' private aims and values as the relevant data for study. As Arrow's *Social Choice and Individual Values* proves, there is no theoretical means to ground a notion of public, public good, or public interest. Collective outcomes can only ever be assessed from the vantage point of individual actors. The public sphere as an arena of orientation toward others or the social whole is rendered theoretically nonsensical, and all that remains as a conceptual tool is a calculation of how collective outcomes affect private interests. Tullock and Buchanan go beyond Arrow by holding that even the attempt to construct a function that can be mapped from the individual to a group will is a misguided effort that smacks of a smothering organicism.[28] Like Arrow, Buchanan and Tullock were concerned with the specter of Marxism, arguing that scientific, value-free analysis of individuals and democracy rules out the "Marxist vision," "class domination," and "historical determinism," as well as any possibility of an "organic conception of the State." One reviewer of *The Calculus of Consent* states explicitly what Tullock and Buchanan voice implicitly, that the individualist approach stands opposed to a Marxist analysis dependent on nebulous concepts like "class exploitation."[29]

Although Buchanan took umbrage when one reviewer suggested that his politics were those of the extreme Right, Tullock and Buchanan's school of public choice has consistently been associated with the conservative political position of fiscal restraint and individualist philosophy consistent with the "pull yourself up by the bootstraps" credo. In response to Mancur Olson's 1964 review, Buchanan wrote to Olson that *The Calculus of Consent* is politically neutral and that furthermore his own politics must be characterized as that of "an old-fashioned or nineteenth century liberal."[30] Still, Tullock and Buchanan's work has continued to be characterized as one of intense political conservatism.[31] In an insightful essay on "Dissent in Economics," Olson identifies the position held by Buchanan's "Virginia school" as of those "economists who object so regularly to the passing of *laissez faire*, to 'Keynesian' and post-Keynesian fiscal policies, to the threat to individual liberties they see in the welfare state, and to the economic analyses and prescriptions that have encouraged a generation or more of 'creeping socialism.' " [32] Olson's essay makes the point that it is economists of the Keynesian persuasion, and not Marxists per se, who are the immediate target of Buchanan's antisocialist arguments. As Hayek had argued, and Buchanan concurred, socialism of any variety lies on the road to serfdom. It followed that Keynesianism, upholding a vestigial notion of an organic state, internally threatened America's future of prosperity and individualism. In personal correspondence to Olson, Buchanan specified that Keynesianism is a doctrine of elite rule by supposedly selfless public servants: "[M]ost mainstream economists act *as if* they are advising the despot, or a despot. . . . [T]he idealized despot whom the mainstream . . . [economists] serve is 'pink' or even a deeper shade than any who might actually be in power." [33] Buchanan's staunch defense of individualism has no room for the Marxist postulate that governments rule in the interests of the dominant social class. Closer to home, he regarded mainstream American economics as tainted with the communist impulse because of its faith in neutral policy officials who serve the public interest.

Buchanan's keen interest in electoral politics is readily apparent from his numerous publications, his assessment of the student protests of the 1960s and 1970s, and in his letters of recommendation wherein he consistently made a point to expressly locate the candidate's place within the political spectrum. [34] Buchanan cites Keynesian economics as the source of the student unrest because, in his estimation, fiscal laxity breeds moral laxity. Referring to "a generalized erosion in public and private manners, increasingly liberalized attitudes toward sexual activities, a declining vitality of the Puritan work ethic, deterioration in product quality, explosion of the welfare rolls, widespread corruption in both the private and governmental sector, and, finally, observed increases in the alienation of voters from the political process," Buchanan indicts Keynesian fiscal policy that, contributing to inflation, leads to a reckless "live for the moment" attitude. [35]

The politics of the public choice school are important because the movement stakes its claim on the proposition that their scientific investigation inform normative, political decisions; public choice scholars, principally Buchanan and Tullock, hold that normative political implications of their work follow as a logical consequence of their objective, scientific analysis. The public choice movement, standing for an individualistic notion of society in which collective good is a meaningless concept and private gain the only measure of effective rule, helped provide the philosophical underpinnings to the late-twentieth-century revitalization of classical liberalism.[36]

The Public Choice Society

Buchanan claims that his presence at RAND in 1954, working on the "criterion problem," as well as his role as consultant through 1958, was largely peripheral to his later research. Despite the fact that the new analytic language of collective decisionmaking as put forward by Arrow and Downs were woven into *The Calculus of Consent,* he and Tullock formed their collaboration quite apart from any established intellectual movement. Immediately after publishing their book, they were centrally involved in creating an interdisciplinary professional society with a much wider scope of operation than the center at the University of Virginia. Named the Public Choice Society in 1967, it would serve as a steady organizational focus for both men, despite their respective nomadic relocation from university to university over the ensuing years. In 1968 Buchanan resigned from the University of Virginia in protest over Tullock's being denied tenure for the third time.[37] The two continued their research and promotion of the Public Choice Society at Virginia Polytechnic Institute, where they established the Center for the Study of Public Choice in 1969. Both the broadly interdisciplinary Public Choice Society and Buchanan and Tulloch's center depended on the organizational coherence and *esprit de corps* generated by Betty Tillman, who has provided administrative support from the early 1960s to the present.

The Public Choice Society, which had originally convened as the "Committee for Non-Market Decision Making," drew together scholars who were working in the same vein as Tullock and Buchanan, all concentrating on positive analyses of nonmarket decisionmaking problems outside the domain of traditional economics. The society became the hub for scholars of disparate academic fields who met yearly to discuss academic papers. Within only three years of the group's founding, it could boast of having among its members a virtual rational choice hall of fame: James S. Coleman, Anthony Downs, John Harsanyi, Roland McKean, Mancur Olson, Vincent Ostrom, John Rawls, Thomas Schelling, and Aaron Wildavsky. In its third year of operation, the political scientist William Riker took on a key organizational role.

The society is noteworthy for several reasons. First, with its prominent and interdisciplinary list of participating members, the society illustrates how the rational choice movement unfolded as a complex of knowledge comprised of an interlocking set of interdisciplinary revolutions. The fields represented in the society included economics, political science, public policy, sociology, mathematics, and philosophy. Rather than having one discipline predominate, the spirit of the enterprise was one of an innovative synthesis that created the field of public choice by generating a new language of political economy in the space between mainstream economics and political science. Meeting yearly, the society helped establish the critical mass necessary to generate a new field. Thus, for example, Anthony Downs, Henry G. Manne, Mancur Olson, and William Riker all reviewed and participated in discussions about the impact of *The Calculus of Consent*.[38] The manuscript for Buchanan's 1967 *Public Finance in Democratic Process* was reviewed by four active members of the Committee for Non-Market Decision Making.[39]

From the publication of the compiled essays presented at the first three meetings of the embryonic society grew the journal *Public Choice*. The title was clearly meant to counter the phrase "social choice," which conjured up images of the welfare economics tradition.[40] It would always convey some tension between the larger community of researchers who met as members of the Public Choice Society and Buchanan and Tullock's Virginia-based school of Public Choice, which capitalized on the same name. With the establishment of the journal, which continues to publish works of formal analysis today, a field of scholarship was born that was dedicated to "the application of essentially economic tools and methods of reasoning to areas outside traditional economics."[41] A new journal was necessary because traditional economics journals failed to recognize the importance to their discipline of what seemed to be a rogue clique of scholars. Mainstream economists were not leading the way toward extending economic analysis to new fields. That trail was blazed instead by the interdisciplinary band of researchers that drew its identity from the commitment to the analysis of self-interested rational action and of collective outcomes of individual decisions. The unique style that coalesced out of public choice scholarship represented a synthesis that, while drawing inspiration from various strands of economic theory, over time would itself influence mainstream economics. Mancur Olson articulates this nuanced transition within economics in his observation that "[i]n recent years . . . economic theory has come to be conceived as a general theory of rational behavior, rather than merely a description of market behavior in capitalist economies."[42]

The newly established public choice tradition challenged basic economic assumptions that drew a clear distinction between political processes and law on the one hand, and the economic marketplace on the other hand. Vincent Ostrom, writing a general memorandum regarding a constitution for the Public Choice Society, noted the group's interest in "the application of economic reasoning to problems of *public choice* or non-market decision making." He also acknowledged that scholars interested in public choice took up questions outside the scope of mainstream economics, and that these scholars "are lifting the veil of the law and order postulate and [are] inquiring about the logic of collective action, the strategies of conflict and of inter-dependent decision-making, the principles of political constraint, the calculus of consent and the calculus of threat systems."[43] Over the following decades, insights and methods germane to public choice scholarship—such as game theory, a focus on the microfoundations of individual decisionmaking, and institutionalized factors constraining market transactions—would become increasingly central to economics. Key to the transition from market to nonmarket decisionmaking was the supersession of the heretofore focal concept of scarcity. Hence, the areas of concern as well as the tools and explanatory tactics of public choice theorists have been incorporated into mainstream economics.

Some observers see the public choice movement to have emerged from a pattern of "economics imperialism," in which mainstream economics extends its domain by routinely encroaching on and appropriating formerly external subject matter, bending it to its own disciplinary methods and standards.[44] However, the clear pattern, which Vincent Ostrom articulates, is of the establishment of a field of study drawing on methodological individualism and self-interested rational action that comes to pose an entirely new set of questions not of interest to most mainstream economists:

> The works of Mancur Olson and of Gordon Tullock have provided devastating critiques of group theory and of the Weberian theory of bureaucracy—two of the old classics in political science and sociology—and pointed the way toward the use of a fundamentally different paradigm in the analysis of collective action. Buchanan and Tullock's introduction of a cost calculus into the analysis of decision rules opens new possibilities for developing a rigorous form of institutional analysis which was never realized by the earlier institutional economists. Together with the work of [Kenneth] Boulding and Schelling in relation to international decision making, Black, Downs, and Riker on elections, parties and coalitions, and [Richard] Musgrave and [William] Baumol in public finance, we have many of the elements which I would expect to grow into a basic paradigmatic revolution in political science, sociology, anthropology and law.[45]

As Ostrom sees it, because the early public choice movement was essentially interdisciplinary, it stimulated a general shift in perception across the social sciences.

The economics discipline did not play host to the revolution thus described by Ostrom, neither by recognizing the new movement's core research concerns nor by providing institutional support for its research initiatives. Nevertheless, according to Ostrom, "[P]rospective members of the Public Choice Society will thus have ties to the variety of social science disciplines which serve as the basis for departmental organization in many universities while sharing theoretical interests based upon a common paradigm that tends to cross disciplinary boundaries."[46] From within the movement it was clear that there was a well-defined community of scholars participating in a shared research enterprise of analyzing collective decisionmaking processes according to the new rules of methodological individualism and self-interested rational action in parametric and strategic environments. As Ostrom understands it, the development of public choice is a single "paradigmatic revolution" that "is occurring within a universe of discourse as wide as the social sciences," and that "can be expected to have a major impact upon work in the various social sciences." Far from representing the colonization of the social sciences by economics, this new intellectual tradition "is essentially inter-disciplinary in its thrust," and has a common source of origin in the interstices between traditionally defined academic fields. Economics, as much as the other social sciences, would feel the impact of the public choice movement as its own set of research questions and methods were altered to face the new challenges raised by the savvy public choice scholars who consistently saw economic transactions as intertwined with nonmarket decisionmaking procedures.[47]

Buchanan's take was similarly emphatic:

> Contributions from organization theory, information theory, the theory of teams, statistical decision theory, game theory, learning theory, theoretical welfare economics, pure theory of government finance, and others point toward a fundamental revision of existing orthodoxy, and an emerging consensus on what may be called a general theory of social structures, which will surely include political organization only as one among an array of forms. These developments should help to break down the barriers among the disciplinary specializations in the social sciences, barriers which have been, at best, arbitrarily erected and maintained.[48]

Thus, it is evident that the set of methods that came together to form rational choice theory did not flow out of mainstream economics but emerged as an exciting new movement attracting scholars in numerous fields across the academy interested in building a consistent social science method focused on individualism and the science of rational decisionmaking.

In fact, James Buchanan holds neoclassical general equilibrium economics in the same disdain as he holds Keynesian and social welfare economics. He believes the general equilibrium efficiency models to have continued down the same blind alley that led astray collectivist-minded thinkers: these models rely on measuring social outcomes according to standards defined independently from individual preferences. Buchanan recognizes that game theory provided a sharp break with neoclassical economics because its solution sets are only defined by the property that no individual has the reason or incentive to select a different course of action.[49] Public choice theory developed outside the concerns of mainstream economics, and only now that it has become an accepted school of thought is it possible to perceive of its development as representing a process of "economics imperialism."

John Rawls, Public Choice, and the Problem of a Normative Consensus

One example of the extraordinary creative impulse of this new interdisciplinary field is the manner in which it added kindling to the creative spark underlying one of the most famous contributions to political theory and moral philosophy in the latter twentieth century—John Rawls's *A Theory of Justice*.[50] Rawls presented a synoptic draft version of that work in his paper "Justice and the Theory of Constitutional Choice," which he read at the October 1964 meeting of the Committee for Non-Market Decision-Making, attended by of Buchanan, Tullock, Downs, Olson, Riker, Ostrom, and Harsanyi. That Rawls presented his work before an audience comprising key members of the founding community of rational choice scholars is historically remarkable. It demonstrates that Rawls's thinking about justice was driven by the same impetus motivating the rational choice inquiry into the founding principles of American constitutional democracy. It is not widely appreciated that Rawls developed his theory of justice in active dialogue with rational choice theorists.[51] Rawls, Tullock, Buchanan, Arrow, Harsanyi, and Riker similarly sought to provide the inner logic of rational choice liberalism: a constitutional framework that, while respecting individuals' liberties, also works to effectively coordinate individuals' self-determined, rationally pursued ends. In Rawls's early formulation, this requires *"those principles which rational persons, who have a concept of the good which they wish to advance and who regard one another as equals and as potential members of a system of cooperation for mutual advantage, would agree upon or consent to unanimously from an original position of equality."*[52] This stands close in spirit to Buchanan and Tullock's question about "what set of rules *should* the fully rational individual, motivated primarily by his own self-interest, seek to achieve if he recognizes the approval of such rules must embody mutual agreement among his fellows."[53] Rational choice liberalism is founded on the dual principles of rationality, as a self-interested calculus, and the primacy of the individual as the final arbiter of personal ends. It is characterized by the attempt to design a nonideological constitutional framework that privileges individual liberty and provides a legal system in which individuals coordinate their actions, to which all participants can in principle unanimously accede. Obviously, rational choice theorists did not invent this project; however, they have contributed a unique interpretation of it.[54]

In his paper presented to the Committee for Non-Market Decision-Making, Rawls challenged the favored status among economists of the Pareto principle specifically because it reinforces the status quo endowment of individuals' resources.[55] Economists working in the tradition of welfare economics had long privileged Pareto optimality as a criterion for deeming one social state as superior to another because it does not rely on interpersonal comparisons of utility, and it strictly relies on voluntary exchange thereby ruling out any form of coercion as an appropriate means to determine social ends. Having said that, the Pareto criterion is also widely acknowledged by economists to affirm the status quo arrangement of resources and, hence, despite its lack of coercive force, tacitly legitimizes the status quo.[56] Rawls departs from Buchanan and Tullock, arguing that in a hypothetical "original position" in which the social contract is hammered out, agents would go further than the Pareto condition to adopt what he calls the "difference principle."[57] Rawls explains that "the difference principle goes beyond the notion of (Pareto) efficiency to a principle of justice," because it adds the requirement that differences of earning potential within a society must always be structured so as to benefit the least well-off person.[58]

Rawls mirrors Tullock and Buchanan in developing his idea of a "veil of ignorance," behind which people reach constitutional agreement without having any knowledge of their station in life, even including their race and gender. Similarly, Tullock and Buchanan maintain that an individual be uncertain as to his "precise role in society" during the process of constitutional design, and that therefore the individual "is considered not to have a particular and distinguishable interest separate and apart from his fellows."[59] Thus, Rawls shares with Buchanan and Tullock the operational starting point of the individual's "uncertainty" or "ignorance" concerning her precise status in society; they share as well the rational calculation of interests that the individual employs to evaluate constitutional

principles. They diverge, however, on the extent of the uncertainty and ignorance involved in this process: Rawls advocates more and Tullock and
Buchanan believe less is more realistic.

Even given their common initiative, other differences between Rawls's
system of justice and rational choice theorists' positions on constitutional
democracy would emerge over time. Thus, while initially believing his
theory of justice to be consistent with rational choice theory, since both
looked to human rationality as foundational, Rawls later denied this consistency.[60] The distance between Rawls and rational choice theorists grew
in part over the question of whether Rawls's theory upheld the prohibition of normative assumptions and the thorough-going commitment to
self-interested strategic reason. Although at the 1964 meeting Buchanan
chose to emphasize his agreement with Rawls, already the seeds of later
schisms between Rawls and rational choice theorists are visible. It could
be asked within the context of Rawls's paper, for example, if his theory
of justice relied solely on the founding premise of self-interested rational
action, or if it demanded normative or deontological assumptions such as
"the good," or "duty."

The question of the normative consensus providing sufficient cohesion
to enact the most basic market transaction remained at the heart of scholarly debate animating rational choice liberalism. Battle lines of pro-West-
ern democratic liberalism versus doctrines of "ideal democracy" or "organic statehood" were drawn: rational choice liberalism depends on a
rationale consistent with individualism and nonnormative, scientific
analysis of rational self-interest in opposition to authoritarian socialism,
which transgresses the basic precept of individualism and possibly also
that of nonideological analysis. Theorists auguring into the debate over
the constitutional design had to accept the guidelines of individualism
combined with scientific analysis, or face the result of being charged with
acting in collusion with totalitarianism or Stalinism.

Buchanan himself claimed that his entire theory of political economy
and constitutional democracy boils down to the basic principle of exchange based on consensual agreement: "The simple exchange of apples
and oranges between two traders—this institutional model is the starting
point for all I have done."[61] However, in the face of the social unrest of
the 1960s and 1970s, Buchanan lamented the loss of the normative consensus that celebrated "hard work, and responsible or rational behavior."[62] He explains:

> My diagnosis of American society is informed by the notion that we are liv-
> ing during a period of erosion of the "social capital" that provides the ba-
> sic framework for our culture, our economy, and our polity—a framework

within which the "free society" in the classically liberal ideal perhaps came closest to realization in all of history.[63]

The ultimate source of "moral anarchy" threatening to dissolve liberal society is "the negation of both moral community and moral order." [64] Borrowing from Kant—the quintessential deontological philospher—the precept necessary to establish moral order, Buchanan approaches the battle line between ideal democracy and individualistic democracy. He observes that moral anarchy "is a setting within which persons violate the basic Kantian moral precept that human beings are to be treated as ends not as means." [65] Thus, in establishing operating principles for constitutional design predicated on self-interested calculus, Buchanan simultaneously lifts a leaf from Kantian moral philosophy that is at least a step in the direction of achieving the consensus on social ends that Arrow had postulated as a way to negate his impossibility theorem.[66] With this impulse to recognize a minimal normative consensus as indispensable to social interactions as basic as trade, Buchanan tacitly endorses the Kantian dictum that individuals must be treated as ends in themselves. However, like all rational choice theorists, he is hard-pressed to derive even this basic normative consensus from the principle of rational self-interest.

Buchanan is forced, by both his view of traditional moral consensus and his view upholding free trade and private property, to support the status quo arrangement of society. As he wrote to W. Samuels:

> I do not especially like the status quo defense that my methodology forces me into, but where can I go. . . . In my vision, the status quo does have a unique place, for the simple reason that it exists, and hence offers the starting point for any peaceful (contractual) change. . . . My defense of the status quo stems from my unwillingness, indeed, inability, to discuss changes other than those that are contractual in nature. . . . The status quo has no propriety at all save for its existence, and it is all that exists. The point I always emphasize is that we start from here and not from somewhere else.[67]

It is James Buchanan's respect for the status quo as resting on historical precedent, his belief in a necessary underlying moral consensus to support the social fabric, uncompromising belief in free trade, and his claims to espouse classical liberalism that makes his theoretical legacy one of political conservatism.

Conclusion

When the 1986 Nobel prize for economics was awarded to James Buchanan, it signaled the arrival of public choice scholarship as an internationally acclaimed body of research. It also signaled the swan song of Buchanan and Tullock's long-term partnership; Buchanan was the sole recipient of the coveted prize, and Tullock's career-long contributions to their joint efforts would for the moment be deemed secondary.[68] Buchanan and Tullock's work specifically and public choice scholarship generally had, since its debut in the 1960s, been considered outside the scope of mainstream economic concerns. But two decades later, after the rebirth of political economy and the attendant study of interrelationships between political decisions underlying the formation of decision rules yielding economic policy, it had found its place in that formerly recalcitrant and entrenched discipline. In addition to constitutional design, public choice scholars analyzed public goods, bureaucracies, the legislature, the behavior of government agencies, and rent-seeking, all from the perspective of rational egoism.[69] By the late 1990s, their approach to political economy had become standard even in Hong Kong's public management curriculum.[70]

Buchanan's essay in which he proclaimed that "socialism is dead" helps give some perspective on the theoretical legacy of public choice and its timely articulation anticipating the global demise of communism. He asks, "How did we, as members of the academies and intelligentsia, come to be trapped in the romantic myth that politically organized authority could direct our lives so as to satisfy our needs more adequately than we might satisfy them ourselves through voluntary agreement, association and exchange, one with another?"[71] Buchanan goes on to say, "I suspect that, literally, thousands of man-years will be spent in efforts fully to answer this question."[72] Recalling the time when the West was caught in the icy grip of the Cold War fear of communism, he reminds us that "the 'fatal conceit' [of socialism] was almost universal . . . there were socialists among us everywhere, in all societies, at all levels of discourse, and . . . there are many who still cannot escape from the socialist mind-set."[73]

Quite the inverse of explaining the long-term staying power of socialism, my task in this book is to chronicle and explain the rise to preeminence of rational choice theory and of rational choice liberalism. Buchanan argues that public choice theory was "influential in providing an intellectual basis which allows observers to understand better what it is they observe[d]" as communist governments floundered and failed.[74] According to Buchanan, in debunking the delusion that government bureaucracy acts in the best interests of constituents, public choice scholarship has provided the more realistic understanding that all government officials are self-interested rational actors, and that government is best designed when each individual's calculus of interests is entered into the equation. Elsewhere Buchanan suggests that public choice scholarship helped to lift the veil of illusion from wide-eyed, naive believers in socialism and welfare economics because of its effectiveness in explaining the actual politics of economic life not just in the United States but worldwide:

> Public choice theory, broadly defined, came along in the 1960s, 1970s, and 1980s to offer intellectual foundations that allowed citizens to understand the political failures they were able to observe at first hand. . . . Once this elementary shift in vision is made . . . the critical flaw in the idealised model of politics and politicians is exposed. No longer could the romanticised model of the workings of the state be tolerated.[75]

It is impossible not to notice that the rise to academic preeminence of rational choice theory in the late twentieth-century paralleled the demise of communism, both by shoring up the foundations of Western liberalism and by explaining the failure of authoritarian regimes wedded to socialism.

Whether or not one believes that the collapse of the Berlin Wall and disintegration of the Soviet Union were inevitable because of their failure to give priority to individual assent and free trade, it is not possible to argue that the development of rational choice theory was inevitable. Rational choice theory grew out of the Cold War environment in which the nightmares of Schumpeter, Popper, and Hayek were daytime reality for millions of people. Public choice theorists were well-placed to explain the inconsistencies and weaknesses of socialism in the 1990s because their theoretical system had negated it from its inception. When the final failure of Soviet communism caught Western observers off-guard, especially given how quick was its collapse, public choice theory could explain ex post facto the inherent inconsistencies and instabilities of planned, authoritarian economies. These shortcomings were far from evident to either 1940s protagonists for liberalism or to the proponents of military buildup in the 1960s, when it appeared all too possible that the Soviet's planned economy might outstrip Western production.[76] In effect, the readiness of public choice advocates to pronounce that "the god that was socialism is *demonstrably* dead," and to posit further that this death was prefigured in the value-free, scientific analysis of rational choice theory, distorts the chronology and causal structure of the historical narrative.[77]

Public choice differs from classical liberalism in its single-minded dedication to the principle of rational self-interest, and in proposing that questions of constitutional design can be settled by recourse to precisely formulated mathematical models reflecting individuals' self-interested calculations. It accepts as a fundamental axiom the sanctity of the individual's preferences over ends, and proposes that constitutional design and daily decisionmaking can be understood as a precise calculation of interests. Public choice also seeks to translate questions of constitutional design into a calculus of expected utilities with the result that decisionmaking rules are legitimized when they coordinate individuals' privately held interests in a manner best approximating voluntary exchange or contractual agreement.

There is an intriguing tension within the historical accounts of the rational choice movement. On the one hand is the tendency to claim theoretical innovation for the movement and for its findings while, on the other, to claim that these theoretical results are somehow internal to the logic of democracy and political economy as understood by the Founding Fathers. This attempt to both claim the intellectual legacy handed down by the founders but to also claim originality in understanding collective decision problems is similar to a related historiographical tension. This second tension results from associating the development of public choice scholarship with the practical demise of socialism, as though both were somehow inevitable, and yet acknowledging that this inevitability is apparent only in hindsight.

The originality of the public choice movement is best appreciated as a direct response to American Cold War concerns. The creative reinterpretation of American liberalism was the hybrid result of drawing on the legacy of Enlightenment liberalism expressed by Adam Smith and America's founders, as Buchanan and Tullock are quick to acknowledge, and transposing these insights into the new, mathematically formulated language of self-interested rational action. It is more appropriate to view the new realism interjected into American analysis of political economy during the Cold War as a positive step toward securing a vision of polity-based self-determination of individual interests than it is to view it as a cynical statement about human nature. However, it is also important to realize that this thorough-going commitment to individuals' utility maximizing calculation in the arena of politics was designed from the beginning in opposition to idealistic democracy, socialist economics, and collectivist sentimentality. Since this opposition is built into the very fabric of public choice theory, it is reasonable to suggest that the theory is well-positioned not just to give an authoritative account of the disintegration of socialism, but also to assume preeminent status as the leading social theory.

CHAPTER 4

William H. Riker's Positive
Political Theory

In the world today two concepts of society are competing, communism and democracy. . . . Of course, I never expected to get to China [Taiwan]—but here I am. But what pleases me even more is to be able to visit the country which has for thirty years been a steadfast opponent of communism.
William H. Riker

THE three schools of rational choice theory discussed in this book—social choice theory, public choice theory, and positive political theory—each differ in their disciplinary status. The economics subfield of social choice theory, with interdisciplinary implications for political science, political theory, and the philosophy of justice, arose without oversight as a consequence of scholars' fascination with the technical sophistication and elegance of Kenneth Arrow's impossibility theorem. No directed, disciplinary coordination structured the growth of social choice theory. By contrast, James Buchanan and Gordon Tullock's school of public choice received attentive nurturing and institutional support from both scholars, who oversaw programs dedicated to its research at the University of Virginia, Virginia Polytechnic Institute, and George Mason University.

The development of positive political theory is different still. Like public choice theory, it was institutionally based, at least initially, but at the University of Rochester. Its development was also carefully fostered by its intellectual progenitor, William H. Riker (1920–93). However, unlike social choice or public choice theory, Riker's positive political theory became central to the entire discipline of American political science. For this reason, it offers the best opportunity for investigating disciplinary transformation along the lines of quantitative formal models of the rational choice variety. The story that unfolds is one of active engagement with central Cold War issues concerning potential Soviet threats to American democracy, both as a global superpower and as a philosophical opponent. Instead of ignoring nuclear weapons and Marxist political philosophy by adopting a language of scientific neutrality, Riker, like Arrow and

156

Buchanan, was centrally involved in defending the American democratic republic by mapping its contours in universally relevant and philosophically minimalist formal models grounded in individualistic, rational self-interest.

Of course, there was no real shift in the underlying attention American social sciences paid to American democracy. The only shift was a generational change in leadership in the post–World War II period that emphasized "scientific"—meaning nonnormative and quantitative—analyses. As discussed in chapter 2 in contrasting Kenneth Arrow's formal model of democracy with John Dewey's concept of a discursive public, a comparable concern to defend liberal Western values against organic statehood and totalitarian communism received different expression. David Hollinger observes that the Dewey-Merton-Popper generation of public intellectuals celebrated the Enlightenment values of science, democracy, and cosmopolitanism in direct opposition to fascism and totalitarianism.[1] In Robert Merton's formulation, these values were universalism, disinterestedness, communalism, and organized skepticism.[2] The Cold War generation as represented by Kenneth Arrow, Gordon Tullock, James Buchanan, and William Riker similarly celebrated Enlightenment values, which they took to be at the core of the American democratic establishment. However, the Cold War generation's Enlightenment values had shifted to emphasize the individual, rationality, objective scientific inquiry, universalism, and democracy. Significantly, "rationality" referred to self-interested calculation instead of reasoned intersubjective discussion, and scientific inquiry itself assumed objectivity to be a matter of course and not arising out of a personal commitment to integrity and impartiality. It is in this shift of focus within the familiar territory of Enlightenment values overlapping with Western liberalism that a key transition in American intellectual history came about: "rational self-interest" became an acceptable expression out of step with the two-century-long skepticism that "self-love" could result in anything more than prejudice and self-indulgence, or that it could help secure the authenticity of scientific results.[3] Under the rational choice approach to knowledge, it became customary to assume the objectivity of scientific results independently from any personal characteristics of the inquirer.

So far in discussing the articulation and development of rational choice theory in the economics subfield of social choice and in the context of the public choice school, I have sought to show how that theory and its methodology were interwoven in the Cold War initiative to undermine communism as an intellectually coherent economic and political philosophy. In the attempt to overcome communist theory, a rethinking of the basis of American democracy and its relationship to economic liberalism was prompted; this reconceptualization relied on a combination of individualism and rational self-interest formulated in the precise language of mathematics. It led to the demolition of the traditional concept of the "public," formerly central to American democracy.[4] It also led to quantitative modeling of collective decisionmaking procedures that transformed the emphasis from one of discursive democratic will formation through reasoned argumentation to an exercise in mathematically amalgamating individual preferences.[5]

The mathematical formalism structuring rational choice theory is impelled by the same academy-wide momentum propelling an increased emphasis on formal models as an indication of scientific standing. This movement has received sustained attention by historians providing accounts of disciplinary transformation in the American social sciences, especially following World War II.[6] The priority given to mathematically articulated research findings has two rationales. First, in the wake of World War II, during which scientific analysis of strategic problems proved useful to the war effort, additional mathematically oriented research was supported as a response to the Soviet Union's successful launch of the *Sputnik* satellites. Money was thus channeled to research endeavors that provided quantitative analyzes of social issues. Second, this preference for mathematical formulas and models served the function, as RAND leaders realized, of depoliticizing research by translating contentious social debates into the "objective" language of mathematics.[7]

The goal of removing both faction and ideology from the design of collective decisionmaking procedures is evident in the origins of RAND's Planning-Programming-Budgeting System and in Arrow's social choice theory. In this chapter's account of William Riker's transformation of the discipline of political science throughout the United States, the favored status of mathematical analysis is again apparent. However, in the case of rational choice theory, arguably the preeminent and paradigmatic example of mathematization of American social science, the two rationales for the ascendancy of mathematically articulated research mentioned above are necessary, but not sufficient, for understanding the powerful role that the theory has come to play both in American academia and increasingly abroad.[8] Therefore, I present a complementary argument exploring the role rational choice scholarship has played since its origins in informing what has now become a formidable and widely accepted theoretical infrastructure of American democracy. This infrastructure is of chief importance because it not only shapes political discourse, but also political practice. Thus, I argue that the particular content of rational choice theory's basis in individualistic rationality served to stabilize thinking about democracy, political economy, and justice during a time of ideological strife against a Cold War adversary. Leading social science theorists were keen to adopt nonnormative theoretical models to ground analyses of democracy and markets, but this was not because they turned their backs on the riveting faceoff between Western liberalism and Soviet communism. Rather, rational choice theorists embraced the constraints of reconceptualizing democracy in a scientific, nonnormative fashion; they restructured democratic theory along the lines of rational choice theory as a direct response to communism. The implicit form of individualism and definition of rationality informing rational choice theory were from the outset fashioned to render authoritarianism and collectivism theoretically moribund. This ostensibly nonideological academic effort to secure the foundations of American constitutional democracy resulted in "rational choice liberalism": the search for a legal framework upholding the "negative liberty" ideal serving to coordinate the actions of self-interested rational agents.

Perhaps it has been the great success of Cold War social scientists in promoting the "value-free" nature of their methods that makes it difficult for later observers to appreciate the extent to which, at least in the case of rational choice scholarship, many scholars were centrally concerned with defeating communism. For example, Thomas Bender finds that "[b]y 1950 the intolerance generated by McCarthyism and the Cold War moved academics and intellectuals generally to make themselves and their work less vulnerable to attack." To this end, he reports that "Marx was replaced by Freud, the world 'capitalism' dropped out of social theory after the war, and class became stratification.... Economics ... turn[ed] ... away from reform and distribution questions."[9] Bender's observation, while acknowledging the impact that competitive Cold War fervor had on American academics, misses the drama underlying the formulation of rational choice theory as a direct response to the intellectual puzzles bequeathed to the Cold War generation by communist Marxists.

"Marx" is surprisingly alive in the early canonical rational choice texts as the "other," who adept liberal theorists sought to debate into submission. Bender claims that the "political scientist David Easton has found in McCarthyism a stimulus for development of a more scientific and objective political science, for it provided a 'protected posture for scholars.'"[10] Rational choice theory, as it developed, certainly embraced objectivity. However, it was not by avoiding the key issues of the confrontation between Western liberalism and Soviet communism that it prospered. Quite to the contrary, it was specifically by facing these concerns head on,

within the "beyond ideology" context of postwar academics, that it triumphed. Instead of assuming "the virtually unchallengeable supremacy
of the nation's liberal-democratic ideology," the early rational choice theorists strove to secure this supremacy in response to the threatening overtones sounded by the Schumpeter-Hayek-Popper trio, and by the actual
Soviet opposition marked in deed and creed. Bender calls for a "precise
chronology and generational succession"[11] in tracing American social
scientists' responses to postwar pressures, and it is to this call for historical specificity that this chapter replies.

Riker's Early Writings

The significance of Riker's early writings is best viewed against the backdrop of the status quo of political science in the 1940s and 1950s. Riker
would supply what the discipline lacked: a vision for how to deliver on the
promise of a "science of politics." Following World War II, political science was in disarray.[12] American political scientists debated continually
over the appropriate method and substance of their field, leading one observer to comment, "The political sciences are a very fair illustration of the
following: as a whole they are sure neither of their methods nor even of
their subject matter, but [are] hesitant and groping; and further, taking it
all in all, can they really boast of a sufficiently abundant harvest of
achievement to resolve doubts about their essential premises?"[13] This la-
ment later would be echoed by Charles Lindblom in a 1990s disciplinary
retrospective capturing the midcentury confusion over method that en-
gulfed American political scientists.[14] In the immediate postwar period
there were two fundamental methodological approaches in the field. Some
political scientists sought to "emulate[e] . . . the natural sciences. . . . Objective description and precise measurement have become their ideals."
Others promoted political science as a normative enterprise in which the
study of particular political institutions is guided by values and ethical
postulates.[15] Variants of the approach to political science included the historical, case study approach that resonated with the then-popular public
law and public administration studies of Leonard D. White; the journal-
istic approach of Walter Lippman; the psychological approaches of
Harold D. Lasswell; the political and democratic theory of John Dewey;
and the growing behavioral approach emphasizing surveys and statistics
as found in the work of Charles E. Merriam.

Although there was already a clear tendency to promote statistical
methods and quantitative techniques, especially evident in the behavioral
school, there was nothing on the intellectual map remotely resembling

what would come to be positive political theory, or rational choice theory. Its seemingly closest cousin, the then-flourishing behavioralist approach, emphasized statistical correlation and empirical testing but lacked the concept of axiomatic treatment of human behavior and reliance on minimalist assumptions to yield general laws. The behavioralist approach instead generally focused on psychological attitudes to derive empirical generalizations. Behavioralism did uphold the standards of scientific rigor and embraced quantitative analysis. When contemplating the waning fortunes of behavioralism in light of the waxing fortunes of positive political theory, it should be remembered that the successes of rational choice theory represent a particular mathematically formulated method that outdueled not just case study-based or normative political science, but also other quantitative approaches. Rational choice theory offered a comprehensive means to reconceptualize capitalist democracy while behavioralism did not.

In 1948, William H. Riker graduated with his doctorate in political science from Harvard University, where he studied under Carl Friedrich. His dissertation, on the Council of Industrial Organizations, reflected the then popular case study approach. In the midst of a poor hiring climate, Riker accepted a faculty position at Lawrence College, Wisconsin, in 1949. There he remained for the next decade, building up a small political science department, and working to articulate his thoughts on political science methodology. During this period he was awarded two fellowships, a Ford Foundation education grant, which he relied on to write his first text, and a Rockefeller fellowship, which he used to assemble his thoughts on a new science of politics. Riker's 1953 text, *Democracy in the United States,* provides no hints of intellectual ferment preceding his adoption of the mathematically articulated language of rational self-interest that would increasingly come to structure his thinking about politics.[16]

Dating back to his days as a graduate student, Riker had been intellectually dissatisfied with the dominant case study approach which political science shared with the overlapping fields of legal history and public administration. He was actively casting about for a new method to serve a platform on which to build a robust science of politics. In 1954 two RAND researchers, L. S. Shapley and Martin Shubik, published a paper in the *American Political Science Review* with a formal treatment of what they referred to as a "power index."[17] Within the context of game theory, this paper defined the "power index" as a mathematical formula expressing a legislator's power as a function of his ability to swing decisions. It exemplified a new type of analysis that spoke about political processes in the language of mathematics, including the work of John von Neumann,

Oskar Morgenstern, Duncan Black, Kenneth Arrow, and Anthony Downs. Riker rapidly worked his way through this body of research, all of which was developed outside of the disciplinary bounds of political science, and introduced it into his curriculum at Lawrence College.

Drawing from such a broad array of work, by the mid-1950s Riker had assembled a stimulating collection of approaches to the study of political phenomenon, including methodological individualism, an emphasis on microfoundations, game theory, spatial models, axiomatic set theoretic treatment of rational action, and generalized Condorcet results questioning the validity of processes for collective decisionmaking. All these approaches, however, were marginal in their own fields, and required disciplined and unifying development before they could serve as building blocks for a new approach to the study of political events. Notably, Riker was the first non-RAND theoretician to recognize the potential of game theory for understanding political interactions. In fact, it was Riker who bestowed on game theory the promise of a new life during a crucial lull: after RAND defense strategists concluded the theory was of little merit for studying warfare, and before economists grasped its promise for grounding a new mathematics of the market, Riker began using game theory to structure empirical studies of coalition formation among his undergraduate students at Lawrence College.

Between 1957 and 1962, Riker wrote three formal papers that contained initial steps toward his eventual theoretical synthesis. Two papers drew on Shapley and Shubik's power index, and a third explored whether Arrow's impossibility theory, which predicted the n-person voting procedures for more than two outcomes demonstrate an inherent instability, pertained to actual voting practices.[18] Whereas these papers presented their findings mathematically and attempted to draw generalized conclusions by combining theoretical deduction with empirical tests, they did not as yet put together the pieces that would later characterize positive political theory. Notwithstanding Riker's mid-1950s experiments on coalition formation using a game-theoretic structure, neither game theory nor an explicit "rational action" model was relevant to these early papers.

Riker also authored two papers in philosophy before the close of the decade. These articles discuss the importance of carefully circumscribing the events defining a scientific study, and the need to base science on "descriptive generalizations."[19] Although these articles were not earth-shattering to the philosophical community, they do reveal Riker's grasp of the philosophical and conceptual issues necessary to ground his developing positive approach to politics. In them, Riker challenged the accepted view in political science that promoted the study of idiosyncratic details of rare and influential events.

The earliest indication that Riker's theoretical synthesis was complete is found in his 1959 application as a nominee to the Center for the Advanced Study in the Behavioral Sciences, housed at Stanford University. In his proposal Riker distances himself from his earlier work on federalism, stating that "I describe the field in which I expect to be working at the Center as 'formal, positive, political theory.'" He elaborates, "By Formal, I mean the expression of the theory in algebraic rather than verbal symbols. By positive, I mean the expression of descriptive rather than normative propositions." [20] This document is telling of Riker's own sense of intellectual development, and his reflective and unabashed program for political science:

> I visualize the growth in political science of a body of theory somewhat similar to . . . the neo-classical theory of value in economics. It seems to be that a number of propositions from the mathematical theory of games can perhaps be woven in to a theory of politics. Hence, my main interest at present is attempting to use game theory for the construction of political theory.[21]

Riker was accepted and spent the 1960–61 academic year as a fellow at the center. During this fertile year away from the responsibilities of teaching Riker wrote *The Theory of Political Coalitions,* which served as the manifesto for his freshly minted positive political theory.[22]

An exchange with another fellow at the center indicates the extent to which Riker's formulation of a new method for studying political phenomenon was sufficiently expansive to reach from politics to evolutionary biology, even at this early date. It is clear from the record of a conversation between Riker and Larry Friedman that Riker suggested a connection between rational action and political success, implying that the "criterion of success or failure meaningfully relate[s] to the rationality or irrationality of a man's behavior." [23] In addition, Riker hypothesized that rational behavior is similarly rewarded in evolution, provoking Friedman to respond:

> [Regarding] your genetic drift hypothesis . . . I think that most geneticists would deny that the gene pool of the human race is vulnerable to such transient and variable changes in the human genetic processes. In any even, the implicit assumption that losers are irrational and that winners are rational strikes me as not only unproven as a hypothesis but an untenable hypothesis.[24]

This wide scope Riker wanted to give his positive political theory, applicable to the achievement of political goals and also pertinent to evolutionary "success," illustrates how ambitious he was in extending its applicability: his new method of political science was consistent with a view of the world in which political rationality, as measured by successful attainment of goals, is in some sense equivalent to evolutionary success in survival and species propagation. This speculative exchange between Riker and Friedman anticipates a feature of the emerging rational choice theory, which over time would draw more explicit connections to evolutionary biology.[25] Riker's recasting of "rationality" was bold. Rather than being a uniquely human trait that separates humanity from the rest of nature, rationality was now a universal "scorecard": any winning course of action is by post facto definition "rational," while any losing course of action is "irrational."

Riker's Theory of Political Coalitions

Riker must first and foremost be recognized as the architect of a coherent methodology for political science that fit the bill of being "scientific," and the one who addressed the concerns voiced from within the field that political science lacked disciplinary unity and analytic rigor. His *Theory of Political Coalitions* is innovative and joins the aforementioned texts by von Neumann and Morgenstern, Black, Arrow, and Downs as part of the rational choice canon. The book's opening chapter serves as a prolegomena for "the Prospect of a Science of Politics," suggesting that science should be built up of deductive structures derived from intuitively justified axioms that are subject to empirical tests.[26] Riker proposed studying politics by analyzing its microfoundations of the decisionmaking of agents, whose actions could be modeled like particles in motion. Just as a particle's trajectory can be predicted if its momentum and the force exerted on it are known, so too can an agent's actions be predicted by knowing her preferences and the environment shaping her choices. Using this information, the political scientist could model the results of collective actions through analysis of the parameters of individual decisionmaking. In proposing and enacting this new method, Riker intended to counter what he took to be the psuedo-science of Marxism and Marx's idea that macroeconomic conditions structure ideas and political relations (5, 9).

Riker adopted David Easton's definition of politics as "the authoritative allocation of value," and made the crucial distinction that set apart his theory of politics from economic theory: whereas collective outcomes that occur in the market place are made in a "quasi-mechanical way," collective outcomes that are the stuff of politics are made by conscious processes (11). This is an important distinction because the rational actor in political arenas intentionally calculates how to achieve aims in a strategic environment with other similarly minded rational agents. Riker also drew heavily on von Neumann and Morgenstern's formulation of human rationality, as well as their zero-sum, n-person game theory (16–31).

Ever methodologically aware, Riker carefully walked the line between "crude" economic rationality measuring agents' utility according to a single standard such as money and the tautological definition of rationality as agents choosing what they prefer, regardless of the content of this choice (20–22). For Riker, the concept of "winning" is as appropriate to political contexts of elections as it is to warfare. In both, winners take all and losers are eliminated, reinforcing the premium on "rational" behavior. Riker reinitiated enthusiasm that would later become contagious over the potential for game theory to be relevant to actual political situations. In the introduction to *The Theory of Political Coalitions,* he referred to the growing disillusionment that early excitement for game theory had resulted in, suggesting that the disappointment in applications of von Neumann and Morgenstern's "minimax theorem" should not detract from the overall usefulness of game theory to political scientists.[27]

Riker's argument in his text is best understood as responding to Downs's *Economic Theory of Democracy* by applying von Neumann and Morgenstern's contention that their "discussion of games of strategy will show that the role and size of 'coalitions' is decisive throughout the entire subject." [28] Downs had presented a protorational choice model relying strictly on marginal economic analysis of the self-interested calculation politicians make in seeking to maximize their votes in order to gain office. In Downs's analysis, politicians design their political agendas not on principle but strictly according to the principle of obtaining the most votes. He concludes that each political party will be induced to announce a centrist platform insofar as this is the best way to attract the most voters.

Riker found Downs's logic to be flawed. He surmised that Downs's model of democracy results in contradiction because its dual premises that citizens vote to maximize their potential gains and that political parties strive to maximize votes cancel each other out. Seeming to acknowledge this inconsistency, Downs concludes that "rational behavior by political parties tends to discourage rational behavior by voters." That is, according to Downs's analysis, in order to gain votes parties not only move to the center but also only vaguely articulate their policies, hence making it difficult for voters to rationally choose a candidate due to the ambiguity of payoffs. Attempting to rescue Downs from sinking into the quicksand of logical contradiction, yet preserving the overall theoretical commitment to agents' self-interested rationality, Riker reiterates the insight of von Neumann and Morgenstern highlighting the importance of the size of coalitions. Where Downs had misstepped, argued Riker, was in finding that politicians maximize votes, regardless of the number of votes required to achieve a winning coalition. Using game theory, Riker derived his "size principle," holding that "[i]n n-person zero-sum games, where side-payments are permitted, where players are rational, and where they have perfect information, only minimum winning coalitions occur."[29] In Downs's model, political actors seek to attain the maximum votes, without limit. Riker deductively argued that party leaders create minimum winning coalitions so that the least compromise is necessary and so that the spoils of victory are divided among fewer coalition members.

In proposing the "size principle," Riker demonstrated what he thought the ideal of political science to be: to progressively gain knowledge of familiar political processes by applying deductive argument and testing conclusions on empirical cases. In addition to the game-theoretic analysis of coalition building, Riker built in to his model concepts of uncertainty, dynamic decision processes, and stability or "equilibrium." He tested the conclusions reached through deductive logic on historical events and processes in the United States, such as the evolution of the American two-party system, which on occasion had briefly comprised three parties. He also analyzed international relations and warfare, hence initiating the field of game-theoretic analysis of international relations as a respectable topic for political scientists.

Far from avoiding reference to either Marxist principles or to the unfolding Cold War bipolar competition to be "the leader of a world-dominating coalition," Riker's manifesto for a coherent study of politics concludes with a chapter entitled "Reflections on Empire: An Epilogue on the United States in World Affairs" (217, 211–43). Riker recognized the tremendous boon to intellectual creativity the Cold War competition bestowed and, acknowledging the Marxist roots of history of science, he acceded that political competition most often provides the spark for scientific invention. Riker saw the Cold War power struggle between the United States and the Soviet Union as flowing naturally from his theory of political coalitions. Criticizing the postwar characterization of the Soviet Union by Western journalism as "an aggressive imperial power . . . constantly upsetting the status quo," and its rationale as following from "the evil motive of Communist leaders," Riker promoted his explanation attributing "a rational (rather than evil) motive . . . to the leaders of both sides" (228). In view of his deductive, predictive, and empirically testable study, Riker offered policy conclusions on the basis that "[i]f politicians act upon them and that action is successful, as I am personally convinced would be the case, then in a pragmatic fashion the theory would be justified" (243). Exhibiting the political realism that his school is famous for, Riker concluded his *Theory of Political Coalitions* with the personal reflection that "I, as a (possibly overoptimistic) citizen in the leader of a world-dominating coalition, would like to see both the leadership and coalition survive . . . at least as long as the lifetime of my children" (243).

William Riker represents an engaged intellectual applying what he took to be nonnormative, scientific analysis to the core political question of his day: how political decisions are made over resource allocation in a zero-sum, winner-take-all world. Riker's writings acknowledge the legacy of Marx and the reality of the communist bid for hegemony, and he responds with the balanced attempt to construct a science of politics capable of generating unprecedented theoretical insights into the merry-go-round of human politics. Riker's contribution to the rational choice canon, like Buchanan and Tullock's *The Calculus of Consent,* methodologically and substantively counters Marxism. In *Theory of Political Coalitions,* Riker advances a scientific, interest-based analysis of politics that challenges Marx's "main proposition of *Capital* . . . [that] 'Capitalism is theft'" (5). In Riker's view, this conclusion of Marx can only rate as pseudo-science because Marx's "description" relies on the norms already implicit within the "positive legal system" defining "theft." For Riker, legitimate political science is only entitled to positive analysis of human institutions relying on deductive models and empirical tests. Riker also counters Marxist "official dogma insist[ing] . . . that all political activity is mere superstructure supported by the really fundamental activity of economic life" (9). Instead of representing politics as epiphenomena driven by economic relations, in Riker's new political science, political events are studied as the deliberate and informed choices of self-interested, rational actors.

Disciplinary Synthesis of Positive Political Theory

It is clear that it took imagination and vision for William Riker to synthesize the leads provided by von Neumann, Morgenstern, Black, Arrow, and Downs into a coherent theory of politics based on the idea of methodological individualism encapsulated in a theory of rational, strategic action modeled by n-person game theory. However, brilliant vision does not inevitably lead to achievement. Riker's ambitious platform for reorienting political science may have gone little further than his personal bibliography had he not tirelessly and deftly built up a graduate program specifically geared toward educating theorists capable of transforming the entire discipline of political science. This achievement required a unique constellation of circumstances that provided Riker with the resources and institutional infrastructure requisite to carry out his program for reform.

Shortly before setting out for the Center for the Advanced Study in the ᴅenavioral Sciences at Stanford in 1960, Riker caught the eye of administrators at the University of Rochester, who were seeking to establish graduate programs in the social sciences with national standing. The University of Rochester, throughout most of the 1960s, was flush with capital provided by the largesse of Joseph Wilson, head trustee of the Haloid-Xerox Corporation, who was committed to science as a means of bettering human lives. This beneficence gave the University of Rochester an endowment that was in the league of Yale and Harvard for part of the decade. Resonating with Wilson's vision for improving society through scientific research, support grew on campus to build up the social science departments by emphasizing programs oriented toward rigorous quantitative analysis resembling the successful programs in the physical sciences. Riker, whose work admirably fit this plan, was hired to create a graduate program in political science. Also newly appointed were Lionel McKenzie, brought in to chair the economics department and build its graduate program, and W. Allen Wallis, formerly dean of the Chicago Business School, to head the university as chancellor. Wallis and McKenzie, too, were committed to the development of analytic and formal social science, and would become close colleagues and active supporters of Riker.

Wallis served as the university's president and chancellor during the 1963–74 period. Previously a denizen of the natural security world, Wallis had already had an impressive career. He had managed the Statistics Research Group of the Applied Mathematics Panel of the Office of Scientific Research and Development during World War II, had served as a member of the Office for Strategic Services, and had been under consideration to head the economics division of RAND, a post that instead was offered to Charles Hitch. Wallis saw a close overlap between the decision theoretic tools of policy science and formal models in the social sciences, and was firmly committed to both. Under his leadership the University of Rochester agreed to oversee the Navy's RAND-style think tank, the Office for Naval Analysis, starting in 1967 and throughout the 1970s. It was in the person of Wallis that Riker's positive political theory met the world of national security policy and prospered. Anecdotes, supported by Riker's track record in faculty recruitment and retention, recount how Wallis was unable to refuse Riker's masterfully constructed cases for securing additional university funds to achieve his departmental goals. The collegial partnership between the two, essential for making the University of Rochester into the social science powerhouse it became in the 1970s and 1980s, exemplified the post–World War II effort to harness quantitative social scientific research to inform rational policymaking.

Upon taking his position, Riker rapidly outlined a strategy for building the university's political science department. His plan emphasized both behavioral methods and positive political theory. He sought to rival what were then the nation's leading programs at Yale, Chicago, Northwestern, MIT, and the Michigan Survey Research Center. The result was fourteen new courses and seminars, an entire new curriculum, that included the study of the scope of political science; theories of strategy; positive political theory; techniques of research in political science; theories of decisionmaking; theories of organization; problems in measurement of political events; political parties; legislative behavior; political sociology; comparative politics; problems in constitutional interpretation; national security policy; and recent political philosophy.

Riker balanced the goal of attracting greater numbers of undergraduates and graduate students into his program against building up his faculty. When he arrived at Rochester, the political science department could only go upward in view of its dismal mark in 1959 of graduating not a single undergraduate political science major. By the early 1970s it had about twenty-five graduate students and four times as many undergraduates. By 1973 the department had graduated twenty-six doctoral students and forty-nine master's students, and it had climbed up the American Council of Education's ratings from being unranked in 1965 to fourteenth place in 1970.

In addition to creating a powerful graduate program that placed its graduates as faculty members in nationally recognized political science departments, Riker further laid the foundation for his new discipline of positive political theory by publishing *An Introduction to Positive Political Theory*, written in collaboration with a former student, Peter Ordeshook, in 1973.[30] The text is aimed at advanced undergraduates and beginning graduate students, and represents an important step in defining positive political theory for a widespread audience. It introduces to its readers the assumption of rationality and the formal account of preference orderings, and it demonstrates the positive approach to political science through its application to such problems as political participation, voting and majority rule, public goods, public policy, and electoral competition. The text also includes discussions of formal theory and deductive results from formal theory including n-person and two-person game theory, the power index, and the size principle. It is not clear that the textbook was introduced into the curriculum of many political science programs, but it proved to be a necessary step in paving the way for a rational choice approach to politics to be widely recognized and well-defined. It provided a resource for those outside Rochester who sought to participate in the research program launched by the Rochester school.

Riker also benefited from Rochester's highly acclaimed economics department, headed by Lionel McKenzie. Economics as a discipline was itself undergoing dramatic transition in the 1960s, as the neoclassical synthesis prompted by long-time RAND consultants Paul Samuelson, Robert Solow, and Kenneth Arrow became the discipline's orthodoxy.[31] Significantly, McKenzie's economics department played an active and leading role in this transformation within economics, which meant that on the same campus and at the same time Riker and McKenzie were leaders in the interlocking development of these disciplines. Riker developed his graduate program for positive political theory in conjunction with McKenzie's efforts to establish a new protocol in economics, which was friendly toward game theory and microfoundations while critical of a Keynesian, macroeconomic approach. Riker had a strong vantage point from which he could build a curriculum that could exert major influence on the entire discipline of American political science because he had strong institutional support, which, not coincidentally, similarly advanced McKenzie's vision of economics. The University of Rochester, with trustees firmly committed to advancing scientific methods within the social sciences, provides a compelling example of how rational choice theory was furthered as a complex of knowledge spanning several independent but interrelated fields of study.

Riker's establishment of a public policy program housed within his political science department in the mid-1970s, with overlapping faculty and course listings, also demonstrates how the development and perpetuation of rational choice theory in the social sciences is inseparable from a more encompassing movement spanning academic research and active policy analysis. Riker was motivated to establish the policy program as a revenue source for the department by providing a popular terminal master's degree. In turn he worked to ensure that graduates of the policy program had a strong track record in landing good jobs. Rational choice theory has in part been successful because of the prestige of its practitioners, who are well placed within the active world of policymaking. The University of Rochester was committed to supporting the interconnected set of disciplinary movements constituting rational choice scholarship evident not only in political science and economics, but also clear in the early law and economics movement. The first program in law and economics, headed by Henry G. Manne in the late 1960s and early 1970s, was also established at the University of Rochester.[32] Riker would have been hard-pressed to have the widespread impact he did without the backing of similarly committed, resource rich, university leaders and department heads.

Riker's legacy in political science was secured by both his personal career successes and by those of his students. He was inducted into the National Academy of Sciences (NAS) in 1974 and thus was among the first political scientists to become a member of the elite society. Riker's election demonstrates his achievement in promoting positive political theory as a readily identifiable scientific method. It also shows the changing standards for scientific research that characterized the postwar era. In 1949 the only social sciences acknowledged by the NAS were anthropology and psychology, because they reflected the then-accepted scientific methods typical of biology and chemistry.[33] Therefore Riker's membership in the NAS signaled not only that political science had achieved the status of "science," but also that standards of scientific achievement themselves had shifted to favor axiomatic and deductive models.

Riker's efforts in helping build the careers of former students was unceasing. Those efforts paid off handsomely, as his first generation of graduates introduced Rochester's unique brand of positive political theory to other departments and made it a national phenomenon. Rochester's doctoral graduates in political science during the 1970s accepted appointments at, among other institutions, Cal Tech, Carnegie Mellon, and Washington University, helping these programs also to become important centers for positive political theory. By 1985, both Morris Fiorina and Kenneth Shepsle had attained appointments at Harvard University, which Riker took to be one of the tell-tale signs that positive political theory had arrived. His alma mater, which had for the longest time insisted on perpetuating what he took to be dated and nonscientific approaches to politics, had at last come around to acknowledge the rightful and leading role that his positive political theory played in defining political science.

Riker's *Liberalism against Populism*

Like Arrow, Riker sought to defeat populism, which he believed to be consistent with the political philosophies of Rousseau, Kant, and Marx, as well as of Stalin, in order to protect liberalism against authoritarian incursions violating the individual. At stake was more than just "Jean Jacques Rousseau versus James Madison," as Riker sketched the debate. According to Riker, who would contribute to a wider debate initiated by Isaiah Berlin over the differences between "negative liberty" and "positive liberty," populism was also subject to Berlin's fear that "positive liberty . . . is the root of tyranny."[34] In the vein of Hayek, Arrow, Buchanan, and Tullock, Berlin argues that "[s]ocialized forms . . . [of] the positive doctrine of liberation by reason . . . are at the heart of many of the nationalist, communist, authoritarian, and totalitarian creeds of our day."[35] Berlin posits that "an ethical doctrine of individual responsibility and individual self-perfection [leads] . . . to an authoritarian state obedient to the directives of an *élite* of Platonic guardians."[36] Berlin realizes that associating Kant's kingdom of ends with Stalin's Soviet Union is a stretch of the imagination, yet insists that the doctrine of moral perfectibility through reason necessarily leaves the door wide open for the rule of experts claiming to have achieved this superior state of knowledge.[37] Hence, any doctrine of rational self-control giving rise to a general will or kingdom of ends must, in Berlin's analysis, be susceptible to the worst form of corruption: coercive authoritarianism, or "a final solution," violating the sanctity of the individual.[38]

Although not arguing that Madisonian liberalism will necessarily result in a social order equivalent to Berlin's government upholding negative liberty, Riker follows Berlin in recognizing the potential "transformation of Kant's notions of individual ethical responsibility by, successively, Hegel and Marx into the justification for a monstrous dictatorship."[39] Riker takes the discussion over positive and negative liberty further by challenging C. B. MacPherson's effort to rescue positive liberty from Berlin's relentless attack.[40] As Riker explains, "MacPherson, as a populist and a socialist, wants to save self-mastery as complementary to and not inconsistent with negative liberty, while banishing coercion, that Stalinist embarrassment to 'democratic' socialists."[41] By equating Mac-Pherson's socialism with populism, Riker effectively constructs his argument in *Liberalism Against Populism* to also negate socialist political philosophies.

In his analysis of the contemporary debate between Berlin and Mac-Pherson over the nature of liberty, Riker adds a degree of philosophical complexity to Rousseau's populism and Madison's liberalism. It is these steps in Riker's argument, seamlessly developing the long-standing discussion over the legitimate constitution of government respecting individual liberty, that require our special attention. First, it is worth assessing Riker's argument against populism, based on Arrow's impossibility theorem combined with empirical findings about strategic voting and agenda setting. No well-read individual with an interest in social choice literature will be surprised by Riker's indictment of Rousseau, Kant, and Marx, since Arrow had explicitly stated that his theorem countered each of their political philosophies. However, it is remarkable that Riker adopts a different strategy to refute Rousseau's populism—one that invokes both Arrow's impossibility theorem and actual voting scenarios to demonstrate the impossibility of achieving collectively rational voting results. Recall that Arrow had acknowledged the possibility that, under the strict requirement that their citizens consider the general welfare,

Rousseauean and Kantian communities may achieve a degree of normative consensus necessary to circumvent the impossibility theorem, thereby achieving a collectively rational result. In both Rousseau's and Kant's schemes for self-ruling communities, it is imperative that citizens supersede their personal desires and whims in order to reach collective decisions that serve the public at large.

Always a pragmatic thinker, Riker ignores this caveat in Rousseau's and Kant's systems and realistically concludes that this demand for ideal citizens is not met in the political world confronting the twentieth-century political scientist. After all, American politics, embracing a vast melting pot of individuals, is a far cry from Rousseau's native Geneva, and it is not unrealistic to observe in twentieth-century political expression the lack of cohesion accepted as the starting point of Arrow's theorem. Therefore, Riker cannot be impugned for neglecting to mention that, as Arrow suggested, if citizen's interests are aligned by common concerns, the impossibility theorem does not apply.

In undermining populist philosophy, which depends on popular voting to result in an expression of the collective will, Riker presents a realistic appraisal of the demos that leads to a measured skepticism that the populist ideal can ever be realized in practice. Riker worries that as long as citizens uphold the ideal of popular sovereignty as a meaningful expression of the collective will, this fervent hope may provide legitimacy for a mode of rulership that would effectively be tyranny. Moreover, Riker is concerned that people may believe that populism could coexist with liberalism. He explores the possibility that whereas citizens may usually believe that election results only reflect the liberal ideal that voting serves the function of removing bad leaders, on occasion citizens may believe that the popular vote does, in fact, give voice to a collective will. Similar to Buchanan and Tullock's caution regarding the meaningfulness of majority rule, Riker insists that it is not appropriate to believe that populism and liberalism can coexist on a premise of partnership; he argues that the populist belief in legitimate democratic will formation is always invalid. Riker worries that any residual belief in populism will lead to the temptation on the part of rulers to exceed the bounds of their authority by enacting policy before the inevitable cycling characterized by social choice theory or the shifting coalitions predicted positive political theory places different leaders in power. Echoing Berlin's fears, he observes that "[p]opulism reinforces the normal arrogance of rulers with a built-in justification for tyranny, the contemporary version of the divine right of rulers." [42] Riker points to the government of the United Kingdom as having fallen to such a fate. [43]

The final aspect of Riker's argument that bears scrutiny is his equation of socialism with populism. Whether this aspect of his analysis is valid or not is immaterial to the integrity of the overarching argument in *Liberalism against Populism,* but it is nonetheless worth examining what prompted this conclusion about socialism. In developing his claim, Riker refers to MacPherson, who in his essay "Berlin's Division of Liberty" argues against Berlin's conclusion that positive liberty of the sort espoused by Rousseau and Kant must necessarily breed totalitarianism.[44] MacPherson's argument is prolix, defining three different versions of positive liberty: one consistent with the philosophies of Rousseau and Kant, one a perversion of Rousseau and Kant, and a third that is a form of democratic sovereignty dependent on voter participation. In his essay, MacPherson does not write much about popular sovereignty apart from concluding that it remains to be determined whether democratic voting does or does not uphold the negative version of liberty so crucial to Berlin. He does, however, note that even Berlin believes that "democracy or self-governance 'may, on the whole, provide a better guarantee of the preservation of civil liberties than other regimes, and has been defended as such by libertarians'" (130). Riker's concern to defend liberalism versus populism does not match up perfectly with Berlin's defense of negative liberty against MacPherson's concept of positive liberty. This is because Riker's liberalism is minimalist in its requirement that the only function democratic voting plays is to remove leaders, while Berlin's negative liberty is a clearer articulation of the liberal ideal of erecting a legal framework that permits individuals the greatest sphere of liberty in selecting their actions without transgressing others' liberties. MacPherson is correct in pointing out that there is not a necessary correlation between democratic voting and negative liberty, though he also charitably concludes that democratic elections may provide the best hope for achieving this minimalist ideal of liberty.

Riker and MacPherson part company earlier in the argument, with MacPherson redefining positive liberty to embody a more inclusive ideal of freedom consistent with a socialist vision of society. According to MacPherson, negative liberty—being free from invasive coercion—does not capture the sense in which most people would like to be free: to develop their capacities and developmental powers (111). Interestingly, here MacPherson resonates with Berlin's claim that it is most individuals' greatest wish to be respected within their community.[45] MacPherson does not believe that either poverty or "the capitalist market economy with the right of unlimited individual appropriation" is consistent with his ideal of positive liberty.[46] It is dubious that MacPherson's positive liberty is consistent with Kant's kingdom of ends insofar as Kant's system, built on negative virtues, is more akin to both the negative liberties framework and with a "night watchman" view of the rule of government. Leaving aside this awkward fit between MacPherson's positive liberty and Kant's kingdom of ends, it is MacPherson's socialist stance, combined with his definition of participatory voting as another form of positive liberty, that leads Riker to associate socialism with populism. This association enables Riker to conclude that socialism, like populism, is flawed because it relies on the moral correctness of the popular vote.

However, as will be apparent with Arrow's cautious defense of socialism, it is not possible to conclude that socialism entails populism. The difference between Arrow's and Riker's attitudes toward socialism stems from their different conclusions about the implications of social choice theory for the market. Arrow consistently argues that his theorem presents as serious an indictment of democracy as it does of the market with respect to achieving collectively rational outcomes. Riker by contrast, much like Buchanan, believes that free market transactions are crucial to an effective democratic society. He also holds that Arrow's theorem does not mire the market in logical inconsistencies as it does either social welfare economics or democratic voting, because he doubts the relevancy of the condition of "independence of irrelevant alternatives" for the market.

The work of Riker, Buchanan, Tullock, and Arrow all illustrate how, using the tools of mathematical analysis, it is possible to reach conclusions about such elusive concepts as freedom, liberalism, and socialism that are unparalleled in previous discourses. These rational choice thinkers were concerned with laying the foundations for an individualistic democracy to protect against the possibility of totalitarian encroachments on individual freedom. Combining individualism with a mathematically delineated theory of rational action, rational choice theory enables precise conclusions about political theory subject to empirical testing. This new method achieved unprecedented results: the intricate and complex discursive arguments of Rousseau, Kant, and Marx were countered by equally intricate and complex mathematical arguments demonstrating the logical and actual possibilities achievable through collective decision procedures. In rejecting the sort of collective decision procedures embodying a "general will" as both impracticable and illegitimate, Riker, Buchanan, Tullock, and Arrow proposed less ambitious aspirations for democracy, and more realistic goals.

CHAPTER 5

Rational Choice and Capitalist Democracy

A THEORY of American Cold War democracy must center on the cross-linkages between RANDs rationality project as it was enunciated in decision theory and game theory, and its foray into decision technologies useful to policy formation.[1] In the 1960s and 1970s, these decision technologies formed the basis of rational choice theory and informed both academic inquiry and public policy.[2] In addition to this close interconnection between the worlds of policy and social scientific inquiry, rational theorists enthusiastically employed the new framework for analyzing collective decisionmaking to secure the foundations of American constitutional democracy by countering the threats posed by authoritarianism and communism. In this conclusion to the book's second part, I discuss the latter initiative.

Part 2 of this book is organized around the rational choice movements of social choice, public choice, and positive political theory—each of which was authoritatively articulated in a classic text: *Social Choice and Individual Values, The Calculus of Consent,* and *The Theory of Political Coalitions.* Other canonical texts are John von Neumann and Oskar Morgenstern's *Theory of Games and Economic Behavior,* Anthony Downs's *Economic Theory of Democracy,* and Mancur Olson's *The Logic of Collective Action.* Whereas von Neumann and Morgenstern's text was germane to all that followed in the development of rational choice theory, and Downs's work directly stimulated Riker's *Theory of Political Coalitions,* Olson's book has yet to receive the same measure of attention because, published in 1965, it signals the end of the early creative phase establishing rational choice theory. Both Olson's work and career however, are important for pointing up the consistent set of factors giving rise to rational choice scholarship.

The professional trajectory of Mancur Olson (1932–98) exemplifies the developmental pattern of rational choice theory itself. He was associated with RAND during the formative stages of his career, when he served as a first lieutenant in the U.S. Air Force during 1961–63.[3] His manuscript for *Logic of Collective Action* greatly benefited from copious comments by RAND's Thomas Schelling. In 1967 Olson accepted the position of deputy assistant secretary for social indications at the U.S. Department of Health, Education and Welfare, where he took part in the efforts to rationalize decisionmaking in government. Then in 1969 he became associate professor of economics at the University of Maryland. It was the height of the Planning-Programming-Budgeting craze in Washington, in the spirit of which Olson was prompted to publish "The Plan and Purpose of a Social Report," discussing the efforts to rationalize American public policy through superior knowledge and methods of analysis.[4] He devoted a section of that essay to "Systems Analysis" and to the "Planning-Programming-Budgeting System," and concluded that there "could have been no hope that an adequate set of social indicators would be collected until someone had defined what they were, and showed that the nation could not have fully rational public policies without them."[5] Thus, he fully endorsed the effort to engage in rational policy analysis of the sort pioneered by RAND.

Olson's *The Logic of Collective Action* resembles the other texts in the rational choice canon by posing a direct challenge to Marxist political philosophy. Friedrich Hayek was sufficiently impressed with Olson's theory refuting Marxist collectivism that he arranged to have it translated into German. In his text, Olson directly opposes "Marxian theories of class action" that suppose "that groups tend to act in support of their group interests [as a consequence of the] . . . widely accepted premise of rational, self-interested behavior."[6] Olson challenges what he takes to be the conventional wisdom that it is rational to cooperate with others, even in great numbers, in order to achieve collective goals. In contrast, Olson finds "it is *not* in fact true that the idea that groups will act in their self-interest follows logically from the premise of rational and self-interested behavior" (2). He reemphasizes his main point, adding a caveat that "unless there is coercion or some other special device to make individuals act in their common interest, *rational, self-interested individuals will not act to achieve their common or group interests*" (ibid.). Thus, Marx was wrong to suppose that a class of individuals will collaborate to achieve a group goal. They will do so only if forced by some external authority. In addition to Marxist theories, Olson seeks in his book to counter the arguments of Arthur Bentley among other American group theorists.[7]

Olson builds his case by presenting an economic model balancing the costs an individual must incur in contributing to a collective action against the gains the individual will receive from his share of the collective enterprise. Olson mathematically demonstrates, according to the calculus of individual economic interests, that it will be in an individual's rational self-interest to shirk on his contributions while continuing to receive his share of the collective efforts. This is because an individual will not appreciably benefit from his own efforts once they are divided among the entire group of members. Therefore, a rational individual will calculate that he is better off standing on the sidelines when it comes to contributing to the group effort, and stepping up to the plate when it comes to receiving from the group. Olson turns the Marxist credo "From each according to his ability, to each according to his need" on its head by demonstrating that rational self-interest cannot support large scale, societywide collective ventures.

Olson is especially keen to defeat the Marxist theory of class interests because of its apparent consistency with the premise of rational self-interest: according to Marx, individuals, especially the bourgeoisie, are inherently governed by economic self-interest. In this respect, therefore, while Marxist theory seems to have the identical starting point of rational choice theory, it reaches the opposite conclusion—specifically, that the liberal capitalist system should be overthrown. Olson stresses:

> It is *not* in fact true that the absence of the kind of class conflict Marx expected shows that Marx overestimated the strength of rational behavior. On the contrary, the absence of the sort of class action Marx predicted is due in part to the predominance of rational utilitarian behavior. *For class-oriented action will not occur if the individuals that make up a class act rationally.*[8]

Thus, Olson advances a new critique of Marx unforeseen by Arrow, Riker, Buchanan, and Tullock. Indeed, in finding that it is not rational to cooperate in large-scale collective projects, despite the resulting collective impoverishment of the group as comprised of individuals, Olson counters centuries of conventional wisdom; in the process he initiates a branch of rational choice theory devoted to collective action problems following the logical structure of his "nonobvious and paradoxical result."[9] In his account of the intellectual history leading up to Olson's finding, Richard Tuck points out that for centuries, according to a diversity of thinkers, it had been considered rational to contribute to social enterprises.[10] Tuck specifically discusses David Hume, for whom the system of justice resembled such a vast collective enterprise that it was rational for each person to contribute to the system, even though each would not benefit appreciably from his own actions. Tuck suggests that in presenting his counterintuitive theory of collective action, Olson in effect reformulates the premises of individual rational action.

In his intellectual history of collective action, Tuck argues that the "free rider" problem is an invention of modern political theorists, and that the problem has "*no* extensive literature . . . until the 1960s," after the publication of Olson's book (1). In contrast to present-day commentators, who generally agree that Olson's new rational choice methodology is path-breaking, Tuck raises the possibility that this shift in reasoning about reasoning is not a new scientific finding so much as it is a new explanation and definition of "rationality." Tuck links his analysis to the two-century-long discussion among economists over whether it is rational to compete or whether instead it is rational to collude, or to combine, one's efforts. Tuck explains that theorists preceding Olson believed it to be eminently rational for individuals to combine their efforts to reach collective goals. Francis Ysidro Edgeworth, for example, dedicates a long passage to the calculations a laborer makes in deciding whether to join a trade union:

> And if, as seems to be implied . . . it is attempted to enforce the argument against Trades Unionism by the consideration that it tends to diminish the *total national produce,* the obvious reply is that unionists, as "economic men," are not concerned with *total produce.* Because the total produce is diminished, it does not follow that the labourer's share is diminished . . . ; much less does it follow (as aforesaid) that there should be diminished that quantity which alone the rational unionist is concerned to increase—*the labourer's utility.* If this view be correct, it would seem as if, in the matter of *unionism,* as well as in that of the predeterminate *wage-fund,* the "untutored mind" of the workman had gone more straight to the point than economic intelligence *mislead by bad method,* reasoning without mathematics upon mathematical subjects.[11]

In Edgeworth's estimation, it is eminently rational for laborers to join trade unions because it is thus that they are able to gain a greater return for their labor. Tuck presents similarly argued cases in which "perfect competition," among large or small communities of members, must be coercively enforced to forestall the natural tendency of members to gain advantage by colluding, or joining their efforts.

Olson, to the contrary, and consistent with his findings about the collective impoverishment of self-interested rational actors underlying public goods and free-rider studies, argues that large-scale collective undertakings, such as labor unions, can only function effectively if they use coercive means to ensure individual compliance. In keeping with the general skepticism of communism, Olson points to a more sinister aspect of Marxist social philosophy, finding that it is not, paradoxically, in an individual's interest to join a labor movement because "the large labor union, though not a part of government, must be coercive, if it attempts to fulfill its basic function and still survive." [12] In Olson's analysis, it is necessary for unions to adopt coercive practices if they are to achieve the coordination required to have impact. Thus, the labor union movement acquires the same authoritarian overtones that had already been associated with communism. Just as socialist economies use force to acquire and distribute public goods, so must unions require compulsory policies to achieve results.

It is through an appreciation of Olson's finding against the backdrop of conventional economic analysis that makes it possible to propose that rational choice theorists' staunch commitment to rational self-interest has reshaped the basic set of premises underlying conventional political theory. Olson and his rational choice colleagues apply basic premises about human action to reveal underlying truths about individuals' collective behavior. However, cast in a different light it is also possible to recognize their efforts as changing the political discourse of Western society by teaching new truths about the essential characteristics of rational action. Riker, Buchanan, Tullock, and Arrow, four of the founding figures of a rational choice theory of politics, were all intent on restructuring thinking about Western liberalism with a program combining positive, nonnormative analysis, individualism, and the concept of rational self-interest expressed in the language of mathematics. They simultaneously harnessed this same framework in order to defeat Marxist philosophy, populism, and any form of organic collectivism that could potentially lead to communism and totalitarianism.

Marxist philosophy, while not at all times focal, was central to this effort to redefine economic and political liberalism, because in the real world of geopolitics it shaped more people's lives than did Rousseau, Kant, and Hegel combined. Marxist philosophy as a whole, however, is difficult to challenge explicitly because of its apparently contradictory features. At times, for example, Marx seems to stress the importance of the individual, whereas at other times he seems to denigrate the integrity of individuals and their ideas to historical determinism and class interests. Also, Marx seems to vacillate between envisioning a society beyond politics, and yet calling for a coercive "dictatorship of the proletariat" in order to ensure this eventuality. To the mid-twentieth-century West, Marxist philosophy represented the ultimate bogeyman because in providing the social and political rationale for the ruling regimes in the Soviet Union and China, it thereby threatened to displace Western liberalism. Marxist philosophy proposed a puzzle to rational choice theorists because at the same time that it was subversive in predicting and attempting to eradicate liberal, capitalist democracy, it also held out tantalizing leads with respect to scientific method and economic analysis of individuals' interests. When William Riker nonchalantly derided the "reduc[tion] . . . of politics to economics . . . as Marxism," [13] he distanced himself from precisely what he and his rational choice cohorts were (and are) often accused of: using tools of economic analysis to explain noneconomic issues of collective decisionmaking such as politics. Defenders of Western liberalism opposed the coercive scheme of "the dictatorship of the proletariat led by its vanguard the communist party," and yet Marx offered what they too sought: to understand the interconnections between government and economic institutions. [14] Marx offered a scientific, interest-based analysis of political economy. Rational choice theorists pursued the same lines of research in the service of liberal democracy instead of communism.

In Olson and Christopher Clague's article "Dissent in Economics: The Convergence of Extremes," the authors argue that there is surprising common ground between the New Left and the *laissez faire* liberalism of James Buchanan's so-called Virginia school. [15] They draw out parallel agreement between the dissenting extremes of mainstream economics by rendering explicit the manner in which public choice theory is in basic agreement with some of the tenets of classical Marxism. Most important, the Virginia school challenged the notion that governmental bureaucracies act in the "public interest." They observe that Buchanan's position is similar to the Marxist conviction that government serves the interests of the ruling class. In Olson and Clague's reading, Buchanan believes that mainstream American Keynesian economics serves the interests of "the liberal establishment" (756). Therefore, in their view, "the effort to incorporate political and governmental behavior explicitly into economic theory is the principal distinguishing feature of the Virginia School" (758), and follows the lead of Marx by interjecting political realism into the otherwise ideal analysis of economic institutions.

Olson was able to make this provocative association between Buchanan's New Right and the New Left because he carefully specifies that the New Left itself is characterized by the rejection of the coercive planning and large-scale centralized bureaucracies that marred the historical track record of Marxism in Eastern bloc nations. He proposes further that due to their increased emphasis on participation and democracy, there is great commonality between Marx's ideal of a classless society and Buchanan's *laissez faire* orientation: both look to individual, voluntary transactions as the basis of social order. Olson was bold and inventive in comparing the Marxist New Left with the Virginia school of political economy, and there is an important historical lesson to be learned from his analysis. In suggesting that the new Marxist radicals share common goals with the New Right against the mainstream middle representing Keynesian economics and large-scale bureaucratic control, Olson renders explicit the fear among some that mainstream academic economics and economic institutions fostered the same authoritarian and collectivist evils characterizing the Soviet state. To some latter-twentieth-century analysts, Keynesian economics seemed to imply the potential subversion of America's commitment to rational individualism from within, making the certitude of a victorious alliance between *laissez faire* economics and liberal democracy premature to pronounce.

The periodical *Commentary* joined in the discussion over the future of American democracy and capitalism in 1978, presenting a symposium exploring Joseph Schumpeter's *Capitalism, Socialism, and Democracy*.[16] *Commentary* posed the very question that had gripped Schumpeter, Karl Popper and Friedrich Hayek, and that looms so large in contemporary discussion of democracy and free trade underlying the "globalization" debates:

> The idea that there may be an inescapable connection between capitalism and democracy has recently begun to seem plausible to a number of intellectuals who would once have regarded such a view not only as wrong but even as politically dangerous. So too with the idea that there may be something intrinsic to socialism which exposes it ineluctably to the "totalitarian temptation." (29)

Respondents were asked, "How significant do you judge this development to be? Do you yourself share in it, either fully or even to the extent to feeling impelled to rethink your own ideas about capitalism and socialism and the relation of each to democracy?" The commentators' responses represented a wide spectrum of views, ranging from Robert Nisbet's observation, "I doubt that there are many intellectuals left who seriously identify themselves as socialist. . . . Totalitarianism is inherent in the modern doctrine of socialism" (62), to Eugene Genovese's claim that "Capitalism as a world system is palpably bankrupt and fighting a rearguard action. . . . Socialism . . . is almost everywhere ascendant" (22). Between these two extremes propounding the possibility of socialist democracy on the one hand and, on the other, the necessary correlation between free trade and democracy, a more centrist chord was struck as well. Charles Frankel pointed out the clichéd association of *laissez faire* economics and democratic politics, stating that Marx's *Communist Manifesto* had long ago claimed "a close connection between capitalism and democracy" (37).

Perhaps the most thought-provoking response to the issue as formulated by *Commentary* came from Kenneth Arrow, who contributed an essay responding directly to Schumpeter's *Capitalism, Socialism, and Democracy* as well as to Hayek's *The Road to Serfdom*. Arrow contended that "it is only relatively recently in the history of the great debate between socialism and capitalism that an allegation of a peculiar association between capitalism and democracy has become a staple of pro-capitalism argument" (29). This is because, of course, Marx had proposed that democracy serves the interests of the bourgeoisie ruling class. Furthermore, as Arrow pointed out, Marxists had long believed that the government serving capitalist interests had to be overcome through a transitional "dictatorship of the proletariat." After socialism was achieved, the future state of democracy was unclear in Marxist political philosophy. If the Soviet Union was taken as paradigmatic, then, according to Arrow, the association of socialism and totalitarianism must be acknowledged as "one overwhelming and very ugly fact" (30).

Arrow, however, is equally unconvinced of the necessary correlation between capitalism and democracy, for the nagging reason that this association, too, smacks of a "Marxoid" determinism, suggesting that, "the political 'superstructure' is basically determined by the 'relations of production.'" In observing that theorists need to study more carefully the relationship between democracy and capitalism, and the causal forces at play underlying the proposed mutual reinforcement of the two, Arrow makes a surprising claim. He observes that while "*political* liberties, freedom of speech and of the press, are so closely inherent in meaningful democracy as to constitute part of the definition, . . . [the] definition of 'democracy' must not include private property" (ibid.) Indirectly challenging Riker's skepticism of the United Kingdom's "constitutional dictatorship," Arrow suggests that in extending the definition of socialism to include "Labor Britain" and "socialist Sweden," "there would be no difficulty in refuting the connection between capitalism and democracy" (ibid.). Arrow concludes that "there is no convincing evidence or reasoning which would argue that a democratic-socialist movement is inherently self-contradictory" (31). Whereas Arrow acknowledges his having put "advocacy of a socialist world . . . on ice" due to the miscarriage of democratic freedoms in the Soviet Union, he still believes that socialism has validity that may more plausibly be explored given the economic stagflation of the 1970s (ibid.).

In closing his essay, Arrow reminds readers that there is a palpable manner in which "[s]ocial theories are also social facts." By this he means that, as Robert Merton earlier had alerted social scientists, theories can have "self-confirming" and "self-denying" properties (ibid.). Therefore, proponents of capitalism and opponents of Marxism should be cautious in their confidence itself having societal repercussions. Perhaps, for example, overzealous fear of socialism may have the opposite effect of reinforcing the Marxist model: "If 'conservatives' believe too strongly that any move to socialism undermines democracy, then they may indeed act in accordance with the 'Marxist' model, and vice versa" (ibid.). In making this observation Arrow hints at the fluidity of political discourse, even that of political theories relying on scientific analysis. Now, half a century after Schumpeter and Hayek's funereal dirges for capitalism and democracy have yielded to the widespread belief in the necessary correlation between democratic governments and free trade, it is timely to assess the degree to which rational choice theory itself has permeated and structured the discourse of American politics.

A recent essay by Edward Harpham and Richard Scotch addressing "economic discourse and policy analysis" seeks to sketch out the means by which economic analysis and economic professionalization have transformed the discourse, and in turn the practices, at the heart of American democratic politics.[17] Citing the examples of the Planning-Programming-Budgeting System and of the law and economics movement, the authors note that "[e]conomic analysis has become one of the principal languages through which we discuss public affairs in the modern democratic state." According to Harpham and Scotch, relying on the concept of self-interested rational man, "economic analysis represents a language of political discourse that has grown up alongside of other modes of discourse," namely, liberalism, civic humanist republicanism, and Marxism (215–17). The authors draw on the methodological work of J. G. A. Pocock and Quentin Skinner to argue that economic theorists who contribute to public policy analysis promote a singular language of political discourse that invests their subject matter with meaning created at the interface between political theory and practice: "The actual political world gives content and historical specificity to a particular language of political discourse" (217). Applied directly to rational choice theory, Harpham and Scotch's argument suggests both that its peculiar style of analysis shapes the political landscape of the Cold War period, and that it grows out of and responds to the concerns characterizing this specific political context.

Although Harpham and Scotch do not provide a detailed analysis of the means by which economic analysis became inseparable from the political discourse of late-twentieth-century American democracy, they are certain that this new movement of public policy analysis has left an indelible impression on public policy formation. This mark is evident in the increased objectivization of political decision procedures, and the manner in which this depoliticization of policymaking proceeds only at the peril of overlooking its own ideological roots. Similarly inspired by the works of Pocock and Skinner, one goal in recounting the origins and development of the rational choice approach to politics has been to recognize it as a rigorous intellectual movement while at the same time demonstrating its entanglement with the Cold War project of both advancing democracy and staving off the potential for authoritarian socialism. The ascendency of rational choice theory is inseparable from efforts to understand American politics and to establish a firm foundation for American constitutional democracy. This entangled, synchronous development does not detract from the intellectual rigor of rational choice theory, but does help to explain that its significance transcends the confines of academic social science departments. From the start, leading figures in the rational choice world both appreciated and enacted the relationship between social scientific inquiry based on individualism and rational self-interest and that based on public policy. Similarly, these theorists contributed to the efforts to provide a theoretical underpinning for democracy while undermining support for totalitarian communism. This coincidence of rational choice pursued as detached scientific inquiry with its defense of American democratic ideals puts into perspective the theory's goal to achieve the status of "objective science," and helps make explicit the interconnections between the late-twentieth-century triumph of liberal, market democracy and the preeminent status of rational choice theory in social science departments and professional schools.

Rational choice theory and its structuring of American political discourse and practice can be perceived as a direct response to Marxist social theory. Throughout the canon's commentaries on Marxism and communism, there is a reverberating ambivalence between the condemnation of Marxism and the acknowledgment that Marxist theory, based on economic self-interest and scientific analysis, can only be condemned at the risk of self-defeat. Hence, Olson equated Buchanan and Tullock's Virginia school with the radical Marxist Left, and Arrow recollected that, after all, Marx himself had claimed an indisputable association between capitalism and democracy. On the basis of their acceptance of individualism and rational self-interest, rational choice theorists were united in repudiating authoritarianism as an illegitimate form of government, yet room remained for rational choice theorists to disagree about nuances concerning the relationship between socialism and democracy. It is possible to conclude that rational choice theory responded to Marx and his followers by appropriating their positive findings in a rational choice theory of politics, while rejecting elements that smacked of coercive collectivism. It is not surprising that in view of the great empirical experiment of modern democracy, from its Jacobin excesses of the French Revolution to the totalitarian nightmare of Stalin's Russia, leading Cold War political and economic theorists positioned themselves to restructure its foundations by reconceptualizing them in explicit opposition to a collectivist or organic view of the state.

Nor is it surprising that in this process, rational choice theorists and policy analysts have themselves presented "a new language for discussing public affairs with its own grammar and vocabulary." [18] Neither is it shocking that in developing a new political discourse, this discourse has become indistinguishable from the world of politics that it describes. Flourishing in public policy schools, business schools, law schools, economics and political science departments, and embodying an approach to international finance and development economics at such familiar prominent nongovernmental organizations as the World Bank and the International Monetary Fund, rational choice theory has found its place at the heart of international and domestic political economy. However, the extent to which the rational choice approach to politics has invested political practices with meaning remains opaque to many observers.

Adding weight to the suggestive claims made by Harpham and Scotch, it is worth focusing on the evocative case of voting to demonstrate the entanglement of political discourse and practice characterizing rational choice scholarship. It is key to recognize the manner in which traditional political actions and concepts, such as voting and the public, are themselves invested with new meanings as rational choice theorists framed their significance in the unfamiliar language of self-interested rational action. We have seen how Tuck contrasts Olson's theory of the rational impossibility of collective action against the backdrop of traditional political discourse on the subject to illustrate a profound shift in the meaning of rational action. It is likewise possible to observe an equally dramatic shift in the meaning of voting and the concept of the "public." Harpham and Scotch criticize these shifts, observing that "[i]n a quest to impose an economic view on the world of the policymaking process, such actors could actually work to undermine the procedural and value foundations upon which the modern democratic state has been built." [19] However, the point here is that in understanding the history of rational choice theory's long-term involvement in articulating the foundations of democratic theory, it is better to be a savvy consumer of political discourse than either naively compliant or overzealously critical.

Rational choice theory dramatically reconstitutes political actions in the case of voting. Casting one's vote is the keystone act in democratic rule of, by, and for the people; for centuries, the privilege and practice of voting, representing a citizen's right to political expression and participation, has been deemed the fundamental legitimating principle of democratic government. Since the 1957 publication of Anthony Downs's *Economic Theory of Democracy,* rational choice theorists have struggled to explain why people vote. Downs proposed that from the individual perspective, since one vote rarely makes a difference, it is irrational to vote. This troublesome result has led, over the ensuing decades, to a vast literature attempting to build rational choice models that explain individuals' voting behavior.[20] Early models built an account of voting on the basis of instrumental action; they strove to assess what an individual stood to gain from casting her vote versus the cost of educating herself about the candidates and traveling to the polling place. Whether using the methods of expected utility theory, decisionmaking under uncertainty invoking regret, or game-theoretic strategic interactions, theorists repeatedly failed to explain voting behavior using an instrumental rational choice model.[21] This result implies that either citizens who vote are irrational according to the precepts of rational choice theory, or that they derive satisfaction from voting in ways other than having a direct effect on the election's outcome.

The inability of rational choice theory to support a model that adequately explains voting became a major source of contention and dismay from the 1970s to the 1990s. Critics of the rational choice method took full advantage of this theoretical impasse.[22] In rational choice terms, the "voters' paradox" seemed to be a classic case of collective action in which the democratic decisionmaking process requires voters' input, but each voter has the incentive to free ride on others' participation given the insignificance of his single vote. And yet voters do participate in the polling process, often at great personal risk, as was the case for African Americans in the Jim Crow south during the 1950s and remains true today in many elections in Latin America. One public choice theorist admits that the "rationality of voting is the Achilles' heel of rational choice theory in political science. Public choice theorists themselves divide over the question of whether turnout can be considered a rational decision."[23]

What is clear in the midst of this theoretical controversy is the malleability of both social practices and theories of those practices. An action—voting—deemed eminently worthwhile and self-justified in early American democracy has taken on an entirely new significance in a rational choice theory of politics. As theorists struggle to make a meaningful fit between models and empirical reality, they participate in enacting the democratic politics in question. Of interest is the direction rational choice models have taken in response to the failure of an instrumental account of voting: it has become standard among practitioners to regard voting as an "act of consumption."[24] In this new approach to understanding voters' behavior, the possibility that individuals derive satisfaction from sources external to the instrumental activity of casting the winning vote has led theorists to surmise that voting is no different from, for instance, showing support to the home team at a baseball game.[25] Thus, instead of a purely instrumental action, voting has come to be regarded by rational choice theorists as an "expressive act," in which a voter's goal is no more than "expressing one's preferences."[26] Voting is regarded as "consumption" because the satisfaction conveyed by the act lies in realizing the opportunity to articulate one's opinion; it is not intended to achieve any result in the polity. With this interpretation of voting, the alleged paradox of voting is purportedly to be resolved.[27]

On the strength of this resolution to the problem posed by voting, rational choice scholars have been able to make progress in interpreting the outcomes of elections.[28] However, what theorists have ended up proposing is akin to a consumer model of democracy in which the democratic process is not a means to participatory government so much as it is a means for individuals to "consume." This may seem like an insignificant matter of semantics, but the interpretive features of this account of voting reach deep into the legitimating principle of democracy, echoing Eric Hobsbawm's claim that traditional models of participatory democracy are yielding to market sovereignty.[29] Consistent with Arrow's *Social Choice and Individual Values,* citizens' sovereignty is defined in terms of their autonomy as consumers, not in terms of the traditional understanding of sovereignty as self-rule. The resolution of the "voter's paradox" by a consumption model of voting is an artifact of a particular historically and culturally localized political discourse that is inseparable from political practice. The change in the significance associated with the act of voting is peculiar to the rational choice interpretation of individual rational action.

It may seem that this invocation of a market language to sustain sovereignty is no more than an expression of the reality that *Homo economicus* is storming the polis. That is, it may give the impression that in the two-century-long history of modern liberal democracies, democracy is yielding to the market as a means of achieving collective social order. This interpretation of the rise of rational choice theory is incorrect insofar as it fails to appreciate that the flux in social practice is not limited to democracy, but is relevant to markets as well. Jürgen Habermas, in his two-volume *Theory of Communicative Action* advances a densely woven argument that, over the past two centuries, markets have increasingly "colonized" spheres of action that were formerly regulated by communicative social practices.[30] This sentiment is not unique to Habermas; it has been similarly argued that "[m]oney dissolves social ties, founds a society based on pure rationality and kills personal relationships . . . it seals the triumph of *gesellschaft* over *gemeinschaft*."[31] The argument that markets represent one form of rationality, and that this instrumental, means-to-an-end approach to action is engulfing traditional networks of association based on communicative exchanges and familial ties, misses the point that rational choice theory is not simply a reiteration of an atemporal, monolithic, self-explanatory, and universal "rationality." It is important to recall that for Adam Smith, market transactions themselves were inherently discursive and dialogic. For Smith, trade was indistinct from reasoning and speaking, and ultimately from the spirit of the Enlightenment.[32] In Smith's words, "the offering of a shilling, which to us appears to have so plain and simple a meaning, is in reality offering an argument to persuade one to do so and so as it is for his interest. . . . And in this manner every one is practising oratory on others through the whole of life."[33] For Smith, writing in the eighteenth century, trade mirrored a conversation in which oratory and monetary structures of meaning were inseparable.

This awareness, that eighteenth-century market exchanges may not be so easily regarded as anonymous transactions between disjunctive individuals whose activities are regulated purely by calculation and money, makes it possible to see that just as political practices have changed over two centuries, so has the market. The understandings of both the market and politics in the early years of the twenty-first century increasingly offer an understanding of human interactions as regulated by rational self-interest and not necessarily mediated through linguistic discussion. Thus, a consumption account of voting is consistent with a definition of sovereignty granted to consumers instead of to citizens. In acknowledging this shift in understanding of the fundamental practice of voting, however, it is important not to reify the market as an atemporal social institution. The rational choice approach to democracy and to political economy is itself distinct from earlier understandings of the market, and yet is entangled with the institutionalized procedures that it studies. Therefore, the growing phenomenon of voting apathy may itself be indistinguishable from the perspective afforded by rational choice theory holding that it is irrational to vote.

PART III

Antecedents to Rational Choice Theory

CHAPTER 6

Adam Smith's System of Natural Liberty

The natural effort of every individual to better his own condition, when suffered to exert itself with freedom and security, is so powerful a principle, that it is alone, and without any assistance, not only capable of carrying on the society to wealth and prosperity, but of surmounting a hundred impertinent obstructions with which the folly of human laws too often incumbers its operations; though the effect of these obstructions is always more or less either to encroach upon its freedom, or to diminish its security.
Adam Smith

The great difficulty, for the political theorists of the enlightened disposition, was how to describe a universe, or a society, in which everybody has opinions and theories and conflicting, changing desires. It was to make a "system" out of the innumerable, swerving *moleculae* of individual reflections and sentiments.
Emma Rothschild

[T]he social order of the market can degenerate into the disorder of anarchy unless market relationships are embedded within a constitutional-legal framework where individual rights of person and property are well-defined, mutually respected and enforced.
James M. Buchanan

IN the mid-1940s, Joseph Schumpeter, Friedrich Hayek, and Karl Popper believed it possible that socialism or communism could triumph over capitalism and democracy, with the consequent loss of both personal freedom and the unfettered ability to pursue truth. For each of them, socialism was inseparable from an authoritarian "Big Brother" regime that threatened individual freedom and even rational inquiry. Schumpeter argued that socialism, which he felt likely to be in store for the United States, would ultimately devolve into monopolist state power unless pluralism were guaranteed by economic competition of diverse interests. Hayek, too, was pessimistic about the future of democracy and economic liberty; he thought that individual freedom was the necessary bulwark against the downfall into first socialism, and then fascism. Popper detested Marx's historical determinism, and believed that democratic social institutions and rational inquiry were the means to obviate the revolutionary discontent bred by economic injustices.

The rational choice approach to politics and policy, the development of which was inextricably bound up with America's Cold War political quest to strategically best the Soviet Union, rested squarely on the three pillars of rational decisionmaking, objective scientific inquiry, and a partnership of democratic and economic freedom. Kenneth Arrow, James Buchanan, and William Riker each sought to avert the potential rise of philosophical idealism and organic conceptions of statehood that they were convinced lead to the subjugation of the human spirit. As a consequence of the vastly different historical and cultural circumstances of the mid-twentieth century compared to the present, the capacity of rational choice theory to methodologically refute an authoritarian or political idealist philosophy goes largely unnoticed. While Buchanan's opposition to Keynesianism, socialism, and collectivism within the American polity is clear, it is less obvious that the underlying target of his analysis is Karl Marx, whose abiding genius is defined by "his acute understanding of the possible reaction of the ignorant intellectual to the workings of the capitalist or market order." [1] Buchanan's antidote to "[t]he community, the society, the organic unity of the group, the state" remains constant throughout his work: a partnership of Adam Smith's political economy with the democratic politics of the Founding Fathers, both celebrating individual freedom. [2]

The goal of this chapter is to describe another aspect of rational choice theory's development. Instead of focusing on the construction of a theory that favored a version of democracy and economic liberalism free from the looming threat of authoritarianism or collectivism, here I consider how it became customary to reassert the foundations of American democracy and free-market economy by looking back to Enlightenment social philosophy. This tendency to promote democracy, science, and capitalism as fundamental building blocks of modern Western civilization that were enunciated between the Renaissance and the Enlightenment is present in Hayek's *Road to Serfdom*. [3] For Hayek, as for rational choice theorists, the crux of the connection between the commitment to liberty in the spheres of economics, politics, and science is that of an individual's freedom to determine her own ends. [4] It is this emphasis on individual freedom that makes it possible to draw a correlation between Cold War visions of freedom cast in opposition to totalitarian repression and Adam

Smith's espousal of the principle of individual liberty. This reflection is aptly expressed by R. S. Downie in commenting on the apparently countervailing principles of "sympathy" and "self-interest" in Smith's *The Theory of Moral Sentiments* (1759) and *An Inquiry into the Nature and Causes of the Wealth of Nations* (1776).[5] Claiming that "free choice" is essential to Smith's view of the self, Downie observes that "[i]nsofar as a person is prevented, either by the might of the State or by its paternalism, from exercising his 'rational will' his humanity will atrophy."[6]

It is historically myopic to presume that the American rational choice theorists reinvented American economic and political liberalism by adopting the template of "Enlightenment thought" and transposing it into the language of rational choice theory. Similarly, however, it is misleading to assume that Arrow, Buchanan, and Riker constructed a vision of liberalism *ex nihilo,* without resort to the long-standing political tradition bequeathed them by both American and European Enlightenment thinkers. As is evident, for example, in the writings of James Buchanan, rational choice theorists have seized upon Enlightenment political and economic theory as having a clarity of insight before its nineteenth-century subversion by romantic notions of statehood and Marx's critique. My principle goal in this chapter, without which this book is not complete, is to explore the continuities and ruptures between the rational choice approach to political economy and liberalism and that of the Enlightenment political economists epitomized by Adam Smith. I depend on clues given by contemporary rational choice scholars to identify Enlightenment themes and values that have been important to their work, and explore ways in which rational choice theory offers a radical departure from previous contributions to liberalism.

In order to make sense of what may otherwise turn into an undifferentiated sea of either "Enlightenment" or "liberal" thought, it is necessary to be precise in setting up our analysis. In exploring the relationship between rational choice theory and classic political economy, it is possible to select from a wide number of representative figures. In addition to James Madison and Thomas Jefferson, other possible candidates are Benedict Spinoza and David Hume, and reaching a little further back in time, John Locke and Thomas Hobbes.[7] More than any other, however, it is Adam Smith's system of natural liberty that offers the clearest instance of Enlightenment ideas against which to measure rational choice liberalism. As will be explored in the context of James Buchanan's writings, Smith, who is commonly thought to have based his analysis of political economy on "self interest" and who put forth the idea that social prosperity is "spontaneously" achieved within a just legal framework, has special relevance to rational choice scholars' concern with collective action problems characterizing government.

Smith's social scientific analysis of the human institutions of justice and political economy is widely thought to be a key blueprint for political economy, and is recognized by rational choice theorists as setting the norm for the study of collective actions problems in terms of individual self-interest. Commenting on the connection between Enlightenment "liberalism" and the present-day world, Gordon Schochet observes:

> For the most part, the principle terms of twentieth-century English-language politics were in place by 1800. . . . This vocabulary came from the newer and increasingly hegemonic juridical discourse and comprised the more-or-less coherent body of doctrine that would come to be known as "liberalism." The so-called "triumph" of that liberal ideology was facilitated by the dominance in British philosophy after Hume of "empiricism," an outlook that is sympathetic to a skeptical individualism in morals and politics. The legal construct "state" eventually replaced the more humanistic "commonwealth," and its members were "citizens" in a modern sense whose "rights," "interest," "properties," and "liberties" were the reasons for political action as well as limitations on public "authority." The point of politics was to protect and enhance rights and liberties—which were now conceived of as *entitlements* that preceded organized politics and government rather than as *privileges* which were their creations—and not civic virtue. . . . The substitution of interest for personal virtue as the ultimate end of *politics* was accompanied by a transformation in the meaning of *justice*.[8]

My point in quoting this passage is not to overstate the commonalties between eighteenth-century society and twentieth-century society, but to draw attention to the profound sense in which present-day concepts and institutions achieved their purchase on the contemporary imagination and practices as a function of their past establishment.

This chapter does not comprehensively discuss either the Enlightenment or liberalism, but instead focuses on the political philosophy of Adam Smith as germane to the set of social innovations constituting liberalism, and hence suitable for comparing to the perspective on liberalism adopted by rational choice scholars. As Schochet observes, this set of entangled theories and practices involves the embrace of individualism, epistemological skepticism about morals and social norms, and an emphasis on an appropriate juridical structure that balances an individual's rights against the rights of others. Adam Smith not only was involved centrally in the eighteenth-century discussion of these ideas, but also is recognized by rational choice theorists as working within the theoretical confines of nonnormative social science, a secularized concept of sovereignty, and self-interested individualism.[9] To best compare the broad category of Enlightenment political philosophy with rational choice theory, I focus on the theoretical resonance between Adam Smith's system of natural liberty and James Buchanan's public choice theory. In addressing the conjunction between these two, it is possible to gain insight into the relationship between classical political economy and rational choice liberalism.

Comparing Smith's system of natural liberty with contemporary rational choice liberalism involves running the risk of historiographical pitfalls. Several perspectives are in play simultaneously: rational choice liberalism as a contemporary branch of scholarship; the relationship between rational choice liberalism and earlier liberal philosophies, in this case Smith's; the relationship that rational choice theorists believe themselves to have with their Enlightenment predecessors; and the question of what type of "authentic" access is available to Enlightenment thought, or Adam Smith's thought, in order to achieve a legitimate vantage point for comparison. Each of these considerations poses a challenge to our goal of uncovering the relationship between rational choice liberalism and Enlightenment ideas of liberty. This goal is facilitated by recent historiography of both the Scottish Enlightenment and Adam Smith.

Scholarly assessments of the work of Adam Smith have varied from the rapid early-nineteenth-century reconstitution of Smith's legacy to be consistent with anti-Jacobin political conservatism, to the late-nineteenth-century German economists' puzzle over reconciling *Theory of Moral Sentiments,* apparently predicated on "sympathy," with *Wealth of Nations,* cast in terms of "self-interest."[10] While there was a lull in Smith studies in the early twentieth century, characterized by the 1926 observation by E. Cannan that "[v]ery little of Adam Smith's scheme of economics has been left standing by subsequent inquirers," the period from the 1920s to the mid-1980s witnessed an exponential growth of interest.[11] Between the 1950s and the 1970s, scholars wrestled with the relationship between the economic and political domains in Smith's works, the one calling for hands-off *laissez faire,* and the other implying some role for active governmental intervention.[12] In the 1970s and early 1980s, new editions of Smith's works were published, indicating the newfound attention they were receiving.[13]

The fascination with Smith has continued past the close of the twentieth century, with recent scholarship divided into two discernible branches, one guided in its mission by the historical effort to understand Smith in eighteenth-century terms, and the other more interested in understanding Smith's relevance to contemporary political economy.[14] Examples of these two branches of study are collected in a group of essays edited by Thomas

Wilson and Andrew S. Skinner, which includes contributions by rational choice theorists Mancur Olson, Charles Rowley, and James Buchanan.[15] This collection of essays, originally presented as part of a conference, makes evident the often close association of Smith scholarship with Cold War concerns of shoring up the theoretical foundations for Western society in view of the threat of communism. Thomas Wilson's essay discussing the principles of sympathy and self-interest in Smith suggests that it may be possible to associate a misguided understanding of sympathy with the underlying principles of communism.[16] Wilson concludes that it is most appropriate to associate self-interest with the market, and sympathy with "private charity . . . [and] the mechanism of the welfare state."[17]

While much of the contemporary effort to revitalize interest in Adam Smith has proceeded from the active ferment of interest in contemporary economics, historians have initiated a renaissance of understanding of Smith by firmly contextualizing his writings within the Scottish Enlightenment. Inspired by J. G. A. Pocock's reexamination of Machiavelli, a number of scholars have explored the competing traditions of civic humanism and natural jurisprudence in Smith's *Theory of Moral Sentiments* and *Wealth of Nations*.[18] This historiographical debate between the two perspectives of civic republicanism versus rights-based jurisprudence, while generating a virtual consensus on the significance of both perspectives, has also produced a cornucopia of insights into Smith work. Many of these insights promise fruitful exploration for the roots of rational choice scholarship in Smith's Enlightenment political economy: Smith is often recognized for his confidence in self-interest as fundamental to social order; he can be understood to have helped establish a rights-based, negative liberties, jurisprudential framework for political economy; he is committed to studying the unintended consequences of human actions; and he is often cited for supporting a view of justice upholding economic efficiency over distributional concerns. Each of these features in Smith's texts could be assessed from the perspective of "[t]he historian, searching the past for the seeds of the present" in the current form of rational choice theory.[19]

James Buchanan is the rational choice theorist who has most explored Enlightenment thought generally, and Adam Smith in particular, and has discussed how his theory of classic liberalism relates to Smith's system of natural liberty as expressed in *Wealth of Nations*. The first section of this chapter traces Buchanan's account of the relationship between public choice theory and Smith's analysis of political economy. In the process, several points of commonality between the two become evident, including the emphasis on individual freedom and on nonnormative and non-teleological methodology, and a supposition of unordered social order that arises within the context of an appropriate legal framework. But in exploring these commonalties, a significant difference between the two becomes equally apparent: whereas Buchanan relies exclusively on the principle of rational self-interest to model political economy, Smith relies on both the sentiments of self-interest and sympathy.

In order to flesh out the comparison between Smith and Buchanan, the second section of this chapter relies on recent contributions to Smith scholarship to better our understanding of Smith's system of natural liberty less colored by present concerns, and more true to its Enlightenment social and political context. This section discusses the role "sympathy" plays in Smith's system of justice: I argue that for Smith justice cannot be translated into the terms of self-interest, whereas for Buchanan the legal framework structuring a society is derived exclusively from individuals' calculated self-interest; for Smith justice arises as the unintended consequence of sympathy.

The first two sections of this chapter discuss Buchanan's interpretation of Smith's writings, and their relationship to public choice theory. A concluding section examines the looser claim of some rational choice theorists that Smith and rational choice scholars are united in their methodological reliance on "rational self-interest." Whereas Buchanan is cautious and modest in his reading of Smith, focusing, for example, on Smith's principle of "bettering one's condition" as providing the underlying motive force of political economy rather than "rational self-interest," others are not so restrained. The concluding section poses the question of the accuracy of locating "self-interested rational actors" in Smith's world. It finds that for Smith, self-interest can corrupt rational deliberation if not mediated by self-command. Even the closest cousin to the self-interested rational actor in Smith, the prudent man, cannot be transposed readily into the vocabulary of rational choice.

James M. Buchanan's "Adam Smith"

In the *Calculus of Consent*, Buchanan, writing with Tullock, believes their investigation into the logic of constitutional design is undertaken in the spirit of the American Founding Fathers and various Enlightenment philosophers. They recognize Hobbes, Spinoza, Hume, and Adam Smith as presenting important precursors to their theory of self-interested rational calculation underlying legitimate constitutional design.[20] In assessing Buchanan's voluminous writings over the better part of half a century, however, one Enlightenment figure looms larger than all the rest for having set forth an analysis of political economy that most closely resembles Buchanan's own theory—namely, Adam Smith. The numerous references to Smith scattered throughout Buchanan's texts leave no doubt that in Buchanan's assessment, crucial similarities characterize the two systems, notwithstanding the two centuries separating them.

Buchanan believes it is necessary to recover Enlightenment principles and ideas that had been lost during the dark times of socialist collectivism, and that the vital importance of public choice theory is that it represents a continuation of classical political economy:

> Warren Nutter was fond of saying in, in the sometimes bleak days of the 1950s and early 1960s [Keynesian digression], that one of our most important functions was to "save the books." . . . Classical liberalism—the ideas and the analysis that nurtured these ideals for a society that became a near reality—need not perish from the earth. As the saying on Fred Galhe's Colorado T-shirt goes, "Adam Smith was right—pass it on." [21]

For Buchanan and other public choice theorists, Marxism, Keynesianism, and any other version of social collectivism are dangerous dead ends that can be avoided by returning to the path blazed by Adam Smith: "[T]here has been a loss of wisdom in this respect, a loss from eighteenth century levels, and the message of Adam Smith requires reiteration with each generation." [22] Buchanan reasserts the fundamental principles of American capitalist democracy by revisiting the wisdom of Smith, who upheld the primacy of self-interest in economic relations and emphasized the importance of individual freedom in exchange. In this way, public choice theorists may be viewed as appropriating basic insights from Enlightenment political economy as they participate in a "project of modernity" engendered by Enlightenment predecessors. Although there may be many other ways to conceptualize this project, within the context of rational choice theory it is best understood as a commitment to individual freedom, a belief in rational inquiry, a secularized notion of sovereignty, and a legal framework coordinating self-interested ends.

Buchanan writes that all he has done, throughout his work, is to apply Smith's basic insight that individuals have the propensity to truck, barter, and exchange; Buchanan insists that "we commence concentrating on the origins, properties, and institutions of *exchange,* broadly considered. Adam Smith's propensity to truck and barter one thing for another—this becomes the proper object for our research and inquiry." [23] Not only is the individual the primary subject of analysis, but for Buchanan, the principle of exchange is key because it focuses on individuals' freely made choices regarding what they prefer; exchange implies voluntary transactions among individuals who make their own decisions about what they want. Each individual, focused on his own ends and achieving his own goals, trades possessions and enters into binding agreement with others, yielding the result that each is better off since voluntary exchange is characterized by mutual advantage. In Buchanan's view, economic freedom to exchange is perhaps the most fundamental form of human freedom that makes others, such as political freedom and freedom of inquiry, possible.

According to Buchanan, through the principle of exchange, Smith and other Enlightenment thinkers came to realize that individuals' self-interested pursuit expressed in voluntary exchanges results in a prosperous and harmonious social order. He sketches the intellectual history of this theoretical development:

> [T]he eighteenth-century contribution was to construct the bridge between *homo economicus* on the one hand and "social welfare" or "group interest" on the other. [Bernard] Mandeville, Hume, and Smith did not invent the notion of self-seeking, autonomous man. Such a person had been around for centuries, and he had been emphatically brought to philosophical consciousness by Thomas Hobbes in the seventeenth century. By building on the Hobbesian contractual insights, and by postulating the possible existence of the limited sovereign in the sense articulated by John Locke, the eighteenth-century philosophers demonstrated that, within constrained behavioural limits, the self-interested motivation on the part of individuals might promote the welfare of the whole community of persons.[24]

In this passage, Buchanan combines the idea of self-interested exchange with the concepts of spontaneous coordination and a duly constituted legal framework, which establishes the parameters for both voluntary exchange and the enhancement of individuals' welfare. In articulating this insight, Buchanan believes he is consistent with Smith, who also proposes a system in which social harmony arises as the consequence of individuals' pursuit of self-interest constrained only by the laws of justice. Reiterating this crucial insight structuring both public choice theory and Smith's system of natural liberty, Buchanan observes:

> The great discovery of the eighteenth-century philosophers was that, within appropriately designed laws and institutions, separately self-interested individual behaviour in the market generates a spontaneous order, a pattern of allocational-distributional outcomes that is chosen by no one, yet which is properly classified as an order in that it reflects the . . . values of the participating persons.[25]

The crucial ideas expressed here are that individuals pursue personal goals by engaging with others in exchanges from which all parties gain, and that for the process of mutual gain to be guaranteed, individuals must obey laws prohibiting the violation of others' personhood and property. Buchanan's reliance on the ideas of individual liberty constrained by a legitimate legal framework that serves to spontaneously coordinate individuals' ends is key not only to understanding rational choice liberalism, but also to understanding the relationship between public choice theory and classical political economy.

Buchanan asks what went astray in social theory as the Enlightenment political economists were followed by nineteenth-century Marxist philosophy, and the twentieth-century experiment with communism and socialism. He finds the answer in the "corruption" of economics following the 1840s.[26] The initial corruption Buchanan here refers to proceeded from Marx's critique of the efficiency of markets, hence "[t]he distributional implications of market coordination were moved to center stage, providing grounds for revolutionary political proposals that were well beyond any mercantilist schemes for political management of national economies" (69). Almost simultaneously, Buchanan claims, Hegel launched a romantic notion of the state, "a model that came to be increasingly dominant, an idealist vision of an omniscient and benevolent collective entity" (ibid.). Alongside political idealism, classic utilitarian philosophy arose and was also swayed by the romantic theory of statehood: "the romantic model of the state became the source for totally unwarranted comparisons between the market order, as observed in operation, and the state as idealized" (ibid.). Buchanan finds classic utilitarian political philosophy flawed in a way similar to idealized political theory because it presupposes the existence of "maximum social well-being" as the sum of individuals' well-being; therefore he denounces this utilitarian enterprise for clinging to idealized concepts of social welfare.[27] For Buchanan, Smith's commitment to individual freedom represents the preventive to various forms of collectivism, whether that of Hegel or Marx, classic utilitarians, Keynes, or even the residual collectivism he finds in general equilibrium theory suggesting an "artificially forced and warranted extension beyond individual choice to collectivities, to macrounits, to society, to the economy."[28]

As Buchanan tells the story, game theory broke social scientists out of the habit of formulating their research initiatives in terms of the mathematics of collective units characterizing marginal economics and post-Marshall economics.[29] Buchanan judges that most contributions to economic theory since Adam Smith are bastardizations of individual freedom realized through trade. For this reason Buchanan claims that in recovering the central principle regarding the primacy of the individual, public choice theory returns to the insights of classical political economy after a two-century exodus in the desert of coercive and sterile social theory. In rescuing the past insights of Enlightenment philosophers, game theory provides contemporary public choice theorists with the mathematical capability to push aside the fixation with collective welfare dogging marginalist and general equilibrium economics. In game theory, collective outcomes can only be assessed from the perspective of whether any individual would have had reason to select a different course of action, thereby resulting in a different overarching outcome.

Buchanan is himself aware of the steps public choice theory takes beyond Smith's system of political economy.[30] In Buchanan's assessment, Smith applies the principles of self-interest and voluntary exchange to markets, but stops short of applying them to political decisionmaking. This reading of Smith coincides with that of Emma Rothschild in *Economic Sentiments*. Rothschild emphasizes that whereas Smith points out the efficacy of individual freedom to trade in the economic sphere, he is doubtful that laws enacted by politicians, more than likely serving merchants' interests, can do more than pervert the system of natural liberty. Rothschild thus finds that whereas Smith celebrates voluntary exchange in markets, he is dubious about the efficacy of political interference of any sort in free trade; Smith's system of natural liberty "requires both good institutions and good norms, whereby individuals pursue their interests within the rules of well-defined games, and not by seeking to influence institutions and rules."[31] According to Rothschild, Smith suggests that political regulation will only serve the interests of rulemakers, and that enlightened statesmen seek to avoid political interference, trusting instead to the free market to coordinate individuals' efforts.

Buchanan agrees with Smith that laws will reflect the interests of politicians; however, he proposes a different solution emphasizing this attribute of human behavior instead of curtailing it. Buchanan extends the principle of self-interested action to politicians, thereby accomplishing two theoretical goals. The first is to denounce the ideas of "public servants" and a "benevolent state." The second is to suggest that all individuals are best served by pursuing their interests as actively in the political arena as they do in the market arena. Only then, Buchanan claims, will individuals achieve the constitution and laws that appropriately reflect their interests. Buchanan realizes that his proposed solution accepting political machination differs from Smith, and he characterizes this shift as a union of Smith's political economy with the democratic theory of James Madison and Thomas Jefferson. Elaborating this element in public choice theory, Buchanan explains:

> When persons are modelled as self-interested in politics, as in other aspects
> of their behaviour, the constitutional challenge becomes one of construct-
> ing and designing framework institutions or rules that will, to the maxi-
> mum extent possible, limit the exercise of such interest in exploitative ways
> and direct such interest to furtherance of the general interest.[32]

Buchanan is suggesting that the process of constitutional design gains legitimacy when it grows out of individuals' self-interest in the same way
that market transactions reflect individuals' interests. Public choice theory preserves the centrality of voluntary exchange in markets and extends
it to the political sphere, in keeping with James Madison's view of democratic politics as a balance of individually expressed self-interests articulated in the Federalist Papers.[33] Therefore, public choice theory is best understood as a combination of Smith's political economy and Madison's
democratic theory: spontaneous political order arises from individuals'
pursuit of self-interest in the political arena. This political order is manifest in the legal framework that structures a society. Game theory is most
useful for modeling this order because it assesses rational self-interest to
determine what legal framework best serves individuals' independently
construed goals. In taking into consideration individuals' self-determined
interests, game theory analyzes the effects of alternative rule sets on
individuals' fates to determine which rule set best reflects individuals'
interests.

As Buchanan is the first to recognize, understanding the political process as mirroring the process of the free market involves a feature of public choice theory that departs from Smith's political economy. Buchanan's
self-acknowledged departure from Smith's system of natural liberty, then,
serves as the marker for clearly distinguishing between public choice theory and classical political economy. Buchanan reveres Smith's dedication
to individual freedom and to spontaneous social coordination within a
framework of just law. However, he departs from Smith in not only building his analysis on individual self-interest as expressed in politics, but also
in arguing that correct analysis of individuals' self-interest leads to the
construction of a legitimate constitution. Thus, Smith and Buchanan differ in their analysis of how justice (in the case of Smith) and constitutional
order (in the case of Buchanan) are brought about. For Smith, justice is the
unintended consequence of individuals' natural tendency to feel sympathy
when one person is wronged by another; for Buchanan, constitutional order arises out of the self-interested agreements individuals reach in considering how constitutional rules will affect their lives. While both theorists uphold the freedom of the individual in trade, look to "unordered
order" instead of to economic prosperity achieved through governmental

regulation, and consider a legal framework of justice necessary, the two differ markedly in their appraisals of how the legal order is affected.

Adam Smith's System of Natural Liberty

While lauding Smith's wisdom as a light still shining after two centuries, Buchanan makes a notable move beyond him in asserting that self-interest is the sole principle sustaining political economy and constitutional order, and the only mover of politics and markets. Thus, Buchanan carries over to present-day understanding only one of the two organizing principles crucial to Smith's *Theory of Moral Sentiments* and *Inquiry into the Nature and Causes of the Wealth of Nations*. As Buchanan would do, Smith upholds both free markets and the regulation of society by law; however, unlike Buchanan, Smith claims that it is the human sentiment of sympathy that gives rise to justice. Furthermore, for Smith, sympathy is neither motivated by self-interest, nor serves self-interest indirectly by grounding justice. It is key that in Smith's theory of justice, sympathy "cannot, in any sense, be regarded as a selfish principle" derived from "self-love."[34] Indeed, unchecked, self-love is the source of many of the disorders of human life" (III.4.6). Therefore, for Smith, justice and morality must originate in features of the human character not bound up with personal ambitions.

Smith's commitment to the dictates of natural philosophy in his reflections on political economy and justice is remarkable. His *Theory of Moral Sentiments* and *Wealth of Nations* are widely considered to be Enlightenment texts because Smith adopts a naturalistic mode of explanation that avoids recourse to theistic or teleological rationales. This commitment to natural philosophy resonates with contemporary rational choice theorists' insistence on nonnormative scientific inquiry. In avoiding theistic or teleological explanations for social institutions, Smith proposes instead an "efficient causes" methodology: whereas the efficient cause of material prosperity is individuals' inclination to better their own circumstances, the efficient cause of justice is sympathy.

According to Smith, if one conceives of human society as a grand system, or machine, akin to the physical universe, finding "in every part of the universe . . . means adjusted with the nicest artifice to the ends which they are intended to produce," it is tempting to explain both the world of nature at large and human society in terms of "final causes," with which all things are imbued and which directs them to a final end. However, natural philosophy dictates that the only valid explanations are of efficient, not final, causes. Thus, for Smith, in studying the process of digestion or blood circulation, explanations resorting to the final end of "the great purposes of animal life" are inappropriate. Similarly, in accounting for the operation of a mechanical watch, it is misguided to look to any desire or intention on the component parts of the watch for its achievement of smooth operation or accurate time-telling. Of course, it is the watch-maker's intent to produce such a mechanism, but "in accounting for the operations of bodies, we never fail to distinguish in this manner the efficient from the final cause" (*TMS* II.ii.3.5). God's final causes are achieved through efficient causes, and "we never ascribe any such desire or intention to . . . [the wheels of a watch], but to the watch-maker, and we know that they are put into motion by a spring, which intends the effect as little as they do" (ibid.). Thus, the principal lesson of natural philosophy, which Smith steadfastly applies to the study of human society, is that aggregate outcomes, or final causes, must be explained as the unintended consequence of individual agents. For Smith, it is not appropriate to propose that social prosperity results from the direct intention of individuals; neither is it accurate to hold that the rule of law is a product of individuals' intention to create a just society. This theme is fundamental to both Smith's *Theory of Moral Sentiments* and *Wealth of Nations,* and is shared James Buchanan and rational choice theorists in general. The primary distinction between Smith's approach and that of rational choice theory is that for the former, both sympathy and self-love animate individuals, whereas for the latter, only rational self-interest explains individuals' actions.[35]

Wealth of Nations might best be considered as a rigorous, empirically informed analysis of the means by which individuals' efforts to promote their own interests result in overall betterment. These means include more effective production through the division of labor that arises "in a society where things were left to follow their natural course, where there was perfect liberty, and where every man was perfectly free both to chuse what occupation he thought proper, and to change it as often as he thought proper." [36] Unregulated trade, or "perfect liberty," permits a commodity's market price rise to its natural price (I.vii.30). Individuals would employ their stock most effectively, and since a society's total annual revenue is "always precisely equal to the exchangeable value of the whole annual produce of its industry," again individuals' efforts on their own behalf add up to overall benefit. Thus, for example, when an individual prefers

> the support of deomestick to that of foreign industry, he intends ownly his own security; and by directing that industry in such a manner as its produce may be of the greatest value, he intends only his own gain, and he is in this, as in may other cases, led by an invisible hand to promote an end which was

no part of his intention. . . . By pursuing his own interest he frequently promotes that of the society more effectively than when he really intends to
promote it. (IV.ii.9)

As Buchanan emphasizes, Smith points to the potential of unleashed individual freedom to pursue one's own interests, thereby profiting all who
participate in the voluntary trade transactions.

Crucially, for Smith as for Buchanan, the "obvious and simple system
of natural liberty" requires that freedom be secured through the imposition of justice. Individuals must be secure in their possessions:

> Commerce and manufactures can seldom flourish long in any state which
> does not enjoy a regular administration of justice, in which the people do
> not feel themselves secure in their possession of their property, in which the
> faith of contracts is not supported by law, and in which the authority of the
> state is not supposed to be regularly employed in enforcing the payment of
> debts from all those who are able to pay. (V.iii.7)

"The rules of justice are accurate in the highest degree, and admit of no
exceptions or modifications," and pertain to the violation of a person
through theft of property, physical attack and murder, or breech of promise.[37] Protecting individual rights to self-betterment through the imposition of justice guarantees "the highest degree of prosperity" for a society:

> That security which the laws in Great Britain give to every man that he shall
> enjoy the fruits of his own labour, is alone sufficient to make any country
> flourish, notwithstanding these and twenty other absurd regulations of
> commerce. . . . The natural effort of every individual to better his own con-
> dition, when suffered to exert itself with freedom and security, is so power-
> ful a principle, that it is alone, and without assistance, not only capable of
> carrying on the society to wealth and prosperity, but of surmounting a hun-
> dred impertinent obstructions with which the folly of human laws too of-
> ten incumbers its operations.[38]

Smith's system forms a seamless, architectonic whole—a sphere of
freedom for individual industry limited only by just laws, which, like the
system of political economy, arise of their own accord. Legitimate laws
protect individuals' rights but do not encroach on individual freedoms in
the attempt to legislate social outcomes. Legitimate laws construct a
framework for the achievement of material prosperity, given the universal
principle of individual industriousness.[39] Put in today's terms, the system
of natural liberty may be described as a "noninterventionist" framework
that guarantees the coordination of interests into a socially beneficial outcome; "the function . . . of the laws of justice is to maximise the compatibility of individual persons' pursuit of their own aims."[40] The passage

just quoted is glib in ascribing the concept of "maximization" to Smith,[41] yet its familiar language cuts through two centuries of political discourse to reveal Smith's path-breaking contribution to political theory. Smith helped set the precedent that the task of the political theorist is identifying an institutional structure that upholds individual freedom and simultaneously coordinates individuals' self-interested actions in a mutually beneficial way within a duly constituted legal system.

Buchanan goes to considerable lengths to make clear that there is great common ground between his and Smith's systems of political economy. Of most significance is the shared belief in individual freedom to pursue one's own economic interests and to enter into voluntary exchanges within the context of a legitimate constitutional order or system of justice. However, as we have seen, Buchanan parts company with Smith over the manner in which the legal order is brought into being. Buchanan relies exclusively on self-interest expressed in political decisionmaking, whereas Smith's analysis rests on the human sentiment of sympathy.

Smith's goal in *Theory of Moral Sentiments* and *Wealth of Nations* is to account for how social order arises and is sustained independently of agents' intentions. In the first of the two books, Smith seeks to explain how justice, which serves as "the main pillar that upholds the whole edifice" of human society, came about. This question has urgency since the laws of justice are a prerequisite for social order; if these laws are removed "the immense fabric of human society . . . must in a moment crumble into atoms."[42] Justice, for Smith, is a particular sort of virtue: a "negative virtue," distinct from other "positive" virtues in so far as its principles are precise and exact. Whereas acts of benevolence are regarded as voluntary, acting in accordance with the principles of justice is strictly necessary and shortfalls are subject to punishment. Justice grows out of the sympathy we, as spectators, feel toward an injured party, and the disapprobation such injury arouses in us toward the injuror. Unlike the sentiment of approbation triggered by observing others' actions of benevolence and charity, the negative virtue of justice draws its precision from the black and white character of injury combined with the heightened sense of sympathy evoked by pain and suffering (II.ii.2.2). The principles of justice attain additional precision because of the transcendental and universalizing assumption Smith makes that individuals can aspire to an "impartiality," whereby we judge an other's actions "neither with our own eyes nor yet with his, but from the place and the eyes of a third person, who has no particular connection with either, and who judges with impartiality between us."[43]

Smith's efficient causes theory of justice provides an explanation for how the rule of law comes about independently from individuals' self-interest or aims; he provides a thoroughly naturalistic account of justice that depends on individuals' empirically evident tendency to experience fellow-feeling in observing the joys and travails of others. Of the entire range of human emotions, negative passions, especially those caused by injury, arouse the greatest sympathy in spectators.[44] After establishing in a variety of circumstances the empirical reality of sympathy—that is, the tendency of individuals to place themselves in another's shoes and vicariously feel their joy or pain—Smith works to establish the notions of the impartial spectator and of justice.[45]

For Smith it is a fundamental feature of both human society and human nature generally that individuals perceive themselves and their actions primarily in relationship with others. By the same token, individuals are quick to judge others' actions and intentions according to their propriety within a given social context.[46] From this process of evaluating the legitimacy of others' actions from a third-person, uninvolved perspective, Smith derives the proposition that it is possible for individuals to apply this third-party perspective of the impartial spectator to their own actions. Just as we are quick to judge others' actions, so during the process of maturation do we learn that we are similarly subject to the judgments of others. Smith, however, readily admits that one is always far more interested in one's own fate than in that of others: in fact, one could easily prefer the preservation of one's little finger to the deaths of multitudes (*TMS* III.3.4). When it comes to evaluating the propriety of one's own actions, the self may prefer to adopt a position of self-love instead of that of third-person impartiality. In view of this undeniable reality of human nature, Smith asks how it is possible, given the constancy of self-love, that a framework of morals and laws could be established (III.3.5).

The tendency of "[e]very man . . . [to be] more deeply interested in whatever immediately concerns himself, than in what concerns any other man" is the most pressing difficulty challenging moral philosophy and jurisprudence. Smith's explanation of how justice comes about is intricate. In acknowledging the individual's tendency to be ruled by self-love, to place himself first, Smith nevertheless claims that "yet he dares not look mankind in the face, and avow that he acts according to this principle" (II.ii.2.2). That is, Smith proposes that it is proper when viewing our own concerns that we adopt the perspective of the impartial spectator—that we view our own affairs as though they were those of a third party. In this case, Smith explains, when an individual

> views himself in the light in which he is conscious that others will view him, he sees that to them he is but one of the multitude in no respect better than any other in it. If he would act so as that the impartial spectator may enter

into the principles of his conduct . . . [then this would] humble the arrogance of his self-love, and bring it down to something which other men can go along with. (Ibid.)

For Smith, it is automatic that in assessing the actions of third parties that we adopt an impartial perspective. It is not automatic that we in turn adopt this impartial viewpoint in evaluating our own actions, but given that each of us is constantly judged by those in society with whom we live, it is natural that we internalize the stance of the impartial spectator, from which we behold ourselves.

Smith builds his theory of justice by moving in two directions simultaneously. First, he observes that through the perspective of the impartial spectator one is able to judge the propriety of one's own acts and to counter flights of self-love. However, he realizes that some individuals made of "less noble clay" may have difficulty in reining in their selfish passions (III.4.1). Thus, second, he observes that justice will be enforced by others who adopt the position of the impartial spectator. On the one hand, the impartial spectator permits individuals the latitude to pursue their personal ambitions: "In the race for wealth, and honours, and preferements, . . . [the individual] may run as hard as he can, and strain every nerve and every muscle, in order to outstrip all his competitors" (III.ii.22). On the other hand, Smith notes:

> But if he should justle, or throw down any of them, the indulgence of the spectators is entirely at an end. It is a violation of fair play, which they cannot admit of. This man is to them, in every respect, as good as he: they do not enter into that self-love by which he prefers himself so much to this other, and cannot go along with the motive from which he hurt him. (Ibid.)

In watching competition among third parties, an impartial observer distinguishes between fair play and injurious conduct. It is this assessment borne out of sympathy with the injured party from a disinterested perspective that establishes the basis for justice.

Thus, even if lacking the wherewithal to appraise one's own behavior impartially, others are able to maintain a third-person perspective on our actions. It is crucial to Smith's theory of justice that theft, personal injury, murder, or breach of promise constitute clear offenses that can be universally acknowledged from the impartial spectator perspective as a transgression against a member of society. Justice itself depends on impartial appraisal of injuries and does not maintain that all individuals be adept or practiced at scrutinizing their own actions by "the supposed impartial and well-informed spectator . . . that man within the breast, the great judge and arbiter of their conduct" (III.2.32). Justice grows out of "[o]ur continual observations upon the conduct of others, [which] insensibly lead us to form to ourselves certain general rules concerning what is fit and proper either to be done or to be avoided" (III.4.7). Feeling sympathy with another's agony, and viewing his situation with the eye of an impartial observer, yields a "general rule . . . [which] is formed . . . by finding from experience, that all actions of a certain kind, or circumstanced in certain manner are approved or disapproved of" (III.4.8). For Smith, it is through the process of sympathy for others from an impartial perspective that the "precise, accurate, and indispensable" rules of justice are discerned (III.6.11).

Whereas we may want to impute to mankind a "refined and enlightened reason" as the efficient cause of "the sentiments and actions" by which justice is achieved, in Smith's mind the actions contributing to justice do not arise from intentional agency predicating the utility or end of justice as the goal.[47] Rather, justice and the social order it makes possible might be thought of as a final cause, with the sympathy spectators naturally feel toward others' injuries and attendant disapproval of the injurer as the efficient cause. Whereas "Nature, indeed, seems to have so happily adjusted our sentiments of approbation and disapprobation to the conveniency both of the individual and of the society . . . it is not the view of this utility or hurtfulness which is either the first or principle source of our approbation and disapprobation."[48] It is not the useful end of justice that motivates the sentiments of approval and disapproval that underlie it, rather it is an individual's innate ability to both sympathize and maintain the perspective of third-person objectivity when approving or disapproving another's actions. Public utility is served by justice, but the sentiments grounding justice do not have that end in mind. Still, with hindsight, public utility that is served by justice grants justice legitimacy since social order constitutes an end with which people can acquiesce.[49]

For Smith, sympathy and self-interest are both dominant forces effecting social order. Buchanan, on the other hand, bases his analysis on individual self-interest, individual choice, and voluntary participation. Thus, for Buchanan, the problem of designing a constitutional order that acquires the consent of its citizens is one of a rational calculation on the part of citizens regarding their personal self-interest. As Smith describes it, sympathy is not so much a "rational choice" as it is a natural, empirically evident outpouring of emotion in response to acts of injustice. Furthermore, sympathy does not entail a rational calculation to achieve agreement on laws such that the individual's stake in society will be best protected. Justice arising out of the principle of sympathy is black and white because, from the point of view of the impartial spectator, sympathy makes exacting pronouncements about matters of injury. Both Smith and Buchanan seek naturalistic explanations, yet each recognizes a different principle as fundamental to the order implicit in the legal framework that governs political economy.

Self-Love, Prudence, and Self-Command versus Rational Self-Interest

This final section of the chapter investigates the claim made by some rational choice theorists that the idea of "rational self-interest" extends back to Adam Smith. Amartya Sen, for example, observes:

> [One common] . . . approach to rational behaviour . . . sees it in terms of reasoned pursuit of self-interest. The origins of this approach are often traced to Adam Smith, and it is frequently asserted that the father of modern economics saw human beings as tirelessly fostering their respective self-interests. As a piece of history of economic thought, this is, to say the least, dubious, since Adam Smith's . . . belief in the hold of self-interest in some spheres of activity (e.g., exchange) was qualified by his conviction that many other motivations are important in human behaviour in general.[50]

Although Sen is dubious about drawing this connection, others want to maintain for rational choice theory this lineage extending back through the marginalist economists to Adam Smith. Kristen Renwick Monroe, for example, states:

> Rational actor theory originated in the classical microeconomics of Adam Smith. In its purest form, it refers to behavior by an individual, be it a person, a firm, or a political entity, designed to further the actor's perceived self-interest, subject to information and opportunity costs. As originally conceived by Smith, the theory provided a powerful creative mechanism whereby the pursuit of individual self-interest would lead to collective welfare. The genius of Smith's invention—the market mechanism, regulated by an invisible hand—solved the problem which had troubled philosophers since Hobbes made his famous argument that there was one basic nature and this nature was self-centered: How can a government of selfish citizens produce collective welfare without authoritarian government.[51]

There are several aspects to Monroe's account of the origins of "rational actor theory" in Smith's "classical microeconomics," as Monroe refers to them. Three themes for further exploration, which will not be discussed here, are the ideas of the "invisible hand," "collective welfare," and "opportunity costs" in Smith.[52] My goal instead is to explore the relevance of the idea of rational self-interest in Smith's writings. This exploration is motivated both by those who claim for rational choice theory a direct lineage from Smith's *Wealth of Nations* and by the popular current idea that "self-interested rational action" is a transparent concept with no further explanation necessary, that it is relevant to individual agents at all times and across all cultures. Thus, it can be used to understand the workings of contemporary Vietnamese peasant culture and the seventeenth-century British civil wars.[53]

Daniel Hausman's introduction to *The Philosophy of Economics,* an edited anthology, puts forward a similar historical narrative for the concept of rational self-interest:

> Since Adam Smith, a particular vision of such [capitalist] economies has dominated theorizing. One conceives of an economy as made up of a number of separate agents—individuals or households or firms—whose only interactions with one another are voluntary exchanges of goods and services. . . . Economic agents are conceived of as well-informed, rational, and self-interested maximizers.[54]

Again, the focus here is on the definition of economic agents as "well-informed, rational, and self-interested maximizers," and on examining the correctness of the claim of a lineage for this definition extending back to Smith's political economy. Hausman puts forward a sketch of how the supposed self-interested rational maximization in Smith and other classical economists became further developed by the marginalist economists and utilitarian theorists.[55]

Albert Hirschman's delightful and breezy look at the concept of self-interest leading up to Smith also helps reinforce the claim that self-interest became a major analytical tool for understanding the institutions shaping political economy, especially once freed from the crumbling structure of virtue theory.[56] Smith stands out among his Enlightenment contemporaries as among the first to understand individual self-interest as the regulative principle of society leading to the wealth of nations. His celebration of self-interest, not just in governing individuals' actions, but also in the wider social context in which it contributes to every citizen's standard of living, was later echoed in James Buchanan's emphasis on individualism combined with self-interested calculations grounding his logic of constitutional choice.

One crucial premise uniting all contemporary rational choice theorists is that the term "rational self-interest" implies that self-interest and reason are related in such a way that an individual is free to determine his or her set of ends, and that rational calculation is used to best achieve those ends. However, ends themselves are not subject to rational reflection;

ends are the expression of agents' freely selected preferences. In rational self-interest, therefore, ends and rational calculation are orthogonal to each other, each performing a different function in rendering an agent's actions predictable to an observer. For Donald Davidson, for example, if we do not impute to those we interact with the quality of being rational actors, then their utterances and actions become opaque and meaningless to us; "[f]or unless an interpreter can discover a rational pattern in the behavior of an agent, he cannot describe or explain that behavior as intentional action."[57] The philosophical framework of rational self-interest, which combines methodological individualism with rational decision-making, works to define the important aspects of one's behavior: an agent's actions are rational when they appropriately reflect the individual's interests given his beliefs about the world and his consistently expressed preferences over ends. Put more sharply, the designation of being a rational actor conveys a pedigree of humanity that divides those fit for civilization and commerce from those barbarians or terrorists on the outside who can only seek nonsense and destruction. The extent to which the term "rational self-interest" has acquired a currency among contemporary Americans and other Westerners cannot be overemphasized.[58]

Because he never used the term, it is difficult to find with precision how "rational self-interest" translates into the language of Smith's eighteenth-century political economy. This problem is made clear if we consider how much more frequently Smith employs the viscerally emotive term "self-love."[59] For Smith, "self-love" conveys passion whereas "rational deliberation" connotes dispassionate contemplation. More than likely in affairs concerning one's self, passion will interfere in the process of dispassionate reflection. In the *Theory of Moral Sentiments,* Smith states that in matters dear to our own hearts, arising out of "our own selfish passions," "every thing appears magnified and misrepresented by self-love" (III.3.1–3). Self-deception growing out of passionate feelings toward our own affairs clouds our ability to reason impartially. Indeed, this "self-deceit, this fatal weakness of mankind, is the source of half the disorders of human life" (III.4.6).

The self-deception Smith talks about pertains to "delusions of self-love" that make it difficult for individuals to appraise their own circumstances dispassionately:

> He is a bold surgeon, they say, whose hand does not tremble when he performs an operation upon his own person; and he is often equally bold who does not hesitate to pull off the mysterious veil of self-delusion, which covers from his view the deformities of his own conduct. (III.4.4)

A contemporary rational choice theorist may find little cause for concern or confusion in Smith's description of delusion arising in matters of passionate personal interest. In the language of rational choice theory, an agent has a well-ordered set of preferences over outcomes, forms rational beliefs about the world, and rationally calculates how best to achieve his preferred ends.[60] From this perspective it is possible to argue that Smith's self-deluded agent simply has false beliefs about the world, and once those are corrected, a rational course of action consistent with the agent's preferences can be adopted. For the contemporary rational choice theorist, it is ultimately in an agent's best interest to assemble an accurate set of beliefs about the world, so that the self-interested actor will rise above the self-delusion Smith worries about.

It was not so simple in Smith's world, however, to make the firm distinction between interests of self-love and reason. The rational choice theorist takes objectivity and impartiality for granted whereas Smith, writing in an age in which the language and tradition of virtue remained compelling, suggests that the achievement of impartiality that results from self-command is the embodiment of virtue. Furthermore, for Smith, the self-command through which one adopts the perspective of the impartial spectator in assessing one's own affairs also regulates the passions of the agent. That is, for Smith, practicing self-command and adopting the position of impartiality serve to censor an individual's passions, and are necessary for reasoning dispassionately about personal affairs. He writes in the *Theory of Moral Sentiments*:

> But though the virtues of prudence, justice, and beneficence, may, upon different occasions, be recommended to us almost equally by two different principles [concern for others and concern for one's self]; those of self-command are, upon most occasions, principally and almost entirely recommended to us by one; by the sense of propriety, by regard to the sentiments of the supposed impartial spectator. Without the restraint that this principle imposes, every passion would, upon most occasions, rush headlong, if I may say so, to its own gratification. (VI.concl.2)

Justice, beneficence, and prudence are the three "perfect virtues" for Smith; the first two embody concern for others, the third expresses concern for one's self. All three virtues require self-command to enable us to act in accordance with the behavioral principles set before us by the impartial spectator: "The man of the most perfect virtue, the man whom we naturally love and revere the most, is he who joins, to the most perfect command of his own original and selfish feelings, the most exquisite sensibility both to the original and sympathetic feelings of others" (III.3.35).

Smith's virtuous man does not sail by the compass of self-interest; his actions are regulated in accordance with the perspective adopted by the impartial spectator and are enacted through recourse to self-command. The virtuous man, then, regulates his passions or interests by adhering to moral principles derived from impartially appraising the situation of others; he "who governs his whole behaviour and conduct according to those restrained and corrected emotions which the great inmate, the great demigod within the breast prescribes and approves of; is alone the real man of virtue, the only real and proper object of love, respect, and admiration" (VI.iii.18). The impartial observer offers a perspective from which to evaluate our own passions and actions; living in accordance with the outlook of the neutral observer censors our emotions and behavior.

By adopting the position of the impartial spectator in assessing our affairs and our actions, and by acting out of self-command, it is possible to achieve the perfect virtues of justice, beneficence, and prudence. Smith has explained how justice is a negative virtue, that its laws are exact, and that it is possible to determine matters of justice because it requires adopting the impartial spectator's perspective with respect to others' affairs, and not one's own. Both justice and beneficence are other-regarding and, as argued above, cannot in Smith's system of natural liberty result from considerations of utility or self-interest. They are derived from the sympathy one feels for others when adopting the perspective of the impartial spectator. It is not feasible to translate the two virtues of justice or benevolence into the language of rational self-interest. Smith is abundantly clear that one adopts self-command in assessing our affairs not due to the utility this impartiality affords but because it is a "splendid and dazzling quality" that is much admired (VI.concl.7). In fact, the virtue of self-command counseled by the impartial spectator does not necessarily have any regard to material fortune and is not necessarily advantageous to the actor.[61]

It may, however, be possible to suggest that Smith's self-oriented virtue of prudence can be understood in accordance with the principles of self-interested rational action. Smith approvingly describes prudence as "[t]he preservation and healthful state of the body [which] seem to be the objects which Nature first recommends to the care of every individual" (*TMS* VI.i.1). Leaving aside his challenging virtues of beneficence and justice, not to mention other virtues of generosity, public-spiritedness, and friendship, the argument can be made that prudence resembles the type of agency characterizing rational choice scholars' self-interested rational action. Smith tells us that prudence rests on the two pillars of reason and self-command:

The qualities most useful to ourselves are, first of all, superior reason and understanding, by which we are capable of discerning the remote consequences of all our actions, and of foreseeing the advantage or detriment which is likely to result from them: and secondly, self-command, by which we are enabled to abstain from present pleasure or to endure present pain, in order to obtain greater pleasure or to avoid a greater pain in some future time. (IV.2.6)

For Smith, the union of reason and self-command constitute the virtue of prudence, "of all the virtues, that which is most useful to the individual" (ibid.).

Smith is careful not to imply that prudence is derived from utility by making it clear that neither the pillars of reason or self-command are based on utility. In the *Theory of Moral Sentiments,* he points out that "superior reason and understanding are originally approved of as just and right and accurate, and not merely as useful or advantageous" (IV.2.7). In the most developed cases of reasoning presented in "the abstruser sciences," "the utility . . . either to the individual or to the public, is not very obvious. . . . It was not, therefore, their utility which first recommended them to public admiration" (ibid.). Similarly, Smith is quick to argue that self-command does not derive from utilitarian considerations. In prudential matters, self-command regulates behavior by overcoming the impulse for instant gratification in favor of future security. However, for Smith, "[t]he pleasure which we are to enjoy ten years hence interests us so little in comparison with that which we may enjoy to-day . . . that the one could never be any balance to the other, unless it was supported by the sense of propriety" (IV.2.8). Self-command, allied with the approbation of the impartial spectator, supplies an impetus for action that cannot be understood in terms of either short or long-term gratification, but in terms of "a sense of propriety quite distinct from the perception of utility." [62]

It is not surprising, therefore, that the virtue of prudence stipulates agents' ends, including a desire for the respect of others, thereby imposing a regulatory set of principles on the agent's selection of ends. For Smith, prudence pertains to "our character and conduct, or upon the confidence, esteem, and good-will, which these naturally excite in the people we live with" (VI.i.4). He goes on to state:

The care of the health, of the fortune, of the rank and reputation of the individual, the objects upon which his comfort and happiness in this life are supposed principally to depend, is considered the proper business of that virtue which is commonly called Prudence. (VI.i.5)

The prudent man is concerned with security, with earnest study, with cautious friendship, with industry and frugality. However, as with Smith's other virtues, humans live their lives in the eyes of others, and to achieve the most judicious courses of action, even in the case of prudence, one must adopt the position of the impartial spectator to properly exert self-command (VI.i.11). In Smith's world, it is not possible to disentangle the idea of rational pursuit of self-interest from a vocabulary of civic virtue that cannot be cast in terms of utility.

Smith denotes two forms of prudence in the *Theory of Moral Sentiments:* the first is more readily attainable by a person who has "reason and understanding" concerning the consequences of his action, and who is able to override the impulse for instant gratification to achieve a longer-term goal; the second is that of "high prudence." In the latter case, "[p]rudence is . . . combined with many greater and more splendid virtues, with valour, with extensive and strong benevolence, with a sacred regard to the rules of justice, and all these supported by a proper degree of self-command" (IV.i.15). The first, and lower, form of prudence might be thought of as that forming the basis of commercial society.[63] It would be a stretch, however, to maintain there is a direct equivalence between Smith's commercial prudence and the self-interested rational actor postulated in rational choice theory.[64] The primary difference between the two is that in rational choice theory every action is evaluated in terms of its payoff for the actor, whereas for Smith even the virtue of prudence is cast in terms of the self-command and character of the agent.

To conclude, it is not possible to translate Smith's analysis of human nature and political economy into the language of self-interested rational action; Smith's commitment to the language of virtue and his depiction of justice, prudence, and self-command as virtues, forestall such a translation.[65] In his political discourse, Smith believes that the most important feature of persons are their characters; "Smith admired Thucydides, above all, for his demonstration that 'nothing gives greater light into any train of actions than the characters of the actors.' "[66] For Smith, knowing the character of agents is the most important step in being able to understand, and explain, their actions. Quite to the contrary, for rational choice theorists, questions of character must be formulated in different terms; for the rational choice theorist all that need be known about agents is their preferences, and their capacity for rational reflection.

Similarly, in matters of justice and constitutional design, rational choice theorists only consider agents' rational pursuit of self-interest. Despite this different emphasis placed on egoism in Smith's system of natural liberty and rational choice liberalism, still it is possible to identify commonalities shared by the two approaches. Both propose a legal framework to coordinate self-motivated ends, a secularized notion of sovereignty, and a nonnormative and nonteleolgical methodology. Therefore, even while acknowledging profound differences, we are correct in concluding that rational choice theorists' contributions to the challenge of constructing a stable society and legitimate rule represent a new chapter in the abiding modern experiment giving priority to individual liberty.

CHAPTER 7

Rational Mechanics, Marginalist Economics, and Rational Choice

> For more than 200 years much of the history of economic thought has centered on the explication of the workability and the desirable properties of the market mechanism. This has continued to be one of the most controversial issues and a considerable source of tensions. Basically, however . . . the notion that economic actors, left to themselves (acting in their own interest and within a given framework that is variously interpreted by different writers), will in some sense promote general welfare or that perfect competition will in some sense achieve a maximum of individual satisfactions . . . this notion runs through most of classical and neoclassical literature.
>
> George R. Feiwel

THE 1870s transnational "marginalist revolution" in economic thought represents a theoretical and chronological midpoint between Adam Smith's system of natural liberty and rational choice scholars' analysis of political economy as consisting of a rational coordination of interests. Whereas Smith assumed that material prosperity is generated within a framework of just laws, the neoclassical economists rigorously sought to prove that in competitive market conditions, individuals' self-interested purchases result in an equilibrium, and that this equilibrium represents optimal social welfare: "[P]erfect freedom of exchange . . . tends to the maximizing of utility"; "[f]ree competition determines the coefficients of production in a way that assures maximum ophelimity." [1]

For the early neoclassical economists, physics provided a methodological point of departure: physics represented *the* exemplary science to be emulated in order to put economics on a respectable footing. Thus, economists of the day modeled economic agency on the variational principles of least action, which describe the motion of particles motion through force fields. Whereas twentieth-century rational choice theory emphasized the rationality of agents, for the nineteenth-century neoclassical economists, "rational" was understood to mean that the discipline of economics had the same sort of scientific legitimacy as did rational mechanics. According to Léon Walras, "[E]conomics, like astronomy and mechanics, is both an empirical and a rational science"; in Vilfredo Pareto's words, "Rational mechanics, when it reduces bodies to simple physical points, and pure economics, when it reduces real men to the *homo oeconomicus*, make use of completely similar abstractions, imposed by similar necessities."[2] Through the appropriation of the mathematical techniques of energy physics, economics emerged as a discipline distinct from classical political economy. Whereas the latter was filled with irregular and unquantifiable elements of political behavior, economics as a more specialized field of study could meet the rigorous analytical standards required of scientific inquiry. Francis Galton's 1877 motion to abolish the Statistics and Political Economy section from the British Association for the Advancement of Science, on the grounds that it failed to uphold scientific standards, was proof that the field's professional status depended on its having scientific credibility.[3] The subsequent emergence of economics as a discipline corresponded to its professionalization, evidenced by the establishment of professional associations, for example, the American Economic Association (1885), and journals such as the *Quarterly Journal of Economics* (1886), and the fact that economic theorists increasingly were being appointed to academic posts.[4]

The marginalist revolution in economics is associated with the transformation of the concept of "value" from a cost of production theory characterizing the classical political economy of Adam Smith, David Ricardo, James Mill, Thomas Malthus, and Karl Marx to a subjective theory of utility promulgated by William Stanley Jevons (1835–1921), Léon Walras (1837–1910), Carl Menger (1840–1921), and the second-generation marginalist Vilfredo Pareto (1848–1923). The marginalists' principles of diminishing marginal utility and equimarginal utility, combined with the formulation of "equilibria," constitute the central core of ideas that shaped neoclassical economic thought and to some extent continues to underlie contemporary orthodox microeconomic theory.[5] The marginalist revolution is most relevant to the history of rational choice theory because it is often thought, as illustrated by the chapter's epigraph, that there is a straight line of development from the marginalists' concept of "maximizing pleasure," or "maximizing utility," to rational choice theorists' idea that rationality means having a complete and transitive set of preferences.[6]

In this chapter I present a detailed exposition of the concept of "rational action," and the mathematical language used to express it, in marginalism and rational choice theory, respectively. The first section presents the key ideas of marginalist thought by discussing Jevons' formulation of the law of one price and his equimarginal principle of exchange. The equation of exchange he develops resembles the fundamental consumer demand equation used throughout marginalist economics. Its importance for this study is in helping show how, in marginal economics, "rational action" was understood along the lines of the theory of virtual velocities borrowed from rational mechanics, and did not point to a theory of rational choice.[7] In the second section, the mathematical equation for consumer demand is compared with the idea of rational choice developed by Kenneth Arrow and Amartya Sen. I argue that the two mathematically defined concepts of "rational action" and "rational choice" are distinct. The third section explores whether either of the two theories can be said to be an instantiation of instrumental means–ends reasoning, as is often claimed for economic theory. In the fourth section I argue that the mathematics of marginalism and of rational choice theory are sufficiently distinct that each can be readily identified; this argument is made with specific reference to cost–benefit analysis, which can be developed using either marginalist or rational choice principles. Together these four sections argue that rational choice theory is qualitatively different from marginalist economics and presents a new definition of rationality in terms of nonmarket decisionmaking without considerations of scarcity.

The marginalist revolution raises two sets of historiographical issues that are worth our consideration before proceeding. Scholars question how revolutionary marginalist thought in fact was—that is, how much of a disjuncture from classical economic thought it represented. Scholars also question the impetus behind marginalist thought, and how marginalism came to dominate economics as a discipline in the early twentieth century. These principal historiographical concerns are easily distilled by contrasting two leading scholars' positions with respect to them. The historian of economics Mark Blaug concludes that "to try to explain the origins of the Marginal Revolution in the 1870s is doomed to failure: it was not a marginal *utility* revolution; it was not an abrupt change but only a gradual transformation of old ideas; and it did not happen in the 1870s"; in effect, the marginal revolution was reconstructed in the twentieth century when the neoclassical orthodox position matured and sought to celebrate its antecedent roots in the early marginalist principles.[8] In his revisionist history *More Heat Than Light: Economics as Social Physics, Physics as Nature's Economics,* the economist-*cum*-historian Philip Mirowski responds directly to Blaug. He reminds us that the original marginalists spoke of their own work as revolutionary, and that these theorists were conscious of their efforts to construct economics as a rational discipline. Mirowski argues that "neoclassical economic theory is best understood as a sharp and severe break with the doctrines characteristic of the classical theory of value, which subsequently implied extensive revisions in most other areas of economic theory." [9] Most significantly, the sharp break Mirowski detects entails "the successful penetration of mathematical discourse into economic theory," and the subsequent separation of the discipline of economics from the more loosely construed field of political economy. [10]

Notwithstanding these historiographical debates, points of consensus exist. First, the marginalist revolution represents an identifiable body of theoretical discourse. It draws scholarly attention specifically because it stands prominently on the direct path leading from classical political economy to "Paretian welfare economics to cost–benefit analysis and dynamic programming." [11] These fields are at the heart of twentieth-century economic theory and social welfare policy, and are critical to the development of rational choice theory. Second, the marginalists receive credit in virtually all texts on the history of economic thought for transforming the theory of value and, consequently, the central concern of economic thought. Whereas political economists concentrated on increased productivity as the objective source of wealth, the marginalists' conceptualized utility as a subjective entity and emphasized the efficient distribution of resources to maximize consumer utility. Now, too, there is general agreement with Mirowski that with the marginalist revolution "economics finally attained its objective to become a science through a wholesale appropriation of the mid-nineteenth-century physics of energy." [12] That agreement notwithstanding, Mirowski's thesis is still criticized by some for emphasizing the history of ideas to the exclusion of contingent social factors and interests. [13]

Jevons's Principle of Equimarginal Utility

Although the early neoclassical economists' development of the principles of diminishing marginal utility and equimarginal utility drew on extant procedures using optimization techniques from calculus, these principles were mostly developed independently and only later was the work of predecessors acknowledged. Among the predecessors were the French civil engineer Jules Dupuit, the German agronomist-farmer Johann Heinrich von Thünen, the Prussian civil servant Hermann Heinrich Gossen, and the French professor of analysis and mechanics Augustin Cournot. Some correspondence did take place among the three principal figures— William Stanley Jevons, Léon Walras, and Carl Menger—but any substantive exchange of ideas appears to have been incidental to one another's theoretical achievements. Notwithstanding the seemingly spontaneous emergence of marginalist thought brought about independently by the three men, there is one prominent factor shared by the contributors to marginal utility theory, including the premarginalist theorists. With the sole exception of the Austrian Carl Menger, all were trained in the physics and mathematics requisite for basic level engineering; all but Menger were fascinated with incorporating the techniques of the mathematical analysis of force fields and energy conservation into their economic explorations.

William Stanley Jevons studied chemistry and metallurgy, but struggled with mathematics, at the University College of London. After a hiatus in Australia where he worked at the Sydney mint, he completed his studies and eventually was able to attain a professorship in political economy at Owen's College in 1866, and then later accepted a professorship at the University College of London in 1876. His major theoretical contribution, which earned him a place among the triumvirate credited with establishing the principles of marginal utility, was *The Theory of Political Economy*, originally published in 1871.[14] Jevons also wrote on logic and scientific methodology, as well as on the coal situation in Britain and the impact of sun spots on the business cycle.

For Jevons, the "theory of economy," as he renamed political economy in the second edition preface to *Theory of Political Economy*, "is purely mathematical in character," "consists in applying the differential calculus to the familiar notions of wealth, utility, value, demand, supply," and can be described as *"the mechanics of utility and self-interest"* (3, 21 [emphasis in original]).[15] Jevons's commitment to the mathematical treatment of economic variables structured his analysis of "marginal utility," and led him to redefine "value" as a ratio of exchange rather than an objective property inherent to goods (*TPE* 76–81). For the classical economists, "value" was a property of a particular good itself that was dependent on the amount of labor required to produce it. However, throughout the history of classical economic theory a tension had long existed between a good's theoretical value and its actual exchange value dictated by market clearance. Jevons and the other neoclassical economists resolved this tension by locating a good's value in the eye of the purchaser: a good's worth is determined by the "utility" it gives a prospective owner, which, in turn, dictates the price the buyer is willing to pay. For Jevons, "cost of production determines supply; supply determines final degree of utility; final degree of utility determines value"; that is, the value of a good is a function of its degree of usefulness per increment consumed. The latter is determined by the availability of a good, which follows from the cost of production.[16]

Jevons states in his *Theory of Political Economy* a "general law" now known as the principle of diminishing marginal utility: that *"the degree of utility varies with the quantity of commodity, and ultimately decreases as that quantity increases"* (53). For example, one glass of water quenching a desperate thirst represents more utility incrementally than that provided by a third, fourth, or fifth glass, with the result that the first glass potentially represents more value in exchange. Jevons combined the principle of diminishing marginal utility with the idea of effective resource allocation to derive the idea that in allocating units of a single resource for various uses, the final unit of consumption for each usage must provide an equivalent increment of utility, or $du_1/dx = du_2/dy$, where u_1 and u_2 represent the utility of the first and second allocations respectively, and x and y represent the amounts of resource used in the two allocations. The most sensible resource allocation requires that the increment of satisfaction derived from the final unit provided for each usage be equal, otherwise increased allocation to one of the uses would be more beneficial. Thus, "the *final degrees of utility* in the two uses [must be] equal" (60). Jevons concludes, anticipating what twentieth-century scholars would refer to as "rational action," that "[t]he general result is that commodity, if consumed by a perfectly wise being, must be consumed with a maximum production of utility" (ibid.).

The revolution of neoclassical economics was centered around the equimarginal principle, which holds that any given individual operating under a budget constraint purchases the final increment of various goods such that these final increments afford the individual the same quantity of "marginal utility" per dollar spent.[17] Jevons essentially states this equimarginal principle as his theory of exchange: *"The ratio of exchange of any two commodities will be the reciprocal of the ratio of the final degrees of utility of the quantities of commodity available for consumption after the exchange is completed."*[18] He goes on to provide equations representing a single individual's equilibrium exchange allocation between two commodities, and the equilibrium exchange ratio resulting from two individuals trading two commodities. Jevons responds to "objections made to the general character of the equations" he employs to model exchange by appeal to the treatment of "virtual velocities" in mechanics. According to Jevons, "The Theory of Economy . . . presents a close analogy to the science of Statical Mechanics, and the Laws of Exchange are found to resemble the Laws of Equilibrium of a lever as determined by the principle of virtual velocities."[19] He reproduces his equations of exchange by quoting Mr. Magnus's derivation of the equation for a lever in equilibrium from the law of energy conservation presented in *Lessons in Elementary*

Mechanics.[20] Just as a lever is in equilibrium when the ratios of the downward forces are inversely equivalent to the ratio of the length of the lever's respective arms, so an individual attains a stable resource allocation when the ratio of the final degrees of marginal utility for two commodities is inversely proportional to the ratio of the total amounts of the commodities traded.

Jevons's early marginalist theory expressed in his equation for exchange has been understood by later historians of economics to represent a nascent form of "rational action." It is through the automatic "rational" balancing among trade-offs that the ideal consumer achieves an optimal resource allocation: "[t]he marginalists saw people as rational balancers (at the margin) of pleasure and pain in a world of perfect competition"; "[m]arginalism permitted the utilitarian vision of human nature, which was considered to consist exclusively of the rational, calculating maximization of utility, to be formulated in terms of differential calculus."[21]

In essence, the concept of "rational" economic behavior was derived from the least action principle first developed in the field of mechanics, as expressed by the calculus of variations: the rational economic man tends to allocate resources "among alternate modes of use in such a way that they will be equally remunerative in all and so will yield the maximum total return,"[22] just as according to the principle of least action a particle selects a path that minimizes its action integral. The trick to applying variational calculus to physics problems was to isolate a variable characteristic of the system in question which could be maximized or minimized, such as with Maupertuis's principle of least action, Hamilton's stationary action, or Gauss's principle of least constraint. Economic theorists similarly sought to identify variables—namely, various expressions of the utility concept—that could be maximized. In *Mathematical Psychics,* the marginalist theorist Francis Ysidro Edgeworth relates how "social mechanics" may aspire to the heights attained by celestial mechanics as a consequence of their shared basis in the maximization of measurable variables:

> "Mécanique Sociale" may one day take her place along with "Mécanique Celeste," throned each upon the double-sided height of one maximum principle, the supreme pinnacle of moral as of physical science. As the movements of each particle, constrained or loose, in a material cosmos are continually subordinated to one maximum sub-total of accumulated energy, so the movements of each soul whether selfishly isolated or linked sympathetically, may continually be realising the maximum pleasure.[23]

In *Mathematical Psychics,* Edgeworth draws an overt analogy between the utilitarian or egoistic "principles of greatest happiness" and "those principles of Maximum Energy which are among the highest generalizations of physics"; "reasoning" applies to the work of the physicist or economist and not to the particle or a pleasure-seeking individual (4).

Writing in 1947, economist Paul Samuelson was keenly aware of the parallel construction of the "constrained maximum problem" characteristic of economic theory and the equations describing particles' trajectories constrained by the conservation of energy in physics:

> In some cases . . . it is possible to formulate our conditions of equilibrium as those of an extremum problem, even though it is admittedly not a case of any individual's behaving in a maximizing manner, just as it is often possible in classical dynamics to express the path of a particle as one which maximizes (minimizes) some quantity despite the fact that the particle is obviously not acting consciously or purposively.[24]

Mathematical solutions required that the variable of interest be maximized (or minimized). As Samuelson recognized in his *Foundations of Economic Analysis,* economists can proceed as long as the equilibrium in question can be associated with "a stable maximum position." The equations demand that some variable be maximized; the economist can later apply meaning to this mathematical term, "[t]hus, we really argue backwards from maximizing economic behavior to the underlying physical data consistent with it."[25] As with the farmer who is thought to grow his crops in accordance with "the validity of the law of diminishing marginal physical productivity," it can later be determined what aspect of field usage is maximized—production per square inch or average yield over the total acreage.[26]

Although Samuelson remained equivocal over whether individuals deliberately maximize the variable of economic interest, enough other mid-twentieth-century economists associated deliberate maximization with rational behavior that, over time, human rationality came to be explicitly defined in accordance with the maximization (or minimization) characteristic of rational mechanics. Thus, in the course of the first half of the twentieth century, the term "rational" came to apply less to the science of economics as a discipline and more to the nature of deliberation on the part of economic actors. Chicago school economist Frank Knight, for example, while retaining the idealized abstraction of "economic man" as "a concept methodologically analogous to the frictionless machine of theoretical mechanics," added that the twentieth-century economic agent is also "individualistically and rationally purposive."[27] The agent is not just assumed to automatically behave in a rationally optimizing fashion, but is also thought to apply means–end reasoning to deliberately select optimal actions.

It is not possible to pinpoint with exactness the first use of "rational" to refer to economic behavior rather than to the discipline as a field of study. Certainly, by 1944, in *The Theory of Games and Economic Behavior,* John von Neumann and Oskar Morgenstern theorized about "rational behavior," for which the principle of maximization was central: "[t]he individual who attempts to obtain . . . maxima is also said to act 'rationally.'"[28] In 1951 Kenneth Arrow could matter-of-factly refer to "the traditional identification of rationality with maximization of some sort."[29] However, despite this gradual transformation in the concept of rationality associated with "economic man," it can only be argued with difficulty that the mathematical concepts of marginalist rational action, and of rational choice, are equivalent.

Although Jevons met with inadvertent success in providing a template for rational action, his mathematical formulation of the exchange problem remained incomplete. Specifically, he did not provide the mathematics requisite for moving from a single individuals' optimal resource allocation to what could be considered optimal for numerous trading parties, since this required the simultaneous solution for prices and quantities traded, both as dependent mathematical variables. Jevons was only able to discuss trade of commodities given prices that were already established. Thus, instead of price's being a dependent variable dictated by supply and demand, Jevons resorted to his "law of one price" wherein quantities exchanged are determined in light of a preestablished price. He does, however, introduce a variation of the classic marginalist equation for consumer demand:

$$\frac{\text{the marginal utility of } x}{\text{the marginal utility of } y} = \frac{\text{final infinitesimal unit of } y \text{ exchanged}}{\text{final infinitesimal unit of } x \text{ exchanged}} = \frac{y}{x}^{[30]}$$

This equation expresses the idea that *"the degrees of utility of commodities exchanged will be in the inverse proportion of the magnitudes of increments exchanged."*[31]

However, only with hindsight can it plausibly be suggested that Jevons's equation represents an expression for rational behavior. Jevons and other marginalists were instead concerned with defending the rationality of their discipline. As the theory was developed by Vilfredo Pareto, replacing the assumption of ostensive psychic pleasure with a more modest dependence on the empirically observable "material fact of choice," the concept of consumer behavior itself changed.[32] Psychological hedonism associated with ostensive utility gave way to a revealed preference approach, and "rational" ceased to refer to the discipline of economics itself and instead came to characterize the norms of decisionmaking for human agents. At the same time there was a transformation in the mathematics used for economic theory. The marginalists strictly copied the differential techniques of maximization from the physics of motion whereas rational choice theorists studied choices among discrete pairs of outcomes and established logically consistent relations pertaining to them.

Is Marginalist Economics a Special Case of Rational Choice Theory?

Marginalist economics and rational choice theory are commonly treated as conceptually equivalent.[33] The goal of this section is to assess this equivalence by exploring the mathematical relationship between the two. Marginalism defines "*rational* [as] efficient, i.e., maximizing output for a given input, or minimizing input for a given output." [34] In contrast, within rational choice theory, "a rational man" behaves in accordance with the following conditions:

> (1) he can always make a decision when confronted with a range of alternatives; (2) he ranks all the alternatives facing him in order of his preferences in such a way that each is either preferred to, indifferent to, or inferior to each other; (3) his preference ranking is transitive; (4) he always chooses from among the possible alternatives that which ranks highest in his preference ordering; and (5) he always makes the same decision each time he is confronted with the same alternatives.[35]

Whereas "maximizing utility" is a generic catchphrase often used in reference to both marginalism and rational choice theory, I argue in this section that the marginalists' calculus-based equations expressing maximization are theoretically distinct from the consistency conditions on sets of choices characterizing rational choice theory. For the marginalists, economics is scientific because it rationally links diminishing marginal utility and scarcity; scarcity is a physical reality and utility maps subjective experience. In rational choice theory the mathematical concepts of completeness and connectedness are fundamental to defining rational action: an agent can make a decision of preference or indifference when confronted by any two choices, and when considered together none of these binary choices is inconsistent.[36]

Thus, while mathematical and conceptual identity between marginalism and rational choice is often presupposed, the distinct formalisms of each theory demonstrate their incommensurability. Whereas marginalist economics expresses its findings in terms of continuous, convex functions, rational choice is expressed in terms of consistency of choices over finite sets. Kenneth Arrow, a principle leader in the development of rational choice theory, outlined his assessment of the relationship between the two in the following self-referential passage:

> Reflection on social choice provided a stimulus for studying individual choice and the meaning of rationality. Jevons, Walras, Menger, and Edgeworth had introduced the hypothesis that consumer choice of commodity bundles was determined by maximization of a utility function subject to a budget constraint. Irving Fisher and Vilfredo Pareto observed that the cardinal nature of the utility function was irrelevant; only an ordering of commodity bundles need be postulated. Samuelson [1938] introduced a change in orientation in his concept of revealed preference. The choices made and not an underlying ordering or utility function were primary. Conditions of rationality were imposed on the choices. As shown by Ville [1946] and Houthakker [1950], suitably strong conditions on the demand functions implied the existence of an underlying ordering which rationalized choices.
>
> Arrow [1959] observed that if choice was assumed to be defined from finite sets [instead of by only budget constraint sets], the equivalence between choice functions defined by maximizing in a given ordering and choices satisfying certain consistency conditions took a somewhat different form. This line of analysis invites taking apart the conditions of the choice function (the function defining the choice or choices made from any given opportunity set) and showing the equivalence of each to some form of rationality weaker than an ordering.[37]

There are three crucial aspects to Arrow's historical narrative. First, there is the marginalists' idea of "maximization of a utility function subject to a budget constraint"; marginalists accepted that agents' utilities could be represented by abstract mathematical functions. Second, there is Paul Samuelson's revealed preference approach: this approach only accepts the data of observed behavior as the starting point for establishing the relations characterizing consumer's choice. Third, there is the transition to rational choice theory that analyzes the choices individuals make on all finite sets of potential outcomes; this analysis is distinct from the marginalists' budget constraint sets circumscribed by commodities, prices, and budgets.

After exploring in this section the work of Paul Samuelson, H. S. Houthakker, Kenneth Arrow, and Amartya Sen, I will conclude that the two forms of rational action characterized by the marginalists' demand equations and by the rational choice axioms are distinct and can only be compared with difficulty. This finding implies that the concepts of "rational action" conveyed by each system cannot be readily translated into the other. This incomparability makes it evident that the notion of "rationality" itself was in flux between the time of the marginalists and rational choice theorists. For the marginalists, the demand equation expresses how *Homo economicus* maximizes utility per last dollar spent. A consumer's rational action is an intricate mathematical function of his pleasure, or "utility," per additional increments of a commodity, his budget, and the price of the commodities. Whether conscious of it or not, *Homo economicus* has his mind full of the appropriate exchange relations, represented in differential calculus, that enables him to maximize pleasure. This agent might be thought of "a lightening calculator of pleasures and pains, who oscillates like a homogeneous globule of desire of happiness under the influence of stimuli that shift him about the area, but leave him intact." [38] It was not relevant to marginalist analysis whether or not individuals deliberately make rational choices.

In 1947, Samuelson explicitly argued that it is dubious that such complex demand equations are at some level consciously calculated by agents, and held that economists should focus on observed consumer behavior to reveal agents' preferences. This move to rely on empirical observation, in addition to postulating abstract laws regulating human consumption, gave economics a more credible scientific basis. According to Samuelson's "revealed preference" approach, all that is known about consumer choice is gleaned from observing choices among various commodity bundles. But with this theoretical innovation came the task of understanding how the revealed preference approach related mathematically to the earlier marginalists' utility function approach. In other words, what mathematical function must govern a consumer's revealed preferences to manifest the same "rational action" captured by the marginalist utility function governing demand under a budget constraint? Somewhat surprisingly, discovering that mathematical expression is no easy task.

Samuelson first proposed that a consumer's choices among respective commodity bundles must reflect the form given by his "fundamental hypothesis" that in his view captures "the entire theory of the standard case of consumer's behaviour":

If $X^a \neq X^b$ *and* $P^a X^b \leq P^a X^a$, *then* $P^b X^b < P^b X^a$. [39]

This equation expresses the fundamental relationship between a batch of goods X^a, bought by a rational consumer at prices P^a, at an income established by prices multiplied by goods, $P^a X^a$, and a second batch of goods *not* chosen by the consumer that costs less, represented by $P^a X^b$. In his analysis of the equation, Houthakker explains that Samuelson's fundamental hypothesis "should imply and be derivable from utility analysis; . . . it should be a necessary and sufficient condition for the existence of ordinal utility." [40]

Again, Samuelson's goal here is to derive a statement about the revealed preferences of a rational consumer that is mathematically equivalent to the marginalists' consumer utility function resembling that of Jevons above. [41] In marginalist economics, this equation is formulated with two additional parameters, namely, "budget constraint" and relative valuations based on scarcity, which create the conditions for a constrained maximization problem. [42] Houthakker argues that Samuelson's hypothesis concerning revealed choices, although a necessary condition, is not sufficient to guarantee its equivalence to the demand equations of a utility function. One feature it is lacking is the all important condition of integrability, which is essential to the differential equations of the marginalists. Samuelson failed to see the weakness of his hypothesis because he limited his analysis to a two-commodity space, and hence did not consider that the integrability requirement is necessary in the case of three or more commodities.

To shore up the weaknesses of Samuelson's fundamental hypothesis, in 1950 Houthakker introduced a new axiom to capture the relationship between a rational consumer's revealed preferences over commodity bundles as a function of price and income, and the marginalists' utility function:

If for every finite t and T $(t = 1, 2, \ldots, T)$ *the inequality* $P^{t-1}X^t \leq P^{t-1}$ X^{t-1} *holds, and if there are numbers i and j such that* $0 \leq i \leq j \leq T$ *and* $X^i \neq X^j$, *then* $P^T X^T < P^T X^0.$ [43]

Houthakker's axiom relies on the property of "semi-transitivity": where transitivity requires three elements, semi-transitivity need only involve $T + 1$ elements, T being any finite number. In Houthakker's expression, the index *t* denotes a series of different commodity bundles expressed as a combination of the price *P* and the allotment of commodity *X*. Houthakker's axiom differs from Samuelson's by incorporating information given by intermediate revealed preferences, while Samuelson only considers end points of a series. Houthakker concludes that his "axiom of semi-transitivity is . . . not a property of curves, but of relations between a finite number of batches." [44] Houthakker's observation is attuned to the difficulty of navigating between the two mathematical perspectives: the marginalists', operating on infinite and continuous sets; and the revealed preference approach pertaining to finite sets of observed consumer's choices.

Writing in 1959, Kenneth Arrow observed that the "language of the theory of consumers' demand is still somewhat confused despite the great progress that has been made in recent years."[45] Arrow alludes to the "good deal of effort [that] has gone into finding assumptions on the demand function which would imply the existence of an ordering from which it could be derived."[46] He notes that both J. Ville and Houthakker found that Samuelson's hypothesis, which in the literature became known as the "Weak Axiom of Revealed Preference," was insufficient to imply the existence of consumer preference ordering from which a demand function could be derived. That is, observed consumer behavior may satisfy the weak axiom—holding that if one commodity bundle is revealed to be at least as good as a second, the second cannot be revealed preferred to the first—and still not uphold the completeness and transitivity conditions. In its place, Ville and Houthakker proposed what came to be called the "Strong Axiom of Revealed Preference." Arrow restated each of these axioms in the set theoretic language that he helped to popularize. The fundamental insight of Arrow's article "Rational Choice Functions and Orderings" is that if the restriction of considering only sets defined by budget constraints, a restriction characterizing marginalist economics, is removed so that all finite sets of possible choices are included, then the strong and weak axioms of revealed preference can be proven to be logically equivalent. Arrow explains:

> The most interesting conclusion is the complete equivalence of the Weak Axiom of Revealed Preference with the existence of an ordering from which the choice function can be derived. This equivalence is demonstrable by very elementary means provided we concede that choices should be definable from finite sets as well as budget constraint sets.[47]

Hence, whereas the strong and weak axioms of revealed preference are equivalent in the case of all finite sets, they are not equivalent in the case of budgetary constraint sets. Arrow goes on to observe, "It is true that very interesting mathematical problems are bypassed by this point of view." By this, Arrow presumably means that the intricacies of the marginalists' concept of marginal utility and constrained maximization have fallen by the wayside in the rational choice focus on binary choices on all finite sets of possible outcomes.

Amartya Sen, writing in 1971, also addressed the relationship between utility theory and revealed preference theory:

> Much of revealed preference theory has been concerned with choices restricted to certain distinguished subsets of alternatives, in particular a class of convex polyhedra (e.g., "budget triangles" in the two commodity case). This restriction may have some rationale for analyzing the preferences of competitive consumers, but it makes the results unusable for other types of

choices, e.g., of government bureaucracies, of voters, of consumers in an imperfect market.[48]

What is notable is that in changing the language from marginal utility functions to revealed preference and establishing the "complete criterion of rationality of choice," the concept of rationality itself has been shifted by the translation of the problem from differentiable marginal utility functions to binary choice sets. In the first case, the rationality condition is strictly defined by the consumer demand equation, subject to a budgetary constraint. In the latter case, a consistency criterion among choice sets determines the rational behavior of the chooser.[49] Sen notes that if the restriction of only considering sets defined by budget constraints is removed, "the axiomatic structure of revealed preference theory changes radically," thus implying that the axiomatic system for revealed choices among budget constraint sets is radically different from the axiomatic system for all finite sets.[50] Sen devotes his attentions to the axiomatic structure of revealed preference theory without budget constraints, and does not compare the axiomatic structure appropriate to marginal utility theory with his axioms of rational choice on unrestricted sets. In the case of rational choice theory, the strong and weak axioms are logically equivalent; however, in the case of budget constraint sets, the two axioms are nonequivalent. How the two systems of axioms are related remains an open question.[51]

What is most clear from the discussion enjoined by Houthakker, Ville, D. Gale, and Sen is that different concerns and different mathematics characterize the endeavors of marginalist economists and rational choice theorists.[52] If it could be known a priori that a consumer's behavior is governed by the marginalist demand function, then it would follow that the agent obeys the rational choice conditions of completeness and transitivity.[53] However, in order to follow the dictates of empiricism, economists must analyze behavior in view of observable behavior. It is the exercise of mapping back from observable choices to the criteria of rational choice that presents the problem in the case of budget constraint sets. If it were possible to move seamlessly between the two worlds of scarcity-based budget constraint sets and nonscarcity-based finite sets, then it would be possible to consider the former as a subset of all finite sets of possible alternatives. In this case, consumer choices in accordance with the weak axiom of revealed preference over all binary pairs within this encompassing set would yield the completeness and transitivity criteria defining rationality. But it is not possible either in principle or in practice to study consumers' choice against the background of all conceivable finite sets of choices; hence revealed consumers' choice peculiar to marginalism requires a distinct axiomatic system.[54] Furthermore, the completeness and transitivity criteria of rational choice themselves need to be augmented by the conditions of continuity and convexity in order to ground the marginalist demand function.[55]

Marginalist economists are unable to say anything about consumer valuations or choices in a world without scarcity. It is specifically this world without scarcity—of nonmarket decisions—that interests rational choice theorists.[56] Preference in the rational choice world takes on an absolute quality independent from public ratios of exchange and quantities consumed: an individual has preferences over steak, beer, or potatoes; the individual can decide between a given commodity bundle or, for instance, increasing his mother's life expectancy by a given percentage over the next three years. In unremitting contrast, the marginalists' concept of "rational action" hinges on the diminishing marginal utility of scarce goods and their ratios of exchange.[57] A marginalist is concerned only with the relative valuation of steak after the consumption of, say, ten beers in view of its ratio in exchange. The worlds of scarcity and nonscarcity are wholly distinct, and navigating between the two systems is mathematically feasible but requires one hundred pages of advanced mathematics.[58]

Marginalist Economics and Rational Choice Theory as Refinements of "Instrumental Reasoning"

Having discussed the mathematics pertinent to marginalism and rational choice theory, it may be asked whether either can be considered an instantiation of "instrumental," means–ends reasoning. Understanding the relationships both marginalist economics and rational choice theory have with instrumental reason is important because it is often argued that economics is a science specifically insofar as it conforms to the means–end or cause–effect principles underlying natural science. Furthermore, it is often held that rational choice theory represents a progressive refinement of marginalist economics. Just as it has been shown in the preceding section that the lack of equivalence between the mathematical systems structuring marginalism and rational choice demonstrates a conceptual disjunction, so here I argue that rational choice theory cannot readily be assimilated into instrumental reason. Rational choice theorists are uninterested in "human behavior as a relationship between ends and scarce means that have alternative uses," a concept that previously both gave economics its unity and made it the science of efficient resource allocation.[59]

In 1943, Joseph Schumpeter proposed a succinct explanation of how "economic reasoning," based on causal relations in nature, linked science and capitalism as the main engine of civilization in the West. For Schumpeter, "the rational attitude presumably forced itself on the human mind primarily from economic necessity."[60] He points out that an important and widespread attitude toward economics developed in the twentieth century: with the decline of the authority of religious and moral precepts, scientific inquiry of the sort undertaken by economists ascended by mid-century to become the positive source of human knowledge and technological progress. Economic reasoning is wholly a part of this scientific outlook insofar as it studies the real-world relations between means and ends and analyzes effective use of resources. This view was shared by Max Weber, who also wrote about modern Western civilization's enthrallment by instrumental reason.[61]

While it is difficult to associate means and ends directly with the marginal economic theories of Jevons, because the nineteenth-century marginalists did not develop a theory of instrumental action, with hindsight Robert Sugden believes that Jevons's theory of maximizing utility is consistent with instrumental reasoning.[62] This is because Jevons argues that human agents strive to maximize pleasure, and that the exchange equation provides the mathematical expression consistent with achieving this goal. In order to think of Jevons's theory as a contribution to instrumental rationality, it is necessarily to hold that an agent's end is to maximize the utility of each increment of commodity bought per dollar spent. Viewed in this way, marginalist economics may be thought of as setting a precedent for requiring that specific conditions structure an agent's extraction of pleasure from additional units of goods: marginalist economics requires that individuals' preferences are continuous, that more is favored to less, and that prices plus a budget constraint specify a rational purchase. If it is possible to consider Jevons's mathematical construction as an instantiation of instrumental reasoning, it is because the agent's overarching goal is to "maximize pleasure," and equations are capable of capturing what it means to maximize this ostensive psychic entity.[63]

It must be remembered that Jevons, Walras, and Pareto were much more concerned with persuading skeptics that economics is a science than they were in putting forward a theory of instrumental reasoning. For them, "rational action" derived its significance from rational mechanics, and not from establishing rules for reasoning. Rational mechanics embodied causal relations, but not instrumental relations because bodies in motion do not choose means consistent with ends. In direct parallel, it may be most appropriate to think of marginal economics as establishing the relations that ideally govern economic agents who have the innate propensity to "maximize pleasure." Thus, it is only retrospectively possible to suggest that the marginalists presented a refinement of means–ends reasoning; some believe that even an instrumental reading of marginalism is a stretch.[64]

There is a significant shift with the emergence of the "rationality project," with its assorted intertwined articulations: von Neumann and Morgenstern's objective expected utility theory, Leonard J. Savage's subjective expected utility theory, and game theory. Unlike the marginalists, the new generation of theorists was keen to establish the normative and prescriptive parameters of rationality.[65] All of these axiomatic systems rely on consistency conditions among preferences, or among choices between actions. It is a moot point in decision theory whether these consistency relations can be extrapolated from means–ends, causal relations thought to inhere in nature, or whether they involve additional assumptions beyond those of a purely instrumental approach to reasoning. This intensely contested debate, with much at stake, has well-demarcated battle lines. Edward McClennen, David Gauthier, Robert Nozick, and William Riker make up the orthodox social science position that decision theory represents no more than the rules for means–ends reasoning: he who wills the end wills the means.[66] On the other side, Jean Hampton and Robert Sugden insist that consistency among preferences is wholly different from acting in a consistent fashion to achieve a single goal.[67] On the middle ground are cautious theorists who uphold rational choice theory as a helpful predictive tool that does not necessarily prescribe rules of reasoning.[68]

What is at stake in the debate over the character of decision theory is whether it is possible for the social sciences to be nonnormative and value free. The insistence that rational choice theory is no more than a refinement of means–ends reasoning is consistent with the endeavor to place social science on a nonideological foundation free from morals, metaphysics, and value-laden commitments. From this perspective, it is necessary to maintain that the consistency criteria such as "transitivity" are a fundamental property of goal-oriented action.

Historically, Hampton and Sugden are on firm ground in pointing to David Hume's characterization of reasoning. For Hume, reason is the slave of the passions; passions are often inconsistent and reason cannot adjudicate between them. It can only dictate the means necessary to achieve a single end, not to optimize given conflicting ends:

> 'Tis not contrary to reason to prefer the destruction of the whole world to the scratching of my finger. . . . 'Tis as little contrary to reason to prefer even my own acknowledg'd lesser good to my greater, and have a more ardent

affection for the former than the latter. A trivial good may, from certain circumstances, produce a desire superior to what arises from the greatest and
most valuable enjoyment; nor is there anything more extraordinary than
in this, than in mechanics to see one pound weight raise up a hundred by
the advantage of its situation. In short, *a passion must be accompany'd
with some false judgment, in order to its being unreasonable;* and even
then, 'tis not the passion, properly speaking, which is unreasonable, but the
judgment.[69]

What is important to Hume is that reason dictates that an agent act consistently toward a desired end, but reason cannot adjudicate between
passions, goals, or preferences. In her analysis of the relationship between expected utility theory and instrumental reason, Hampton argues
that "Hume and his followers have tended to think of means/end reasoning as occurring with respect to a *particular* desire for a *particular*
end, establishing what actions objects are necessary for the attainment
of that end." Quite to the contrary, the consistency axioms characterizing rational choice theory "apply to a *set* of such desires or preferences;
they concern the *relationship among* desires or preferences."[70] Therefore, rational choice theory with its focus on consistency relations
among preferences is wholly distinct from Hume's or Immanuel Kant's
characterization of means–ends reasoning. Eliding any reference to
means and ends, Debra Satz and John Ferejohn acknowledge that the
"theory of formal rationality . . . [suggests that] 'rationality' pertains
only to the relations among . . . [an agent's] preferences."[71]

It may illuminate the discussion to understand that in the case of classic instrumental reason, given the goal of constructing a brick wall, it provides the steps necessary for building one. Marginalist economics could
additionally specify the appropriate ratios of brick and mortar required
to build the wall with utmost efficiency in view of utility, prices, and a
budget constraint. Rational choice theory, in this example, stipulates
pairs of preferences, with consistency among sets of all possible outcomes, over any sorts of walls that could be imagined.

The only plausible way to argue that decision theory conforms to
means–ends reasoning is to assert that preference rankings are not
among conflicting goals, but that they function as a means of ordering
choices according to their potential for achieving one overarching goal—
for example, "winning," or obtaining the greatest financial payoff.[72] Expected utility theory has been mired in controversy because of questions
about the plausibility of basic axioms such as Leonard Savage's "sure
thing principle."[73] Leaving aside the more complicated cases of decisions
under risky and uncertain conditions, it is fruitful to focus on the most

basic of the consistency conditions undergirding rational choice theory: transitivity. Under this condition, if an agent prefers an apple to an orange and an orange to a banana, it is not rational for her to prefer a banana to an apple. What motivates the consistency requirement of transitivity is a deep philosophical question. Luce and Raiffa acknowledge that there are several motivations: that transitive preference orderings are the appropriate concern of decision theorists who are in the position to define rational decisionmaking; that actual human agents exhibit transitive preferences, at least in close approximation; and that decision theory is the province of idealized action. They add that in all likelihood, the most important consideration in upholding transitivity is "the traditional mathematician's hedge: transitive relations are far more mathematically tractable than intransitive ones."[74] In other words, the requirement of transitive preference orderings is the most basic ingredient to a theory of rational choice, and thus may be motivated more by the necessity of the theory than by the necessity of preference relations that in fact obtain (or that are hoped to obtain) to human agency.

The typical defense of the set of rationality axioms, including that of transitivity, is that "anyone who violates the axioms 'could have a book made against him by a cunning bettor, and would then stand to lose in any event.'"[75] Whereas this observation is levied at decisionmaking in risky and uncertain circumstances, a similar argument is mounted in the case of intransitive preference orderings: the person violating the axiom of transitivity will lose out to a shrewd trader. In this "Money Pump" example, a person who prefers an apple to an orange to a banana to an apple will be exploited by a rational dealer who consistently offers to take back a fruit, plus some money, until the individual ends up penniless with the same fruit she started with. This defense of transitivity appeals to rational choice theorists because it attempts to ground the theory entirely in payoffs for choices. Hence, the theory is thought to introduce no normative standards that are not strictly required by means–ends relations: agents without transitive preferences are thought to lose satisfaction or "utility" because they fail to comply with a basic reality that intransitive preferences logically entail wasteful dissipation of effort dedicated to achieving goals.

The difficulty with the Money Pump defense of transitivity is that it fails to render explicit the relationship between transitivity and means–ends reasoning: it remains unclear how transitivity relates to either an agent's goals or to her means of achieving them.[76] That is, either it must be part of an agent's ends to obey transitive relations or it must be a means to an end to obey them. The Money Pump example works by supposing that an agent must have consistent preferences in order to best fulfill her entire set of desires. It is opaque, however, if the rational agent adopts consistent preferences as a means to fulfilling all her desires simultaneously, thereby violating the Humean stipulation that reasoning cannot dictate preference, or whether instead it must be characteristic of a rational agent to arrange her preferences transitively. In the latter case, it must be acknowledged that this new consistency condition is a step beyond strictly Humean instrumental reasoning that only pertains to achieving a single goal and not to balancing all goals in a rationally consistent fashion.[77]

Coming from another perspective, Robert Sugden has argued that agents with intransitive preferences may be incorporating other considerations into their decision process, such as avoidance of regret. In his example, a person's choices between two outcomes may be influenced by the consideration of regret: that is, if a person's choice is governed both by potential satisfaction and potential regret, then it is possible that such a person could be rational and hold intransitive preferences.[78] This philosophical debate over the motivation underlying the transitivity axiom is far from resolved. The only conclusion that can be put forward at this time is admittedly tentative—namely, that the transitivity condition as used by Kenneth Arrow in *Social Choice and Individual Values* and throughout decision theory does not in any transparent manner refer to an agent's means and ends: "If x is preferred or indifferent to y and y is preferred or indifferent to z, then x must be either preferred or indifferent to z."[79] This statement of the principle of transitivity refers only to relations that must obtain among an agent's preferences, and conveys no information about an agent's goals and means of achieving them.[80] Hence at this time it is premature to conclude that rational choice theory represents a refinement of instrumental reasoning.

Marginalist Cost–Benefit Analysis versus Rational Choice Cost–Benefit Analysis

In the final section of this chapter I consider how discussions of social welfare evolved from the marginalists' concern with general equilibrium and individual achievement of utility through trade to Arrow's formulation of "collective rationality" and the development of cost–benefit analysis. The first part of the section discusses the transformation of the concept of "Pareto optimality" from Pareto's original formulation through Samuelson's take on it and finally to Arrow's formulation in social choice theory. The second part specifically discusses the development of cost–benefit analysis, which had both European and American adherents and demonstrated varying degrees of congruence with the rationality project.

The Pareto condition, despite its moral ambiguity, as explained above, and its definitional distinction between questions of distribution and of efficiency, has been broadly used in welfare economics, in social choice theory, and in cost–benefit analysis.[81] This widespread application of the principle makes it worthwhile to reflect briefly on the intellectual migration the concept has undergone as it has been applied in varied and new circumstances of analysis. Pareto's original formulation of his idea of "maximum ophelimity" was meant to capture the conditions necessary for a free-trade economy in which parties participating in voluntary exchange each gain. The key aspect of his formulation of optimality is that of ensuring that each person is potentially better off, and no one worse off, as an outcome of their trading activities. Since markets are envisioned as voluntary, postulating that individuals must either gain through trade, or abstain, renders Pareto's definition of optimality unproblematic. Pareto further argues, by using the same mathematical analysis of individuals' indifference curves intersecting to produce a set of socially preferred outcomes, that a collectivist society is at least as able as a free-market society to obtain these optimal conditions of exchange. Thus, even from its inception, Pareto's idea of optimality could be used to evaluate the outcomes of voluntary exchange or of collectivized production.[82]

Arrow's initial statement of his impossibility theorem in *Social Choice and Individual Values* does not use Pareto's optimality, although subsequent theorists find the principle to be implied in his conditions of citizens' sovereignty (condition 4) and positive association of social and individual values (condition 2).[83] Arrow had used the Pareto principle in an auxiliary proof more consistent with the individualistic assumptions better corresponding to the new welfare economics.[84] In his impossibility theorem, Arrow permits individuals to have preferences over end states that precisely qualify how all individuals fare. This formulation of individual choice over final end states differs from the new welfare economics in which individuals are only concerned with the commodity bundles each personally receives.[85] This auxiliary proof in *Social Choice and Individual Values* is most directly comparable to the welfare economics tradition, and it is possible to draw individuals' indifference curves to replicate the manner in which Arrow derives collective irrationality from the individualistically oriented preferences of two persons.[86] The subsequent interpretation of Arrow's impossibility theorem in which the Pareto principle was substituted for conditions 2 and 4 became the standard treatment.[87] In Arrow's rendering, the Pareto principle is one of unanimity, holding that if outcome x is preferred to y by every member of society, then the group prefers x to y.[88] Instead of having reference only to each individual's commodity bundle, Arrow's version of the Pareto principle establishes a precedent for considering unanimous agreement over social states affecting all members of society.

In his rendering of the Pareto principle, Amartya Sen gives a slightly modified version that permits collective choice to be based on less than unanimity. Sen provides two rules to be followed in establishing his Pareto criterion. First, if each member of a society is indifferent between two outcomes x and y, then society is also indifferent. Second, "if at least one individual strictly prefers x to y, and every individual regards x to be at least as good as y, then the society should prefer x to y."[89] In Sen's version of the Pareto criterion, a group decision can be based on less than unanimous agreement in cases where some individuals are indifferent, and one individual's preferences are aligned in one direction.

In these post-Arrovian formulations of the Pareto principle, it is little appreciated that Pareto's original concept of optimality has been modified to take on a new significance.[90] As originally devised by Pareto, voluntary exchange is the key attribute of his idea of optimality because it guarantees mutual gain and eliminates the possibility of degradation of individuals' welfare. In welfare economics from Pareto to Samuelson, the concept of Pareto optimality was strictly used in reference to an individual's subjective preferences regarding his or her own commodity bundle. In the social choice tradition, however, individuals' preferences over social outcomes include consideration of the fate of others. Because of this fundamental difference between self-oriented and globally oriented preferences, it is not strictly possible to compare Pareto's optimality with social choice theorists' Pareto principle. In Pareto's analysis, a society of individuals left to trade on their own terms would automatically achieve a Pareto optimal outcome due to individuals' initiative to achieve greater satisfaction. In this scenario, the introduction of "unanimity" is entirely superfluous, because each individual is only concerned with his own goods. In the world of social choice theorists, where individuals are thought of as choosing among outcomes affecting everyone, unanimity among a pair of choices directly relates to all society members. Sen exploits the new Pareto condition, which he defines as unanimous preference over collective outcomes, to introduce his "Paretian Liberal Paradox," discussed in chapter 8.

The prominence of the Pareto condition in welfare economics and policy analysis makes it a convenient point of departure for exploring how the development of the rationality project affected public policy. This discussion offers clear criteria for distinguishing between an approach to policy based on marginalist economics and one based on the decision-making tools of the rational choice. The story is best told by starting with the welfare economics procedure of cost–benefit analysis, which relies on marginalist economics, and the idea of Pareto efficiency related to it. This narrative is a somewhat fragmented because of the tremendous ferment in policy analysis in the 1950s, and because there were separate developments in the British and American traditions.[91]

The earliest instance of cost–benefit analysis is most often associated with the idea of Pareto efficiency taken from marginalist economics, and with the Kaldor–Hicks compensation principle articulated in the late 1930s.[92] Recall from chapter 2 J. R. Hicks's contribution to welfare economics that promoted a strict division between facts and values, and utilized an efficiency criterion for making welfare judgments that was supposedly distinct from distributional judgments. The central characteristic of cost–benefit analysis as it developed out of the work of Kaldor and Hicks is that of achieving maximal economic efficiency using the Pareto concept to evaluate between social states. The steps used in achieving a policy choice are the following:

1. The project or projects to be analyzed are identified.
2. All the impacts, both favorable and unfavorable, present and future, on society are determined.
3. Values, usually in dollars, are assigned to these impacts. Favorable impacts will be registered as benefits, unfavorable ones as costs.
4. The *net benefit* (total benefit minus total cost) is calculated.
5. The choice is made.[93]

Decisions are made according to one fundamental rule: "In any choice situation, select the alternative that produces the greatest net benefit."[94] This mode of analysis uses the Pareto concept that any movement to the "Pareto frontier" through net gain is accepted as a legitimate social decision. The Pareto idea used here is not that of unanimity, but instead is that of having achieved greater economic efficiency regardless of the distribution of the benefits: "The fundamental rule guarantees that the benefits of any project undertaken will be large enough so that those who gain by the project *could* compensate those who lose, with everyone thus made better off," regardless of the result that compensation need not actually be made.[95] Marginalist economics is invoked in this analysis, and Edith Stokey and Richard Zeckhauser restate the fundamental rule in marginalist terms: "Expand the size of the project to the point where marginal benefit equals marginal cost."[96] Cost–benefit analysis derived from the Kaldor–Hicks compensation principle is inseparable from marginalist economics, and the goal of the decisionmaker is to achieve the greatest economic efficiency as indicated by Pareto optimality, regardless of distributional consequences.[97] It is true that the Kaldor–Hicks compensation principle may be thought of as a perverse adaptation of Pareto optimality, because winners do not actually compensate losers, yet it has been used to inform policy decisions.

The greatest shift between the cost–benefit approach relying on the concept of Pareto efficiency and public policy analysis based on rational choice theory is a movement away from the idea of efficiency engineering. Roland McKean of the RAND Corporation wrote a transitional book based on the systems analysis research initiative at RAND. The focus of his book, *Efficiency in Government through Systems Analysis,* is the "criteria problem" that had absorbed the attention of many RAND theorists. RAND researchers sought to break through the confines of the basic optimization techniques characteristic of marginalist economics by broadening the scope of their decision tools. Formerly, decision problems had well-defined criteria for optimization, such as net monetary gain or less resources, and were typical of " 'scientific management' or 'efficiency engineering' wherein F. W. Taylor focused attention on factory layout and time-motion studies." [98] The concept of efficiency could be defined using mathematics developed by physicists, as was typical of the rational action of marginalist economics. Wanting to move beyond the constrained maximization paradigm, McKean sought means to determine decision criteria for problems not neatly circumscribed by efficiency considerations. He focused on decision situations with competing goals wherein the decisionmaker must prioritize and make trade-offs among goals. In a water management project these may include increases of the nation's real income, expected benefits as a function of time, and effects on national wealth distribution.[99] McKean could only reach a negative result because he was not able to resolve the criteria problem: "Utility, the label for whatever should ultimately be maximized, depends upon a vast number of variables. . . . Since such functional relationships, and indeed many of the variables, are not fully known to us, the analyst cannot devise any perfect, complete criterion." [100] Leaving the criteria problem theoretically unresolved, McKean proposed general criteria that the decisionmaker must consider, one of which is "changes in the personal distribution of wealth." [101]

While McKean was in the end unable to resolve the criteria problem he put forward, policy analysis was developed on a firm footing by using a combination of techniques from the rationality project. Most ingeniously, while the criteria problem remained irresolvable for the policy analyst, decision theory provided a clear-cut framework for the assertion that individual decisionmakers can make choices over any two disparate outcomes. In the decision theory articulated by von Neumann and Morgenstern, Arrow, Luce and Raiffa, and Savage, individuals are treated as though they can make pair-wise and transitive choices among any set of alternatives offered to them.[102] The new version of cost–benefit analysis, fully congruent with the rationality project, deferred as much as possible to the individual decisionmaker for whom "we postulate that all choices are consistent with an ordering, a transitive and complete relation."[103] Thus, individual rational agents are immune from the criteria problem that daunted policy analysts who were tasked with deciding among competing objectives with differential consequences for members of the community.[104] Policy analysis that incorporated the results of decision theory forged ahead by using individuals' preferences over outcomes instead of the policy maker's criteria.

The result of this new brand of rational choice policy analysis is best articulated in Stokey and Zeckhauser's *A Primer for Policy Analysis*, and in an important essay of Arrow's addressing the implications of decision theory for public policy.[105] Arrow's characteristically concise paper sets forth the outlines of the American approach to cost–benefit analysis that was inseparable from the rationality project. In his view, cost–benefit analysis was not a part of American policymaking until the 1950s, when it emerged within the framework of individual rational choice as explicated by decision theory. What is notable in Arrow's discussion is that policymaking pertaining to potentially risky outcomes, such as building a nuclear power plant, is couched entirely in the language of individual decisionmaking in uncertain circumstances. Arrow notes that "[b]enefit-cost analysis under certainty of course requires not only measures of willingness to pay but also measures of the costs of alternative policies."[106] Public decisions regarding a nuclear power plant raise new issues due to the possibility of a nuclear core meltdown. Specifically, in this case, "we need rationality hypotheses about probability judgements," and hence must consult decision theory in risky and uncertainty situations.[107] It is here that Arrow links decision theory with his social choice theory, combining the two to propose a logically consistent approach to public policy.

Arrow's approach to public decisions encompassing uncertain outcomes is critical for understanding the relationship between the rationality project, as encapsulated in both decision theory and social choice theory, and policy science. Arrow's impossibility theorem had demonstrated the logical contradiction of satisfying five minimalist conditions: individuals' latitude to express any set of transitive preferences; positive association of individual and social preferences; independence of irrelevant alternatives; citizens' sovereignty; and nondictatorship. However, in the public policy problem involving uncertainty, Arrow "ignore[d] all the additional complications due to the difficulties of social choice," and instead supposed "that there is a representative individual." [108] This individual's preferences are to be used in making a rational public policy decision. Arrow then examines the difficulties in probabilistic decision theory, arguing that policymakers must be aware of individuals' propensity to miscalculate probabilities, to exhibit intransitive preferences, and to evaluate outcomes on the basis of the way they are linguistically framed.

It may seem that with the foundational problems marring social choice theory, and the theoretical paradoxes and behavioral anomalies tainting probabilistic decision theory, that rational choice theorists would despair of making progress. This situation led Amartya Sen to remark:

> It seems easy to accept that rationality involves many features that cannot be summarized in terms of some straightforward formula, such as binary consistency. But this recognition does not immediately lead to alternative characterizations that might be regarded as satisfactory, even though the inadequacies of the traditional assumptions of rational behaviour standardly used in economic theory have become hard to deny.[109]

In other words, rational choice theorists have had to accept the logical and behavioral limitations inherent in their approach. This acceptance is made palatable because, as Sen further observed, "[i]t will not be an easy task to find replacements for the standard assumptions of rational behavior . . . and . . . there is little hope of finding an alternative assumption structure that will be as simple and usable as the traditional assumptions of self-interest maximization, or of consistency of choice." [110] Rational choice continues to be the mainline standard bearer in social science and public policy because, despite its limitations, no other system offers equivalent or superior results.

Stokey and Zeckhauser's *A Primer for Policy Analysis* sets forth the rational choice approach to public policy. As with other studies advocating the rationality project, it proceeds by distinguishing between methods of analysis relying on marginalist economics and on the rational choice framework.[111] Choices made on the criterion of efficiency derived from Pareto optimality square with the marginalist paradigm of maximizing resource subject to a budget constraint and ignore distributional consequences. By contrast, in the rational choice framework, decisionmaking criteria are all-encompassing. Indeed, one major task of public policy analysts is to settle on decision criteria among competing objectives (116). Notwithstanding the logical and behavioral perplexities such as Arrow's impossibility theorem, Maurice Allais's paradox, and Daniel Kahneman and Amos Tversky's framing hypothesis, it is possible to see how a coherent mode of policy analysis has been derived from rational choice theory.

Rational choice theory pushes beyond the boundaries of "efficiency engineering" circumscribing marginalist economists to encounter the criteria problem discussed by McKean. By focusing attention exclusively on individuals' sets of well-ordered preferences, the criteria problem could be offset by only requiring information about individuals' wants, regardless of the policymaker's. Thus, for example, Stokey and Zeckhauser look to a "complete, formalized depiction of a decision maker's preferences." This formalized depiction, referred to as an "objective function," "is an explicit statement of how each attribute that is a consequence of a particular choice situation contributes to a single overall index of that choice's desirability" (131). In setting up a decision problem using expected utility theory, all the familiar assumptions are required: an individual is able to make a decision over any pair of choices, including one of indifference; his preferences obey transitivity; he also obeys the rules of probabilistic decisionmaking stipulated by von Neumann and Morgenstern (253). Thus, a policymaker is able to choose decision criteria, and then obtain information about preferences over outcomes from her constituency.

Having obtained this information about preferences, and taking pains to eliminate strategically misstated preferences, the policy analyst has three options from which to choose in making a sound public decision. One of the three options relying on the traditional efficiency criterion is only available if the decision problem conforms to old-style, cost–benefit analysis in accordance with the fundamental rule yielding the greatest net benefit, though failing to take into consideration redistributional effects (137). As applied, however, this method contradicts the social choice rule of the Pareto principle defined as unanimous agreement. A second choice is to follow Arrow in simplifying the decision problem in cases involving uncertainty, or criteria not readily resolvable into monetary quantities. This option negates Arrow's impossibility theorem by permitting some degree of interpersonal comparison of utilities, either by using a representative individual's preferences or the notion of extended sympathy.[112] A third solution open to the policy official is to submit the decision to a public referendum. This relinquishes the idea of collective rationality, and looks to due process as the means of legitimating the decision rather than to logical consistency with the social choice axioms.[113]

The firm hold of the policy analyst is not thwarted by the impossibility theorem nor by foundational problems underlying decision theory. Public policy analysts have well-defined mathematical formulas resting on the premise of individual rationality to guide them in their quest for successful public decisions. Circumventing the criteria problem that limited the reach of public decisionmaking based on Pareto efficiency, rational choice policy analysts assume that individuals can make transitive choices among all sets of outcomes. Arrow's impossibility theorem is then obviated by either permitting some degree of interpersonal comparisons, or by subjecting decisions to elections not predicated on the idea of "collective rationality." Marginalist economics, though still taught as a means of achieving economic efficiency in cost–benefit problems subject to "willingness to pay," is offset by the rational choice framework looking to individual preferences over disparate and uncertain outcomes. Despite the profound theoretical questions lying at the foundation of decision theory, rational choice theory remains a technocrat's dream for achieving public decisions based on individuals' preferences and avoiding disruptive public displays.

PART IV

Rational Choice Liberalism Today

CHAPTER 8

Consolidating Rational Choice Liberalism 1970–2000

The purpose of rational choice is to provide a grand theoretical framework for designing human institutions. . . . [T]he primary motivation for practitioners of rational choice theory, in the course of its evolution since the 1950s, has been to create an integrated, empirical theory of market and polity that would serve the normative purpose of designing "good" institutions.
Norman Schofield

Justice is thought of as a pact between rational egoists the stability of which is dependent on a balance of power and similarity of circumstances. . . . Justice is the virtue of practices where there are assumed to be competing interests and conflicting claims, and where it is supposed that persons will press their rights on each other.
John Rawls

The central part of Rawls's theory [of justice] is a statement of fundamental propositions about the nature of a just society, what may be thought of as a system of axioms. On the one side, it is sought to justify these axioms as deriving from a contract made among rational potential members of society; on the other side, the implications of these axioms for the determination of social institutions are drawn.
Kenneth J. Arrow

THE past chapters have discussed the early development of rational choice theory as an overlapping set of multidisciplinary movements. RAND was identified as a quintessential Cold War organization providing a key locus for generating decision theory and rational policy analysis. Later we saw how social choice, public choice, and positive political theory are best understood as independent and interrelated movements with shared concepts, theorists, and institutional support networks. It is clear that there are no impermeable borders between rational choice in social science, formal decision theory, and public policy analysis. More-

251

over, each of these intellectual endeavors was inseparable from the Cold War initiative to secure the foundations of capitalist democracy. Finally, the continuities and ruptures between rational choice theory and its theoretical predecessors in Adam Smith's system of natural liberty, and the marginalist economists' concept of constrained maximization have been explored.

Rational choice theory, first recognized as a field of research within the social sciences in the 1970s, and then as an established paradigm by the early 1980s, achieved methodological security just as the Cold War drew to an end. Since the conclusion of the Cold War, the motivating force behind the rationality project has become increasingly obscured and forgotten. Rational choice appears to be successful precisely because of its claim to offer objective, nonnormative social scientific analysis independent of ideological concerns over capitalism and democracy. Because rational choice theory itself evinces no historical awareness, even of its own evolution as a scientific discipline, it is often difficult to apprehend the source of the deep divisions between proponents and critics of the research method.

Within the field of political science, institutional victories and the high-profile status of rational choice theory, as well as consistent determination on the part of some Rochester school members to displace other approaches to political science, have positioned positive political theory at the center of much heated debate. As William Riker boldly and antagonistically asserted, "the rational choice paradigm is the oldest, the most well established, and now, . . . the one that by its success is driving out all others."[1] Donald P. Green and Ian Shapiro's 1994 *Pathologies of Rational Choice Theory: A Critique of Applications in Political Science* served to both underscore the widespread acceptance of the rational choice method as a practice within political science, and to articulate reservations about its explanatory powers. Debate over the efficacy of a rational choice theory of politics was continued in the journal *Critical Review,* which devoted an entire issue in 1995 to the controversy generated by Green and Shapiro's widely cited book. The collected essays make it clear that debate over the merits and efficacy of a rational choice theory of politics is engaged on three levels. As in Green and Shapiro's critique, scholars disagree whether positive political theory's theoretical findings and empirical evidence provide meaningful insight into political phenomena. At a second level, scholars disagree over the definition and legitimate practice of social science generally and political science, particularly. At an even more inclusive level, the heated nature of the debate is due to a fundamental disagreement as to whether the rational actor model is sufficient to explain all facets of human behavior.

Despite the articulation of this debate provided by the essays in *Critical Review,* it remains difficult to get a full sense of the reasons why the rational choice approach has provoked such profound disagreement. As a tentative explanation, I would suggest that the heat of this controversy is generated by the relevance of rational choice research to concerns that exceed the bounds of social science methodology and spill out into visions of science and democracy, not just in the United States, but increasingly worldwide. This instance of disciplinary turmoil is a manifestation of a larger set of debates that are inevitable because rational choice theory has a wider scope and a more comprehensive mission than its innocuous identity as a social science methodology would suggest. Due to the dramatic divide between the actual scope of rational choice and its assumed status as merely another method for doing political science, it is helpful to contextualize rational choice scholarship by viewing it against the backdrop of American political scientists' long-standing interest in their disciplinary history and in the dialectical relationship between their field and American democracy.[2] To that end, this chapter first discusses rational choice theory with respect to the enduring Enlightenment project of modernity, and the relationship between rational choice and classic republicanism. Next, I explore how John Rawls's landmark theory of justice serves as a touchstone for the characteristic concepts used by rational choice theorists in their construction of liberal democratic theory. After providing a clear sense of the parameters of rational choice liberalism, Amartya Sen's "Paretian Liberal" paradox pitting social welfare against individual rights is addressed. Finally, I consider the contributions to a liberal theory of democracy made by the second generation of rational choice theorists. Russell Hardin's institutional utilitarianism, David Gauthier's status quo contractarianism, and Ken Binmore's whiggish reformism demonstrate the comprehensive manner in which each puts forward a vision of how to achieve a stable social order. These normative projects, resting on scientific analyses of self-interested rational action, represent differing versions of rational choice liberalism.

Science, Democracy, and the Enlightenment Project of Modernity

Rational choice theory has been at the center of a heated controversy over methodology in political science, and to a lesser degree in other social sciences, because of its theory of human action predicated solely on self-interested rational action, a theory principally expressed in mathematical language. This debate over method is related to other debates concerning political ideology and, ultimately, debates about human life. Despite the high-profile character of much of this controversy, it is difficult from these discussions alone to grasp why there is so much fervor in the exchanges.[3] The pages ahead make the case that rational choice theory is linked to concerns that exceed the bounds of social science methodology, thereby enabling its encompassing vision for how social order and justice should be achieved.

The first step in contextualizing rational choice theory is to ask how it relates to the long-standing conviction that science and democracy are allies in the Enlightenment project of modernity. Obviously, the vast amount of literature on this point cannot be reviewed here. However, one can quickly get a sense of how rational choice fits in this tradition from David A. Hollinger's work on Robert Merton, John Dewey, and other American public intellectuals of the 1930s and 1940s. They, among others, were keen to promote both scientific inquiry and democratic government as allies countering Christian provincialism on the one hand and Nazi fascism on the other.[4] Science and democracy, according to these thinkers, share an ethos of "universalism," "disinterestedness," "communalism," and "organized skepticism." In both, reasoned discussion among equals leads to agreement, either on research findings or on communal ends.

Political scientist John G. Gunnell similarly focuses on the traditional American identity of science and democracy as sharing the values of tolerance, skepticism, and pragmatism. Given the close relationship between American political science and American government, it is not surprising that U.S. political science traditionally promoted both as shared endeavors, much as Hollinger describes in the work of Merton and Dewey. However, Gunnell argues, the influx of fleeing European émigrés in the 1940s destabilized this comfortable partnership between science and democracy that had been central to the ethos of American political scientists since the dawn of American democracy. Such newcomers to America as Leo Strauss, Hannah Arendt, Hans Morgenthau, Theodor Adorno, Eric Voegelin, Franz Neumann, Arnold Brecht, Max Horkheimer, and Herbert Marcuse, each of whom would become a significant political theorist, challenged the comfortable relationship between science and democratic liberalism. They argued that the liberal values underlying science and democracy were specifically those that were unable to halt, and were even complicit in encouraging, the rise of fascism and totalitarianism in Continental Europe of the 1930s and 1940s.[5] In Gunnell's words, "The assessment advanced by émigré scholars . . . was that the problem of totalitarianism was at root a problem of science, liberalism, and relativism."[6]

Gunnell argues that the émigrés' challenges to American liberalism resulted in the distillation of "political theory" as an isolated field within American political science, an isolation still very evident today, as émigrés staked out their territory of commentary and American political scientists reasserted the alliance of science and democratic liberalism characteristic of their field. Gunnell finds that chief among these efforts to reclaim the Enlightenment ties linking scientific inquiry and democratic values were those of David Easton, the leader of the nascent behavioral movement. Easton, and others such as Harold D. Lasswell and Herbert Simon, reformulated the epistemology of the social sciences in keeping with a traditional American instrumental pragmatism combined with logical positivism.[7] Easton's opening chapter of his famous 1953 work *The Political System* echoed the interests of Dewey and Merton in advancing an empiricist and skeptical epistemology that simultaneously sustained and grounded liberal democratic values.[8]

Even though William Riker was adamant in disassociating positive political theory from the burgeoning behavioral movement, he was nonetheless captivated by Easton's vision of a science of politics, and he often used Easton's definition of politics as "the authoritative allocation of values."[9] As argued in part 2 above, Riker, too, was an enthusiast of democratic values in opposition to any which could be construed as totalitarian, fascist, organicist, or socialist; Kenneth Arrow and James Buchanan similarly were keen to advance science and liberal democratic values in opposition to those seemingly responsible for communism or fascism.[10] Gunnell's argument about political theory and the behavioralism, while perhaps not necessarily helpful in all respects for assessing the forces behind the rise of Riker's positive political theory, social choice theory, or the public choice movement, still draws attention to an important point: rational choice theory represents a continuation of the Enlightenment project of promoting scientific inquiry and democratic government.

An emphatic enunciation of this point is provided by political scientist Simon Jackman, who is determined to stave off postmodernism with a joint commitment to science and Enlightenment liberalism:

> I . . . link[ed] both science and liberalism as complementary products of the Enlightenment. I remarked that both science and liberalism are relativist and pragmatic—liberals and scientists make few assumptions about absolute truth. The arguments within social science that I survey . . . show liberalism is actually fairly accommodating of "conditionality" or "contingency," concepts dear to postmodernists, and, as it turns out, concepts that are actually at the heart of science as well. The admission of a contextualized basis for knowledge is not an abandonment of science, but rather an

acknowledgement of the richness of the world that is, if anything, an invitation to inquiry. This admission was the mutual origin of both science and liberalism, the source of their resilience, and will ensure their safe passage through the postmodernist "storm." [11]

Jackman's defense of the partnership of science and liberalism against the threat of postmodernism represents a different context from the postwar concern with totalitarianism, but the single-minded devotion to seeing science and democracy as partners remains constant.

Rational choice theory represents a contribution to a modernist epistemology that supports democratic liberalism by upholding the values of free inquiry, universalism, individual autonomy, and government by trade and negotiation, as opposed to autocratic tyranny or irrational mob rule. Many rational choice scholars also uphold a liberalism of free-market trade, and believe there is a strong correlation between democratization and free markets. In *The End of History and the Last Man,* written largely at RAND, Francis Fukuyama clearly articulates the position.[12] For scholars such as Fukuyama, the fall of the Berlin Wall and the demise of the Soviet Union are seen as victories for freedom, liberal democracy, and free markets. Their understanding is that science, democratic liberalism, and capitalism are based on toleration; free trade and free association; personal autonomy permitting subjective moral standards; an experimental epistemology based on universal laws subject to empirical test; and legitimate rule as a reflection of individuals' interests.

While it is important to recognize that rational choice theory continues the Enlightenment project of advancing knowledge and liberal government, it is also necessary to remember that it represents one specific way of understanding the relationship between scientific epistemology and the legitimating principles of democratic rule. In chapters 6 and 7, I explored how the rational choice account of human action differs from that of both Adam Smith and marginalist economists. The conclusions reached there are that rational choice theory pivots on a historically unprecedented, axiomatically formulated definition of rational self-interest.

American Political Science and Classic Republicanism

Besides understanding that rational choice theory is very much an active participant in furthering a commitment to scientific inquiry and democratic government as joint ventures, it is also helpful to understand the location of rational choice theory within the centuries-old debate between two familiar traditions of political discourse: classic republicanism emphasizing virtuous citizenship, and natural jurisprudence catering to property rights and commerce. In the wake of the impressive works by J. G. A. Pocock and Quentin Skinner, much attention has been drawn to the interplay between these two traditions, and to the key role played by classic republicanism in establishing American democracy.[13] It has been widely recognized that although the classic republic tradition was important to early American democracy, this tradition waned over the nineteenth-century in favor of a tradition favoring commerce, property rights, contracts, and an institutionalized version of virtue.[14] Because of the close relationship between American political scientists and American government, this declining fortune of republicanism has been reflected within the academic pursuits of political scientists. James Farr writes about this interlocking transformation in American statehood and American political science, suggesting that the latter responded to the ebbing of civic republicanism by reciprocally relinquishing its tendency toward a civic-minded pedagogy that sought to instill republican values in citizen-students. Farr observes that "in the course of its first century, American political science was transformed from a political discourse in the service of republican principles to a professional discipline in the service of the administrative state."[15]

As much as it seems appropriate to see rational choice theory as implicated in the furtherance of a specific type of democratic liberalism that counters either Pocock, Skinner, and James T. Kloppenberg's emphasis on classic republicanism, or the community-oriented reinvocation of the virtue-based civic humanist tradition in the works of Charles Taylor, Michael J. Sandel, and Alasdair MacIntyre, there has been a surprising failure to recognize the close association of rational choice theory and the rights-centric liberalism characteristic of John Rawls.[16] Political scientist Rogers M. Smith, in his disciplinary retrospective "Still Blowing in the Wind: The American Quest for a Democratic, Scientific Political Science," comes closest to recognizing the association of rational-choice-driven political theory with a contractarian and rights-oriented liberalism standing in clear opposition to civic republicanism.[17] It is this position of rational choice scholarship within the midst of mainstream, contemporary discussions over liberalism, and as a logical step in the language of natural jurisprudence emphasizing commerce, natural law, and rights, that needs to be further explored. This need is all the more urgent given that rational choice theory is already germane to American political practices insofar as it informs the conceptual foundations of public policy analysis and has become increasingly significant to American jurisprudence through the success of the rational choice-based law and economics movement.

John Rawls's *A Theory of Justice*

The publication in 1971 of *A Theory of Justice* by John Rawls (1921–2002) is widely regarded as a crucial point in political theory that kindled interest in the social contract as a means of achieving a constitution.[18] The densely argued book became the landmark text against which all American political theorists measured their own work; it presented a new point of departure for political theory, seamlessly combining political and economic analyses in a single theory of justice. Kenneth Arrow wrote that "Rawls's major work has been widely and correctly acclaimed as the most searching investigation on the notion of justice in modern times." He further observed that Rawls's facility with economic theory was remarkable, and unique among philosophers and social scientists.[19] Rawls's sophisticated knowledge of economic theory generated an interdisciplinary discussion between economists and political theorists over the basic principles of justice and constitutional democracy. Newly sparked academic interest in the moral bases of politics filled the pages of the recently established journals *Political Theory, History of Political Thought,* and *Philosophy and Public Affairs.*

The intersection of Rawls's project with rational choice theorists' analysis of political economy, and the dependency of both on shared convictions, is not well known. Rawls's stature as a leading twentieth-century philosopher was in part secured through his discourse with prominent rational choice theorists, who developed their own theories as they challenged Rawls to advance his. There are three distinct positions within the rational choice camp whose views are informed by their encounter with the work of Rawls: utilitarianism, social choice, and public choice. As a fully engaged partner in this dialogue, Rawls's idea of justice as fairness was likewise influenced by the growing rational choice approach to political economy.[20] As will be recalled from chapter 3, Rawls presented an early version of his theory at the Meetings for Non-Market Decision Making in 1964 at which John Harsanyi was present. Kenneth Arrow wrote two penetrating critiques of Rawls's *Theory of Justice* in 1973; and Arrow, Rawls, and Amartya Sen together offered a seminar on rationality and justice in 1968 at Harvard University.[21] Though it may come as a surprise given their different political orientations, it is fair to assert that of any two theorists working in the area of contractual constitutional design, John Rawls and James Buchanan had the most similar approaches.[22] The debate between John Harsanyi's rational choice rendition of utilitarianism and John Rawls's rights-based approach to justice provided a steady reference point for subsequent theorists.[23]

This is not the place for a detailed study of the development of Rawls's *Theory of Justice;* that intellectual archaeology would be the subject of a text at least as substantial as the original. The goal here is to provide an overview of the intersection between the various approaches to rational choice liberalism and Rawls's theory of justice. The pertinent approaches include John Harsanyi's utilitarianism, Arrow and Sen's social choice, and Buchanan and Robert Sugden's public choice. During its early years, rational choice theorists were jealously protective against what they perceived to be the encroachment of idealistic, collectivist, or authoritarian philosophical approaches. In the 1960s and early 1970s, the wrangling continued as Arrow and Harsanyi charged Rawls with leaving a door ajar for the entrance of totalitarianism[24]; Buchanan accused Arrow and the utilitarians of sustaining organic social philosophy[25]; Rawls insisted that he did not invoke "a perfectionist or an organic conception of society," and he challenged the presumed sanctity surrounding the notion of the efficiency of market society, though he accepted "a property-owning democracy."[26] What emerges from this early positioning is the overriding impulse to create a social philosophy of justice within the bounds of non-normative scientific analysis. Such positive analysis was believed to provide a secure epistemological basis for social theory and to protect against the excesses of philosophical idealism and organicism. Like rational choice theorists, Rawls strove to make his principles of justice consistent with the premise of rational self-interest that maintains the primacy of the individual to determine personal ends.

Rawls developed his theory of justice in opposition to utilitarianism, a position he believed both to be prevalent in nineteenth- and twentieth-century intellectual history and to underlie much economic theory.[27] Rawls opposed all utilitarian philosophy, from Jeremy Bentham's to Henry Sidgwick's, and including its latest rational choice iteration by John Harsanyi.[28] The basic principle of utilitarianism is that as the individual is best served by rationally pursuing his ends to achieve maximal satisfaction, so "the well-being of society is to be constructed from the fulfillment of the systems of desires of the many individuals who belong to it."[29] Hence, the well-known classic utilitarian principle of "the greatest happiness for the greatest number." Rational choice theory, with its formal expressions of individual utility, provided a consummate tool for investigating individuals' fates in a society given their propensity to rationally pursue self-interest. Demonstrating the widespread currency of rational choice, Rawls accepted this perspective, observing that "[i]t is natural to think that rationality is maximizing something and that in morals it must be maximizing the good."[30] He takes issue, however, with the utilitarian's exclusive emphasis on consequences of actions instead of the sanctity of individuals' rights. In what ends up being a central debate between him and Harsanyi, Rawls disagrees over the appropriate distribution of resources among individuals. He further is at odds with Harsanyi's dependence on an idealized "impartial spectator" as a way of aggregating individuals' satisfaction.

John Harsanyi (1920–2000), formerly at the University of Budapest, adopted John von Neumann and Oskar Morgenstern's axioms of expected utility under conditions of uncertainty to construct his theory of utilitarianism. In 1994 he would be awarded the Nobel prize in economic sciences, shared with John Nash and Reinhard Selton, for his contributions to noncooperative game theory. In two ground-breaking essays in the early 1950s, Harsanyi defended the idea of a minimalist basis for comparing individuals' welfare in accordance with "factual propositions based on certain principles of inductive logic" as a starting point for his utilitarian ethic of maximizing the average utility level of members of society.[31] He follows the suggestion of John Stuart Mill and Knut Wicksell that the overriding social goal is to maximize average welfare among individuals, instead of maximizing total utility, as had been suggested originally by Bentham. Combining von Neumann and Morgenstern's expected utility theory with the idea that "value judgments concerning social welfare are a special class of judgments of preference, inasmuch as they are impersonal judgments of preference," Harsanyi derives his utilitarian ethic.[32] He reasons that individuals are rational decisionmakers in accordance with expected utility theory, and that individuals regularly make interpersonal comparisons of well-being. In his view, public policy judgments should be based on the ethical premise that individuals adopt a position of provisional uncertainty over how they themselves will be affected by policy outcomes. Thus, in evaluating policy, a posture of impartiality is adopted whereby each individual assesses outcomes "as an expression of what sort of society one would prefer if one had an equal chance of being 'put in the place of' any particular member of the society."[33] Given this equiprobability of assuming the identity of any one of society's members, Harsanyi argues that it is appropriate to think of collective decisionmaking as a problem of maximizing utility under the conditions of risk.

Thus, Harsanyi constructs a deductive argument showing that such rational individuals will endorse a principle of maximizing average expected utility, because this provides each member of the community with the greatest likelihood of achieving maximum well-being. The axiomatic system Harsanyi applies in drawing this conclusion resolves the paradox of

Arrow's impossibility theorem by permitting minimalist interpersonal comparisons of utility; that is, Harsanyi permits judgments of the sort that person 1 is better of in condition x than person 2 is in condition y.[34] This allows for trade-offs to be made when the preferences of two individuals conflict as to the desirability of a given social state. Despite the great disrepute into which such attempts to compare individuals' welfare had fallen following the positivist critiques of J. R. Hicks, Lionel Robbins, and Arrow, Harsanyi strenuously argues that "interpersonal comparisons of utility are not value judgments based on some ethical or political postulates but rather are factual propositions based on certain principles of inductive logic."[35] This minimal standard for comparing individuals' well-being became known as the principle of "extended sympathy," and ultimately in 1984 achieved Arrow's cautious and begrudging acceptance.[36]

The building blocks of Harsanyi's deductive argument are rational individuals obeying the axioms of expected utility; minimal interpersonal comparison of utility; and the idea that social choice essentially resembles a situation in which an individual must select a social policy not knowing who among that society's members he will end up being. Because human psychology exhibits biological and cultural regularities and because people routinely make interpersonal comparisons, Harsanyi believes that his philosophy is on firm ground and avoids any normative assumptions. The indubitable conclusion of this combination of facts and axioms is that "our social welfare function must take the form of a weighted sum (weighted mean) of all individual utility functions, with more or less arbitrary weights chosen according to our own value judgments."[37] Thus, Harsanyi finds that scientific analysis can serve as a guide for determining public policy, and concludes that the utilitarian ethic of maximizing average utility per individual wins out over other alternative social ethics.

Rawls devotes chapters 27 and 28 of *A Theory of Justice* to refuting Harsanyi's utilitarian philosophy; he challenges Harsanyi's use of expected utility theory and the soundness of the means used to compare individuals' welfare. The two most significant features of the unfolding discussion between Rawls and Harsanyi are Rawls's adoption of a similar perspective upholding uncertainty over personal fate within the social system, and his substitution of his well-known "maximin" principle for Harsanyi's average utility. In order to lay out the broader dialogue between rational choice theorists and Rawls, it is necessary to distinguish between two levels of discussion. On the one hand, rational choice theorists such as Harsanyi readily accepted Rawls's maximin principle as consonant with the basic premise of rational self-interest, and debated its merits accordingly. On the other hand, a more general debate ensued over whether Rawls's overall system of justice is consistent with rational choice theorists' exclusive reliance on rational self-interest as an explanatory device. I explore the nature and outcome of the first level of discussion before examining the broader question of Rawls's congruence with the principles of rational choice theory.

In the introduction to his study of justice, Rawls explicitly states that "[t]he theory of justice is a part, perhaps the most significant part, of the theory of rational choice."[38] His theory is meant to be as consistent as possible with the assumption of individuals as rational egoists.[39] Indeed, Rawls seeks to justify the basic structure of his theory by insisting that rationally self-interested individuals would accept the basic principles of justice as fairness: "[T]he guiding idea is that the principles of justice for the basic structure of society are the object of the original agreement. They are the principles that free and rational persons concerned to further their own interests would accept in an initial position of equality as defining the fundamental terms of their association."[40] While the individuals Rawls considers are not necessarily egoists bent on wealth and domination, they conform to a "concept of rationality [that] must be interpreted as far as possible in the narrow sense, standard in economic theory, of taking the most effective means to given ends."[41] Rawls stresses that he works to uphold this concept of rationality as much as possible because "one must try to avoid introducing into it any controversial ethical elements."[42]

Rawls's general congruence with rational choice theory is more fully discussed below; here it is important to note his awareness that only departure from the concept of rational self-interest puts his theory at risk of rejection on the basis of incorporating metaphysical elements not consistent with the dictates of nonnormative social science. Rawls's and rational choice theorists participated in a major turf battle over the norms of valid scientific inquiry, wherein it was feared that the admission of ideological or metaphysical assumptions could support communism or totalitarianism. Rawls was so successful in presenting his theory of justice as consistent with self-interested rational action that an avid public choice theorist was led to remark that "Rawls starts from the position that men are rational solipsists searching for principles of justice that reflect considerations exclusively of personal advantage."[43]

Accepting the necessity that justice be manifest in an institutional arrangement to which all self-interested individuals would each agree, Rawls further proposes that there be a "veil of ignorance" as to each citizen's place or status in society. This feature is not unlike Harsanyi's idea of ethical impartiality, which as we saw requires that each individual evaluate social states as though she has an equiprobability of being any member of society.[44] Rawls explains:

> The principles of justice are chosen behind a veil of ignorance. This ensures that no one is advantaged or disadvantaged in the choice of principles by the outcome of natural chance or the contingency of social circumstances. Since all are similarly situated and no one is able to design principles to favor his particular condition, the principles of justice are the result of a fair agreement or bargain.[45]

The veil of ignorance obscures individuals' knowledge of the details of their circumstances so that they are forced to reason about the principles of justice "solely on the basis of general considerations." Individuals do not know their prospective social status, their fortune, their natural abilities, or even their physical aptitudes. Therefore, they must consider how the rules of justice will affect all members of the society, even across generations.[46]

In their "original position" under the veil of ignorance, individuals will agree to two principles to regulate their affairs justly, Rawls argues. These two principles, which he had already articulated in the paper he presented to the 1964 Meetings for the Committee on Non-Market Decision Making, are the following:

> First: each person is to have an equal right to the most extensive basic liberty compatible with similar liberty for others.
> Second: social and economic inequalities are to be arranged so that they are both (a) reasonably expected to be to everyone's advantage, and (b) attached to positions and offices open to all.[47]

The first principle, pertaining to rights, did not receive the full attention of rational choice theorists until Amartya Sen's first attempt to provide an axiomatic definition of rights within the social choice framework, to be discussed below. Harsanyi, for example, responded to Rawls that within his averaged utilitarian ethic, individuals' utility for freedom could easily be integrated into the calculation for determining how to organize a society.[48] Rawls second principle, referred to as the "maximin" or the "difference" principle, was derived from decision theory.[49]

Rawls arrives at his second principle through extensive argument aimed at convincing readers that in reaching agreement on social rules, and in not knowing what role one will play in the social order, rational individuals will hedge their bets and ensure that the least well-off member of society is cared for. In making his case, Rawls argues in his *Theory of Justice* against a society run according to market efficiency because it "permits the distribution of wealth and income to be determined by the natural distribution of abilities and talents," which do not ensure the welfare of society's least well-off members.[50] He seeks to build "fair equality of opportunity" into the basic structure of society (75). His method for achieving this is to insist that inequality of expectations among society's population is only justified when the inequality in question results in "material benefits spread throughout the system and to the least advantaged" member (78). And he believes his system has the added benefit of not straying far from the ideal of efficiency characterizing discussions of free-market economics (79).

In his argument for equality of opportunity, Rawls takes a crucial step by focusing on "primary social goods as the basis of expectation," instead of on individuals' utility, as is the case for utilitarian theorists (90–95). He believes his system has the advantage of not requiring either cardinal or interpersonal comparisons of utility, as does, for example, Harsanyi's system.[51] In his *Theory of Justice*, Rawls defines primary goods as those resources that "are things which it is supposed a rational man wants what ever else he wants." [52] These include rights, liberties, opportunities, powers, income, and wealth; they are the conditions that must be met in order for a person to carry out "the most rational long-term plan of life given reasonably favorable circumstances (92–93). The underlying idea here is that regardless of one's walk in life or one's goals and ambitions, primary goods are equally valuable for one person as for another. In this way, primary goods provide Rawls with an objective basis for comparing individuals' social states, without the need to compare subjective utilities (91).

Rawls was fully aware that he had to make his case for the difference principle with specific reference to Harsanyi's defense of the principle of average utility, because the latter regulative idea could also plausibly achieve the assent of rational agents (150). Rawls reminds readers that "the general conception of justice as fairness requires that all primary social goods be distributed equally unless an unequal distribution would be to everyone's advantage (ibid.). He appeals to decision-theoretic arguments to persuade readers that given the original position of ignorance regarding one's social position, "it is rational for parties to adopt the conservative attitude expressed by . . . [the maximin] rule." In decision theory, the maximin criterion refers to a decision strategy of maximizing one's minimum payoff.[53] Rawls approves of this decision rule because it does not evaluate the likelihood of achieving a minimum payoff; it only maximizes the payoff in the worst possible outcome, even if the probability that this outcome obtains is only one in one hundred. Rawls's reticence to enter into calculations of probabilities stems from his doubt that meaningful estimates can be made in most cases of interest under the veil of ignorance.[54] Thus, his choice of the word "ignorance" rather than "uncertainty" helps to distance his theory of justice from Harsanyi's utilitarian ethic, which depends entirely on von Neumann and Morgenstern's expected utility axioms pertaining to uncertain outcomes.

After putting forth his argument for the maximin decision rule ensuring that all social inequalities benefit the least-advantaged members, Rawls directly challenges the principle of average utility, even while admitting that in many practical circumstances it will lead to the same results as the maximin rule (161). He states that the "average principle appeals to those in the initial situation once they are conceived as single rational individuals prepared to gamble on the most abstract probabilistic reasoning in all cases" (166). Rawls calls into question the averaging utilitarian's premise that it is possible to make probabilistic calculations concerning the likelihood of ending up in the position of any one member of society, high or low, and believes that Harsanyi's entire position depends on such dubious probabilistic estimates (169). However, in developing his parallel arguments—the one supporting his difference principle and the other repudiating Haranyi's average utilitarian ethic—Rawls found himself in a tight corner requiring intricate argument thrusts at not just Harsanyi but also decision theory generally. He notes that Harsanyi's equiprobability concept must ultimately rely on Laplace's principle of insufficient reason (168–71). But not wanting to relinquish to mathematicians the responsibility for making moral judgments, Rawls remarks that

> it may be surprising that the meaning of probability should arise as a problem in moral philosophy, especially in the theory of justice. It is however, the inevitable consequence of the contract doctrine which conceives of moral philosophy as a part of the theory of rational choice. Considerations of probability are bound to enter in given the way in which the initial situation is defined. The veil of ignorance leads directly to the problem of choice under uncertainty. (172)

This passage is telling for three reasons. First, it acknowledges the tremendous epistemological force decision theory had come to have, even in moral philosophy, by the time Rawls constructed his theory. Second, it serves as an acknowledgment that to a large extent Rawls strove to be consistent with rational choice theory in designing his theory. Third, it indicates that, despite Rawls's reservations about using probability theory in conditions of unknown probabilities, he was well aware of how close philosophically his veil-of-ignorance approach was to Harsanyi's theory of average utility. In fact, given Rawls's admission of these three points, it is fair to ask why rational agents, in their state of "ignorance," would prefer the maximin criteria over Harsanyi's average utility principle.

One key aspect of Rawls's argumentative strategy is that he navigates around the features of decision theory with sufficient precision to assuage rational choice theorists, without conceding that the axioms for decision-making under uncertainty must have the final say over matters of justice.[55] He accomplishes this by taking a stand on decision theory as it had developed from von Neumann and Morgenstern's axioms based on objective probabilities, and L. J. Savage's neo-Bayesian approach based on subjective probabilities.[56] He also takes a stand on the distinction between attitudes toward risk in which some individuals prefer taking chances over known probabilities of outcomes, and other situations of uncertainty in which individuals must reach a decision without being clear on the probabilities of outcomes. In Rawls's opinion, justice should not hang in the balance, dependent upon individuals' willingness to gamble; for him, the principles of justice should be independent from considerations of risk because behind the veil of ignorance individuals do not know what their attitudes toward gambling might be. Furthermore, he argues that the probabilities in question for justice must be those that have "an objective basis, that is, a basis in knowledge of particular facts."[57] By relying only on objective probabilities to reach judgments about justice, and by deeming irrelevant subjective attitudes toward risk, Rawls ensures that expected utility theory of von Neumann and Morgenstern, or of Savage, is of little help (173).

As part of his argument for the maximin principle over the theory of average utility, Rawls questions whether it is possible to achieve any meaningful measure of utility across individuals by assuming a representative individual. This is because the subjective perspective of each individual is so strong as to render it impossible to put "oneself in another's shoes" (174). He also urges his readers to consider the types of agreements it would be rational to reach in the original position behind the veil of ignorance. He stresses that "for an agreement to be valid, the parties must be able to honor it under all relevant and foreseeable circumstances" (175). Here Rawls touches on a theme that would occupy the attention of rational choice theorists interested in social justice and constitutional design: How is compliance with the social contract guaranteed? Rawls anticipates the significance of this question and proposes the social covenant based on his difference principle, which he asserts will be the least taxing once one realizes, for example, that one's social position is that of a hourly paid laborer instead of an investment banker. Rawls believes that by ensuring the welfare of the least advantaged of society's members it is more likely that individuals will honor their original commitment and that the society will enjoy greater stability. He argues that the principle of maximizing average utility falls short on these two counts:

it would permit a society in which there were ninety-nine free men and one slave because given the assessment of odds in the process of impersonally considering each individual's utility, it is possible that such an arrangement would best yield average utility. However, once one's condition materialized into being that of a slave, the social organization may not seem so worthy of acquiescence or compliance.[58]

Harsanyi and Rawls engaged in an active debate over the merits of their two approaches. Harsanyi wrote a long response to Rawls's *Theory of Justice,* which was so closely followed by Rawls's defense of his maximin principle that Harsanyi's postscript to his original critique applied to that defense.[59] With each repeatedly cross-referencing Arrow, the intense intellectual effort that went into assessing the fundamental principles and axioms of a rational choice theory of justice is readily apparent to readers of this exchange.[60] In his essay "Can the Maximin Principle Serve as a Basis for Morality," Harsanyi granted to Rawls that the "only alternative to using subjective probabilities, as required by Bayesian theory, would be to use a decision rule chosen from the maximin-principle."[61] But his argument against Rawls rests on two pillars. One is Arrow's argument that, in most cases, Rawls's maximin principle and his own average utility principle have the same social consequences (605). The other is that, where the two principles diverge, Rawls's leads to unpalatable decisionmaking. For example, in the case of two patients requiring heart surgery, the one at death's door and the least likely to survive the procedure would be operated on, while the one with a better prognosis would be passed over.

Harsanyi adamantly defends his use of Bayesian theory, and of the von Neumann–Morgenstern expected utility axioms. He explains: "In my model, every person making a moral value judgment will evaluate any institutional arrangement in terms of the average utility level it yields for the individual members of the society, i.e., in terms of the arithmetic mean of these individuals' von Neumann-Morgenstern (= vNM) utility functions" (600). In case there is any doubt, Harsanyi goes on to clarify that "[t]his means that, under my theory, people's vNM utility functions enter into the very definition of justice and other moral values" (ibid.). He believes that Rawls has misinterpreted the significance of the von Neumann–Morgenstern axioms because Rawls does not understand that, whereas expected utility theory is related to behavior under risk and uncertainty, its primary function is to express subjective importance of goals instead of attitudes toward risk. Harsanyi reaffirms his staunch defense of these axioms as a basis for moral philosophy, concluding that "vNM utility functions have a completely legitimate place in ethics because they express the subjective importance people attach to their various needs and interests" (ibid.). Harsanyi's vindication of his argument is consistent with the rational choice approach to political theory: it attempts to reach normative conclusions from an objective starting point; it is committed to individuals' self-determined goals; it claims to be universally valid; and it relies on rationality defined as instrumental pursuit of goals.

Harsanyi doubted that Rawls's theory of justice is fully consistent with the conclusions of rational choice theory because he believes that Rawls promotes a view of "a society where citizens and legislators are never motivated by their own selfish interests" (603), contrary to what Anthony Downs had established in his *Economic Theory of Democracy*. Thus, he incriminates *A Theory of Justice* for being idealistic. Ultimately, Harsanyi mistrusts what he takes to be Rawls's moralizing and perfectionist approach, fearing that it suggests that way of thinking responsible for the totalitarian threats in the mid-twentieth century. He concludes his review with the remark:

> One thing that all of us must have learned in the last fifty years is that we must never commit ourselves seriously to moral principles or political ideologies that are bound to lead to morally utterly *wrong* policies from time to time—however great the advantages of these principles or ideologies may be in terms of administrative convenience, easy of application, and readier understandability. (605)

Harsanyi puts great stock in what he considers to be scientifically vindicated expected utility axioms as a source of moral philosophy that serves as a bulwark against dangerous political ideologies. That he accuses Rawls of potentially being on the wrong side of the divide illustrates how punctilious social scientists had become about defending their nonnormative method as a platform for building a stable society free of political ideologies.

Arrow brings attention to other features of Rawls's system in his review of *A Theory of Justice*. He is most concerned with Rawls's use of primary goods; his reliance on ordinal, interpersonally comparable well-being to establish the maximin principle; and the epistemological problems potentially marring his "original position." Arrow is extremely skeptical of the meaningfulness of any concept of utility of welfare that involves interpersonal comparisons. Furthermore, he argues that Rawls's attempt to use primary goods as an objective measure of welfare backfires, because in his view it, too, ultimately relies on interpersonal comparisons; moreover, in an extreme case considering only a single primary good, Rawls's maximin criteria does not differ from the sum of utilities approach of the utilitarians.[62] As Harsanyi points out, Arrow mathematically proves that the two approaches are also equivalent in the case where a society's members in the original position are risk adverse.[63]

Also like Harsanyi, Arrow is concerned that the epistemological implications of Rawls's original position have totalitarian consequences. He believes that the original position permits individuals the latitude to hold any view over religion and politics; therefore, it is possible that an individual may hold that, for example, "Catholicism is the true religion, that is part of the knowledge which all sensible people are supposed to have in the original position, and that it insists on it for the salvation of all mankind." But, Arrow asks, "How could this be refuted?" and he argues:

> Indeed, just this sort of argument is raised by writers like [Herbert] Marcuse, not to mention any totalitarian state, and within wider limits, any state. Only those who correctly understand the laws of society should be allowed to express their political opinions. I feel I know that Marxism (or *laissez-faire*) is the truth, therefore, in the original position, I would have supported suppressing other positions. Even Rawls permits suppression of those who do not believe in freedom.[64]

Arrow asserts his own commitment to "very wide toleration," but expresses his doubt that Rawls's original position is sufficient to support it. Thus, with Harsanyi, Arrow is concerned that the ramifications of *A Theory of Justice* may justify authoritarianism on the basis of superior insight. This worry that a social philosophy may embrace totalitarianism by incorporating idealistic elements inconsistent with methodological individualism and rational inquiry has been a consistent theme throughout the development of rational choice theory, and is evident in the writings of Arrow, Tullock and Buchanan, and Riker. It is reminiscent of Arrow's discussion in *Social Choice and Individual Values* of the idealism of Rousseau's general will, Kant's categorical imperative, and Marx's dictum "to each according to his ability, from each according to his need."[65] Rawls had specifically addressed Arrow's claim "that the assumption of unanimity is peculiar to the political philosophy of idealism," arguing that his philosophy of justice was not prone to this foible.[66] Yet the scientifically minded rational choice theorists were not reassured by Rawls's assertion that his "two principles of justice provide an Archimedean point for appraising existing institutions," and that they "provide an independent standard for guiding the course of social change without invoking a perfectionist or organic conception of society."[67]

In his response to Arrow, and by extension to Harsanyi, in his 1974 essay "Some Reasons for the Maximin Criterion," Rawls accepts that attitudes toward risk may appropriately be admitted into a theory of justice, and argues that individuals faced with the task of hammering out the guiding principles of a society will be risk averse. In accepting risk-based argumentation as valid, he adopts Arrow's proof that classic utilitarians will be forced to adopt the maximin principle as "risk aversion increases without limit."[68] During the 1970s, a consensus was reached among rational choice theorists that, as both Harsanyi and Arrow maintained, the maximin and average utility criteria were the two main contending principles for organizing social institutions with distributional consequences.[69] In 1977, Arrow wrote a milestone paper titled "Extended Sympathy and the Possibility of Social Choice," in which he came around to accepting that some degree of interpersonal comparison of utility, as required by both Rawls and Harsanyi, is permissible. With this admission of Arrow, a leading figure in the rational choice community who had previously barred any allowance for interpersonal comparison, various solutions to Arrow's impossibility theorem became possible. Edward Mc-Clennen, an astute participant in the unfolding discussions of social choice and justice, notes that with Arrow's acceptance of "extended sympathy" as a means of achieving valid interpersonal comparisons, solutions to the social choice problem came in two forms: Rawls' maximin criterion and Harsanyi's average utility criterion.[70] Unfortunately, since both systems are derived from axiomatized arguments, there is no way to definitively resolve the debate between the two polar positions since each is based on different underlying assumptions.

Rawls himself was tempted by the development of the social choice discussion to harness Arrow's extended sympathy argument as a means by which to buttress his maximin principle.[71] However, in the long run it seems that Rawls rejected not only the strategy of basing his argument on the fundamental axioms of rational choice theory, but also the entire rational choice project as a worthwhile basis for a theory of justice. This change in his thinking was made clear in his crucial 1985 essay "Justice as Fairness: Political not Metaphysical."[72] This essay opens the door for more fully exploring Rawls's consistency with the principle of rational egoism. Although having all along affirmed a Kantian constructivist approach in his writings on justice, Rawls had also attempted to square his theory of justice with the premise of rational self-interest. But in articulating his commitment to Kantian moral philosophy in the 1985 essay, he wrote "Thus it was an error in *Theory* [*of Justice*] (and a very misleading one) to describe a theory of justice as part of the theory of rational choice."[73]

Rawls's retraction of his earlier commitment to work within the parameters of rational choice is a key moment in the intellectual history of the late-twentieth-century attempt to construct a universal, objective, individualist, and rational political theory. It also provides a helpful point of departure for assessing what falls within the ambit of rational choice liberalism, and what lies beyond its bounds. Rawls overlapped with the rational choice community in his acceptance of universal principles, the necessity for objectively derived judgments, and the importance of individuals' self-determined ends. Up until his 1985 recantation, it could also plausibly be argued that Rawls accepted the premise that individual citizens be considered self-interested rational actors, and that their decisions be consistent with rational choice theory. It was, however, reservations concerning his commitment to the concept of rational action that became the major cause of his break with rational choice theorists; Rawls henceforth endorsed what he referred to as "the Reasonable" in addition to and prior to "the Rational." He explained: "What I should have said is that the conception of justice as fairness uses an account of rational choice subject to reasonable conditions to characterize the deliberations of the parties as representatives of free and equal persons; and all of this within a political conception of justice, which is, of course, a moral conception." [74] For Rawls, then, rational choice theory falls short insofar as it is incapable of supplying the necessary normative ideas and principles essential to justice. He added, "There is no thought of trying to derive the content of justice within a framework that uses an idea of the rational as the sole normative idea." [75]

Rational choice theorists, already worried by the initial publication of *A Theory of Justice,* shunned Rawls's new step of incorporating into his theory a concept of human reason transcending purely instrumental and strategic rational self-interest. To further pursue the reasons behind this reaction requires delving more deeply into rational choice theory as a form of instrumental reason; one possible approach not explored by Rawls is to reexamine whether the fundamental axioms of rational choice can legitimately be said to conform to means–ends, scientifically vindicated reasoning.[76] Rawls, however, removed himself from the mainstream discussion of rational choice, seeking a nonmetaphysical argument for his principles of justice that was not limited to merely instrumental reason. It is no accident that Rawls's rejection of rational choice as a point of departure for justice was accompanied by the assertion that his "conception of justice avoids certain philosophical and metaphysical claims." [77]

Rational choice theory is built on the premise that the fundamental axioms of choice, including transitivity and the von Neumann–Morgenstern axioms (or modifications thereof), are privileged because they rely on scientific laws of cause and effect to ground each person's pursuit of her own goals. Hence, the value of rational choice theory is its ability to extend instrumental rationality to decisionmaking situations of uncertainty and strategic interactions. Human beings are accepted as they are and are not presumed to evince behavioral characteristics contrary to their personal preferences over ends; any normative assumptions introduce an idealism that may leave the door open to authoritarianism.[78] Thus, the rational actor will always pursue his advantage, however he defines it, no matter what the circumstances; concepts of duty and responsibility are alien to the instrumental agent pursuing his goals.

Rawls points up his differences with rational choice theorists by stating that justice is captured by the "fundamental intuitive idea . . . of society as a fair system of cooperation between free and equal persons."[79] This "fair system" comprises "the Reasonable," which he claims "presupposes and subordinates the Rational."[80] Whereas "the Rational" corresponds exactly to rational choice theory, hinging on "rational advantage," "the Reasonable" introduces a new element of commitment on the part of a society's members: "if the participants in a practice accept its rules as fair, and so have no complaint to lodge against it, there arises a prima facie duty . . . of the parties to each other to act in accordance with the practice when it falls upon them to comply."[81]

It is the Kantian constructivism underlying Rawls's assertion of an individual's duty to comply with agreements reached in the past that caused the irreparable rift between him and rational choice theorists. For Rawls it is crucial that parties entering into agreement by mutual consent would be moved, if not by rationality then by reason, to uphold their bargain, regardless of whether it suited them in particular instances encountered later: "[a]s with any moral duty, that of fair play implies a constraint on self-interest in particular cases; on occasion it enjoins conduct which a rational egoist strictly defined would not decide upon."[82] It is fair to observe that while for rational choice theorists it is axiomatic that rational individuals obey the law of transitivity and the axioms of expected utility theory, for Rawls it is axiomatic that reasonable persons will play by the rules to which they originally agreed. For Rawls, reasonable individuals by definition agree on a set of rules to organize their society, and subsequently comply with them. The rational choice theorist, however, presupposes that whatever individuals may agree to at one point, they may later choose to breach when it suits their interests. As will be investigated further with respect to Russell Hardin's *Morality within the Limits of Reason,* David Gauthier's *Morals by Agreement,* and Ken Binmore's *Game Theory and the Social Contract,* it is this problem of compliance counterbalanced against rational self-interest that has come to form a central focus for rational choice theories of politics.

Amartya Sen's Paretian Liberal Paradox

A crucial development in rational choice liberalism was the attempt to ax-iomatically define the concept of "rights" within the social choice tradi-tion. This attempt was first made by Amartya Sen in his 1970 essay "The Impossibility of a Paretian Liberal." [83] With Sen's arrival on the scene of social choice theory, the theory can be said to have come full circle from Arrow's initial formulation of the social choice problem in dialogue with economists during the 1930s and 1940s. Sen, originally from West Ben-gal, India, took up graduate studies at Trinity College, Cambridge Uni-versity, where he studied economics with Maurice Dobb.[84] Dobb, as will be recalled from chapter 2, was one of the economists to whom Arrow re-sponded in specifying that a social choice function must obviate the pos-sibility for ethical absolutism.[85] Dobb had expressed concern over the sanctity of consumer sovereignty, whereas Arrow had endorsed it in his notion of "citizens' sovereignty." [86] Dobb, who himself was not trained in the new set-theoretic language of social choice theory, encouraged Sen to pursue his interest in Arrow's impossibility theorem, even against the ad-vice of Joan Robinson and Piero Sraffa, who thought it a waste of time.[87] Close observers of Sen's work report that "[i]n many ways, Sen has spent his career trying to overcome the limitations imposed by the impossibil-ity theorem on economic theory and policy." [88] It is not possible here to do justice to Sen's contributions to the theories of social choice and wel-fare distribution, for which he was awarded the Nobel prize in econom-ics in 1998. However, one of the remarkable features of Sen's work that should be noted is his indefatigable effort to further the understanding of social choice and collective welfare by working within the boundaries of the rational choice approach, while simultaneously presenting an unre-lenting critique of rational choice.[89] His entrance onto the field of social choice secured it international status.

Sen's construction of the Paretian Liberal paradox resembles Arrow's impossibility theorem. Arrow's fundamental result pertains to a society of three or more members who must decide among three or more outcomes, and demonstrates that it is impossible to uphold five minimal decision conditions: universal domain, positive association of social and individ-ual values, independence of irrelevant alternatives, citizens' sovereignty, and nondictatorship (assuming that transitivity is upheld individually and collectively). Sen's paradox involves a society of two members—

"Mr. Lewd" and "Mr. Prude"—who must make a collective social choice from among three outcomes; he demonstrates that it is impossible to obey three minimal requirements: universal domain, the Pareto condition, and a new condition referred to as minimal liberalism. The three possible outcomes are as follows: Mr. Prude reads *Lady Chatterley's Lover* and Mr. Lewd does not (outcome *a*); Mr. Lewd reads the book and Mr. Prude does not (outcome *b*); neither reads the book (outcome *c*). According to Sen, Mr. Prude's preferences are for *c* over *a* over *b*, because second to neither reading the novel, he would rather read the book of questionable decency himself than let Mr. Lewd revel in it. Mr. Lewd's preferences are for *a* over *b* over *c*, because he would rather broaden Mr. Prude's horizons than read the book himself, and considers neither reading it least favorable.[90] However, given this arrangement of preferences permitted by universal domain, then the Pareto criterion that *a* must be preferred to *b* by unanimous group preference collides with the rights of the individual to read what he wishes. Sen reasons that in making a choice between social state *a* and *c*, that is between only Mr. Prude reading the book or neither reading the book, according to the criterion of minimal liberalism permitting at least one private choice (affecting no one else and to be made by the affected individual), Mr. Prude's choice must be decisive. Therefore, since he clearly prefers that no one read the book to his reading it, *c* is preferable to *a*. However, similarly in the case of making a choice between social states *b* and *c*, that is between only Mr. Lewd reading the book or neither reading it, Mr. Lewd's choice must be decisive. Therefore, since he clearly prefers that he read the book to no one reading it, *b* is preferable *c*. This leads to the irrational collective outcome that, by the Pareto condition and in accordance with the condition of minimal liberalism, *a* is preferred to *b*, *b* is preferred to *c*, and *c* is preferred to *a*.[91]

The crucial feature of Sen's paradox is the demonstration that individual rights are incompatible with collective welfare as defined by the Pareto criterion. Given the widespread enthusiasm for the Pareto condition as a means of making any assessments of social welfare, this result appeared crippling for any hope of reconciling the two goals of pursuing social welfare and securing individuals' rights. There was, in response, an explosion of interest in tackling the formal relationship between rights and the Pareto principle.[92]

The most telling reaction to Sen's paradox was initiated by Robert Sugden, who became recognized by members of the public choice community as the champion of rights versus collective rationality. Sugden's 1983 appraisal of Sen's Paretian Liberal impossibility theorem is illuminating because he links the paradox to the basic premises of social choice theory extending back to Arrow's 1951 *Social Choice and Individual Values*, I. M. D. Little's 1952 critique of Arrow's impossibility theorem, and Arrow's eventual 1967 restatement of the impossibility theorem in response to Little.[93] In assessing the significance of the irreconcilable tension between rights and Pareto optimality, Sugden challenges the entire social choice protocol for arriving at a decisionmaking procedure or a social choice. He capitalizes on Arrow's 1967 admission that social choice theory is meant to be used as a way to help an impartial government official select social outcomes.[94] Given that the social choice procedure can therefore lie in the hands of an arbitrary individual, Sugden argues that "[a]n 'Arrow constitution' is a procedure used by a dictatorial decision-maker to form a value system." By this he means that an Arrovian social choice process reaches decisions above and beyond individual members of society. Just as Harsanyi and Arrow expressed concern lest Rawls's theory of justice result in authoritarianism, so Sugden concludes that "in Arrow's social choice theory the existence of coercion is axiomatic."[95]

One way of making sense of Sugden's critique of the Paretian Liberal paradox is to focus on the concept of Pareto optimality, which as argued above had taken on a new connotation in the hands of social choice theorists.[96] As originally worked out by Pareto, his idea of optimality implies that

> [i]f one . . . [of various combinations of two commodities], say P, was produced and distributed among a group of individuals, these persons could no doubt do some trading that would be mutually advantageous. That is, by free exchange, the satisfaction of some could be increased without decreasing that of others. When no further exchanges would be mutually advantageous, the group would have made the most of the possibilities, given combination P and its initial distribution.[97]

The main point to notice in this definition of Pareto optimality is that individuals voluntarily better their states by trading with others to obtain more desirable commodity bundles. In this criterion for assessing social welfare, individuals consider only their own commodity bundles, and do not hold preferences over end states concerning others. By contrast, the Pareto criterion formulated by Sen, characteristic of social choice literature, pertains to individuals' preferences over the end state of each member of society. For Sen, the two rules defining the Pareto criterion are as follows:

> (a) if everyone in the society is indifferent between two alternative social situations x and y, then the society should be indifferent too; and (b) if at least one individual strictly prefers x to y, then the society should prefer x to y.[98]

On the surface, it appears that Sen's Pareto criterion resembles Pareto optimality; it further appears to amply protect individuals' rights under the proviso that if all but one member of a society are indifferent between two alternatives, and one individual has a strict preference for x over y, then Sen's principle requires that x will be selected, seemingly protecting the individual's right to x. However, the difficulty with the Pareto criterion particular to social choice is that it is not about two-way trades among individuals, but instead involves each individual's preferences over all potential end states, even those differing only by outcomes affecting others.

Sen's Paretian Liberal paradox is reached because in attempting to derive a social choice from the three alternatives "You read the book," "I read the book," "Neither reads the book," preferences over others' actions are included as primary social data into the decision function. Thus, the decision procedure dutifully makes note of my preferences over your actions. Sen's paradox arises as a consequence of both Mr. Prude and Mr. Lewd agreeing that Prude's reading the book is superior to Lewd's reading it, hence by the Pareto principle, making the former superior to the latter. However, when the decision problem is considered to be one of individual rights, then obviously Mr. Lewd chooses to read the book, while Mr. Prude does not. The conflict arises from assuming that one individual's preferences over another's actions in the domain of rights is relevant to reaching a collective decision; this basic assumption is inherent to the Pareto condition standard in social choice theory involving individuals' preferences over everyone's end state.[99] Many writers believe that rights should be given priority over a social welfare criterion even as minimalist as the Pareto condition used in social choice theory.[100] Insofar as rights in some instances are felt to unconditionally trump social welfare, James Buchanan and other public choice theorists can be seen to reach a position close to Rawls's, who persistently argued that individual liberty must take precedence over any measures of social welfare.

However, even in accepting the primacy of rights over the most minimal condition of social welfare captured by the Pareto criterion, the conflict characterized by the Paretian Liberal paradox cannot be dismissed as inconsequential. Explaining away the source of the logical inconsistency does not detract from the fact that individuals' full use of their rights may, in some instances, even under unanimous agreement, result in a state less preferred. Furthermore, it is basic to social choice theory that individuals' preferences determine social outcomes independently of who actually implements the decision. Perhaps the most significant outcome of Sen's paradox is that rational choice theorists across the spectrum have had to consider how rights are most appropriately represented in axiomatic choice theory, and what emphasis to give to individual rights versus collective social welfare.[101]

Second-Generation Rational Choice Liberalism: Hardin, Gauthier, Binmore, and McClennen

My discussion of rational choice liberalism now turns toward more recent formulations of a rational choice approach to politics that rest on the work of the early pioneers: Black, Arrow, Downs, Buchanan and Tullock, Riker, and Olson. Here the focus is on Russell Hardin, David Gauthier, Ken Binmore, and Edward McClennen. Each theorist is committed to the centrality of the concept of rational self-interest: that "the rational person . . . seeks the greatest satisfaction of her own interests," and that reason is inseparable from "interest . . . , advantage, benefit, preference, satisfaction, or individual utility." [102] Individualism remains a key component of analysis; "[a] person is conceived as an independent centre of activity, endeavoring to direct his capacities and resources to the fulfillment of his interests." [103] Binmore's vindication of individualism is more personal: "I see no reason to over-rule the judgments of mature adults about their personal tastes. I certainly want nobody doing this to me." [104]

For Hardin, Gauthier, and Binmore, the rational choice approach is deemed to come as close to complete objectivity as is humanly possible, and "it is almost universally accepted and employed in the social sciences." [105] Moreover, the methodological assumptions and processes of rational choice theory are thought to be universally applicable across epochs and civilizations: "The supposition that to conceive of a human being as a maximizer of expected utility is to conceive of him in a limited way, determined by the particular conditions of our own Western society, but neither generally applicable nor ideally appropriate, is mistaken." [106] Other social schemes that do not begin with the basic assumption of rational self-interest represent idealistic longings for utopia that can only miscarry. Thus, it is recommended:

> In responding to such utopian critics, the first step is to challenge their claim to the moral high ground by pointing out that you share their dislike of objective fact that only second-best societies are consistent with what evolution has made of human nature, but what we like or dislike is irrelevant to what is true.[107]

Rational choice liberalism adopts decision theory and seeks to discover an objective and universally valid framework for social coordination under the assumption of the individual's rational self-interest. Hardin, Gauthier, and Binmore each promote one such framework for social theory: progressive institutional utilitarianism, status quo contractarianism, and whiggish realism, respectively.

Russell Hardin's 1982 text *Collective Action* is the natural successor to Mancur Olson's *Logic of Collective Action*. [108] Using precise marginalist calculations of what an individual stands to gain and lose from participating in collective actions, Olson had demonstrated that it is irrational to cooperate to achieve common goals. Hardin endorses Olson's conclusion, while basing his analysis entirely on game theory. Hardin argues that all possible cases of collective action, whether involving a few or many people, can be analyzed using the "Prisoner's dilemma," developed by RAND researchers Merrill Flood and Melvin Dresher in 1950. [109] The Prisoner's dilemma game usually is set up by assuming two individuals convicted of conspiring to commit a crime who have been imprisoned in isolation from each other and are given the same options: each person has the choice of either confessing his crimes or not, with four possible outcomes, depending on what course of action the other prisoner opts for. If both individuals choose to cooperate with the jailer, each confessing his participation, then each is sentenced to five years in prison. If neither individual chooses to talk, then each will be sentenced to one year. However, if one individual opts to confess, and the other does not, then so much the better for the confessor who walks away with no jail time, while his ex-partner is imprisoned for ten years. This scenario has received close attention from game theorists because of the apparent paradox that the seemingly mutually superior outcome of neither confessing, and both serving a one-year sentence, is universally regarded as an irrational course of action for either to take. [110] The reasoning is that from the perspective of each isolated individual, his "payoff" is better if he confesses *regardless* of the decision made by the other prisoner. Therefore, one can be certain that if caught up in a Prisoner's dilemma situation with a game theorist as one's fellow inmate, he will confess. [111] The paradox that both individuals end up worse off by this joint action is a consequence of both individuals serving five years rather than serving one; each person selecting to maximize personal utility ends up in a suboptimal outcome, considering the range of possibilities.

Hardin finds the Prisoner's dilemma to be a superb tool for studying collective action because "it is evidently to [the] Individual's advantage to choose the strategy of not paying toward the purchase of the collective good," and therefore "no matter what [the] Collective does, [the] Individual is better off not [cooperating]." [112] Thus, using game theory instead of marginal analysis, Hardin concurs with Olson that it is not rational for the individual to participate in collective action, because the individual is always better off "free riding" on the efforts of others. Therefore, on the premise of self-interested reason, collective actions are doomed to fail.

Hardin uses the Prisoner's dilemma to undertake an exhaustive analysis of all types of collective action problems—from small communities to anonymous populations, from single interactions to repeated interactions. He points to the irony that, despite his analysis, some of the prominent social movements of the 1960s and 1970s were successful, most significantly the civil rights movement. Thus, part of his work in *Collective Action* is devoted to understanding why the application of the Prisoner's dilemma analysis fails in some instances. Hardin concludes that successful collective actions result as a consequence of one of three features. First, individuals may be ignorant as to their rational strategies of action, and therefore contribute as an error in judgment. Second, individuals may believe in a Hegelian spirit of history, and therefore reevaluate their personal payoffs by interpreting participation in the collectivity as its own reward. Third, in settings that involve smaller communities and repeated interactions, or in which sanctions can be applied to social dropouts, individuals' payoff assessments are altered to make it in each individual's best interest to cooperate.[113]

Hardin's *Collective Action* served as a springboard for his more comprehensive exploration of social order in *Morality within the Limits of Reason*.[114] Here he argues for an institutional utilitarianism, which grows out of his finding that the Prisoner's dilemma characterizing large-scale collective action problems such as government can be solved through the application of sanctions. His approach is thoroughly utilitarian insofar as it holds that only the outcomes of actions are pertinent to assessing morality, social well-being, and effective government. His argument, true to a rational choice theorist, depends only on the assumption of rational self-interest.

To frame his analysis, Hardin posits three societies of different sizes: two-party dyads, small groups, and large groups with social anonymity among members. He then considers which of three types of games from game theory are useful for his analysis: coordinating games, conflict games, and mixed games. In a coordination game, like choosing which side of the road to drive on, each person benefits, so according to Hardin, this class of social interactions is not a candidate for moral analysis. However, both conflict games, in which one person's gain is another's loss, and mixed games, such as the Prisoner's dilemma, are key to moral and utilitarian concerns. While Hardin discusses these two game types with respect to all three differently sized societies, the key two categories he discusses are large-scale mixed strategy games and large-scale pure conflict situations, which Hardin argues are at the heart of the social contract and justice. He incorporates the possibility for ongoing, repeated interactions into his investigation.

In *Morality within the Limits of Reason,* Hardin examines the mixed coordination and conflict game represented by the Prisoner's dilemma, and draws on the findings of his former analysis of collective action that the Prisoner's dilemma exemplifies large-scale collective action problems pertaining to government: "if not coerced by government, the [rational] citizen faces a severe problem of the logic of collective action" (46), since it is in her self-interest not to cooperate. In his discussion of the problem of social cooperation, Hardin includes basic exchange transactions as typical of the Prisoner's dilemma so that even when individual anonymous members of society transact business with each other, there is the constant possibility that one will "defect" and steal the other's goods, failing on her promise to follow through on the trade. For Hardin, the Prisoner's dilemma is ubiquitous in social interactions. His institutional utilitarian solution to this social cooperation dilemma is to impose external sanctions to motivate citizens' compliance, whether in honoring private contracts or paying taxes.

Hardin holds that the issue of rights are best analyzed using the Prisoner's dilemma because rights must be mutually binding in order for all parties to benefit. Recall that Sen's Paretian Liberal paradox introduces a quandary for the utilitarian theorist by demonstrating that an irreconcilable tension exists between aggregate social welfare and individuals' rights. Hardin argues, like Harsanyi before him, that he can incorporate the consideration of rights into his utilitarian framework because the "point of traditional legal rights is to secure the aggregation of individual benefits" (81). Rights pertain at the dyadic, group, and collective levels, and to the issues of privacy, exchange, and free speech. For Hardin, the core issue that Sen attempts to address in his Paretian Liberal paradox is not between general welfare and individual rights, but among "strategic interactions and severe limits of reason and information that require that we create institutional devices to handle them" (111). Hardin proposes that the Paretian Liberal paradox is better perceived as a potential trade relation among two parties in which Mr. Prude promises to Mr. Lewd that he will read *Lady Chatterley's Lover.* In this reading of Sen's problem, the focus shifts from an insuperable paradox to whether or not Mr. Prude will come through on his promise to read the what for him is a disturbing novel. Thus, for Hardin, rights issues such as Sen's ultimately "boil . . . down to a special case of a more general logic of collective action" (ibid.). Thus, in the situation of individuals' rights, Hardin recommends the same institutional solution as before—that institutions apply a sanction structure to enforce rights. Oddly, with this proposal, his solution may best be thought of as an institutional enforcement of what Rousseau and Kant had proposed as a matter of individual voluntary commitment: "There is surely no paradox in the action of constraining our own actions in advance in order strategically to make ours a better world, considered from our own interests." [115]

Hardin's large-scale collective action problem, represented by the mixed game form of the Prisoner's dilemma involving mutual benefit with the possibility for exploitation, maps well the traditional category of the enforcement of negative liberties. That is, how do we draw a line between an individual's rights and his encroachment on another's rights, as in the case of smoking tobacco, and how is the line enforced after it is drawn? His institutional solution provides a means of enforcing the social contract, but is ultimately in each individual's self-interest. Moreover, Hardin believes that such institutions have evolved socially to solve the problem that a precise, case-by-case adjudication of rights is impossible due to limits of human knowledge and reason. Thus, he suggests that institutions provide rule of thumb resolutions of rights that on average benefit all members of society.

In our account thus far, Hardin has proceeded without requiring interpersonal comparisons of welfare, and he has not yet tackled the concern of distributive justice. In his analysis, distributive justice is best understood as a game type of pure conflict because it involves beneficence, that is to say, wealthier individuals giving to less-advantaged individuals. Here Hardin is in the province of Rawls's primary goods, his maximin principle, and Harsanyi's average utility principle. Hardin acknowledges that within the rational choice approach to justice, without any interpersonal comparison of utility or well-being, nothing can be said about redistributive goals. However, he accepts that even a minimal standard for interpersonal comparisons is sufficient to motivate either Rawls's maximin or Harsanyi's average utility criterion. Hardin does not find it fruitful to resort to a hypothetical original position for hammering out an ideal constitution, instead arguing from present-day, real-world expectations that the maximin rule is pertinent to a society with many worse-off people, whereas the average utility principle is pertinent to a society with few worse-off people. In either case, however, just as in the case of rights and the social contract, institutional sanctions are necessary to guarantee compliance with whichever rule is chosen.

David Gauthier is a contractarian theorist who makes a case for enlightened self-interest. Like Hardin and other rational choice theorists, he endorses the view that rational individuals are self-interested maximizers. Like James Buchanan, he looks to the status quo arrangement of society as the only meaningful ground for arriving at a social contract because it is the only realistic starting point. He rules out redistributional concerns as relevant to the social contract, because in his view, no one would agree to a contract in which he may end up bearing the cost of redistribution. Gauthier believes his approach to the social contract upholds the Western liberal tradition by emphasizing individual freedom. In his central text *Morals by Agreement,* he observes:

> Moral relationships among the participants in a co-operative venture for mutual advantage have a firm basis in the rationality of participants. And it has been plausible to represent the society that has emerged in western Europe and America in recent centuries as such a venture. For Western society has discovered how to harness the efforts of the individual, working for his own good, in the cause of ever-increasing mutual benefit.[116]

Given this view of Western society as an arrangement for mutual benefit based on the prospect for ever-increasing gains, Gauthier is emphatic that individuals who do not contribute to the net sum benefit should be overlooked when seeking the terms of the social contract:

> From a technology that made it possible for an ever-increasing proportion of persons to increase the average level of well-being, our society is passing to a technology, best exemplified by developments in medicine, that make possible an ever-increasing transfer of benefits to persons who decrease that average. Such persons are not party to the moral relationships grounded by a contractarian theory. (18)

Gauthier's morals by agreement only concern individuals capable of engaging in mutually beneficial exchange relationships. His position is consistent with his unqualified reluctance to incorporate any notion of interpersonal comparison of utility or welfare into his theory (63, 104).

Gauthier upholds the free-market system as paradigmatic for ensuring individuals' freedoms without imposing any moral constraints on their actions. Here he differs from Hardin, who suggests that even market transactions embody the uncompromising logic of the Prisoner's dilemma because each individual has the incentive to break his commitment to the bargain, and to steal from the other. For Gauthier, free-market society unproblematically expresses the ideal of impartial spectators selecting from an array of social forms; certainly, he argues, the "ideal actor is . . . not a socialist" (261). In his analysis, the only potential difficulties requiring special attention in the social contract arise as well-known cases of market failures yielding "externalities," or negative payoffs not accounted for in anyone's incentive structure, and the provision of public goods falling afoul of the collective action problem.

In order to address these failures of the free-market system, Gauthier seizes on the Prisoner's dilemma as the most fruitful tool of analysis: How is it rational for a self-interested utility maximizer to cooperate socially when, as has been established as axiomatic among rational choice theorists, it is *always* in an individual's immediate self-interest to defect from cooperative ventures. Gauthier's answer is that a rational individual will carefully calculate her expected benefits versus concessions from cooperation, and will arrive at the principle of "maximax relative concession," which holds that "in any co-operative interaction, the rational joint strategy is determined by a bargain among the co-operators in which each advances his maximal claim and then offers a concession no greater in relative magnitude than the minimax concession" (145). This principle isolates what rational bargainers will agree to because their expected mutual benefits outweigh their potential concessions. Since all bargainers are rational, he argues that each will agree on the identical strategy of action. Most importantly, each individual agrees in the original bargain to constrain his behavior to reach better outcomes for each member. In this crucial argument, Gauthier dismantles von Neumann and Morgenstern's expected utility theory, because a von Neumann–Morgenstern actor must necessarily defect in the Prisoner's dilemma (182). Instead, Gauthier substitutes his own concept of "constrained maximization" to capture the idea that self-interested rational maximizers will enter into agreements to constrain their own behavior in order to achieve superior mutually beneficial outcomes. Gauthier capitalizes on the circulating concept of "constrained maximization" introduced by the marginalist economists, but transforms it from constraint under a budget to rational self-constraint to achieve better ends in conjunction with other like agents (182–89).

Thus, under a typical Prisoner's dilemma analysis, individuals decide it is in their self-interest to cooperate if each stands to gain. People follow through on their agreement because it is ultimately in their self-interest. Given that Gauthier has assumed jointly symmetrical actions on the part of his rational participants, he only has to worry about excluding those von Neumann–Morgenstern actors who have not yielded their understanding of rational action to his. Such actors will be inclined to make false promises, to lie, and to cheat the system whenever it offers better expected benefits. Gauthier proposes two mechanisms for excluding those actors following their narrow self-interest: one is through signaling among enlightened rational actors so that they may recognize each other, and cooperate accordingly; the other is to exclude cheaters from all social commerce.

Although starting from the identical premise of rational self-interest, Hardin and Gauthier reach different conclusions about the most effective means of ordering society. Hardin solves the Prisoner's dilemma, which presents an obstacle to social order, by proposing institutionally applied external sanctions to achieve the desired and mutually beneficial behavioral results. Gauthier argues that it is rational for individuals to regulate their own maximizing behavior because "when we correctly understand how utility-maximization is identified with practical rationality, we see that morality is an essential part of maximization" (184). Enlightened self-interest pays off, and thus provides a rationale for social cooperation, given assurances of not conceding more than one stands to gain and of eliminating unenlightened von Neumann–Morgenstern actors from the group.

The final rational choice liberal up for consideration, like Hardin and Gauthier, promotes a political agenda, though his is most accurately regarded as reality-driven Whiggish reformism. Of the three, Ken Binmore is the most ambitious, entering into dialogue with nearly every rational choice theorist to date and, more fancifully, with the entire tradition of Western philosophy. His major contribution to rational choice liberalism is *Game Theory and the Social Contract,* comprising two volumes entitled *Playing Fair* and *Just Playing.* He has little patience for practically all his predecessors with the exception of John Rawls and John Harsanyi, for whom, despite what he considers to be their idealistic and utopian shortcomings, he evinces respect and even fondness.

Binmore's two-volume work has three goals that together give it a vast scope: to be a rational choice primer, to engage other leading theorists in scholarly debate over nuances of rational choice theory, and to provide a comprehensive argument for his Whiggish reform position. Binmore proceeds by inviting the reader to observe Adam and Eve in the Garden of Eden as they negotiate the terms of their marriage. While Adam and Eve are the primal protagonists in a Rawlsian original position, Binmore replaces God with Darwinian evolution, thus creating an anthropological state of primitive nature. Binmore then de-idealizes Rawls's position by incorporating such elements as the biological evolution of genes, the social evolution of norms and customs, and the historical development of entrenched status quo arrangements that establish a de facto social contract. He thus creates a new, seemingly scientific argument for rational choice liberalism.

Binmore deviates from other rational choice theorists in his understanding of rationality, locating it in consistency of action, either at the genetic or the individual level. For him, individuals and processes are rational so long as they are consistent.[117] Evolution and society favor those who consistently survive, so rational self-interest is inherited as part of the process. In fact, for Binmore, individuals' preferences are most likely supplied to them as a function of biological and social evolution. Therefore, we are not surprised to read that while Eve desires to feed her starving children, Adam needs to buy a red Porsche with fully reclining seats. Both Adam and Eve "are to respond optimally to their genetic imperatives." Adam's "ultimate aim is to get laid as often as possible, so that his genes can be spread far and wide."[118]

The question arises as to what sort of society people might hope for given the lack of an omnipotent power to enforce those bargains that are made, and given their murky past countenancing all sorts of only now apparent social injustices. Binmore's response is an intricate argument that rests on expected utility theory, bargaining theory, Harsanyi-style interpersonal comparisons of utility, the concept of Pareto improvements, and game-theoretic equilibria. He argues that any social arrangements reached in primitive society involved extended sympathy, that is, placing oneself in another's shoes to determine if agreements were fair. What is considered "fair," of course, has differed throughout history and has resulted in various social arrangements. The chief feature of these arrangements is their stability, which is "the prime need of a society" (500). Stability signified that an "equilibrium" had been reached; this is not necessarily an optimal equilibrium, but is at least one that individuals had sufficient self-interest to participate in, given their ultimate worry of social anarchy.

Reasoning in the language of markets, Binmore concludes in *Just Playing* that social evolution over time inevitably produces a surplus. Because this surplus is not accounted for as part of the equilibrium of the status quo, it becomes the subject of a modified social contract. It is here that Binmore's whiggish reformist inclinations come into play. He argues that in order to ensure social stability, people will agree to distribute this surplus in such a way that the least advantaged benefit. Thus, he endorses Rawls's maximin principle, although he claims to have removed from it any traces of Kantian idealism and to have deduced the principle purely from the scientific analysis of concerns about social stability. Like Rawls, Binmore argues that the maximin principle is attractive specifically because it fosters social stability rather than breeding the anger and potential revolutionary spirit of marginalized members of society. In considering his version of the maximin principle as conducive to social stability, it is key that it not be read as a redistributive principle, but only as a careful deployment of newly generated sources of social wealth that were previously unaccounted for. Binmore's "whig proposal is that we select whichever of the *Pareto-efficient* contracts in our current feasible set is *fairest* according to current thinking" (506). He explains:

> My pragmatic suggestion is that we adapt the fairness norms that are in daily use for settling small-scale coordination problems to large-scale problems of social reform. I argue that the underlying fairness algorithm was probably biologically fixed when we lived in anarchic hunter-gatherer communities, at which time any workable fairness understandings would necessarily have been self-enforcing. The structure of instinctive fairness intuitions [that reflect maximin and not average utility] is therefore well suited for application to the problem of constitutional reform, where external enforcement is absent by the very nature of the problem. (500)

Binmore believes that an instinct for fairness has become part of the human species biological endowment. He is a staunch believer in the power of scientific investigation and deductive logic to deliver sound social policy recommendations.

The second generation rational choice liberals reserve half a breath for extinguishing any remaining credibility that Marxism has as a social philosophy.[119] Binmore asserts, on the basis of his argument for an evolved standard of fairness, that "an authority governing on the socialist principles advocated by utopian levelers from John Ball to Karl Marx cannot avoid creating destabilizing resentment."[120] In his view, socialism sanctions an unrealistic deployment of resources to unworthy members of society, those who may need but who cannot contribute: "[h]ence the misery and abuse endured by the aged who outlive their resources, by uncuddly animals, by evil-smelling and foul-mouthed street people, by friendless orphans and the mentally handicapped."[121]

Given this relentless attack on the Marxist philosophy by rational choice theorists who deem it irrational to gratuitously give up any expected utility by entering into relations with others, it is worth briefly assessing the status of contemporary Marxist theory. Marxist philosophy may be said to have followed two different responses to the rational choice critique. One is to continue to assert that "[p]ositivist social science and analytical philosophy . . . [are] prime instances of 'instrumental reason'" that Marxists have sought to subvert.[122] The other response is one recently taken by a small contingent of rational choice theorists seeking to reconstruct Marxism as a viable philosophy, or, perhaps more accurately, by a group of Marxist theorists seeking to harness rational choice. In either case, it is acknowledged there is a lack of consensus among Marxists about the core of their position leading "many commentators to consider this a period of profound theoretical crisis within Marxism." [123]

The rational choice variant of Marxism, which since 1986 has been referred to by its practitioners as "analytical Marxism," emerged in the United States and Great Britain in the 1970s. However, this group of theorists has not yet to produce a coherent revised Marxist philosophy; one participant notes "[t]heoretically, there is considerable disagreement over virtually all issues within this group." [124] More significantly, in nurturing a new strand of Marxist theory, they have entered into surprisingly little dialogue with mainstream rational choice theorists. Another close observer of the fledgling movement reports:

> The elusiveness of RCM's [rational choice Marxism's] distinctive identity may have something to do with a certain lack of critical self-awareness among its practitioners. They are remarkably insensitive to the history and context of ideas in general, and to their own ideas in particular; and they have generally inclined to remain within a very narrow universe of debate. [125]

Startlingly, we are told, "RCMists, to judge by the extent of their mutually self-confirming footnoting and the restricted range of controversy encompassed by their writings, seem to talk largely to each other." [126] Analytic Marxists have not responded, or even systematically catalogued, the major challenges to their position mounted by Mancur Olson, James Buchanan and Gordon Tullock, Kenneth Arrow, and William Riker; they do not seem to notice that by and large rational choice theory has systematically dismantled Marx's slogan "From each according to his ability, to each according to his need." However, as with the liberal project whose fate was lamented by Joseph Schumpeter, Friedrich von Hayek, and Karl Popper, it may be possible to underestimate "the remarkable tendency of Western Marxism to renew itself, despite everything." [127]

To conclude this discussion of rational choice liberalism, I briefly consider the work of Edward F. McClennen, who is constructing his own theoretical framework analyzing individuals' potential for resolute commitment and their attitudes toward risk. [128] Like Binmore, McClennen has a sense of the wide-reaching significance of rational choice liberalism seen against the backdrop of earlier philosophical theories of social contract. He writes:

> It is unfashionable in this post-enlightenment age to speak of the enlightenment ideal of progress toward a more rational ordering of relations between persons. In fact, however, economic approaches to the setting of pri-

orities—the rational ordering of scarce resources to meet ordinary needs and desires, and the organization of human energies to pursue such mundane ends—has had an enormous impact on social and political relations in the modern world.[129]

McClennen refers to the postmodern critique of knowledge and science waged in the "science wars" between natural scientists and humanists.[130] For the most part, in a way that is difficult to explain except as the result of the McCarthy-era "cleansing" that served to align economics and political science with the prerogatives of American capitalist democracy, the social sciences generally and rational choice theory specifically have not drawn the focus of this postmodern critique. As McClennen suggests, belief in instrumental rationality embedded in market practices utilizing resources to meet human needs and desires has become an entrenched principle of social life. Instrumental rationality, modified by game theory and expected utility theory to analyze how other individuals' actions can be incorporated as means into the strategic and uncertain pursuit of ends, has gained worldwide practical and theoretical assent.

McClennen associates the rise of market practices as a way of conducting human affairs and the theoretical structure of instrumental reason with the erosion of traditional philosophical and religious metaphysics and morality. He observes:

> This [rational desire fulfillment] has led to the increasing erosion of the staying power of traditional ideologies.
>
> But with that erosion, as suggested above, the issue of justice as fairness, and the issue of the justification of inequalities, becomes all the more pressing. It is ironic (but then in its own way quite predictable) that the economic rationalization of relations has been accompanied by a sustained effort to marginalize considerations of fairness and (economic) equality. The liberal credo in recent years has involved an increasing stress on the *deregulation* of economic activity, and a call to reduce redistrubutive measures, but it also does so in the face of the fact that the increasing acceptance of the "economic" approach creates the conditions under which these very issues cannot be so easily finessed.[131]

Binmore's description of this erosion is more graphic: "The market is . . . the final step in a process that first leaches out the moral content of a culture and then erodes the autonomy of its citizens by shaping their personal preferences."[132] Both rational choice theorists point to the power of markets and rationality to weaken traditional socially enforced value structures that once served to moderate individuals' behavior in order to generate prized equilibria: self-sustaining outcomes that form the bases of stable social order.

Confronted with the bare-bone reality of the human condition, postreligious men and women have lost the innocence that once led them to allow morality plays of hellfire and brimstone to inform their actions. Once stripped of their innocence, people face an new coordination problem because their earlier belief systems had effected socially coherent equilibria. The market, believed to require nothing other than minimalist means–ends reasoning, is thought to best mimic humanity's prehistorical condition in which individuals learned to cooperate in response to the biological imperatives for individual survival.[133] Overlooked by many economists, however, is the residual concern that even the market requires a basic level of normative consensus to prevent its succumbing to the ever-present temptation, as seen in the Prisoner's dilemma, to resort to theft. Given this composite situation, McClennen hopes that the erosion of traditional worldviews will give increased urgency to the imperative to build a just society because social injustices are no longer obscured by tradition and defy rational explanation. The problem of creating a just society within the constraints of rationality has urgency because in McClennens's view only scientific reasoning can provide a sound basis for social philosophy and social order.

According to the brave new world of rational choice liberalism, the findings of natural science and objective imperatives of means–ends rationality counter Kantian and Marxist efforts to sustain idealist philosophy. Suggesting that the scientific objectivity of rational choice theory provides an antidote to fascism and communism, Binmore remarks:

> David Hume was right to predict that superstition would survive for hundreds of years after his death, but how could be have anticipated that his own work would inspire Kant to invent a new package of superstitions? Or that the incoherent system of Marx would move vast populations to engineer their own ruin? Or that the infantile rantings of the author of *Mein Kampf* would be capable of bringing the world to war?[134]

The liberal challenge, answered in various ways by Hardin, Gauthier, Buchanan, Binmore, and McClennen, has been to devise an organization for social coordination as a function of the "goals or ends espoused by the persons whose activities are to be regulated by those institutions."[135]

It is worth briefly reviewing how rational choice theory found success over more traditional social philosophies expressed by the phrases "love thy neighbor as thyself," "from each according to his ability, to each according to his need," and "act only on the maxim that you would at the same time will to be a universal law." Its ascendancy is primarily the result of the strict assertion for itself of scientific objectivity while charging its opponents with having unfounded normative and ideological assumptions. Thus, whereas it is commonplace for rational choice findings themselves to be used in normative and prescriptive contexts, this normative content is deemed to be justified by its having been derived from minimalist assumptions. These assumptions, discussed at length above, are a thorough-going individualism upheld in the principle of citizens' sovereignty, the view that the natural world is objectively available and that social scientific laws are universally applicable, and the norm that agents seek personal ends using means–ends reasoning in uncertain, and strategic environments. It has been argued above, with Rawls's *Theory of Justice* serving as a central touchstone, that any trespass beyond the well-patrolled borders of scientific rationality necessarily results in the incrimination of the violator who has strayed into the territory of metaphysical idealism or ideology. Thus, rational choice liberalism puts forth theories explaining past developments of human society and proposes criteria that social policies must meet given the realities of human nature and evolution.

To keep this intellectual project afloat, each of several key basic assumptions must be defended. Thus, for social scientists using rational choice theory, much is at stake in defending expected utility theory and game theory as forms of scientifically vindicated, means–ends rationality. Similarly, the distinction between the objectivity of science and the ideological or idealistic nature of alternative philosophies must be strictly upheld. Moreover, the individual as the source of personally relative calculations of utility must be defended, even if it is no longer clear whether "individual self-interest" functions at the level of the gene, the "meme," the biological individual, or even the group.[136]

It remains to be seen how rational choice theorists will meet the foundational challenges at the core of their discipline and to what extent their theory will continue to prosper as the nonideological support of capitalist democracy. It also remains to be seen if the realism characteristic of rational choice theory will lead to a rational and just society as envisioned by McClennen, or whether it will underwrite injustices inherent in the stats quo as a corollary of the assumption that agents are self-interested rational actors.

From the Panopticon to the Prisoner's Dilemma

IN *The End of Ideology*, Daniel Bell presents a powerful image of America governed by the god of efficiency, best represented by Jeremy Bentham's Enlightenment-era Panopticon prison. Bentham's Panopticon was designed to be half prison, half factory, with a central observation deck to oversee the activities of its inhabitants. This system was organized according to an elaborate "calculus of incentives which, if administered in exact measures, would stimulate the individual to the correct degree of rectitude and work."[1] Over the ensuing two centuries of industrialization, "efficiency engineers," most notably Frederick W. Taylor, designed means to increase workers' efficiency in production. Taylor, for instance, taught a laborer in his charge to more than double the amount of pig iron shoveled per day by precisely monitoring the shape of the shovel and the details of his motion. Industry hired other social engineers, including sociologists and psychologists, to extract optimal performance from workers. Key to this approach was the analysis of time, space, and motion, which were subsequently organized within a hierarchical order to achieve the well-defined end of efficient production. The calculus of least action, determining the path of lowest energy connecting two points in space, served as the model of efficiency engineering

The Panopticon, which Bentham petitioned the British Parliament to construct, embodies an idealized central organization applicable to the crucial institutions of modern civilization. Human agents, now an extension of inanimate bodies in motion, could be tasked to efficiently attain ends through vigilant observation and calculated application of incentives to motivate appropriate behavior. Whether in the military, schools, factories, or prisons, individuals' behavior could be modified through tactics of surveillance and carefully measured corrective punishments. Within such institutions, the attainment of efficient action is a top–down process; managers dominate the hierarchy, and subjects comply with management's dictates in response to a system of incentives. It is telling that the same systems of surveillance and disciplinary tactics can be used to govern hospitals, factories, and prisons. The god of efficiency, whose presence is embodied in the central all-seeing eye, regulates human behavior in accordance with the institutionalized goals of patient recovery, worker productivity, and criminal reform. The principle of least action that guides the utilitarian inclinations of Bentham also informs the marginal utility theory of William Stanley Jevons, Léon Walras, and Vilfredo Pareto, who use the norm of efficiency to "rationalize" individual behavior in order to specify equations of market exchange.

Daniel Bell's essay addressing "The Cult of Efficiency in America" recounts the early-twentieth-century American experiment with efficiency engineering, and documents the widespread extent to which the average worker's life had been transformed by the relentless attention given to time and motion. Frank Gilbreth, Charles Bedeaux, Elton Mayo, the Ford Company, U.S. Steel Corporation, Western Electric, and the Bell Telephone System were all committed to improving production through well-honed management techniques for optimizing employees' actions. However, by 1960, Bell observed cracks in the facade of the efficiency system caused by a new-found emphasis on consumption and leisure: "Success at one's job becomes less important than success in one's style of life." [2] Though not using the phrase, Bell points to the dawning age of "consumers' sovereignty," in which individuals are characterized more by their leisure desires than by their employment, because the automation of production processes demand less of their physical effort. In Bell's analysis, the traditional discipline of work maintained a continuity with past values that conveyed meaning to individuals' lives. "As *homo faber*, man could seek to master nature and to discipline himself. Work, said Freud, was the chief means of binding an individual to reality." But with changes in work processes, the connection to those past values is fast becoming obsolete. Bell asks, "What will happen, then, when not only the worker but work itself is displaced by the machine?" [3]

The development of rational choice theory is often regarded as continuous with the efficiency calculus of the marginalist economists, and by extension with the efficiency engineering governing familiar modern institutions. To see its evolution in this light, however, is mistaken. Rational choice theory supersedes the theoretical principles defining "efficiency" in engineering, in scientific management, and in economics as constrained maximization. It is an unprecedented system, informing human practices and governing them by an internal rationale built on basic logical principles. The most rudimentary of these principles—that individuals' preferences obey transitive orderings—has only a tenuous relationship with the means–ends rationality characterizing the older concept of efficiency that requires well-specified criterion for maximization such a psychic pleasure. Because rational choice theory is highly abstract, the best way to appraise its break from the exclusive concern for "efficiency" is to consider what has become its central expression: the Prisoner's dilemma.

Contrasting the Prisoner's dilemma with the Panopticon demonstrates that rational choice theory conjures up a human world at odds with that of modern efficiency theorists. An inmate in a Panopticon is centrally observed and is subject to external punitive measures that reform his actions. The Prisoner's dilemma does not embody any such unified or hierarchical effort to achieve efficient outcomes. Instead it represents society as an individualist enterprise in which other agents are partners in a strategic game to achieve personal goals. One man's loss may well be another's gain, and at the end of the day the achievement of individual goals, even at the cost of collective impoverishment, is the only measure of "success." In this respect, the Prisoner's dilemma is wholly different from the Panopticon in form and function, and it signifies a practical shift away from the well-established assumption that efficiency is the organizing principle for modern social institutions. It is true that in factories, hospitals, schools, and prisons, efficiency formerly was pursued through centralized surveillance, hierarchy, and disciplinary measures. But today, from a perspective of society structured in terms of the Prisoner's dilemma, each person is seen to participate in a decentralized game in which efficient resource allocation is replaced by potentially suboptimal equilibrium of actors' strategies.

It is impossible to map the concept of efficiency onto the Prisoner's dilemma, just as it is to span the gap between orchestrated behavioral modification in the Panopticon and the lack of centralized control over individuals' self-determined choices characterizing the Prisoner's dilemma. Efficiency is defined and established in accordance with externally determined criteria for constrained maximization; equilibrium outcomes in game-theoretic forms like the Prisoner's dilemma are a function of individuals' intrinsic objectives. Yet, in both cases, the standards of appropriate conduct or rational action derive from norms that provide the rationale for behavior. It is crucial to recognize that these two sets of norms of conduct are conceptually and mathematically distinct.

Just as the Prisoner's dilemma represents a break with a social system of subordination and control established to achieve economic goals, so it signifies a profound breach with the political discourse formerly animating democratic republicanism. One way to appreciate the new point of departure is to consider the Prisoner's dilemma in the context of George Orwell's 1949 novel about totalitarian repression, *Nineteen Eighty-Four*.[4] The story is set in the fictional Oceania, a totalitarian state that is run in accordance with the principles of total surveillance characteristic of the Panopticon. In Orwell's dramatic conclusion to the book, the main character, Winston Smith, has been captured by Big Brother and still, after months of brutal torture, refuses to renounce his forbidden love for his paramour and confidante, Julia. His jailors then attach a cage to Winston's head that, when trap doors inside the cage are opened, would allow two starving rats to "bore into" Winston's face. Confronted with this visceral threat, Winston finally submits, screaming, "Do it to Julia! Do it to Julia!" [5] The implication of this ending is that Big Brother, by resorting to ultimate terror, is able to utterly break Winston's spirit; the sign of this surrender is his renunciation of his loyalty to his dearest friend. For Orwell, loyalty, love, and friendship are the most basic ingredients of civilization; they require no "reasons" and represent the antithesis to totalitarian repression. Big Brother's victory is only complete when individuals relinquish their loyalty to their fellow man.[6] In *Nineteen Eighty-Four,* Winston is almost superhuman in his ability to withstand physical torture. In the end, though, his fragile humanity dictates that he surrender in the face of his deepest fears made manifest.

To place the Prisoner's dilemma in this context, imagine a different ending in which Big Brother exploits that relentless logic to extract what he wants from Winston and Julia. Loyalty, trust, and commitment between individuals present the greatest challenge to game theorists because, in their view, the ever-present incentive for individuals to cheat on each other renders cooperation an unstable equilibrium. In our alternative rational choice conclusion to *Nineteen Eighty-Four,* the jailer, whose goal is to rehabilitate the co-conspirators, informs Winston of the following payoff matrix that guarantees Big Brother's preferred outcome *if* Winston and Julia are self-interested rational actors: "If neither of you confess, you will both be summarily executed, taking your hatred of Big Brother with you to the grave intact. If you confess and Julia does not, then you will be banished from Oceania. However, if you do not confess and Julia does, then you will face the starving rats without recourse. If you both confess, then you each will be considered rehabilitated, and will become full members of the State."

If Winston considers only his own fate, as is typical in analyzing the outcome of a Prisoner's dilemma, then his preferences fall in the following order: leaving Oceania, being shot with his conscience intact, becoming an accepting member of Big Brother's totalitarian order, being eaten headfirst by rats. As the standard logic of the dilemma goes, Winston and Julia each stand to gain by confessing because not only does this potentially offer immediate freedom, but it also avoids incurring the risk that the other's loyalties may waver, resulting in excruciating death. If Julia and Winston are rational actors, they will betray one other, even with the knowledge that if both retained their loyalty, each will be free of Big Brother.

This alternative ending to *Nineteen Eighty-Four* brings into the foreground the question of loyalty and commitment to other individuals. A Prisoner's dilemma culmination to Big Brother's effort to crush Winston's spirit would be an unimaginable and startling conclusion to *Nineteen Eighty-Four*, because in the book, the loyalty of friendship is precisely what distinguishes Winston and Julia's relationship from those sanctioned by the totalitarian state. In Orwell's novel, friendship and loyalty are the principal defenses against authoritarian repression; loyalty needs no reasons, and only fails in the face of the ultimate and most hideous forms of physical torture. In *Nineteen Eighty-Four*, friendship and love are the defining characteristics of humanity and are crucial for vibrant civilization. Winston is ready to relinquish truth, that two plus two equals four, before he reneges on his love for Julia; and, even then, it is only out of biological weakness that his superlative fortitude is compromised.[7]

In the world of rational choice theory, betrayal in the Prisoners' dilemma, which is thought to characterize many aspects of human relationships, is not just commonplace, but the rationally sanctioned norm. This complete transformation in political discourse and practice in a single generation, between World War II and the Cold War, is extraordinary. Orwell's worst fear is that totalitarian regimes are able to force individuals to yield their loyalties, the basic substance of human existence, because biological weakness ultimately undermines self-command in face exacting torture. In his view, a totalitarian regime can only exist if it thwarts normal human concourse by breaking the human bonds sustaining society. In contrast, during the Cold War rational choice theorists feared that individuals' freedom to determine their own ends might be restricted by an authoritarian government that assumed it knew what was best for everyone. For Orwell, the defense against totalitarianism is the nonquantifiable principle of fidelity; rational choice theorists base their hope for freedom on the principle of consumers' or citizens' sovereignty. While for Orwell, the litmus test identifying a member of a totalitarian order is one who betrays his loyalties, for rational choice theorists, the litmus test for a rational choice liberal is one who defects when confronted by a Prisoner's dilemma, and cheats in collective action scenarios unless it is clearly in his interest to do otherwise. It is impossible to reconcile these two staunchly anticommunist positions that are equally opposed to totalitarianism yet contradict one another.

It may be objected that Orwell's *Nineteen Eighty-Four* is indeed a fictional concoction, that individuals subjected to a real-life Prisoner's dilemma would defect out of self-interest and self-preservation. However, it turns out to be the case that people who have not been exposed to the logic of rational choice theory do not readily defect, even when paired with strangers. Similarly, in field tests of the pie-sharing Ultimatum game, actors often fail to express the behavior predicted by rational choice theory and do not press their advantage in order to acquire more pie for themselves.[8] Rational choice theory as a conceptual tool cuts both ways: it claims to accept people as they are without censure, *and* proposes specific standards of rational behavior. Whereas Kenneth Arrow scrupulously adheres to the principle of citizens' sovereignty, most of his rational choice compatriots are quick to accept a narrow version of self-interest under which "accepting people as they are" requires accepting that they are focused on personal ends, and not the well-being of those around them. Hence, while presenting itself as nonnormative, rational choice theory both proposes logical tenets of rationality and assumes the presence in society of individual pursuit of self-interest. Both of these theoretical stances are normative.

The promise of rational choice theory to construct a nonnormative and knowledge-accumulating social science has won it many adherents. Likewise, it provided a critically important way to reconceptualize capitalist democracy during a time of concern over the stability of its theoretical foundation. In mapping out the social landscape in contour lines of rational self-interest, rational choice theorists have at times been hegemonic in insisting that the rational choice approach is not only a valuable methodological tool for social science, but that it is the only cogent method for making progress. Its many contributions to social theory, especially in situations where questions of self-interest dominate (such as in negotiation and coalition formation) should not make us deaf to the way the language of rational choice theory can sound like INGSOC in Oceania: the state-condoned language of Big Brother that continually strikes words, and hence concepts, meanings, and practices, out of existence. To insist that human behavior be understood, even predicted, in terms of a well-ordered set of transitive preferences combined with strategic calculations of how to maximize expected utility is to nullify modes of existence not structured around payoffs; love, sympathy, respect, duty, and valor fall by the wayside. Transitivity, completeness, and the axioms of expected utility theory become the defining characteristics of rationality whereas the dictum of treating individuals as ends in themselves has no basis in reason.

NOTES

Introduction

1. William Greider, *One World, Ready or Not: The Manic Logic of Global Capitalism* (Simon and Schuster, 1997), 36.

2. John Dewey, *The Public and Its Problems* (Chicago: Swallow Press, 1927); Jürgen Habermas, *The Structural Transformation of the Public Sphere: An Inquiry into a Category of Bourgeois Society,* trans. Thomas Burger (Cambridge: MIT Press, 1989); for discussion see Robert B. Westbrook, *John Dewey and American Democracy* (Ithaca: Cornell University Press, 1991).

3. Alexis de Tocqueville, *Democracy in America,* trans. Henry Reeve (Cambridge, England: Sever and Frances, 1863); John Stuart Mill, *On Liberty* (Boston: Ticknor, 1864).

4. Walter Lippmann, *The Phantom Public* (New York: Harcourt Brace, 1925).

5. Kenneth J. Arrow, "Mathematical Models in the Social Sciences," in *The Policy Sciences: Recent Developments in Scope and Method,* ed. Daniel Lerner and Harold D. Lasswell (Stanford: Stanford University Press, 1951), 131; Mancur Olson, *The Logic of Collective Action* (Cambridge: Harvard University Press, 1965).

6. Eric Hobsbawm, "Democracy Can Be Bad for You," *New Statesman,* 5 March 2001, 26.

7. Ibid.

8. See the recent biography by Sylvia Nasar, *A Beautiful Mind: A Biography of John Forbes Nash, Jr., Winner of the Nobel Prize in Economics* (New York: Simon and Schuster, 1998); see also Philip Mirowski, *Machine Dreams: Economics Becomes a Cyborg Science* (Cambridge: Cambridge University Press, 2002), at 331–48.

9. "Economic Focus: Never the Twain Shall Meet," *Economist,* 2 February 2002, 82.

10. Anthony Downs, *An Economic Theory of Democracy* (New York: Harper, 1957), 27.

11. See, e.g., Richard A. Posner, "Wealth Maximization and Judicial Decision-Making," *International Review of Law and Economics* 4 (1984): 131–35; regarding the "Washington Consensus" and its position within economic theory, see Joachim Ahrens, Government and Economic Development: A Comparative Institutional Approach (Cheltenham, England: Edward Elgar, 2001), 1–21. Regarding game theory's overriding role in analysis at the World Bank, see com-

mentary in "Sustaining Hope: Is the World Bank Turning Marxist?" *Economist*, 24 August 2002, 56.

12. Hendrik Hertzberg, "Comment: Tuesday, and After," *New Yorker*, 24 September 2001, 27.

13. Robert J. Leonard, "Creating a Context for Game Theory," in *Toward a History of Game Theory: Annual Supplement to History of Political Economy* (Durham: Duke University Press, 1992), 29–76; see also William Poundstone, *Prisoner's Dilemma: John von Neumann, Game Theory, and the Puzzle of the Bomb* (New York: Anchor Books, 1992).

14. R. Duncan Luce and Howard Raiffa, *Games and Decisions: Introduction and Critical Survey* (New York: Wiley, 1957).

15. Ibid., vii–viii.

16. John von Neumann, *The Computer and the Brain* (New Haven: Yale University Press, 1958); Herbert Simon, *The Sciences of the Artificial*, rev. 2nd ed. (Cambridge: MIT Press, 1981); and Herbert Simon, "Two Heads are Better than One: The Collaboration between AI and OR," *Interfaces* 17 (July): 8–15; for discussion see Robin E. Rider, "Operations Research and Game Theory: Early Connections," in *Toward a History of Game Theory: Annual Supplement to History of Political Economy* (Durham: Duke University Press, 1992), 225–40.

17. Von Neumann and Morgenstern, *Theory of Games and Economic Behavior*; Leonard Savage, *The Foundations of Statistics* (New York: Wiley, 1954); Kenneth J. Arrow, *Social Choice and Individual Values* (New York: Wiley, 1951).

18. See the collection of papers edited by David E. Bell, Howard Raiffa, and Amos Tversky, *Decision Making: Descriptive, Normative, and Prescriptive Interactions* (Cambridge: Cambridge University Press, 1998).

19. James S. Coleman, *The Mathematics of Collective Action* (Chicago: Aldine, 1973); Amos Tversky and Daniel Kahneman, "Rational Choice and the Framing of Decision," in *Decision Making*, ed. Bell, Raiffa, and Tversky, 167–92.

20. John Maynard Smith, *Mathematical Ideas in Biology* (London: Cambridge University Press, 1968); John Maynard Smith, *Evolution and the Theory of Games* (Cambridge: Cambridge University Press, 1976); Richard Dawkins, *The Selfish Gene* (New York: Oxford University Press, 1976).

21. For attempt to make sense of the "rationality project" from an entirely different perspective, see Philip Mirowki, *Machine Dreams: Economics Becomes a Cyborg Science* (Cambridge: Cambridge University Press, 2002).

22. Thomas Schelling, *Strategy of Conflict* (Cambridge: Harvard University Press, 1960).

23. For more on Ellsberg, see his recent book *Secrets: A Memoir of Vietnam and the Pentagon Papers* (New York: Viking, 2002); see also Nicholas Lehmann, "Paper Tiger: Daniel Ellsberg's War," *New Yorker*, 4 November 2002, 96–99.

24. Daniel Ellsberg, "Risk, Ambiguity, and the Savage Axioms," *Quarterly Journal of Economics* 75 (1961): 643–69.

25. For a light-hearted discussion, see James Ryerson, "Games People Play: Rational Choice with a Human Face," *Linguafranca* 9, no. 6 (December–January 2000): 60–71.

26. The tools of rational choice decisionmaking only became normalized at the World Bank and International Monetary Fund after McNamara's tenure, see Joseph Stiglitz, *Globalization and Its Discontents* (New York: Norton, 2002).

27. Gabriel A. Almond, "Rational Choice Theory and the Social Sciences," in *A Discipline Divided: Schools and Sects in Political Science* (London: Sage, 1990), 117–37; see also Donald P. Green and Ian Shapiro, *Pathologies of Rational Choice Theory: A Critique of Applications in Political Science* (New Haven: Yale University Press, 1994); Steven G. Medema, "'Related Disciplines': The Professionalization of Public Choice Analysis," unpublished manuscript of paper presented at a Duke University history of economics conference, spring 1999.

Prologue

1. Fritz Machlup, "Capitalism and Its Future Appraised by Two Liberal Economists," *American Economic Review* 33 (1943): 301.

2. Compare Schumpeter's discussion of the reasons capitalism is untenable while socialism presents a viable economic system, in Joseph Schumpeter, *Capitalism, Socialism, and Democracy* (London: Allen and Unwin, 1943), 59–200; see Hayek on the need for social insurance, in Friedrich Hayek, *The Road to Serfdom* (Chicago: University of Chicago Press, 1944), 89–91; see also Popper on piecemeal social engineering, in Karl Popper, *The Open Society and Its Enemies*, vol. 2, *The High Tide of Prophecy: Hegel, Marx, and the Aftermath* (London: Routledge, 1945), 222.

3. Schumpeter, *Capitalism, Socialism, and Democracy*, at ix.

4. Ibid., ix–x.

5. Ibid., 302.

6. Ibid., 196–302.

7. For a similar reading of Schumpeter, see Machlup, "Capitalism and Its Future Appraised by Two Liberal Economists," 301–20, esp. 318–20.

8. Anthony Downs, *An Economic Theory of Democracy* (New York: Harper and Row, 1957), ix.

9. Ibid.

10. Schumpeter, *Capitalism, Socialism, and Democracy*, at 269, 271.

11. Hayek, *The Road to Serfdom*, at 44; see also 1–15.

12. Ibid., 101.

13. Kenneth J. Arrow, *Social Choice and Individual Values* (New York: Wiley, 1951).

14. Hayek, *The Road to Serfdom*, at 42–43; for a similar argument, see Schumpeter, *Capitalism, Socialism, and Democracy*, at 250–53.

15. Arrow, *Social Choice and Individual Values*, 81–86.

16. Hayek, *The Road to Serfdom*, at 29.

17. For an interpretation of contemporary readings of Plato and Socrates, see Melissa Lane, *Plato's Progeny: How Plato and Socrates Still Captivate the Modern Mind* (London: Duckworth, 2001).

18. Karl Popper, *The Open Society and Its Enemies,* vol. 1, *The Spell of Plato* (London: Routledge, 1945), 33.

19. Popper, *The Open Society and Its Enemies,* at vol. 2, pp. 91–98; there is consistent ambiguity and at times open disagreement over whether Marx upheld methodological individualism; Schumpeter finds that he supported organic group theory in the form of his idea of class interest. See Schumpeter, *Capitalism, Socialism, and Democracy,* at 20.

20. Popper, *The Open Society and Its Enemies,* at vol. 2, pp. 224.

21. Hayek, *The Road to Serfdom,* at 10.

22. Schumpeter, *Capitalism, Socialism, and Democracy,* at 254.

Chapter One

1. Kenneth J. Arrow, *Social Choice and Individual Values,* 2nd ed. (New York: Wiley, 1963 [1951]).

2. Interview of Robert S. McNamara by Brian Lamb, "In Retrospect: The Tragedy and Lessons of Vietnam," 23 April 1995, Booknotes Transcript, C-SPAN.

3. Examples of this position include Joseph Kraft, "RAND: Arsenal for Ideas," *Harper's Magazine* (July 1960): 69–76; Stewart Alsop, "Our New Strategy: The Alternatives to Total War," *Saturday Evening Post,* 1 December 1962), 13–18; Fred M. Kaplan, *The Wizards of Armageddon* (New York: Simon and Schuster, 1983); Peter J. Roman, *Eisenhower and the Missile Gap* (Ithaca: Cornell University Press, 1995).

4. Guy Alchon, *The Invisible Hand of Planning: Capitalism, Social Science, and the State in the 1920s* (Princeton: Princeton University Press, 1985).

5. Kraft, "RAND: Arsenal for Ideas," at 69.

6. Frank Collbohm, oral history interview, 28 July 1987, RAND History Project, National Air and Space Museum, 17.

7. From RAND's charter, set forth by General Curtis E. LeMay, Deputy Chief of Staff for Research and Development, often quoted in early days. Cited in James Digby, "Strategic Thought at RAND, 1948–1963: The Ideas, Their Origins, Their Fates," RAND NOTE, N-3096-RC, June 1990, 4.

8. Curtis E. LeMay, interview by John T. Bolen, 9 March 1971, March AFB, CA, Air Force Historical Research Center, Maxwell, AL, K239.0512-736, 6, cited in David Raymond Jardini, "Out of the Blue Yonder: The RAND Corporation's Diversification into Social Welfare Research, 1946–1968" (Ph.D. diss., Carnegie Mellon University, May 1996), 119.

9. Jardini, "Out of the Blue Yonder, at 120–21.

10. J. A. Stockfisch, "The Intellectual Foundations of Systems Analysis" (Santa Monica: RAND, 1987), P-7401.

11. *Preliminary Design of an Experimental World-Circling Spaceship,* Douglas Report No. SM-11827, 1946.

12. Francis X. Sutton, "The Ford Foundation: The Early Years," *Dædalus* (winter 1987), 52.

13. Henry Ford II resigned from the foundations board of trustees in 1976, formally ending Ford family involvement in foundation affairs.

14. Henry Ford II to Kart T. Compton, 23 October 1951, Gaither Series VI, Box 11, folder 134, Ford Foundation Archive, Ford Foundation (hereafter FFA).

15. Sutton, "The Ford Foundation," at 48.

16. Ibid.

17. *Report for the Study of the Ford Foundation on Policy and Program* (Detroit: Ford Foundation, 1949), 28.

18. Gaither, "Comments on Bill Greenleaf's Manuscript," 23 January 1959, Gaither Series VI, box 11, folder 134, FFA, 1–2.

19. Sutton, "The Ford Foundation," at 52.

20. For Hutchins and the Ford Foundation, see Harry S. Ashmore, *Unseasonable Truths: The Life of Robert Maynard Hutchins* (Boston: Little, Brown, 1989), 311–53.

21. Gaither, "Comment's on Bill Greenleaf's Manuscript," at 1–2.

22. Sutton, "The Ford Foundation," at 73.

23. Memorandum drafted by Hutchins, quoted in Ashmore, *Unseasonable Truths,* at 330.

24. Ibid., 324–25.

25. "Notes on Conference with Beadle Smith, Allen Dulles and Others," 3 April 1951, FFA: "Hoffman: we cannot contribute to subversive activities." Gaither's response to a CIA request to channel funds through the Ford Foundation makes it clear that he refused not as a matter of principle, but to avoid legal difficulties.

26. Documents on "Political Warfare," and Program Area I, Gaither Series I, box 1, folder 4, dated 3 May 1951 and 23 May 1951, FFA.

27. See Robert E. Gleeson and Steven Schlossman, "George Leland Bach and the Rebirth of Graduate Management Education in the United States, 1945–1975," *Magazine of the Graduate Management Admission Council* (spring 1995): 8–46, esp. 20, 25.

28. Memo and document regarding "A Research Program in the Field of National Security," from Franklin A. Lindsay to H. Rowan Gaither, 10 June 1955, Gaither Series VII, box 13, folder 155, FFA; Gaither's rapport and agreement with Allen Dulles regarding national security objectives is also reflected in Gaither's memo discussing a "Conference with Allen Dulles," 22 October 1956, Gaither Series VI, box 12, folder 141, FFA.

29. Gerald J. Lynch of Ford Motor Company to Henry Ford II, 1 May 1952, Gaither Series VI, box 11, folder 129, FFA, 2.

30. Gaither Series VI, box 12, folder 140, FFA.

31. Memo from Gaither to W. A. Nielsen, 10 August 1953, Gaither Series VI, box 12, folder 145, FFA.

32. Kraft, "RAND: Arsenal for Ideas," at 75. At least half of RAND's physicists took Edward Teller's side in his dispute with Robert J. Oppenheimer.

33. *Report of the Study for the Ford Foundation on Policy and Program,* at 113.

34. Charles Hitch, who was brought in to head the economics division at RAND in 1948, had served on the War Production Board, as a staff economist with the Mission for Economic Affairs (1941–42), and then with the OSS in Britain. John Williams, who was appointed in 1948 to head the mathematics division, had run the Strategic Bombing Section of the Princeton Statistics Research Group during the war. Edward Barlow, who would become head of engineering in 1953, had worked on radar at Sperry Gyroscope, which contracted with MIT during the war. Hans Speier, who was appointed in 1948 to head up RAND's nascent social sciences division, had worked at the Federal Communications Commission analyzing Nazi propaganda. Speier would remain at RAND in the 1950s and would also work closely with Gaither during his presidency of the Ford Foundation.

35. Jardini, "Out of the Blue Yonder," at 35.

36. Ibid., 37.

37. Edward Barlow, oral history interview, 10 February 1988, RAND History Project, National Air and Space Museum, 23.

38. For a more detailed discussion, see Jardini, "Out of the Blue Yonder," at 77–80.

39. Barlow, oral history interview, at 33.

40. The chart is reprinted in Jardini, "Out of the Blue Yonder," at 35.

41. *Comparison of Airplane Systems for Strategic Bombing,* RAND Report R-208, September 1950. Paxson had earlier served as the scientific advisor of the U.S. Army Air Forces Proving Ground Command in 1942, technical aide to the Applied Mathematics Panel of the Office for Scientific Research and Development from 1943–45, and a consultant to the U.S. Strategic Bombing Survey in 1945–46.

42. Edward Quade, oral history interview, 18 February 1988, RAND History Project, National Air and Space Museum, 15; Jardini, "Out of the Blue Yonder," at 42–62.

43. Quade, oral history interview, at 13.

44. Jardini, "Out of the Blue Yonder," at 61.

45. For fuller discussion, see ibid., 44–64.

46. Novick's wartime employment was as a staff member of the War Production Board from 1940 to 1947, and as a program officer for the National Resources Board from 1947 to 1949.

47. David Novick, oral history interview, 24 February 1988, RAND History Project, National Air and Space Museum, 15.

48. Edward Barlow, "Preliminary Proposal for Air Defense Study," RAND Limited Document D(L)-816, 2 October 1950, RAND Classified Library, cited in Jardini, "Out of the Blue Yonder," at 68.

49. Relegated to a footnote in Smith, *The RAND Corporation* (Cambridge: Harvard University Press, 1966), 105.

50. I am grateful to Martin Collins who helped me draw this conclusion.

51. These lectures were later published as *Analysis for Military Decisions* (Chicago: Rand McNally, 1964).

52. Quade, oral history interview, at 21–24.

53. Ibid., 31, 37.

54. Wohlstetter's study was written with Fred S. Hoffman, R. J. Lutz, and Henry S. Rowen, *Selection and Use of Strategic Air Bases*, RAND Corporation, R-266, April 1954.

55. Gregg Herken, *The Counsels of War* (New York: Knopf, 1987), 94–98, 81.

56. David Novick, oral history interview, 20 June 1988, RAND History Project, National Air and Space Museum, 31–33.

57. Kaplan suggests not (*The Wizards of Armageddon*, 93, 104–6); and Herken suggests that the Air Force opted for less reliance on overseas bases (*The Counsels of War*, 93).

58. For U.S. Air Force attitude toward counterforce strategy, see Herken, *Counsels of War*, at 82.

59. Smith, *The RAND Corporation*. An even earlier version of this account is given in Kraft, "RAND: Arsenal for Ideas," at 69–76.

60. Kaplan, *The Wizards of Armageddon;* Robert J. Leonard, "Creating a Context for Game Theory," in *Toward a History of Game Theory*, ed. E. Roy Weintraub (Durham: Duke University Press, 1992); to some extent Jardini, "Out of the Blue Yonder." Because other writers only have this account to refer to, it is perpetuated at all other levels of the discussion; see, e.g., Deborah Shapley, *Promise and Power: The Life and Times of Robert McNamara* (Boston: Little, Brown, 1993).

61. Shapley, *Promise and Power*, at 104.

62. Charles J. Hitch, *Decision-Making for Defense* (Berkeley: University of California Press, 1966), 1–5.

63. Letter of transmittal, 9 April 1976, "Deterrence and Survival in the Nuclear Age," printed for the use of the Joint Committee on Defense Production, 94th Cong. (Washington, D.C.: Government Printing Office, 1976). The other documents of similar caliber mentioned by Proxmire include George Kennan's article on containment, "The Source of Soviet Conduct," authored by "X," *Foreign Affairs*, July 1947, 566–82; NSC-68 (penned by Paul H. Nitze, 1950); and Albert Wohlstetter, "The Delicate Balance of Terror," *Foreign Affairs*, January 1959.

64. See, e.g., Roman, *Eisenhower and the Missile Gap*. Roman uses "The Gaither Report," reprinted by Joint Committee on Defense Production, 92nd Cong., Washington, D.C., Government Printing Office, 1976 [1957], 20, and its vulnerability thesis as the backbone of his argument countering Eisenhower revisionists, who contend that Eisenhower was friendly to arms control and judiciously interpreted intelligence gathered from the U2 spy flight program to maintain a measured approach to U.S. national security policy. In making his case, Roman presents the Gaither committee's findings as reasonable in view of then-available intelligence estimates. In putting his seal of approval on the Gaither Report's alarmist conclusions, he neither submits them to the scrutiny of historical judgment nor questions their basis. Thus, the Gaither Report provides Roman's framework without itself being contextualized and recognized as a historically motivated document; instead it provides the "factual" backdrop to which Eisenhower responded, and its authors are given a blanket endorsement as strategic

experts. In introducing his thesis, Roman inaccurately states that the Gaither panel was organized "to investigate the contributions of active and passive defense" (p. 2), while it is clear that Eisenhower organized the panel to study passive defense in the form of fallout shelters, and strictly admonished the panel to stay focused on passive defense.

65. S. Everett Gleason, Document 114, *Foreign Relations* 19 (1955–57): 462–64.

66. Interview with Gaither, *New York Times,* 25 December 1957, 1, 24.

67. Kaplan, *The Wizards of Armageddon,* at 129.

68. Ibid., 128; Herken, *The Counsels of War,* at 113–14.

69. This aspect of the report prompted Eisenhower to remark that its authors seemed to have in mind a planned economy. S. Everett Gleason, "Memorandum of Discussion at the 343d Meeting of the National Security Council, Washington, Nov. 7, 1957," *Foreign Relations* 19 (1955–57): 632.

70. "The Gaither Report," at 20.

71. In his detailed analysis of the Gaither committee's role in the Eisenhower administration, David L. Snead similarly concludes that given the committee's membership, its finding were not surprising. See Snead, *The Gaither Committee, Eisenhower, and the Cold War* (Columbus: Ohio State University Press, 1999), 114–17, 49.

72. See the account of Digby, "Strategic Thought at RAND."

73. The unique flavor of the Gaither Report's strategic counsel is readily apparent when contrasted with other conservative strategic proposals, such as that published by the Rockefeller Brothers Fund on January 6, 1958, titled *International Security: The Military Aspect.*

74. For an exhaustive listing of missile estimates printed in the public record, see Edgar M. Bottome, *The Missile Gap: A Study of the Formulation of Military and Political Policy* (Madison: Farleigh Dickinson University Press, 1971), 221–34. Regarding the Gaither Report's role in establishing the credibility of the missile gap, see ibid., 44–46, 181.

75. Herken, *The Counsels of War,* at 81, 94–98.

76. See, e.g., *New York Times,* 6 October 1957.

77. The Soviet Union issued a statement to this effect on August 27, 1957, as noted in John Prados, *The Soviet Estimate: U.S. Intelligence Analysis and Russian Military Strength* (New York: Dial Press, 1982), 56–57; see Harlow Shapley, "Satellite Hysteria," *Nation,* 26 October 1957; David Lawrence, "Coming Down to Earth," *U.S. News and World Report,* 18 October 1957, 160; Albert Parry, "Why Should We Have Been Surprised?" *Reporter,* 31 October 1957, 13–15.

78. See the prodefense editorial by Max Ascoli, "Thank you, Sputnik!" *Reporter,* 31 October 1957, 10–12; see also the letter from Lyndon B. Johnson in ibid.

79. Samuel Lubell, "Sputnik and American Public Opinion," *Columbia University Forum,* winter 1957, I, 15–21.

80. Evening meeting of Gaither Committee members, mid December, Nitze and Nixon in attendance, wrangling over getting document published, Foster's re-

marks. Morton H. Halperin, "The Gaither Committee and the Policy Process," *World Politics*, April 1961, 374.

81. For Eisenhower's awareness of the explosive media potential of *Sputnik,* see his comments in Gleason, "Memorandum of Discussion," at 632.

82. Ibid., 630–35.

83. Halperin, "The Gaither Committee," at 368; see also Chalmers M. Roberts, untitled article in *Washington Post and Times Herald,* 20 December 1957, reprinted in *Congressional Quarterly Weekly Report* 15 (1957): 1238. For information regarding Lovett and McCloy's careers, and leading roles in formulating a pro-active defense policy countering isolationism, see Walter Isaacson and Evan Thomas, *The Wise Men: Six Friends and the World They Made; Acheson, Bohlen, Harriman, Kennan, Lovett, McCloy* (New York: Simon and Schuster, 1986), esp. 182–209, 482–504. I am grateful to Kurt Beyer for pointing out to me the new pro-active defense stance evolving out of the pre–World War II isolationist versus internationalist axes.

84. J.F.D., "Memorandum of a Conversation between the President and the Secretary of State White House, Washington D.C., November 7, 1957," Document 157, *Foreign Relations* 19 (1955–57): 638.

85. G., "Memorandum for the Record of a Meeting Held at the White House, Washington, November 4, 1957," Document 154, *Foreign Relations* 19 (1955–57): 624–28. For documents pertaining to the organization and reorganizations of DOD, see Alice C. Cole et al., eds., *The Department of Defense: Documents on Establishment and Organization 1944–1978* (Washington, D.C.: Office of the Secretary of Defense Historical Office, 1978).

86. Halperin, "The Gaither Committee," at 369, also points out that in the normal procedure this would have been the end of the line for the report; Snead argues that Eisenhower's failure to maintain control of the Gaither committee demonstrated weakness of leadership. *The Gaither Committee, Eisenhower, and the Cold War,* at 11.

87. Halperin, "The Gaither Committee." Not all committee members took an active role in this campaign, including Gaither.

88. See, e.g., Jardini, "Out of the Blue Yonder," 159–60. For Snead's conclusions on this point, see *The Gaither Committee, Eisenhower, and the Cold War,* at 106–10, 125–28; also compare his discussion at 171 with 192–93.

89. Eisenhower's consistently expressed doubt about the Soviet's missile capabilities are in keeping with his experience with the short-lived "bomber gap" (see Prados, *The Soviet Estimate,* 41–50), and are found sporadically throughout the document record. For example, "The President said that, shooting from the hip, he would be inclined to think the Soviets were having some missile trouble." Marion W. Boggs, "Memorandum of Discussion at the 351st Meeting of the National Security Council," 16 January 1958, *Foreign Relations* 3 (1958–60): 25; on the U-2 flights and the Gaither committee, see Herken, *The Counsels of War,* at 128–29.

90. On November 26 and 27, CIA director Allen Dulles was asked to testify to the Senate Preparedness Subcommittee (the records of which were not de-

classified even at the time of the compilation of *Foreign Relations* (1955–57) about Soviet capabilities. Dulles then sent a memo to the executive secretary of the NSC (Lay) to catalogue the discrepancies between his assessment and the assessment put forth in the Gaither Report. The substance of these discrepancies remains classified. Further progress is pending freedom of information requests for access to this material as well as to the still-classified documents from the file NSC5724 (NSC business pertaining to the Gaither Report), NND959008, box 111.

91. "Editorial Note," Document 159, *Foreign Relations* 19 (1955–1957): 661; see *Public Papers of the Presidents of the United States: Dwight D. Eisenhower, 1957,* 789–99 for the text of the radio address, and at 799 the text of the White House's summary of this organizational change.

92. Halperin, "The Gaither Committee," at 370.

93. Mentioned in ibid. at 371; also evident in National Security Policy document record for the relevant time period, *Foreign Relations* 19 (1955–57), *Foreign Relations* 3 (1958–60).

94. Note Halperin's observation that the thrust of the Gaither committee was its proposed "new, more 'rational' method of splitting up the defense pie" (Halperin, "The Gaither Committee," at 373); for a historiography of the Gaither committee's relevance to U.S. policy, see Snead, *The Gaither Committee, Eisenhower, and the Cold War,* at 4–11.

95. Halperin, "The Gaither Committee," at 381.

96. "Memorandum of Conversation" (no author cited), Washington, 3 January 1958, Document 1, *Foreign Relations* 3 (1958–60): 1–3.

97. Halperin, "The Gaither Committee," at 376; *New York Herald Tribune,* 23 November 1957, 1–8; Roberts, untitled article in *Washington Post and Times Herald,* 20 December 1957.

98. Stewart Alsop, "How Can We Catch Up?" *Saturday Evening Post,* 14 December 1957, 27.

99. "Memorandum of a Conversation between the President and the Secretary of State, Washington, December 26, 1957," with footnote containing "A memorandum of Dulles' telephone conversation with Senator Johnson on December 23," Document 174, *Foreign Relations* 19 (1955–57): 712.

100. S. Everett Gleason, "Memorandum of the discussion of the 350th Meeting of the NSC," 6 January 1958, Document 2, *Foreign Relations* 3 (1958–60): 8.

101. Ibid., 7.

102. See, e.g., testimony of Admiral Chester W. Nimitz, USN (retired), former chief of naval operations testimony, Hearings before the Preparedness Investigating Subcommittee, Senate Committee on Armed Services Inquiry into Satellite and Missile Programs (Washington, D.C.: Government Printing Office, 1958, vol. 2, pt. 1, 1339. (Date of testimony unclear.)

103. CED publications state, "CED's by-laws emphasize that its work must be thoroughly objective in character and that each issue must be approached, not from the viewpoint of any particular economic or political group, but with regard for the general welfare." Committee of Economic Development, The Problem of

National Security: Some Economic and Administrative Aspects (New York: CED, 1958).

104. Ibid., 52.

105. Ibid., 34–35, 48–49.

106. Ibid., 20–21, 34–35, 41, 43, 48, 55.

107. Bottome, *The Missile Gap*, at 83.

108. Digby, "Strategic Thought at Rand," at 20 n. 21.

109. Joseph Alsop, "The New Balance of Power: War and Peace in a Strange World," *Encounter* 10 (May 1958): 5; Edward L. Katzenbach Jr., "Ideas: A New Defense Industry," *Reporter*, 2 March 1961, 2; Kraft, "RAND: Arsenal for Ideas."

110. Digby, "Strategic Thought at Rand," at 20.

111. E.g., Bottome, *The Missile Gap*, 202; interview of Robert S. McNamara by Brian Lamb; for Kennedy's exploitation of the missile gap and reference to the Gaither Report, see Snead, *The Gaither Committee, Eisenhower, and the Cold War*, at 174–76.

112. Herken, *The Counsels of War*, at 132.

113. Ibid., 133.

114. Shapley, *Promise and Power*, at 82–83.

115. Cited in ibid., 389, 515.

116. Ibid., 98.

117. For a close chronicle of the emerging and disintegrating missile gap hypothesis following contemporary press reports, see Bottome, *The Missile Gap*. He concludes, "Surprisingly, there have not been many published reports that attempt to explain 'Where the Missile Gap Went,' or to assess the blame for its creation" (ibid., 192).

118. Ibid., 193.

119. "Planning-Programming-Budgeting: Initial Memorandum," prepared by the Subcommittee on National Security and International Operations, Committee on Government Operations, U.S. Senate (Washington, D.C.: Government Printing Office, 1967), 3, bound in *Planning Programming Budgeting*, Subcommittee on National Security and International Operations, Committee on Government Operations, U.S. Senate, 91st Cong. (Washington, D.C.: Government Printing Office, 1970) (hereafter *Planning Programming Budgeting*).

120. Shapley, *Promise and Power*, 104–9.

121. Seymour Melman, *Pentagon Capitalism: The Political Economy of War* (New York: McGraw-Hill, 1970), 72.

122. Samuel P. Huntington, *The Common Defense* (New York: Columbia University Press, 1961), 146.

123. The first quotation is from Shapley, *Promise and Power*, at 237; the second is from "The Gaither Report," at 20.

124. Charles J. Hitch and Roland N. McKean, *The Economics of Defense in the Nuclear Age* (Cambridge: Harvard University Press, 1963), reprint of original 1960 RAND publication.

125. This is a constant theme in Shapley, *Promise and Power*.

126. The documents generated by Enthoven's Office of Systems Analysis remain classified.

127. See Enthoven's discursive attempt to define "systems analysis" in "Testimony of Alain C. Enthoven, Assistant Secretary of Defense (Systems Analysis)," 27 September 1967, *Planning Programming Budgeting,* at 226–29.

128. Shapley, *Promise and Power,* at 327.

129. Ibid., 327–28.

130. See Gregory Palmer, *The McNamara Strategy and the Viet Nam War: Program Budgeting in the Pentagon, 1960–1968* (London: Greenwood Press, 1978).

131. Aaron Wildavsky, "Rescuing Policy Analysis from PPBS," *Public Administration Review* 29 (March/April 1969): 2, repaginated in Subcommittee on National Security International Operations, Committee on Government Operations, U.S. Senate, 91st Cong. (Washington, D.C.: Government Printing Office, 1969), 5.

132. Hearings before the Committee on Armed Services, 18 January 1961, U.S. Senate, 87th Cong. 1st Sess. (Washington, D.C.: Government Printing Office, 1961), 15–16.

133. See Hitch's stress on RAND as the source of PPBS in his testimony before H.R. Subcommittee on Military Operations, House Committee on Government Operations Systems Development and Management, 87th Cong., 2nd Sess., 25 July 1962, pt. 2, 513–47, esp. 518, 542–43.

134. Enthoven's testimony, 27 September 1967, in *Planning Programming Budgeting,* at 256; for sample budget preparations, see Statement of Elmer B. Staats, Comptroller General of the U.S., 26 March 1968, in ibid., 334–35.

135. For recognition and acknowledgement of this restructuring, see Charles L. Schultze's testimony, 23 August 1967, in ibid., 192.

136. Hitch and McKean, *The Economics of Defense,* at 47.

137. Presentation prepared for the Special Subcommittee on the Utilization of Scientific Manpower, Senate Labor and Public Welfare Committee, 89th Cong., 2d Sess., 17 May 1966, with excerpts from Industrial College of the Armed Forces, in *A Modern Design for Defense Decisions—A McNamara-Hitch-Enthoven Anthology,* ed. Samuel A. Tucker (Washington, D.C.: Industrial College of Armed Forces, 1966), reprinted in *Planning Programming Budgeting,* 565.

138. "Decision-Making in Large Organizations," Royal Society Nuffield Lecture, London, England, 25 October 1966, in *Planning Programming Budgeting,* at 574–81.

139. Frederick C. Mosher, "Program Budgeting in Foreign Affairs: Some Reflections," a memorandum prepared at the request of the Subcommittee on National Security and International Operations, Committee on Government Operations, U.S. Senate, Miscellaneous Publications, 90th Cong. (Washington, D.C.: Government Printing Office, 1968), 17.

140. Hitch's quote in "Decision-Making in Large Organizations," at 575; see also Aaron Wildavsky, "The Political Economy of Efficiency: Cost-Benefit Analysis, Systems Analysis, and Program Budgeting," originally printed in *Public Administration Review* 26 (December 1966): 4, reprinted in "Planning-Programming-Budgeting: Selected Comment," Committee on Government Operations, U.S. Senate, Miscellaneous Publications, 90th Cong. (Washington, D.C.: Govern-

ment Printing Office, 1968), 63; Jackson's questioning during Enthoven testimony, 18 October 1967, *Planning Programming Budgeting*, at 309.

141. Schelling's statement is in a memorandum prepared at the request of the Subcommittee on National Security and International Operations, Committee on Government Operations, U.S. Senate, Miscellaneous Publications, 90th Cong. (Washington, D.C.: Government Printing Office, 1968), 3.

142. Schultze's testimony, in *Planning Programming Budgeting*, at 192; Mosher, "Program Budgeting in Foreign Affairs," at 3, 2.

143. Mosher, "Program Budgeting in Foreign Affairs," at 3; Schultze's testimony, *Planning Programming Budgeting*, at 197.

144. Richard Austin Smith, "The $7-Billion Contract That Changed the Rules," *Fortune*, March 1963, 96.

145. *The TFX Contract Investigation: Hearings before the Subcommittee on Investigation of the Committee on Government Operations*, 88th Cong., 1st Sess. 1971 (1963) (hereafter *TFX Hearings*); Shapley, *Promise and Power*, at 212.

146. *TFX Hearings*, pt. 1, 208–9.

147. Korth testimony, *TFX Hearings*, pt. 6, at 1502–74, 1852.

148. Shapley, *Promise and Power*, at 217.

149. Questioning on this point resulted in a heated outburst (*TFX Hearings*, pt. 8, at 2105).

150. Memorandum of a GAO interview with McNamara, 16 April 1963, *TFX Hearings*, pt. 3, 902. Even Robert J. Art's *The TFX Decision: McNamara and the Military* (Boston: Little, Brown, 1968), which is sympathetic to McNamara, draws the same conclusion (137–39).

151. In his recent book *The Dark Side of Camelot* (Boston: Little, Brown, 1997), Seymour M. Hersh brings forth new information regarding the TFX decision, alleging that General Dynamics blackmailed the Kennedy administration using evidence of Kennedy's affair with Judith Exner gathered in August of 1962 (295–96, 317–20, 344). Hersh makes the case that the TFX decision had nothing to do with cost-effectiveness and everything to do with blackmail. While I do not dispute the possibility that blackmail on the part of General Dynamics may have played a role in swinging the decision in its favor, a potential blackmail incident in August 1962 is insufficient to explain (a) McNamara's original insistence on "commonality," or (b) that an unprecedented three-stage bidding process, with McNamara overruling the military evaluations at each stage, had already been completed by June 1962.

152. Memorandum detailing the Source Selection process and how to alter it, 18 August 1962 and 2 October 1962, *TFX Hearings*, pt. 5, 1292, 1300.

153. DIAC appears sporadically in the *TFX Hearings*, and in H.R. Subcommittee on Military Operations, House Committee on Government Operations Systems Development and Management, 88th Cong. (Washington, D.C.: Government Printing Office, 1963), vol. 4, 100–103.

154. 27 September 1967, *Planning Programming Budgeting*, at 235.

155. "Initial Memorandum," ibid., 3–4.

156. "Cost-Effectiveness Studies," testimony before the Subcommittee on De-

partment of Defense, House Committee on Appropriations, 11 May 1966, reprinted in *Planning Programming Budgeting.*

157. "Initial Memorandum," ibid., 6.

158. PPB Hearings, opening statement of Senator Henry M. Jackson, 28 March 1968, *Planning Programming Budgeting,* at 321.

159. Letter to Editor-in-Chief, *Public Administration Review* 27, no. 1 (March 1967), in response to "Planning-Programming-Budgeting Symposium," ibid., 26, no. 4 (December 1966), 243–310. Also in "Planning-Programming-Budgeting: Selected Comment," quotations from 25, 26. Regarding the supporting role of philanthropy in the U.S. technocracy of the 1920s and 1930s, see Alchon, *The Invisible Hand of Planning.*

160. E.g., Henry S. Rowen, "Bargaining and Analysis in Government," in "Planning-Programming-Budgeting: Selected Comment," 46.

161. Discussion of Program Memorandum and question of providing information to Congress in Comptroller General Staats's testimony, 26 March 1968, *Planning Programming Budgeting,* at 327–28, 338–51; need for secrecy discussed by Enthoven, ibid., 274.

162. "Statement by the President to Cabinet Members and Agency Heads on the New Government-Wide Planning and Budgeting System, August 25, 1965," in ibid., 508.

163. "PPBS Excerpt from the President's Message to the Congress, the Quality of American Government, 17 March 1967, in PBB Hearings, "Official Documents," 6.

164. Alain C. Enthoven, "The Systems Analysis Approach," *Planning Programming Budgeting,* at 566.

165. Melvin Anshen, "The Program Budget in Operation," in *Program Budgeting: Program Analysis and the Federal Budget,* ed. David Novick (Cambridge: Harvard University Press, 1965), 370.

166. Roland N. McKean and Melvin Anshen, "Limitations, Risks, and Problems," ibid., 289.

167. "Initial Memorandum," and "Interim Observations," *Planning Programming Budgeting,* at 9–25; Mosher, "Program Budgeting in Foreign Affairs;" Frederick C. Mosher, "PPBS: Two Questions," in "Planning-Programming-Budgeting: Selected Comment"; Wildavsky, "The Political Economy of Efficiency."

168. Mosher, "PPBS: Two Questions," at 25.

169. Wildavsky, "The Political Economy of Efficiency," at 63, quoting McKean and Anshen, "Limitations, Risks, and Problems," at 286–87.

170. Thrust of Johnson's introductory statement of 25 August 1965, *Planning Programming Budgeting,* at 503–4.

171. Jardini, "Out of the Blue Yonder," esp. chaps. 6 and 7.

172. Direct lineage of defense-style "systems analysis" and broader purview "policy analysis" are discussed by Quade, oral history interview, at 45.

173. J. P. Roos, *Welfare Theory and Social Policy. A Study in Policy Science* (Helsinki: Societas Scientiarum Fennica, 1973), 76–105, esp. 85.

174. This internal serial publication is mentioned in *The Pentagon Papers; the*

Defense Department History of the United States Decisionmaking on Vietnam (Boston: Beacon Press, 1971–72), vol. 3, 507.

175. See Jürgen Habermas, *The Structural Transformation of the Public Sphere: An Inquiry into a Category of Bourgeois Society,* trans. Thomas Berger (Cambridge: MIT Press, 1989).

176. See Enthovan's testimony, 17 October 1967, *Planning Programming Budgeting,* at 296–97; see also Staat's testimony, 26 March 1968, ibid., 370–71, and Staat's testimony to the effect that the cost of PBB remained unknown, ibid., 361–62.

177. Katzenbach, "Ideas: A New Defense Industry," at 20–21.

178. Mosher, "Program Bugeting in Foreign Affairs," at 16.

179. Staat's testimony was to the U.S. Senate, Subcommittee on National Security and International Operations, Committee on Government Operations, 26 March 1968, *Planning Programming Budgeting,* at 369.

180. Werner Jann, "From Policy Analysis to Political Management? An Outside Look at Public-Policy Training in the United States," in Peter Wagner et al., eds., *Social Sciences and Modern States* (Cambridge: Cambridge University Press, 1991), 110–30.

181. For discussion of the Ford Foundations' involvement in establishing the New Look management program at Stanford Business School between 1958 and 1963, see Robert E. Gleeson and Steven Schlossman, "George Leland Bach and the Rebirth of Graduate Management Education in the United States, 1945–1975," *Magazine of the Graduate Management Admission Council,* spring 1995, 35.

182. *Report to the Study of the Ford Foundation on Policy and Program,* at 113.

183. For an account of rational choice analysis at the World Bank and International Monetary Fund that occurred after McNamara's watch, see Joseph Stiglitz, *Globalization and Its Discontents* (London: Norton, 2002).

184. See, e.g., Alain C. Enthoven, "Systems Analysis and Decision Making," *Military Review* 43 (January 1963): 7–17.

185. Quote of Charles Hitch to this effect in Kraft, "RAND: Arsenal for Ideas," at 76.

186. John von Neumann and Oskar Morgenstern, *Theory of Games and Economic Behavior* (Princeton: Princeton University Press, 1944). See also Robert J. Leonard, "Creating a Context for Game Theory," in *Toward a History of Game Theory,* ed. E. Roy Weintraub (Durham: Duke University Press, 1992), 29–76.

187. For P. M. S. Blackett's recognition of game theory's usage in devising national security strategy and attendant skepticism about that use, see Blackett, "Critique of Some Contemporary Defense Thinking," *Encounter* 16, no. 4 (April 1961): 16.

188. See Philip Mirowski and Wade Hands on Arrow and Samuelson's roles in the neoclassical synthesis in "A Budget of Paradoxes: The Postwar Stabilization

of American Neoclassical Price Theory," paper presented to the conference "Transformation of American Postwar Economics," Duke University, April 1997.

189. P. M. S. Blackett refers to both von Neumann and Morgenstern's Theory of Games and Economic Behavior and Thomas Schelling's Strategy of Conflict in this context. See Blackett, "Critique of Some Contemporary Defense Thinking," at 16.

190. Memo from Adie Suehsdorf to Gaither and Newton, 5 April 1956, Gaither Series VI, box 12, folder 145, FFA.

191. *Report of the Study for the Ford Foundation on Policy and Program,* at 22.

192. Ibid., 18.

193. Ibid., 72.

Chapter Two

1. E. J. Mishan, *Welfare Economics: Ten Introductory Essays,* 2nd ed. (New York: Random House, 1964), 61.

2. This quote happens to be from Gary Hart, "The Big, Lethal Sleep: Why America was Caught Napping on 11 September," *New Statesman,* 17 December 2001, 47; similar quotes abound.

3. Ibid., 48.

4. Arrow's security clearance application submitted by RAND to the U.S. government, Kenneth J. Arrow Papers, Box 36, Rare Book, Manuscript, and Special Collections Library, Duke University, Durham, N.C.

5. Arrow served as a weather officer in the U.S. Army Air Corps, achieving the rank of captain.

6. See the four-volume set of Arrow's collective papers: *Social Choice and Justice* (Cambridge: Harvard University Press, 1983); *General Equilibrium* (Cambridge: Harvard University Press, 1983); *Individual Choice under Certainty and Uncertainty* (Cambridge: Harvard University Press, 1984); *The Economics of Information* (Cambridge: Harvard University Press, 1984). For an insightful assessment of Arrow's contributions, see George R. Feiwel, ed., *Arrow and the Foundations of the Theory of Economic Policy* (New York: New York University Press, 1987); and George R. Feiwel, ed., *Arrow and the Ascent of Modern Economic Theory* (New York: New York University Press, 1987).

7. Kenneth J. Arrow, "Behavior under Uncertainty and its Implications for Policy," in *Decision Making: Descriptive, Normative, and Prescriptive Interactions,* ed. David E. Bell, Howard Raiffa, and Amos Tversky (Cambridge: Cambridge University Press, 1988).

8. Press release, Sveriges Riksbank (Bank of Sweden) Prize in Economic Sciences in Memory of Alfred Nobel for 1972, Royal Swedish Academy of Sciences, 25 October 1972.

9. The earliest publication of Arrow's result following the RAND report is "A Difficulty in the Concept of Social Welfare," *Journal of Political Economy* 58 (1950): 328–46.

10. David A. Hollinger, "The Defense of Democracy and Robert K. Merton's Formulation of the Scientific Ethos," in David A. Hollinger, *Science, Jews, and Secular Culture* (Princeton: Princeton University Press, 1996).

11. Frank H. Knight, *The Dilemma of Liberalism* (Ann Arbor: Edwards Brothers, 1933), 43.

12. Knight titled his essay "The Case for Communism from the Standpoint of an Ex-liberal," in ibid. at 1.

13. Ibid., 44; this argument is made throughout the essay.

14. Lionel Robbins, *Economic Planning and International Order* (London: Macmillan, 1937), 227, 229; Henry C. Simons, *Economic Policy for a Free Society* (Chicago: University of Chicago Press, 1948), 42.

15. F. A. Hayek, *The Road to Serfdom* (Chicago: University of Chicago Press, 1944); Joseph Schumpeter, *Socialism, Capitalism, and Democracy* (London: Allen and Unwin, 1943); Karl Popper, *The Open Society and Its Enemies*, 2 vols. (London: Routledge, 1945).

16. Maurice Dobb, "Economic Theory and the Problems of a Socialist Economy," *Economic Journal* 43 (December 1933): 585–98.

17. A. P. Lerner, "Economic Theory and Socialist Economy," *Review of Economic Studies* 2 (1943): 51–61.

18. Ibid., 55; Lerner cites L. C. Robbins, *The Scope and Significance of Economic Science*, 113n, but presumably means *An Essay on the Nature and Significance of Economic Science*, 2nd ed. (London: Macmillan, 1935).

19. Ibid., 58–59; Lerner quotes from L. D. Trotsky, *Soviet Economy in Danger* (New York: Pioneer Publishers, 1933), 29–30.

20. Maurice Dobb, "Economic Theory and Socialist Economy: A Reply," *Review of Economic Studies* 2 (1943): 144–51.

21. A. P. Lerner, "A Rejoinder," *Review of Economic Studies* 2 (1943): 152–54, 152.

22. Ibid., 153.

23. O. Lange, "The Scope and Method of Economics," *Review of Economic Studies* 13, no. 1 (1945–46): 19–32; K. W. Rothschild, "The Meaning of Rationality: A Note on Professor Lange's Article," *Review of Economic Studies* 14, no. 1 (1945–46): 50–52.

24. Lange, "The Scope and Method of Economics," at 22–23.

25. Popper, *The Open Society and Its Enemies*, at vol. 2, p. 213.

26. Lange, "The Scope and Method of Economics," at 24.

27. Oscar Lange, "The Foundations of Welfare Economics," *Econometrica* 10 (July–October 1942), 215–28.

28. Ibid., 222; see also Lange's *Economic Theory of Socialism* (Minneapolis: University of Minnesota Press, 1938), 101–2.

29. Rothschild, "The Meaning of Rationality," at 50.

30. Ibid., 51.

31. Ibid.

32. Ibid.

33. Arrow, *SCIV*, at 21.

34. S. Moos, "Laissez-Faire, Planning and Ethics," *Economic Journal* 55 (April 1945): 17–27.

35. Ibid., 24.

36. See Arrow's preface, "A Difficulty in the Concept of Social Welfare" (1950), in *Social Choice and Justice* (Cambridge: Harvard University Press, Belknap Press, 1983), 2.

37. J. R. Hicks, "The Foundations of Welfare Economics," *Economic Journal* 49 (1939): 696.

38. Ibid.

39. Ibid., 698.

40. Ibid., 711.

41. This continues to be the standard in cost–benefit analysis despite the additional fact that attaching welfare measures to dollar amounts is contested, since it is generally deemed that the value of a dollar must be related to the number of dollars an individual has.

42. William J. Baumol, "Community Indifference," *Review of Economic Studies* 14, no. 1 (1945–46): 44–48, 44 (Baumol is quoting Hicks).

43. Robert Cooter and Peter Rappoport, "Were the Ordinalists Wrong about Welfare Economics?" *Journal of Economic Literature* 22 (June 1984): 507–30.

44. Arrow uses the term "capitalist democracy" to refer to the subject matter of his text; see *SCIV*, at 1.

45. See Arrow's preface to "A Difficulty in the Concept of Social Welfare," at 2–3.

46. Arrow, *SCIV*, at 48–51; see also Arrow, "A Difficulty in the Concept of Social Welfare," at 20.

47. Although Arrow does not graphically illustrate his scenario, it focuses on distribution points typical of an Edgeworth box (unlike his later compensation example); the spatial presentation of this problem was familiar to Arrow, see Hicks, "The Foundation of Welfare Economics," at 702.

48. Arrow, "A Difficulty in the Concept of Social Welfare," at 20.

49. Although it is unnecessary for his general proof, in this specific instance Arrow introduces the additional example that individuals' indifference curves are smooth and convex.

50. Paul Samuelson, *Foundations of Economic Analysis* (Cambridge: Harvard University Press, 1948), 244.

51. See Arrow, *SCIV*, notes on pages 2–8.

52. See Arrow, "A Difficulty in the Concept of Social Welfare," at 5; Arrow, *SCIV*, at 3.

53. Arrow, *SCIV*, at 51–59.

54. For a fuller statement of Arrow's methodological commitments, see his "Mathematical Models in the Social Sciences," in *The Policy Sciences: Recent Developments in Scope and Method,* ed. Daniel Lerner and Harold D. Lasswell (Stanford: Stanford University Press, 1951), 129–54.

55. Maurice Dobb, "Economic Theory and the Problems of a Socialist Economy," at 589–98; for a contemporary take on Marx's critique of science, see

Lange, "The Scope and Method of Economics," at 22–24; and Popper, *The Open Society and Its Enemies,* at vol. 2, p. 213.

56. See, e.g., L. M. Fraser, "Notes and Memoranda: The Doctrine of Consumers' Sovereignty," *Economic Journal* 49 (September 1939): 544–48.

57. Arrow, *SCIV,* at 17.

58. Fraser, "Notes and Memoranda," at 545.

59. *SCIV,* 28.

60. Lerner, "Economic Theory and Socialist Economy," at 54–59.

61. Arrow, *SCIV,* at 19.

62. Ibid., 13.

63. Lange, "Scope and Method of Economics," at 30.

64. Arrow, *SCIV,* at 19.

65. Ibid., 16.

66. Ibid., 3.

67. Samuelson, *Foundations of Economic Analysis,* at 97–98.

68. Arrow, "Mathematical Models in the Social Sciences," at 131.

69. Arrow, *SCIV,* at 16.

70. Arrow uses the term "rational choice" in 1950 ("A Difficulty in the Concept of Social Welfare," at 4).

71. Arrow, *SCIV,* at 21; Arrow anticipates the implications of the game-theoretic formulation of rationality for his theorem demonstrating that his axioms of reason differ from those of von Neumann and Morgenstern (ibid. at 20).

72. Ibid., 59.

73. Ibid., 29.

74. Ibid., 59.

75. For an excellent overview of these efforts, see Amartya Sen, "*Social Choice and Justice:* A Review Article," *Journal of Economic Literature* 23 (December 1985): 1764–76.

76. Arrow, *SCIV,* at 81–86.

77. Ibid., 84.

78. Ibid.

79. Ibid., 26–28; Murray Kemp and Yew-Kwang Ng, "Arrow's Independence Condition and the Bergson-Samuelson Tradition," in *Arrow and the Foundations of the Theory of Economic Policy,* ed. George R. Feiwel (New York: New York University Press, 1987), 224.

80. Arrow, *SCIV,* at 59.

81. Arthur Smithies, "Economic Welfare and Policy," in *Economics and Public Policy* (Washington, D.C.: Brookings Institution, 1955), 9.

82. James M. Buchanan, "Social Choice, Democracy, and Free Markets," *Journal of Political Economy* 62 (1954): 122. The paucity of response to Arrow's work from the perspective of the marketplace is a topic ripe for both analytic and historical investigation. For further discussion, see Amartya Sen's essay discussing how Arrow's impossibility theorem holds even when the condition of collective rationality is dropped; Sen's proof hinges on the property of "decisiveness." Sen, "Rationality and Social Choice," *American Economic Review* 85, no. 1 (1995): 1–24.

83. Buchanan, "Social Choice, Democracy, and Free Markets," at 123.

84. Reviews commenting on Arrow's *Social Choice and Individual Values* include Abram Burk Bergson, "On the Concept of Social Welfare," *Quarterly Journal of Economics* 68 (1954): 233–51; Irving M. Copi, "Social Choice and Individual Values," *Ethics* 62 (1952): 220–22; Richard G. Davis, "Comment on Arrow and the 'New Welfare Economics,'" *Economic Journal* 68 (1958): 834–35; Leo A. Goodman, *American Sociological Review* 18 (1953): 116–17; Murray C. Kemp, "Arrow's General Possibility Theorem," *Review of Economic Studies* 21 (1953–54): 240–43; I. M. D. Little, *Journal of Political Economy* 60 (1952): 422–32; Gerald J. Schnepp, "Social Choice and Individual Values," *American Catholic Sociological Review* 12 (1952): 243; Harold M. Somers, "Social Choice and Individual Values," *Journal of Political Economy* 69 (1952): 170–71.

85. Copi, "Social Choice and Individual Values," at 221; Goodman, "Social Choice and Individual Values," at 116–17.

86. Goodman, *American Sociological Review* (1953), 117.

87. Copi, "Social Choice and Individual Values," at 221.

88. Somers, "Social Choice and Individual Values," at 171.

89. Schnepp, "Social Choice and Individual Values," 243.

90. For a historical overview and analysis of the social welfare tradition, see Samuelson, *Foundations of Economic Analysis,* at 203–53.

91. Abba Lerner, *Economics of Control: Principles of Welfare Economics* (New York: Macmillan, 1944). For the late-1940s "planned economy" debate in which economists argued over the theoretical possibility of creating a planned economy that would lead to overall social welfare, see Theo Surányi-Unger, "Individual and Collective Wants," *Journal of Political Economy* 61, no. 1 (February 1948): 1–22. The social welfare economists accepted discussion of interpersonal comparisons of utility *if* it were recognized that such discussion introduced value judgments.

92. Samuelson, *Foundations of Economic Analysis,* at 250.

93. Even so, it was stated in the literature that cardinal measures could be introduced if one were aware of the normative judgments implied. See Abram B. Bergson, "A Reformulation of Certain Aspects of Welfare Economics," *Quarterly Journal of Economics* 52 (February 1938): 310–34.

94. Samuelson, *Foundations of Economic Analysis,* at 250.

95. See Bergson, "A Reformulation of Certain Aspects of Welfare Economics, at 7: "The object of this paper is to state in a precise form the value judgments required for the derivation of the conditions of maximum economic welfare . . . ."

96. Arrow referred to his theorem in this way, though a consensus now finds it more appropriately referred to as the "impossibility theorem."

97. While it is possible to draw conceptual similarities between Arrow's *Social Choice* and Bergson's essay, their arguments are encoded in such different languages and are represented by such different questions that they are difficult to compare directly.

98. See, e.g., Bergson, "A Reformulation of Certain Aspects of Welfare Economics," at 15.

99. Little, "Social Choice and Individual Values," at 425; Kemp, "Arrow's General Possibility Theorem," at 240.

100. Bergson, "On the Concept of Social Welfare," at 240.

101. Mishan, *Welfare Economics,* at 61.

102. For another discussion of Arrow's reception among welfare economists, see J. P. Roos, *Welfare Theory and Social Policy: A Study in Policy Science* (Helsinki: Societa Scientiarum Fennica, 1972), 131–34.

103. Bergson, "On the Concept of Social Welfare," at 240–51; Little, "Social Choice and Individual Values," at 422–32. The problem of the "tyranny of the majority" is often cited to distinguish between social welfare concerns and the procedures of majority rule, which, if the majority so desired, could exploit a minority for its own gain.

104. See especially Bergson, "On the Concept of Social Welfare," at 240–49.

105. For the internal critique of the social welfare economics tradition, see Roos, *Welfare Theory and Social Policy;* I. M. D. Little, *A Critique of Welfare Economics* (Oxford: Clarendon Press, 1957); Jan de V. Graff, *Theoretical Welfare Economics* (Cambridge: Cambridge University Press, 1957); Mishan, *Welfare Economics.*

106. See, e.g., Bergson, "On the Concept of Social Welfare," at 245: "But in welfare economics objection is usually made not to interpersonal comparisons, but to the contention that these comparisons can be made without the introduction of ethical premises. No such contention has been or need be made here. The individual members of the community all are supposed to order social states on the ethical premise that distribution should be according to need."

107. See Bergson, "A Reformulation of Certain Aspects of Welfare Economics," at 310–34.

108. Little, "Social Choice and Individual Values."

109. Sen, "*Social Choice and Justice,*" at 1764–76.

110. Ibid., 1765.

111. Charles K. Rowley, ed., *Social Choice Theory* (Hants, England: Edward Elgar, 1993).

112. Duncan Black, *The Theory of Committees and Elections,* 2nd rev. ed., ed. Iain McLean, Alistair McMillan, and Burt L. Monroe, with a foreword by Ronald H. Coase (Amsterdam: Kluwer, 1998), 360.

113. Duncan Black, "On the Rationale of Group Decision Making," *Journal of Political Economy* 56 (1948): 23–24.

114. Black, *The Theory of Committees and Elections,* 389.

115. Ibid.

116. For the details of the priority dispute, see Ronald H. Coase's foreword to Black, *The Theory of Committess and Elections,* at x–xv.

117. Duncan Black, "On the Rationale of Group Decision Making," at 23–34; *The Theory of Committees and Elections* (Cambridge: Cambridge University Press), 1958.

118. Arrow's preface to "A Difficulty in the Concept of Social Welfare," at 2.

119. Ibid.

120. First published in the *Journal of Political Economy* 58 (1950): 328–46.

121. Conclusion reached after numerous conversations with RAND archivists who routinely send out the cover page from the original report, RAND Report RM-291, 28 July 1949, appended to a copy of the 1951 publication.

122. Coase's foreword to Black, *The Theory of Committees and Elections,* at xiii.

123. Black, *The Theory of Committees and Elections* (1998), at 354.

124. Arrow, *SCIV,* at 7, 23.

125. Arrow, "A Difficulty in the Concept of Social Welfare," at 12.

126. Arrow's belief that his theory is consistent with political democracy and *laissez faire* economics is stated in *SCIV* at 23.

127. Charles K. Rowley, introduction to *Social Choice Theory,* vol. 1, *The Aggregation of Preferences* (Hants, England: Edward Elgar, 1993), xiii (emphasis added). Rowley refers to Robert Nozick's "minimal state" (Nozick, *Anarchy, State, and Utopia* [Oxford: Basil Blackwell, 1974]).

128. See, e.g., Kenneth J. Arrow, "A Cautious Case for Socialism," *Dissent* (fall 1978): 472–80; this is discussed at length in chapter 5.

129. Hollinger, "The Defense of Democracy," at 80.

130. Ibid.

131. Hollinger, "Science as a Weapon in *Kulturkämpfe* in the United States during and after World War II," 155.

132. John Dewey, *The Public and Its Problems* (Chicago: Swallow Press, 1988 [1927]).

133. Kenneth J. Arrow, *The Limits of Organization* (New York: Norton, 1974).

134. Dewey, *The Public and Its Problems.*

135. William H. Riker, "The Paradox of Voting and Congressional Rules for Voting on Amendments," *American Political Science Review* 52 (1958): 349–66.

Chapter Three

1. James M. Buchanan, "Socialism Is Dead But Leviathan Lives On," in James M. Buchanan, *Post-Socialist Political Economy* (Lyme, Conn.: Edward Elgar, 1997), at 85.

2. See Dennis C. Mueller, *Public Choice II* (New York: Cambridge University Press, 1989); and Charles K. Rowley, ed., *Public Choice Theory,* vol. 1 (Hants, England: Elgar Reference Collection, 1993) for further readings in the theoretical achievements of public choice; for insightful discussion of James Buchanan's version of public choice theory, see David Reisman, *The Political Economy of James Buchanan* (London: Macmillan, 1990).

3. James M. Buchanan, "The Pure Theory of Government Finance: A Suggested Approach," *Journal of Political Economy* 57 (December 1949): 496–506.

4. Ibid., 497.

5. Ibid., 496.

6. Ibid., 505, 498.

7. James M. Buchanan, "Social Choice, Democracy, and Free Markets," *Journal of Political Economy* 62 (April 1954): 114–23; "Individual Choice in Voting and the Market," *Journal of Political Economy* 62 (August 1954): 334–43.

8. Buchanan, "Social Choice, Democracy, and Free Markets," at 116.

9. James M. Buchanan, *Public Principles of Public Debt: A Defense and Restatement* (Homewood, Ill.: Richard D. Irwin, 1958).

10. Ibid., 158.

11. This observation also holds even in view of James Buchanan's, "Positive Economics, Welfare Economics, and Political Economy," *Journal of Law and Economics*, 2 (October 1959), 124–38, which while wholly adopting a stance of methodological individualism as yet does not contemplate voting mechanisms as a function of rational self-interest amenable to mathematical modeling.

12. Correspondence between Buchanan and Tullock is part of the James M. Buchanan Collection, Center for Study of Public Choice, Buchanan House, George Mason University, Fairfax, Virginia (hereafter JMB Papers).

13. James M. Buchanan and Gordon Tullock, *The Calculus of Consent: Logical Foundations of Constitutional Democracy* (Ann Arbor: University of Michigan Press, 1962); Anthony Downs, *An Economic Theory of Democracy* (New York: Harper and Row, 1957).

14. Downs, *An Economic Theory of Democracy*, at 140. For a discussion of the research in the public choice tradition that Downs's argument inspired, see Charles K. Rowley, introduction to *Public Choice Theory* (Brookfield, Vermont: Edward Elgar, 1993), xiv–xvi.

15. Buchanan and Tullock, *The Calculus of Consent*, at 130.

16. Steven G. Medema provides an in-depth discussion of these reviews in his "'Related Disciplines': The Professionalization of Public Choice Analysis," unpublished manuscript of paper presented at a Duke University history of economics conference, spring 1999; a shorter version of Medema's paper is published in *History of Applied Economics: History of Political Economy Annual Supplement* 32 (2000): 289–323. The authors and publications for the most important reviews include the following: Anthony Downs, *Journal of Political Economy* 72 (February 1964): 87–88; Irwin N. Gertzog, *American Political Science Review* 63 (December 1964): 973–74; Henry G. Manne, *George Washington Law Review* 31 (June 1963): 1065–71; R. J. May, *Australian Quarterly* (December 1963): 111–13; Robert McGinnis, *Annals of the American Academy of Political and Social Science* 346 (March 1963): 188; James E. Meade, *Economic Journal* 73 (March 1963): 101–4; Mancur Olson Jr., *American Economic Review* 52 (December 1962): 1217–18; C. M. P., *Ethics* 75 (October 1963): 65–68; William H. Riker, *Midwest Journal of Political Science* 6 (November 1962): 408–11; Kenneth Vines, *Journal of Politics* 25 (February 1963): 160–61; Benjamin Ward, *Southern Economic Journal* 29, no. 4 (1963): 351–53.

17. Sidney S. Ulmer, "The Role of 'Costs' in Political Choice: A Review of James M. Buchanan and Gordon Tullock, *The Calculus of Consent*," *Conflict Resolution* 7, no. 2 (1963): 171–76.

18. Correspondence from Buchanan to Tullock, 9 September 1959, in JMB Papers.

19. See Buchanan and Tullock, *The Calculus of Consent*, at chaps. 11–13. It is frequently claimed that Buchanan's background in the public finance tradition of Knut Wicksell and R. A. Musgrave is also important. See R. E. Wagner, "The Calculus of Consent: A Wicksellian Retrospective," *Public Choice* 56 (1988): 153–66.

20. For evidence of the continuance of this contrasting style, see Arrow's reformulation of Tullock's *Toward a Mathematics of Politics* (Ann Arbor: University of Michigan Press, 1967) in "Tullock and an Existence Theorem," *Social Choice and Justice: Collected Papers of Kenneth J. Arrow* (Oxford: Basil Blackwell, 1984), 81–87, reprinted from *Public Choice* 6 (1969): 105–12.

21. Their analysis is presented in explicitly anti-Keynesian terms and also stands opposed to the Chicago school's approach to political economy; see Rowley, introduction to *Public Choice Theory*, at xi–xii.

22. The center's pamphlet includes the following as part of its general aims: "The Center is organized to promote scholarly discussion of the basic ideals of Western civilization and of the solutions to modern social problems most in accord with those ideals. The Center is a community of scholars who wish to preserve a social order based on individual liberty. The Center will encourage students to see the philosophical as well as the technical issues entering into problems of social organization" (undated).

23. Buchanan and Tullock, *The Calculus of Consent*, at 25.

24. Ibid., 306; see also 25.

25. Buchanan's appendix, ibid., 308.

26. Ibid., 250; for a more general comment of Buchanan's sense of working in Adam Smith's tradition of political economy, see his manuscript "Virginia's Decade in Political Economy: Positive Elaboration of an Academic History," JMB Papers, 6; see also "Special Session: The Founding Fathers," 24 March 1995 meeting of the Public Choice Society, at 2.

27. See Buchanan and Tullock, *The Calculus of Consent*, esp. at 317–20.

28. Ibid., 12, 26; see also James M. Buchanan, "An Individualistic Theory of Political Process," in *Varieties of Political Theory*, ed. David E. Easton (Englewood Cliffs, N.J.: Prentice Hall, 1966), 25–29.

29. R. J. May, review of *The Calculus of Consent*, at 112.

30. Draft of letter from Buchanan to Olson in file containing reviews of *The Calculus of Consent*, undated, in JMB Papers.

31. For commentary, see Rowley, *Public Choice Theory*, at xiii–xiv.

32. Mancur Olson Jr. and Christopher K. Clague, "Dissent in Economics: The Convergence of Extremes," *Social Research* 38, no. 4 (winter 1971): 753.

33. Letter cited in ibid., 757.

34. See, e.g., Buchanan's *The Limits of Liberty: Between Anarchy and Leviathan* (Chicago: University of Chicago Press, 1975); *Wall Street Journal* article of July 31, 1970, 6; see also copies of assorted letters of recommendation in JMB Papers.

35. James M. Buchanan and Richard E. Wagner, *Democracy in Deficit: The Political Legacy of Lord Keynes* (San Diego: Academic Press, 1977), 65.

36. For Buchanan and other public choice scholars response to "Reaganomics," see James M. Buchanan et al., *Reaganomics and After* (London: Institute of Economic Affairs, 1989).

37. Buchanan mentions the Tullock tenure decision, which was also embroiled in 1960s university politics regarding student protests, as the most significant factor in his decision. Buchanan to Leland Yaeger, 15 January 1968, JMB Papers. For discussion of UVA politics in the 1960s, see "Special Session: The Founding Fathers," Public Choice Meeting, 24 March 1995, 2.

38. Robert McGinnis, professor of sociology at Cornell, also reviewed the book and attended meetings; Manne was a leader in the law and economics movement and established a center first at University of Miami, then at Emory, and later at George Mason University's law school.

39. James M. Buchanan, *Public Finance in Democratic Process: Fiscal Institutions and Individual Choice* (Chapel Hill: University of North Carolina Press, 1967).

40. William C. Mitchell claims to have coined the phrase, a claim that is corroborated by Buchanan's recollections in "Special Session: The Founding Fathers," 5.

41. Draft of proposal to the National Science Foundation to fund publication of *Papers on Non-Market Decision Making*, undated, in the file "Papers on non-market decision making," JMB Papers.

42. Mancur Olson Jr., review of *The Calculus of Consent, American Economic Review* 52 (December 1962): 1217–18.

43. Memorandum from Vincent Ostrom to Members and Prospective Members of the Public Choice Society, 10 September 1969, JMB Papers, 2.

44. Gary J. Miller, "The Impact of Economics on Contemporary Political Science," *Journal of Economic Literature* 35 (September 1997), 1173–1204; Dennis C. Mueller, "Public Choice: A Survey," *Journal of Economic Literature* 14, no. 2 (June 1976): 395–433.

45. Memorandum from Vincent Ostrom to Members and Prospective Members of the Public Choice Society, at 2.

46. Ibid., 3.

47. All quotes are from ibid.

48. Buchanan, "An Individualistic Theory of Political Process," at 37.

49. See James M. Buchanan, "Economic Theory in the Post-Revolutionary Moment of the 1990s," in Buchanan, *Post-Socialist Political Economy*, at 63–74.

50. John Rawls, *A Theory of Justice* (Cambridge: Harvard University Press, 1971).

51. For an indication of how little understood is Rawls's relationship to rational choice scholarship, see Rogers Smith informative essay "Still Blowing in the Wind: The American Quest for a Democratic, Scientific Political Science," in *Dædalus: American Academic Culture in Transformation: Fifty Years, Four Disciplines* 126, no. 1 (winter 1997): 265.

322   Notes to Pages 149–153

52. Abstract to Rawls's paper, "Proceedings of the Big Meadows Conference," 12–13 October 1964, 7.

53. Buchanan and Tullock, *Calculus of Consent*, at 312.

54. See David Held, *Models of Democracy*, 2nd ed. (Stanford: Stanford University Press, 1996), 299–305.

55. Abstract to Rawls's paper, at 6.

56. Reisman, *The Political Economy of James Buchanan*, 43; Daniel M. Hausman and Michael S. McPherson, "Economics, Rationality, and Ethics," in *The Philosophy of Economics: An Anthology*, 2nd ed., ed. Daniel M. Hausman (Cambridge: Cambridge University Press, 1994), 252–77, esp. 260–64.

57. Abstract to Rawls's paper, at 8.

58. Ibid.

59. Buchanan and Tullock, *Calculus of Consent*, at 78.

60. See chapter 8.

61. James M. Buchanan, "Better than Plowing," *Banca Nazionale Del Lavoro Quarterly Review* 159 (1986): 374.

62. James M. Buchanan and Nicos E. Devletoglou, *Academia in Anarchy: An Economic Diagnosis* (New York: Basic Books, 1970), 103.

63. James M. Buchanan, *Liberty, Market and State: Political Economy in the 1980s* (Brighton, England: Wheatsheaf Books, 1986), 108.

64. Ibid., 110.

65. Ibid.

66. Kenneth J. Arrow, *Social Choice and Individual Values* (New York: Wiley, 1951), 82; for discussion, see Reisman, *The Political Economy of James Buchanan*, 98–101.

67. Letters from Buchanan to W. Samuels, 18 May 1972, 27 March 1973, and 8 August 8 1973, quoted in Reisman, *The Political Economy of James Buchanan*, at 43.

68. On Tullock's contributions, see Gordon Brady, "Gordon Tullock: His Development as an Unconventional Economist, 1947–1962," in *Public Choice Essays in Honor of a Maverick Scholar: Gordon Tullock*, ed. Price Fishback et al. (Boston: Kluwer Academic Press, 2000), 1–22.

69. Examples of this work include Mueller, "Public Choice: A Survey," 395; Mancur Olson Jr., *The Logic of Collective Action* (Cambridge: Harvard University Press, 1965); Gordon Tullock, *The Politics of Bureaucracy* (Washington, D.C.: Public Affairs Press,1965); Anthony Downs, *Inside Democracy* (Boston: Little, Brown, 1967); William A. Niskanen, *Bureaucracy and Representative Government* (New York: Aldine-Atherton, 1971); A. Breton, *The Economic Theory of Representative Government* (Chicago: Aldine, 1974); R. D. Tollison, "Public Choice and Legislation," *Virginia Law Review* 74 (1988): 339–71; Charles K. Rowley, *The Right to Justice* (Cheltenham: Edward Elgar, 1992); Kenneth Shepsle, *The Giant Jigsaw Puzzle* (Chicago: University of Chicago Press, 1978); Kenneth Shepsle and Barry Weingast, "Structure-Induced Equilibrium and Legislative Choice," *Public Choice* (1981): 503–20; Charles K. Row-

ley and M. Vachris, "*Why Democracy in the U.S. May Not Produce Efficient Results* (Fairfax: Center for the Study of Public Choice, George Mason University 1990); Barry Weingast and N.J. Moran, "Bureaucratic Discretion or Congressional Control," *Journal of Political Economy* 91 (1983): 764–800; Gordon Tullock, *The Economics of Special Privilege and Rent-Seeking* (Boston: Kluwer, 1980).

70. Ka Ho Mok, "Impact of Globalization: A Study of Quality Assurance Systems of Higher Education in Hong Kong and Singapore," *Comparative Education Review* 44, no. 2 (May 2000): 148.

71. Buchanan, "Socialism Is Dead but Leviathan Lives On," in Buchanan, *Post-Socialist Political Economy,* at 86.

72. Ibid.

73. Ibid.

74. Ibid., 90.

75. James M. Buchanan, "Post-Reagan Political Economy," in James M. Buchanan et al., *Reaganomics and After* (London: Institute of Economic Affairs, 1989), 9.

76. James R. Schlesinger, *The Political Economy of National Security: A Study of the Economic Aspects of the Contemporary Power Struggle* (New York: Praeger, 1960), 31–40.

77. Buchanan, "Socialism Is Dead," at 85.

Chapter Four

1. David Hollinger, "The Defense of Democracy and Robert K. Merton's Formulation of the Scientific Ethos," in David A. Hollinger, *Science, Jews, and Secular Culture* (Princeton: Princeton University Press, 1996), 80–96; see also Thomas Bender, "Politics, Intellect, and the American University, 1945–1995," *Dædalus: American Academic Culture in Transformation: Fifty Years, Four Disciplines* 126, no. 1 (winter 1997): 11.

2. Hollinger, "The Defense of Democracy and Robert K. Merton's Formulation of the Scientific Ethos," at 81.

3. For the presumption that impartiality and scientific inquiry were at odds with the promotion of self-interest, see ibid., 80–96.

4. As found, e.g., in John Dewey's *The Public and Its Problems* (Chicago: Swallow Press, 1927).

5. For a history of the traditional dependence of democracy on "public opinion" formulated in a "public sphere," see Jürgen Habermas, *The Structural Transformation of the Public Sphere,* trans. Thomas Burger (Cambridge: MIT Press, 1989).

6. For detailed analysis of the forces behind increasing formalization of the American social sciences during the twentieth century, see the collection of essays edited by Samuel Z. Klausner and Victor M. Lidz, *The Nationalization of the Social Sciences* (Philadelphia: University of Pennsylvania Press, 1986).

7. Bender, "Politics, Intellect, and the American University, 1945–1995," at 12; Theodore M. Porter, *Trust in Numbers: The Pursuit of Objectivity in Science and Public Life* (Princeton: Princeton University Press, 1995); see also Dorothy Ross, *The Origins of American Social Science* (Cambridge: Cambridge University Press, 1991); Mark C. Smith, *Social Science in the Crucible: The American Debate over Objectivity and Purpose, 1918–1941* (Durham: Duke University Press, 1994).

8. For a detailed analysis of rational choice theory's global reach, see Ka Ho Mok, "Impact of Globalization: A Study of Quality Assurance Systems of Higher Education in Hong Kong and Singapore," *Comparative Education Review* 44, no. 2 (May 2000): 148.

9. Bender, "Politics, Intellect, and the American University, 1945–1995," at 13.

10. Ibid., 14.

11. Ibid.

12. For the best sense of this, see the collection of essays published in *Contemporary Political Science: A Survey of Methods, Research and Teaching* (Paris: UNESCO, 1950).

13. Charles Eisenmann, "On the Matter and Methods of the Political Sciences," in ibid., 91.

14. Charles E. Lindblom, "Political Science in the 1940s and 1950s," in *Dædalus: American Academic Culture in Transformation*, at 225–52.

15. Thomas I. Cook, "The Methods of Political Science, Chiefly in the United States," in *Contemporary Political Science*, at 72.

16. William H. Riker, *Democracy in the United States* (New York: Macmillan, 1953).

17. L. S. Shapley and M. Shubik, "A Method of Evaluating the Distribution of Power in a Committee System," *American Political Science Review* 54 (1954): 787–92.

18. William H. Riker and Ronald Schaps, "Disharmony in Federal Government," *Behavioral Science* 2 (1957): 276–90; William H. Riker, "A Test of the Adequacy of the Power Index," *Behavioral Science* 4 (1959): 120–31; William H. Riker, "The Paradox of Voting and Congressional Rules for Voting on Amendments," *American Political Science Review* 52 (1958): 349–66.

19. William H. Riker, "Events and Situations," *Journal of Philosophy* 54 (1957): 57–70; William H. Riker, "Causes of Events," *Journal of Philosophy* 56 (1959): 281–92.

20. "Supplemental Statements," application to the Center for Advanced Study in the Behavioral Sciences (CASBS), undated, in the collection William H. Riker Papers, Department of Rare Books and Special Collections, University of Rochester, Rochester, New York (hereafter WHR Papers).

21. William H. Riker curriculum vitae, submitted to CASBS, fall 1959, WHR Papers, 2.

22. William H. Riker, *The Theory of Political Coalitions* (New York: Yale University Press, 1963).

23. Letter from Larry Friedman to Riker, 24 February 1961, WHR Papers, 2.

24. Ibid.

25. For examples of such research, see John Maynard Smith, *Mathematical Ideas in Biology* (Cambridge: Cambridge University Press, 1968), and *Evolution and the Theory of Games* (Cambridge: Cambridge University Press, 1976); Richard Dawkins, *The Selfish Gene* (New York: Oxford University Press, 1976); Robert Axelrod and William D. Hamilton, "The Evolution of Cooperation in Biology," in *The Evolution of Cooperation,* ed. Robert Axelrod (New York: Basic Books, 1984), 88–108.

26. Riker, *Theory of Political Coalitions,* at 3–9.

27. Ibid., 5. For one such disappointed theorist, see Thomas C. Schelling, *The Strategy of Conflict* (Cambridge: Harvard University Press, 1960).

28. John von Neumann and Oskar Morgenstern, *Theory of Games and Economic Behavior* (Princeton: Princeton University Press, 1944), 15.

29. Riker, *Theory of Political Coalitions,* at 32.

30. William H. Riker and Peter C. Ordeshook, *An Introduction to Positive Political Theory* (Englewood Cliffs, N.J.: Prentice Hall, 1973).

31. RAND records indicate Solow was a consultant from 1951 to 2002 with only a year's hiatus; Samuelson was a consultant from 1948 to 1990.

32. See Henry G. Manne, *An Intellectual History of the School of Law, George Mason University* (Arlington, Va.: Law and Economics Center, George Mason University School of Law, 1993).

33. For discussion, see Ernest R. Hilgard and Daniel Lerner, "The Person: Subject and Object of Science and Policy," in *The Policy Sciences: Recent Developments in Scope and Method,* ed. Daniel Lerner and Harold D. Lasswell (Stanford: Stanford University Press, 1951).

34. William H. Riker, *Liberalism against Populism: A Confrontation between the Theory of Democracy and Social Choice* (San Francisco: Freeman, 1982), 12–13.

35. Isaiah Berlin, *Four Essays on Liberty* (London: Oxford University Press, 1969), 144.

36. Ibid., 152.

37. Ibid.

38. Ibid., 167.

39. Riker, *Liberalism against Populism,* at 12.

40. C. B. MacPherson, *Democratic Theory: Essays in Retrieval* (Oxford: Clarendon Press, 1973).

41. Riker, *Liberalism against Populism,* at 13.

42. Ibid., 249.

43. Ibid., 248.

44. C. B. MacPherson, "Berlin's Division of Liberty," in *Democratic Theory,* at 95–119.

45. See Berlin's essay "Two Concepts of Liberty," in *Four Essays on Liberty,* at 156.

46. MacPherson, "Berlin's Division of Liberty," at 114.

Chapter Five

1. See, e.g., R. Duncan Luce and Howard Raiffa, *Games and Decisions: Introduction and Critical Survey* (New York: Wiley, 1957).
2. Edith Stokey and Richard Zeckhauser, *A Primer for Policy Analysis* (New York: Norton, 1978), esp. 257–90.
3. RAND records indicate Olson was a consultant from October 1963 to September 1967 and from June 1969 to September 1973.
4. Mancur Olson Jr., "The Plan and Purpose of a Social Report," *Public Interest* 15 (spring 1969): 85–97.
5. Ibid., 96.
6. Mancur Olson Jr., *The Logic of Collective Action* (Cambridge: Harvard University Press, 1965), at 1.
7. Arthur Bentley, *The Process of Government* (Evanston, Ill.: Principia Press, 1949).
8. Olson, *The Logic of Collective Action*, at 105.
9. Douglas Muzzio and Gerald De Maoi, "Formal Theory and Prospects of Policy Science," in *Handbook of Political Theory and Policy Science*, ed. Edward Portis and Michael Levy (New York: Greenwood Press, 1988), 127–45, at 130.
10. Richard Tuck, "The Imperfect History of Perfect Competition," Centre for History and Economics, Kings College, Cambridge University (April 1999).
11. F. Y. Edgeworth, *Mathematical Psychics: An Essay on the Application of Mathematics to the Moral Sciences* (London: C. K. Paul, 1881), at 45.
12. Olson, *The Logic of Collective Action*, at 96.
13. William H. Riker, *Liberalism against Populism: A Confrontation between the Theory of Democracy and Social Choice* (San Francisco: Freeman, 1982), preface.
14. Quote from ibid., 4.
15. Mancur Olson Jr. and Christopher K. Clague, "Dissent in Economics: The Convergence of Extremes," *Social Research* 38, no. 4 (winter 1971): 751–76.
16. "Capitalism, Socialism, and Democracy, A Symposium," *Commentary*, April 1978, 29–71.
17. Edward J. Harpham and Richard K. Scotch, "Economic Discourse, Policy Analysis, and the Problem of the Political," in *Handbook of Political Theory and Policy Science*, ed. Portis and Levy, 215–30.
18. Harpham and Scotch, "Economic Discourse, Policy Analysis, and the Political," at 221.
19. Ibid., 229.
20. See, e.g., William H. Riker and Peter Ordeshook, "A Theory of the Calculus of Voting," *American Political Science Review* 67 (1968): 753–66; Richard D. McKelvey and Peter C. Ordeshook, "A General Theory of the Calculus of Voting," in *Mathematical Applications in Political Science*, vol. 6, ed. James F. Herndon and Joseph L. Bernd (Charlottesville: University of Virginia Press, 1972), 32–79; John A. Ferejohn and Morris P. Fiorina, "The Paradox of Not Voting: A Decision Theoretic Analysis," *American Political Science Review* 68 (1974): 525–

46. For an overview of the effort to understand voting behavior, see the critical discussions in Donald P. Green and Ian Shapiro, *Pathologies of Rational Choice Theory: A Critique of Applications in Political Science* (New Haven: Yale University Press, 1994); Morris P. Fiorina, "Voting Behavior," in *Perspectives on Public Choice: A Handbook,* ed. Dennis C. Mueller (Cambridge: Cambridge University Press, 1997), 391–414.

21. John H. Aldrich, "When Is It Rational to Vote?" in *Perspectives on Public Choice,* 375–85.

22. Green and Shapiro, *Pathologies of Rational Choice Theory,* at 47–71.

23. Aldrich, "When Is It Rational to Vote?" at 373.

24. Fiorina, "Voting Behavior," at 403.

25. Aldrich, "When Is It Rational to Vote?" at 387.

26. Ibid.

27. Ibid., 385–90; Fiorina, "Voting Behavior," at 402–3.

28. Fiorina, "Voting Behavior," at 404–14.

29. Eric Hobsbawm, "Democracy Can Be Bad for You," *New Statesman,* 5 March 2001, 26.

30. Jürgen Habermas, *The Theory of Communication Action,* vol. 1, *Reason and the Rationalization of Society,* trans. Thomas McCarthy (Boston: Beacon Press, 1984), and vol. 2, *Lifeworld and System: A Critique of Functionalist Reason,* trans. Thomas McCarthy (Boston: Beacon Press, 1987).

31. Michel Callon, introduction to *The Laws of the Markets,* ed. Michel Callon (Oxford: Blackwell, 1998), at 33. On the rationalization of society, see also Max Weber, *The Protestant Ethic and the Spirit of Capitalism* (London: Allen and Unwin, 1971); Weber, "Science as a Vocation," in *From Max Weber,* ed. H. H. Gerth and C. W. Mills (New York: Oxford University Press, 1972, 129–56.

32. For the development of this argument, see Emma Rothschild, *Economic Sentiments: Adam Smith, Condorcet, and the Enlightenment* (Harvard: Harvard University Press, 2001), 7–51.

33. Adam Smith, *Lectures on Jurisprudence,* ed. R. S. Mee, D. D. Raphael, and P. G. Stein (Oxford: Clarendon Press, 1978), at 352.

Chapter Six

1. James M. Buchanan, *Liberty, Market and State* (Brighton, England: Edward Elgar, 1986), at 4.

2. Ibid., 6; to get an overview of this emphasis in Buchanan's essays, see "Liberty, Market, and State," and "Political Economy: 1957–82," in ibid., 3–7, 19–27.

3. Friedrich A. Hayek, *The Road to Serfdom* (Chicago: University of Chicago Press, 1944), 15.

4. William H. Riker and Peter C. Ordeshook, *An Introduction to Positive Political Theory* (Englewood Cliffs, N.J.: Prenctice Hall, 1973), 1–7.

5. Adam Smith, *The Theory of Moral Sentiments,* ed. A. L. Macfie and D. D. Raphael (Indianapolis: Liberty Press, 1985) (hereafter *TMS*); Adam Smith, *An In-*

quiry into the Nature and Causes of the Wealth of Nations, 2 vols., ed. R. H. Campbell and A. S. Skinner (Indianapolis: Liberty Press, 1976) (hereafter *WN*).

6. R. S. Downie, commentary to Thomas Wilson's "Sympathy and Self-Interest," in *The Market and the State: Essays in Honour of Adam Smith,* ed. Thomas Wilson and Andrew S. Skinner (Oxford: Clarendon Press, 1976), 103.

7. Dennis C. Mueller, "Public Choice: A Survey," *Journal of Economic Literature* 14, no. 2 (June 1976): 395–433.

8. Gordon Schochet, "Why Should History Matter? Political Theory and the History of Discourse," in *The Varieties of British Political Thought, 1500–1800,* ed. J. G. A. Pocock (Cambridge: Cambridge University Press, 1993), 333.

9. For discussion of Smith's and Enlightenment "secularized sovereignty," see Charles L. Griswold, *Adam Smith and the Virtues of Enlightenment* (Cambridge: Cambridge University Press, 1999), 266–92.

10. For the initial historical assessment of Smith, see Dugald Stewart, "Account of the Life and Writings of Adam Smith, LL.D" (1793), in Adam Smith, *Essays on Philosophical Subjects,* ed. W. P. D. Wightman and J. C. Bryce (Oxford: Clarendon Press, 1980); for commentary see Emma Rothschild, *Economic Sentiments: Adam Smith, Condorcet, and the Enlightenment* (Cambridge: Harvard University Press, 2001), 1–71; for late-nineteenth-century Smith in Germany, see A. Oncken, "Das Adam Smith-Problem," in *Zeitschrift für Sozialwissenschaft,* ed. J. Wolf (Berlin, 1898), 1:25–33, 101–8, 276–87; for recent commentary on the "Adam Smith problem," see Laurence Dickey, "Historicizing the 'Adam Smith Problem': Conceptual, Historiographical, and Textual Issues," *Journal of Modern History* 58 (September 1986): 579–609; Richard Teichgraeber III, "Rethinking *Das Adam Smith Problem,*" *Journal of British Studies* 20 (1981): 106–23. The last two articles cited appear in *Adam Smith,* ed. Knud Haakonssen (Sydney: Ashgate Dartmouth, 1998), 457–88, 489–506.

11. E. Cannan, "Adam Smith as an Economist," *Economica* no. 17 (1926): 123–34; numeric study of articles by J. M. A. Gee, reviewing *Adam Smith Critical Assessments,* ed. I. C. Wood, in "Adam Smith: Critical Assessments," *Scottish Journal of Political Economy* 32, no. 2 (June 1985): 209–18.

12. Three major works addressing these concerns are Joseph Cropsey, *Polity and Economy: An interpretation of the Principles of Adam Smith* (The Hague: Martinus Nijhoff, 1957); William Grampp, *Economic Liberalism,* vol. 2 (New York: Random House, 1965); and Donald Winch, *Adam Smith's Politics: An Essay in Historiographic Revision* (Cambridge: Cambridge University Press, 1978).

13. Smith, *TMS;* Smith, *WN;* Adam Smith, *Lectures on Jurisprudence,* ed. R. L. Meek, D. D. Raphael, and P. G. Stein (Oxford: Clarendon Press, 1978); Adam Smith, *Essays on Philosophical Subjects,* ed. W. P. D. Wightman and J. C. Bryce (Oxford: Clarendon Press, 1980); Adam Smith, *Lectures on Rhetoric and Belles Lettres,* ed. J. C. Bryce (Oxford: Clarendon Press, 1983). All these works were republished by Liberty Fund (Indianapolis) virtually simultaneously in 1976, 1976, 1982, and 1982, respectively.

14. The Smith pursued by historians follows in the tradition initiated by

J. G. A. Pocock in his *The Machiavellian Moment* (Princeton: Princeton University Press, 1975), and is exemplified by Istvan Hont and Michael Ignatieff, eds., *Wealth and Virtue: The Shaping of Political Economy in the Scottish Enlightenment* (Cambridge: Cambridge University Press, 1983); the economists' Smith comes to life in Edwin G. West, *Adam Smith: The Man and His Works* (Indianapolis: Liberty Press, 1976); and Edwin G. West, *Adam Smith and Modern Economics: From Market Behaviour to Public Choice* (Hants, England: Edward Elgar, 1990).

15. Wilson and Skinner, eds., *The Market and the State;* see also Andrew S. Skinner and Thomas Wilson, eds., *Essays on Adam Smith* (Oxford: Clarendon Press, 1975).

16. Thomas Wilson, "Sympathy and Self-Interest," in *The Market and the State,* ed. Wilson and Skinner, at 73–99, esp. 82–83.

17. Ibid., 92.

18. For the two sides of this discussion, see "Needs and Justice in the *Wealth of Nations:* An Introductory essay," in *Wealth and Virtue,* ed. Hont and Ignatieff, at 1–44; Knud Haakonssen, *The Science of a Legislator: The Natural Jurisprudence of David Hume and Adam Smith* (Cambridge: Cambridge University Press, 1981); Donald Winch, "Adam Smith and the Liberal Tradition," in *Adam Smith,* ed. Haakonsseen, at 359–80; Neil MacCormick, "Adam Smith on Law," in ibid., 189–209; Griswold, *Adam Smith and the Virtues of Enlightenment.*

19. Rothschild, *Economic Sentiments,* at 88.

20. James M. Buchanan, "Marginal Notes on Reading Political Philosophy," appendix to James M. Buchanan and Gordon Tullock, *The Calculus of Consent* (Ann Arbor: University of Michigan Press, 1962), 297–322.

21. Buchanan, "Political Economy: 1957–82," at 17; "Keynesian digression" mentioned at ibid., 8.

22. James M. Buchanan, *The Limits of Liberty* (Chicago: University of Chicago Press, 1975), at 91–92.

23. James M. Buchanan, "The Public Choice Perspective," in Buchanan, *Liberty, Market, and State,* at 20.

24. James M. Buchanan, "The Related by Distinct 'Sciences' of Economics and Political Economy," in Buchanan, *Liberty, Market, and State,* at 32.

25. James M. Buchanan, "Notes on Politics and Process," in Buchanan, *Liberty, Market, and State,* at 87–88. Buchanan refers to the "maximization of values"; however, since he, too, strives to get beyond the language of "maximization," I here emphasize individuals' self-determined ends.

26. James M. Buchanan, "Economic Theory in the Post-Revolutionary Moment of the 1990s," in Buchanan, *Post-Socialist Political Economy* (Lyme, Conn.: Edward Elgar, 1977), 68.

27. Buchanan, *Liberty, Market, and State,* at 25.

28. Buchanan, "Economic Theory in the Post-Revolutionary Moment of the 1990s," at 70.

29. Buchanan, *Post-Socialist Political Economy,* at 70.

30. For commentary on Buchanan's contractarian break with Smithian politics, see Winch, "Adam Smith and the Liberal Tradition," at 370–73.

31. Rothschild, *Economic Sentiments*, at 127; see 126–28.

32. Buchanan, *Liberty, Market, and State*, at 26.

33. Ibid.

34. Smith, *TMS* VII.iii.1.4; see also Griswold's discussion in *Adam Smith and the Virtues of Enlightenment*, at 76–83.

35. It is key for Smith that sympathy "cannot, in any sense, be regarded as a selfish principle" derived from "self-love" (*TMS* VII.iii.4).

36. Smith, *WN* I.x.a.1.

37. Smith, *TMS* III.6.10; see also *TMS* II.ii.2.3.

38. Smith, *WN* IV.v.b.43.

39. There is considerable debate over the extent to which Smith argued for state intervention on the part of the poor: as stringently as Istvan Hont and Michael Ignatieff argue that Smith strictly upholds free trade in grains, Emma Rothschild argues that Smith is a proponent of legislation to aid the poor. See Hont and Ignatieff, "Needs and Justice in the *Wealth of Nations*, at 1–44; Rothschild, *Economic Sentiments*, at 61–64, 87–115.

40. Knud Haakonssen, "What Might Properly Be Called Natural Jurisprudence," in *The Origins and Nature of the Scottish Enlightenment*, ed. R. H. Campbell and Andrew S. Skinner (Oxford: Clarendon Press, 1990), 212.

41. See Rothschild, *Economic Sentiments*, at 144.

42. Smith, *TMS* II.ii.3.4.

43. Ibid., III.3.3; for an analysis of Smith's argument, see Andrew S. Skinner, "Moral Philosophy and Civil Society: Ethics and Self-Love," in his *A System of Social Science: Papers Relating to Adam Smith*, 2nd ed. (Oxford: Claredon Press, 1996), 51–75.

44. For further discussion of the concept of sympathy in Smith, see Griswold, *Adam Smith and the Virtues of Enlightenment*, at 76–112.

45. The first section of Smith's *TMS* is devoted to an analysis of sympathy.

46. Smith, *TMS* III.1.4; III.3.22.

47. For a discussion of utility and Smith's theory of justice, see Haakonssen, *The Science of a Legislator*, at 67–74; for an alternative perspective reaching the same conclusion, see Athol Fitzgibbons, *Adam Smith's System of Liberty, Wealth, and Virtue: The Moral and Political Foundations of* The Wealth of Nations (Oxford: Clarendon Press, 1995), 45–57.

48. Smith, *TMS* IV.2.3.

49. Ibid., III.5.7–8, VII.ii.2.13, VII.iii.1.2, VII.iii.3.16. "When we approve of any character or action, the sentiments which we feel, are, according to the foregoing system, derived from four sources, which are in some respects different from one another. First, we sympathize with the motives of the agent; secondly, we enter into the gratitude of those who receive the benefit of his actions; thirdly, we observe that his conduct has been agreeable to the general rules by which those two sympathies generally act; and, last of all, when we consider such actions as making a part of a system of behaviour which tends to promote the happiness ei-

ther of the individual or of the society, they appear to derive a beauty from this utility, not unlike that which we ascribe to any well-contrived machine" (ibid.).

50. Amartya Sen, "Rational Behaviour," in *The New Palgrave: A Dictionary of Economics,* ed. J. Eatwell, M. Milgate, and P. Newman, vol. 4 (London: Macmillan, 1987), 69.

51. Kristen Renwick Monroe, introduction to *The Economic Approach to Politics: A Critical Reassessment of the Theory of Rational Action,* ed. Kristen Renwick Monroe (New York: HarperCollins, 1991), 1.

52. For extended discussion of the reference to the "invisible hand" in Smith, see Rothschild, *Economic Sentiments,* at 116–56.

53. Douglass North and Barry Weingast, "Constitutions and Commitment: The Evolution of Institutions Governing Public Choice in Seventeenth Century England," *Journal of Economic History* 49, no. 4 (1989): 803–31; Barry Weingast, "The Political Foundations of Democracy and the Rule of Law," *American Political Science Review* 91, no. 2 (June 1997): 245–64; Samuel L. Popkin, *The Rational Peasant: The Political Economy of Rural Society in Vietnam* (Berkeley: University of California Press, 1979).

54. Introduction to *The Philosophy of Economics: An Anthology,* 2nd ed., ed. Daniel M. Hausman (Madison: University of Wisconsin Press, 1994), 29.

55. Ibid., 30–33.

56. Albert O. Hirschman, *The Passions and the Interests: Political Arguments for Capitalism before Its Triumph* (Princeton: Princeton University Press, 1977).

57. Donald Davidson, "A New Basis for Decision Theory," *Theory and Decision* 18 (1985): 90.

58. See Hendrik Hertzberg, "Comment: Tuesdays and After," *New Yorker,* 24 September 2001, 27; William Blum, *Rogue State: A Guide to the World's Only Superpower* (Monroe, Me.: Common Courage Press, 2000), 30; "Preparing for Terror," *Economist,* 30 November 2002, 11. See also, for example, Mortimer Zuckerman's observation that "[t]errorism has supplanted reason and even self-interest," in "Sheep, Wolves, and Reality," *U.S. News and World Report,* 16 December 2002, 60.

59. See index to Smith, *TMS.*

60. For the decision theorist, the task is to provide a coherent and consistent theory incorporating these elements; see, e.g., Davidson, "A New Basis for Decision Theory," at 92.

61. See Smith's discussion of self-command, *TMS* VI.iii.3, at 237–64; see also the analysis in Griswold, *Adam Smith and the Virtues of Enlightenment,* at 179–227.

62. Smith, *TMS* IV.2.5; Smith also rejects the possibility that approbation can be reduced to self-love, *TMS* VII.iii.I.1–4.

63. See Smith, *WN* II.iii.16, IV.vii.c.61, IV.ix.13.

64. For a discussion, see Griswold, *Adam Smith and the Virtues of Enlightenment,* at 202–7.

65. For a more comprehensive argument about Smith's rejection of the tradition represented by Hobbes and Mandeville that may be described as "instru-

mental, utilitarian, individualistic, egalitarian, abstract, and ration," see Donald Winch, "Adam Smith: Scottish Moral Philosopher as Political Economist," *Historical Journal* 35 (1992): 91–113, reprinted in *Adam Smith,* ed. Haakonssen, at 507–29, quote at 517.

66. Rothschild, *Economic Sentiments,* quoting Smith at 114.

Chapter Seven

1. The first quotation is from William Stanley Jevons, *Theory of Political Economy,* 2nd ed., ed. R. D. Collison Black (Baltimore: Penguin, 1970), 173; the second quotation is from Vilfredo Pareto, *Manual of Political Economy,* ed. Ann S. Schwier and Alfred N. Page, trans. Ann S. Schwier (New York: Augustus M. Kelley Publishers, 1971 [1927]), 266.

2. Léon Walras, *Elements of Pure Economics or The Theory of Social Wealth,* trans. William Jaffé (London: Allen and Unwin, 1954 [1926]), 47; Pareto, *Manual of Political Economy,* at 12. Joseph Persky believes the term *Homo œconomicus* was likely coined by Pareto in 1906 to denote abstract economic man; "The Ethology of *Homo Economicus*," *Journal of Economic Perspectives* 9, no. 2 (spring 1995): 222.

3. Philip Mirowski, *More Heat Than Light: Economics as Social Physics, Physics as Nature's Economics* (Cambridge: Cambridge University Press, 1989), 265.

4. Jürg Niehans, *A History of Economic Theory: Classic Contributions, 1720–1980* (Baltimore: Johns Hopkins University Press, 1990), 162. For a superb discussion of the professionalization of economics, see John Maloney, *Marshall, Orthodoxy and the Professionalisation of Economics* (Cambridge: Cambridge University Press, 1985).

5. Mirowski, *More Heat Than Light,* at 222–31; Hunt, *History of Economic Thought,* at 358.

6. For the concept of maximizing pleasure, see William Stanley Jevons, *The Theory of Political Economy,* 4th ed. (London: Macmillan, 1931), 37.

7. Ibid., 102.

8. Mark Blaug, *Economic Theory in Retrospect,* 4th ed. (Cambridge: Cambridge University Press, 1985), 307; for extensive discussion, see "Papers on the Marginal Revolution in Economics," 4, no. 2 (fall 1972). See also Niehans, *A History of Economic Theory,* at 159–63. For the standard neoclassical reconstruction of the marginal revolution, see Paul A. Samuelson, *Foundations of Economic Analysis* (Cambridge: Harvard University Press, 1948), 90–96.

9. Mirowski, *More Heat Than Light,* at 195.

10. Ibid., 195–97.

11. Blaug, *Economic Theory in Retrospect,* at 106. For a nuanced historiographical review of the junction between classical and neoclassical economics, repeating the standard emphasis on the distinction reflected in marginalist theory, see William O Thweatt's introduction to *Classical Political Economy: A Survey of*

Recent Literature, ed. William O. Thweatt (Boston: Kluwer Academic Publishers, 1988), 1–12.

12. Mirowski, *More Heat Than Light,* at 196.

13. See the papers presented at the 1991 conference at Duke University on Mirowski's *More Heat Than Light,* collected in *Non-natural Social Science: Reflecting on the Enterprise of* More Heat Than Light, ed. Neil de Marchi *History of Political Economy* 25 (ann. supp., 1993); see esp. Robert J. Leonard's "Chalk and Cheese: Mirowski Meets Douglas and Bloor," ibid., 249–70.

14. Jevons, *The Theory of Political Economy* (hereafter *TPE*). For discussion of Jevons, see R. D. Collison Black, "W. S. Jevons and the Foundation of Modern Economics," *History of Political Economics* 4, no. 2 (fall 1972): 364–78.

15. See also a paper Jevon's read before Section F of the British Association for the Advancement of Science, which contained his ideas in discussion form, published as "Brief Account of a General Mathematical Theory of Political Economy," *Journal of the Royal Statistical Society* 29 (1866): 282–87.

16. Jevons, *TPE,* at 165.

17. For further discussion, see Michael White, "Why Are There No Demand and Supply Curves in Jevons," *History of Political Economy* 21, no. 3 (fall 1989): 425–56.

18. Jevons, *TPE,* at 95; for the relationship between Jevons's equation of exchange and the equimarginal principle, see Blaug, *Economic Theory in Retrospect,* 310, 338–39; see also Margaret Schabas's discussion of Jevons's statement of his equimarginal principle in her *A World Ruled by Number: William Stanley Jevons and the Rise of Mathematical Economics* (Princeton: Princeton University Press, 1990), 39–43.

19. Jevons, *TPE,* at vii.

20. Ibid., 102–6.

21. Ray E. Canterbery, *The Making of Economics,* 3rd ed. (Belmont, Calif.: Wadsworth, 1987), 100; Hunt, *History of Economic Thought,* at 238.

22. Frank H. Knight, *On the History and Method of Economics* (Chicago: University of Chicago Press, 1956), 25.

23. Francis Y. Edgeworth, *Mathematical Psychics: An Essay on the Application of Mathematics* (London: C. K. Paul, 1881), 12.

24. Samuelson, *Foundations of Economic Analysis,* at 23.

25. Ibid., 23.

26. Ibid.

27. Knight, *On the History and Method of Economics,* at 26; see also Frank Knight, "Economics and Human Action," in *The Philosophy of Economics,* ed. Daniel M. Hausman (Cambridge: Cambridge University Press, 1984), 114.

28. John von Neumann and Oskar Morgenstern, *Theory of Games and Economic Behavior,* 3rd ed. (Princeton: Princeton University Press, 1953), 8–33.

29. Kenneth J. Arrow, *Social Choice and Individual Values,* 2nd ed. (New Haven: Yale University Press, 1963), 3.

30. Jevons, *TPE*, at 105.

31. Ibid., 99.

32. Vilfredo Pareto, "Sul principio economico," *Giorale degli Economisti* 22 (February 1901): 131–38, translated as "On the Economic Principle," *International Economic Papers* 3 (1953): 183. See also Vincent Tarascio, "Vilfredo Pareto and Marginalism," *History of Political Economy* 4, no. 2 (fall 1972): 406–25.

33. For the best example of this outlook, see Anthony Downs, *An Economic Theory of Democracy* (New York: Harper and Row, 1957), 4–6.

34. Ibid., 5.

35. Ibid., 6.

36. For a statement of choice rules in terms of completeness and transitivity, see Amartya K. Sen, *Collective Choice and Social Welfare* (San Francisco: Holden-Day, 1970), 8.

37. Correspondence from Kenneth J. Arrow to Ragnar Bentzel, 27 January 1986, Kenneth J. Arrow Papers, Rare Book, Manuscript, and Special Collections Library, Duke University, Durham, N.C., Box 36, 9–10; Arrow's citations refer to Samuelson, 1938; J. Ville, "Sur les conditions d'existence d'une ophélimité total et d'un indice du neveau des prix," *Annales de l'Université de Lyon* 9 (1946): 32–39; H. S. Houthakker, "Revealed Preference and the Utility Function," *Economica*, n.s., 17 (May 1950): 159–74; and Kenneth J. Arrow, "Rational Choice Functions and Orderings," *Economica*, n.s., 26 (May 1959): 121–27.

38. Thorstein Veblen, "Why Is Economics Not an Evolutionary Science," in *The Portable Veblen*, ed. M. Lerner (New York: Viking Press, 1948), 232.

39. Houthakker, "Revealed Preference and the Utility Function," at 161.

40. Ibid.

41. Jevons, *TPE*, at 105; see Samuelson's alternative statement of this equation in *Foundations of Economic Analysis*, at 98–99.

42. See Samuelson, *Foundations of Economic Analysis*, at 98–99.

43. Houthakker, "Revealed Preference and the Utility Function," at 163.

44. Ibid., 173; despite his detailed discussion of the relationship between Samuelson's revealed preferences and ordinal utility functions, Houthakker's analysis lacks the clarity necessary to be the final statement on this relationship. It is not made clear, for example, what is the relationship between integrability of utility functions on the one hand, and the condition of semi-transitivity of revealed preferences on the other; it is not clear if the semi-transitivity condition guarantees integrability, or if continuous derivatives are assumed, as implied in ibid., 165.

45. Arrow, "Rational Choice Functions and Orderings," at 121.

46. Ibid.

47. Ibid., 126. For further discussion see Andreu Mas-Colell et al., *Microeconomic Theory* (New York: Oxford University Press, 1995), at 11–13.

48. Amartya K. Sen, "Choice Functions and Revealed Preference," *Review of Economic Studies* 38 (1971): 307.

49. See Arrow's reference to "rational behaviour" in "Rational Choice Functions and Orderings," at 123.

50. Sen, "Choice Functions and Revealed Preference," at 307.

51. Ibid., 311, 312.

52. D. Gale, "A Note on Revealed Preference," *Economica*, n.s., 27 (November 1960): 348–54.

53. Mas-Colell et al., *Microeconomic Theory*, at 40–52.

54. Ibid., 14; Sen, "Choice Functions and Revealed Preference," at 312.

55. For discussion see Mas-Colell et al., *Microeconomic Theory*, at 40–50; see also Kenneth J. Arrow, *Social Choice and Individual Values*, 2nd ed. (New Haven: Yale University Press, 1963), at 16–17.

56. Sen, "Choice Functions and Revealed Preference," at 307.

57. For an extensive discussion of this, see Lionel Robbins, *An Essay on the Nature and Significance of Economic Science* (London: Macmillan, 1932), at 12–15, 96.

58. Mas-Colell et al., *Microeconomic Theory*, at 5–104.

59. Robbins, *An Essay on the Nature and Significance of Economic Science*, at 15.

60. Joseph A. Schumpeter, *Capitalism, Socialism, and Democracy* (London: Henderson and Spalding, 1943), 122.

61. See Max Weber, "Science as a Vocation," in *From Max Weber*, ed. H. H. Gerth and C. W. Mills (New York: Oxford University Press, 1972), 77–128. For discussion, see David Held, *Models of Democracy*, 1st ed. (Stanford: Stanford University Press, 1987), 145–48.

62. Robert Sugden, "Rational Choice: A Survey of Contributions from Economics and Philosophy," *Economic Journal* 101 (July 1991): 751–85.

63. Jevons, *TPE*, at 37.

64. For an argument that even in retrospect it is not possible to relate means–end reasoning to the enterprise of marginalist economists, see Phillippe Mongin, "Value Judgments and Value Neutrality in Economics: A Perspective from Today," Centre for Philosophy of Natural and Social Science, Discussion Paper Series 60102, December 2001, 18–28.

65. See Sen, "Rational Behaviour."

66. See Edward McClennen, *Rationality and Dynamic Choice* (Cambridge: Cambridge University Press, 1990), esp. chap. 1; David Gauthier, *Morals by Agreement* (Oxford: Oxford University Press), 25–26; Robert Nozick, *The Nature of Reality* (Princeton: Princeton University Press, 1993), 133, 140; William Riker and Peter C. Ordeshook, *An Introduction to Positive Political Theory: A Synthesis an Exposition of Current Trends in Political Theory Based on Axiomatic and Deductive Reasoning* (Englewood Cliffs, N.J.: Prentice Hall, 1973), 12–19.

67. Jean Hampton, *The Authority of Reason*, ed. Richard Healey (Cambridge: Cambridge University Press, 1998); Sugden, "Rational Choice," at 751–85.

68. See, e.g., Debra Satz and John Ferejohn, "Rational Choice and Social Theory," *Journal of Philosophy* 91, no. 2 (1994): 71–87.

69. David Hume, *A Treatise of Human Nature*, ed. L. A. Selby-Bigge, rev. P. H. Nidditch (Oxford: Oxford University Press, 1888), II.III.iii, 416.

70. Jean Hampton, "The Failure of Expected-Utility Theory as a Theory of Reason," *Economics and Philosophy* 10 (1994): 215–16.
71. Satz and Ferejohn, "Rational Choice and Social Theory," at 73. For a discussion of the consistency conditions pertaining to rational choice theory, see Amartya Sen, "Internal Consistency of Choice," *Econometrica* 61, no. 3 (May 1993): 495–521; note that Sen makes scant reference to agents' means–ends considerations in evaluating consistency of choice. See Immanuel Kant on the "categorical imperative," *Groundwork of the Metaphysic of Morals*, trans. H. J. Paton (New York: Harper Torchbooks, 1964), 82–84.
72. Riker and Ordeshook, *An Introduction to Positive Political Theory*, at 8–19.
73. For discussion, see Leonard J. Savage, "The Sure-Thing Principle," in *Decision, Probability, and Utility: Selected Readings*, ed. Peter Gärdenfors and Nils-Eric Sahlin (Cambridge: Cambridge University Press, 1988), 80–85; M. Allais, Le Comportement de l'homme Rationnel Devant le Risque: Critique des Postulats et Axioms de L'ecole Americaine," *Econometrica* 21 (1953): 503–46; Daniel Ellsberg, "Risk, Ambiguity, and the Savage Axioms," *Quarterly Journal of Economics* 75 (1961): 643–69; Edward F. McClennen, "Sure-Thing Doubts," in *Decision, Probability, and Utility*, ed. Gärdenfors and Sahlin, at 245–69; Jean E. Hampton, "Expected Utility Theory and Instrumental Reasoning," in Hampton, *The Authority of Reason*, at 217–50; G. Loomes and Robert Sugden, "Regret Theory: an Alternative Theory of Rational Choice under Uncertainty," *Economic Journal* 92 (1982): 805–24.
74. Luce and Raiffa, *Games and Decisions*, at 26.
75. Peter Gärdenfors and Nils-Eric Sahlin, introduction to *Decision, Probability, and Utility*, ed. Gärdenfors and Sahlin, at 7, quoting Frank Ramsey.
76. For a discussion of the failure of the Money Pump independent of any consideration of means–ends reasoning, see Frederic Schick, "Dutch Bookies and Money Pumps," *Journal of Philosophy* 83, no. 2 (1986): 112–19.
77. See Nozick, *The Nature of Rationality*, at 140; Hampton, "The Failure of Expected-Utility Theory as a Theory of Reason," 212. For the additional complication of context-dependent choice, see Sen, "Maximization and the Act of Choice," at 47–58.
78. Original argument in Loomes and Sugden, "Regret Theory"; for discussion, see Sugden, "Rational Choice," at 751–53; Hampton, *The Authority of Reason*, at 260–61.
79. Arrow, *Social Choice and Individual Values*, at 13.
80. For another statement of the definition of a "rational preference relation" making this point, see Mas-Colell et al., *Microeconomic Theory*, at 6.
81. See the earlier discussion of the Pareto principle in chapter 3.
82. See Pareto, *Manual of Political Economy*, at 266–69; for further discussion, see Samuelson, *Foundations of Economic Analysis*, at 212–19.
83. See Arrow, *Social Choice and Individual Values*, at 96–97.
84. Ibid., 96, 34–35.

85. Samuelson's *Foundations of Economic Analysis* remains the best source for understanding the new welfare economics.

86. Arrow, *Social Choice and Individual Values,* at 34–45, esp. 44.

87. Luce and Raiffa, *Games and Decisions,* at 339; Amartya Sen, *Collective Choice and Social Welfare* (London: Oliver and Boyd, 1970), 27.

88. Arrow, *Social Choice and Individual Values,* at 96.

89. Sen, *Collective Choice and Social Welfare* (London), at 21.

90. J. P. Roos acknowledges this shift in meaning, though does not follow up on his promise to explicate it in *Welfare Theory and Social Policy: A Study in Policy Science* (Helsinki: Societas Scientiarum Fennica, 1973), 143; for a clear statement of the new use of "the Pareto principle, [by which] the group of all individuals is decisive," see Amartya Sen, "Rationality and Social Choice," *American Economic Review* 85, no. 1 (March 1995): 4.

91. British project evaluation varied between macro approaches, and micro approaches more dependent on individual welfare, see E. J. Mishan, *Cost–Benefit Analysis: An Introduction* (New York: Praeger Publishers, 1971); Partha Dasgupta, Amartya Sen, and Stephen Marglin, *Guidelines for Project Evaluation* (New York: United Nations, 1972); and Robert Sugden and Alan Williams, *The Principles of Practical Cost–Benefit Analysis* (Oxford: Oxford University Press, 1978).

92. Nicholas Kaldor, "Welfare Propositions of Economics and Interpersonal Comparisons of Utility," *Economic Journal* 49 (September 1939): 549–52; J. R. Hicks, "The Foundations of Welfare Economics," *Economic Journal* 49 (December 1939): 696–700, 711–12.

93. Edith Stokey and Richard Zeckhauser, *A Primer for Policy Analysis* (New York: Norton, 1978), 136.

94. Ibid., 137.

95. Ibid.

96. Ibid., 141.

97. See Mishan, *Cost–Benefit Analysis,* at 316–21; Sugden and Williams, *The Principles of Practical Cost–Benefit Analysis,* at 95, 180–81.

98. Roland N. McKean, *Efficiency in Government through Systems Analysis: With Emphasis on Water Resources Development* (New York: Wiley, 1958), 7.

99. Ibid., 201.

100. Ibid., 72.

101. Ibid., 201.

102. See, e.g., Stokey and Zeckhauser, *A Primer for Policy Analysis,* at 122–24.

103. Kenneth J. Arrow, "Behavior under Uncertainty and Its Implications for Policy," in *Decision Making: Descriptive, Normative, and Prescriptive Interactions,* ed. David E. Bell, Howard Raiffa, and Amos Tversky (Cambridge: Cambridge University Press, 1988), 497.

104. In the literature of rational choice this is taken for granted. For a helpful discussion, see Stokey and Zeckhauser, *A Primer for Policy Analysis,* at 127–30.

105. Ibid.; Arrow "Behavior under Uncertainty and Its Implications for Policy."

106. Arrow, "Behavior under Uncertainty and Its Implications for Policy," at 498.

107. Ibid., 499.

108. Ibid.

109. Sen, "Rational Behaviour," at 72.

110. Ibid.

111. In Stokey and Zeckhauer, *A Primer for Policy Analysis,* compare 28–44 and 137–42 with 122–24 and 237–54.

112. Arrow, "Behavior under Uncertainty and Its Implications for Policy"; Kenneth J. Arrow, "Extended Sympathy and the Possibility of Social Choice," in *Social Choice and Justice: Collected Papers of Kenneth Arrow* (Oxford: Basil Blackwell, 1984), 147–61. Despite Arrow's reservations, some degree of interpersonal comparisons is generally accepted to be necessary for making progress on social decisions involving collective welfare. This is discussed more fully in the concluding chapter; see also Sen, "Rationality and Social Choice," at 1–24.

113. James M. Buchanan is an advocate of democratic decisionmaking processes as a means of due process instead of as a means to achieve "collective rationality." See his "Social Choice, Democracy and Free Markets," *Journal of Political Economy* 62 (1954): 114–23; see also William H. Riker, *Liberalism against Populism: A Confrontation between the Theory of Democracy and Social Choice* (San Francisco: Freeman, 1982).

Chapter Eight

1. William H. Riker, "A Paradigm for Politics," unpublished manuscript of a 1983 lecture presented in Taiwan, in William H. Riker Papers, Department of Rare Books and Special Collections, University of Rochester, Rochester, N.Y. (hereafter WHR Papers).

2. For earlier texts taking up this set of concerns, see Albert Somit and Joseph Tanenhaus, *The Development of Political Science: From Burgess to Behavioralism* (Boston: Allyn and Bacon, 1967); David M. Ricci, *The Tragedy of Political Science: Politics, Scholarship and Democracy* (New Haven: Yale University Press, 1984); Raymond Seidelman, with Edward J. Harpham, *Disenchanted Realists: Political Science and the American Crisis, 1984–1984* (Albany: State University of New York Press, 1985); Gabriel A. Almond, *A Discipline Divided: Schools and Sects in Political Science* (London: Sage, 1990); Rogers Smith, "Still Blowing in the Wind: The American Quest for a Democratic, Scientific Political Science," *Dædalus; American Academic Culture in Transformation: Fifty Years, Four Disciplines* 126, no. 1 (winter 1997): 253–88. For social science more generally, see Andrew C. Janos, *Politics and Paradigms: Changing Theories of Change in Social Science* (Stanford: Stanford University Press, 1986); Thomas Bender, "Politics, Intellect, and the American University, 1945–1995," *Dædalus; American Academic Culture in Transformation: Fifty Years, Four Disciplines* 126, no. 1 (winter 1997): 1–38.

3. See, e.g., Donald P. Green and Ian Shapiro, *Pathologies of Rational Choice Theory: A Critique of Applications in Political Science* (New Haven: Yale Uni-

versity Press, 1994); *Critical Review: Rational Choice Theory* 9, nos. 1–2 (winter/spring 1995); James Johnson, "How Not to Criticize Rational Choice Theory: Pathologies of 'Common Sense,'" *Philosophy of the Social Sciences* 26, no. 1 (March 1996): 77–91.

4. David A. Hollinger, "The Defense of Democracy and Robert K. Merton's Formulation of Scientific Ethos," and "Science as a Weapon in *Kulturkämpfe* in the United States during and after World War II," in Hollinger, *Science, Jews, and Secular Culture: Studies in Mid-Twentieth-Century American Intellectual History* (Princeton: Princeton University Press, 1996), 80–96, 155–74.

5. John G. Gunnell, "American Political Science, Liberalism, and the Invention of Political Theory," *American Political Science Review* 82, no. 1 (March 1988): 73; see, e.g., Max Horkheimer and Theodore W. Adorno, *Dialectic of Enlightenment*, trans. John Cumming (New York: Continuum, 1989).

6. Gunnell, "American Political Science, Liberalism, and the Invention of Political Theory," at 77.

7. Ibid., 83.

8. David Easton, *The Political System* (New York: Knopf, 1953), 10–11.

9. This definition is rooted in the work of Max Weber. Riker uses it in William H. Riker, *Theory of Political Coalitions* (New Haven: Yale University Press, 1962), 10–11.

10. See Daniel Lerner and Harold D. Lasswell, *The Policy Sciences: Recent Developments in Scope and Method* (Stanford: Stanford University Press, 1951), to which Arrow contributed "Mathematical Models in the Social Sciences," 129–54.

11. Simon Jackman, "Liberalism, Public Opinion and their Critics," in *The Flight from Science and Reason*, ed. Paul R. Gross et al. (Baltimore: Johns Hopkins University Press, 1996), 362.

12. Francis Fukuyama, *The End of History and the Last Man* (New York: Harper Business, 1992).

13. See J. G. A. Pocock, "Authority and Property: The Question of Liberal Origins," in his *Virtue, Commerce, and History: Essays on Political Thought and History, Chiefly in the Eighteenth Century* (Cambridge: Cambridge University Press, 1985); James Tully, ed., *Meaning and Context: Quentin Skinner and His Critics* (Princeton: Princeton University Press, 1988).

14. Seidelman, *Disenchanted Realists,* at 222–41.

15. James Farr, "Political Science and the State," in *Discipline and History: Political Science in the United States,* ed. James Farr and Raymond Seidelman (Ann Arbor: University of Michigan Press, 1993), 66.

16. See James T. Kloppenberg, *The Virtues of Liberalism* (Oxford: Oxford University Press, 1998); Charles Taylor, *Human Agency and Language* (Cambridge: Cambridge University Press), 102–5; Alasdair MacIntyre, *After Virtue,* 2d ed. (Notre Dame: University of Notre Dame Press, 1984); Michael J. Sandel, *Liberalism and the Limits of Justice* (Cambridge: Cambridge University Press, 1982); Michael J. Sandel, introduction to *Liberalism and Its Critics,* ed. Michael J. Sandel (Oxford: Blackwell, 1984).

17. Smith, "Still Blowing in the Wind," at 264–65.

18. For an overview of Rawls's sweeping impact, see Ian Shapiro, *Political Criticism* (Berkeley: University of California Press, 1990), 3–16.

19. Arrow, "Some Ordinalist-Utilitarian Notes on Rawls's Theory of Justice," at 96.

20. For Rawls's own acknowledgment of how his work developed in parallel with that of Buchanan and Tullock, see "Constitutional Liberty and the Concept of Justice," in *John Rawls: Collected Papers*, ed. Samuel Freeman (Cambridge: Harvard University Press, 1999), 74 n. 1.

21. Ibid.; see also "Rawls's Principle of Just Saving," in *Social Choice and Justice: Collected Papers of Kenneth J. Arrow* (Oxford: Basil Blackwell, 1984), 133–46; seminar mentioned in Amartya K. Sen, *Collective Choice and Social Welfare* (London: Oliver and Boyd, 1970), 145.

22. For discussion and comparison, see Charles K. Rowley, *Social Choice Theory*, vol. 1, *The Aggregation of Preferences*, ed. Charles K. Rowley (Hants, England: Edward Elgar, 1993), xxxii–xxxix.

23. See, e.g., Ken Binmore, *Game Theory and the Social Contract*, vol. 2, *Just Playing* (Cambridge: MIT Press, 1998); E. F. McClennen, "Constitutional Choice: Rawls vs. Harsanyi," in *Philosophy in Economics*, ed. J. C. Pitt (Dordrecht: Reidel, 1981), 93–109.

24. Arrow, "Some Ordinalist-Utilitarian Notes on Rawls's Theory of Justice," at 107.

25. James M. Buchanan, "Social Choice, Democracy and Free Markets," *Journal of Political Economy* 62 (1954): 114–23.

26. John Rawls, *A Theory of Justice* (Cambridge: Harvard University Press, 1971), 520, 272, 274.

27. Arrow concurs, writing that "the implicit ethical basis of economic policy judgment is some version of utilitarianism." Arrow, "Some Ordinalist-Utilitarian Notes on Rawls's Theory of Justice," at 97.

28. See Rawls, *A Theory of Justice*, at 22–23.

29. Ibid., 23.

30. Ibid., 24–25.

31. John C. Harsanyi, "Cardinal Utility in Welfare Economics and in the Theory of Risk-Taking," *Journal of Political Economy* 61 (1953): 434–35; Harsanyi, "Cardinal Welfare, Individualistic Ethics, and Interpersonal Comparisons of Utility," *Journal of Political Economy* 63 (1955): 309–21; quote from ibid., 319–20.

32. Harsanyi, "Cardinal Utility," at 434.

33. Ibid., 435.

34. On Arrow's impossibility theorem, see Harsanyi, "Cardinal Welfare," at 321.

35. Ibid., 319–20.

36. Kenneth J. Arrow, "Extended Sympathy and the Possibility of Social Choice," in *Social Choice and Justice*, at 147–61, esp. 160.

37. Harsanyi, "Cardinal Welfare," at 321.

38. Rawls, *Theory of Justice*, at 16.

39. See John Rawls, "Justice as Fairness," in *John Rawls: Collected Papers*, at 52–53.

40. Rawls, *Theory of Justice,* at 11.
41. Ibid., 14.
42. Ibid.
43. Rowley, introduction to *The Aggregation of Preferences,* at xxxiv.
44. For a detailed comparison of Rawls's and Harsanyi's use of ignorance about one's social fate, see Sen, *Collective Choice and Social Welfare,* at 141–46.
45. Rawls, *Theory of Justice,* at 12.
46. Ibid., 136–42.
47. Ibid., 60.
48. John C. Harsanyi, "Can the Maximin Principle Serve as a Basis for Morality? A Critique of John Rawls's Theory," *American Political Science Review* 69 (1975): 601–2.
49. See R. Duncan Luce and Howard Raiffa, *Games and Decisions: Introduction and Critical Survey* (New York: Wiley, 1957), 278.
50. Rawls, *Theory of Justice,* at 67–74.
51. Ibid., 90; see also Harsanyi, "Cardinal Welfare."
52. Rawls, *Theory of Justice,* at 92.
53. Rawls refers readers to Luce and Raiffa, *Theory of Games and Decision,* chap. 13.
54. Rawls, *Theory of Justice,* at 155, 168.
55. See, e.g., Sen's axiomatization of Rawls' maximin criterion in Sen, *Collective Choice and Social Welfare,* at 156–58; for a helpful discussion of this point, see Ken Binmore, *Game Theory and the Social Contract,* vol. 1, *Playing Fair* (Cambridge: MIT Press, 1994), 315–33.
56. For a concise and pointed discussion of the issues at stake involving decision theory, see Arrow, "Some Ordinalist-Utilitarian Notes on Rawls's Theory of Justice," at 102.
57. Rawls, *Theory of Justice,* at 172.
58. For Rawls's discussion about slavery on this point, see ibid., 158; for further analysis, see Sen, *Collective Choice and Social Welfare,* at 142–43.
59. Harsanyi, "Can the Maximin Principle Serve as a Basis for Morality?" at 594–606; John Rawls, "Some Reasons for the Maximin Criterion," in *John Rawls: Collected Papers,* at 225–31.
60. See Arrow, "Some Ordinalist-Utilitarian Notes on Rawls's Theory of Justice."
61. Harsanyi, "Can the Maximin Principle Serve as a Basis for Morality?" at 599.
62. Arrow, "Some Ordinalist-Utilitarian Notes on Rawls's Theory of Justice," at 103–5.
63. Ibid., 106–8.
64. Ibid., 106.
65. Arrow, *Social Choice and Individual Values,* 2nd ed. (New Haven: Yale University Press, 1963), 84–86.
66. Rawls, *A Theory of Justice,* at 263.
67. Ibid., 520.
68. Rawls, "Some Reasons for the Maximin Criterion," at 229.

69. For a discussion of alternatives, see Sen, *Collective Choice and Social Welfare,* at 131–51.

70. Edward F. McClennen, "Constitutional Choice: Rawls vs. Harsanyi," in *Philosophy in Economics,* ed. J. C. Pitt (Dordrecht: Reidel, 1981), 93–109.

71. Draft of supplement to Stanford lectures, read by Edward McClennen, 1978, conversation with author.

72. John Rawls, "Justice and Fairness: Political not Metaphysical," *Philosophy and Public Affairs* 14, no. 3 (summer 1985): 223–51.

73. Ibid., 237; for commentary on Rawls's position, see Okin, "Reason and Feeling in Thinking about Justice."

74. Ibid.

75. Ibid.

76. For two perspectives, see David Gauthier, *Morals by Agreement* (Oxford: Clarendon Press, 1986); Jean Hampton, *The Authority of Reason* (Cambridge: Cambridge University Press, 1998).

77. Rawls, "Justice and Fairness: Political not Metaphysical," at 223.

78. This has been discussed at length with respect to Arrow's *Social Choice and Individual Values;* Buchanan and Tullock's *The Calculus of Consent;* Riker's *Liberalism against Populism* in part 2.

79. Rawls, "Justice and Fairness: Political not Metaphysical," at 231.

80. John Rawls, "Kantian Constructivism in Moral Theory," in *John Rawls: Collected Papers,* 317; for another view of reason as a basis for political and social theory, see Jürgen Habermas, *The Theory of Communicative Action,* vol. 1, *Reason and the Rationalization of Society,* trans. Thomas McCarthy (Boston: Beacon Press, 1984), and vol. 2, *Lifeworld and System: A Critique of Functionalist Reason,* trans. Thomas McCarthy (Boston: Beacon Press, 1987).

81. John Rawls, "Justice as Fairness," in *John Rawls: Collected Papers,* 60.

82. Ibid., 61.

83. Amartya K. Sen, "The Impossibility of a Paretian Liberal," *Journal of Political Economy* 78, no. 1 (1970): 152–57; see also Sen, *Collective Choice and Social Welfare,* at 78–88.

84. For further information on Dobb's contributions to economic theory, see Amartya K. Sen, "Maurice Herbert Dobb," in *The New Palgrave: A Dictionary of Economics,* ed. J. Eatwell, M. Milgate, and P. Newman, vol. 2 (London: Macmillan, 1987), 910–12.

85. Arrow, *Social Choice and Individual Values,* 84.

86. Maurice Dobb, "Economic Theory and the Problems of a Socialist Economy," *The Economic Journal* 43 (December 1933): 588–98; Arrow, *Social Choice and Individual Values,* at 28–30.

87. Steven Pressman and Gale Summerfield, "The Economic Contributions of Amartya Sen," *Review of Political Economy* 12, no. 1 (2000): 91.

88. Ibid.

89. See, e.g., Amartya K. Sen, "Rational Fools: A Critique of the Behavioural Foundations of Economic Theory," *Philosophy and Public Affairs* 6, no. 4 (1977):

317–44; Sen, *On Ethics and Economics* (Oxford: Basil Blackwell, 1987). For an overview of Sen's works, see Pressman and Summerfield, "The Economic Contributions of Amartya Sen."

90. In the attempt to make this logical discussion textually appealing, I have made a simplification by presenting *a, b,* and *c* as a three-way comparison, whereas technically the only comparison used in Sen's proof is between pairs of alternatives.

91. Sen has another version of his Paretian Liberal paradox that does not require the concept of collective rationality; see "Internal Consistency of Choice," *Econometrica* 61, no. 3 (May 1993): 504–7.

92. See Sen's overview "Liberty, Unanimity and Rights," *Economica,* n.s., 43 (August 1976): 217–45; see also Jerry S. Kelly, *Arrow's Impossibility Theorems* (New York: Academic Press, 1978); Kotaro Suzumura, *Rational Choice, Collective Decisions and Social Welfare* (Cambridge: Cambridge University Press, 1983); Kotaro Suzumura, "Alternative Approaches to Libertarian Rights," in Kenneth J. Arrow, ed., *Markets and Welfare* (London: Macmillan, 1991), 215–42; John Wriglesworth, *Libertarian Conflicts in Social Choice* (Cambridge: Cambridge University Press, 1994); Paul Seabright, "Social Choice and Social Theories," *Philosophy and Public Affairs* 18, no. 4 (fall 1989): 365–87; Prasanta K. Pattanaik and Kotaro Suzumura, "Rights, Welfarism and Social Choice," *American Economic Review* 84, no. 2 (May 1994): 435–39. For a recent overview of where the discussion stands, see Prasanta K. Pattanaik, "Some Paradoxes of Preference Aggregation," in *Perspectives on Public Choice: A Handbook,* ed. Dennis C. Mueller (Cambridge: Cambridge University Press, 1997), 215–21.

93. See Arrow, *Social Choice and Individual Values;* Kenneth J. Arrow, "Values and Collective Decision-Making," in *Philosophy Politics and Society,* ed. P. Laslett and W. G. Runciman (Oxford: Basil Blackwell, 1967); I. M. D. Little, "Social Choice and Individual Values," *Journal of Political Economy* 60 (1952): 422–32.

94. In Arrow, "Values and Collective Decision-Making," at 225.

95. Robert Sugden, "Social Choice and Individual Liberty," in *Contemporary Economic Analysis,* ed. M. J. Artis and A. R. Nobay (London: Croon Helm, 1983), 250.

96. See chapter 7.

97. This formulation of Pareto optimality is by Roland N. McKean, *Efficiency in Government Through Systems Analysis* (New York: Wiley, 1958), 128; it is possible to extract a similar understanding of the Pareto condition from Buchanan and Tullock, *The Calculus of Consent,* at 171–80.

98. Sen, *Collective Choice and Social Welfare,* 21.

99. Note that Sugden's rights-oriented resolution of the Paretian Liberal paradox does not involve individuals' preference orderings as it common to social choice theory, "Social Choice and Individual Liberty," at 262; see also Pattanaik, "Some Paradoxes of Preference Aggregation," at 219–20.

100. Sugden, "Social Choice and Individual Liberty"; Robert Nozick, *Anar-*

chy, State, and Utopia (Oxford: Basil Blackwell, 1974), 164–66; Charles K. Rowley and Alan T. Peacock, *Welfare Economics: A Liberal Restatement* (London: Martin Robertson, 1975).

101. For Sen's comprehensive rejoinder to various comments on his Paretian Liberal paradox, see Amartya Sen, "Liberty and Social Choice," *Journal of Philosophy* 80, no. 1 (January 1983): 4–28; and "Minimal Liberty," *Economica*, n.s., 59 (May 1992): 139–59.

102. Gauthier, *Morals by Agreement*, at 7, 6.

103. Ibid., 9.

104. Binmore, *Just Playing*, at 462.

105. Gauthier, *Morals by Agreement*, at 8.

106. Ibid., 335.

107. Binmore, *Just Playing*, at 501.

108. Russell Hardin, *Collective Action* (Baltimore: Johns Hopkins University Press, 1982); Mancur Olson Jr., *The Logic of Collective Action* (Cambridge: Harvard University Press, 1965).

109. See personal communication between Merrill M. Flood and Russell Hardin (1975), cited in Hardin, *Collective Action*, at 16; Binmore, *Playing Fair*, at 102.

110. Richmond Campbell and Lanning Sowden, eds. *Paradoxes of Rationality and Cooperation: Prisoner's Dilemma and Newcomb's Problem* (Vancouver: University of British Columbia Press, 1985).

111. Hardin, *Collective Action*, at 146.

112. Ibid., 26–27.

113. Ibid., 106, 108, 170–72.

114. Russell Hardin, *Morality within the Limits of Reason* (Chicago: University of Chicago Press, 1988).

115. Ibid., see also at 150.

116. Gauthier, *Morals by Agreement*, at 17–18.

117. Binmore, *Playing Fair*, at 153; *Just Playing*, at 513.

118. Binmore, *Just Playing*, at 462.

119. Gauthier, *Morals by Agreement*, at 99, 110–12, 115–16.

120. Binmore, *Just Playing*, at 452.

121. Ibid., 456.

122. Terrell Carver and Paul Thomas, introduction to *Rational Choice Marxism*, ed. Terrell Carver and Paul Thomas (London: Macmillan, 1995), 2; see Leszek Kolakowski, *The Alienation of Reason*, trans. Norton Guterman (New York: Doubleday/Anchor, 1969).

123. Erik Olin Wright, "What is Analytical Marxism," in *Rational Choice Marxism*, ed. Carver and Thomas, at 12; leading texts include G. A. Cohen, *Karl Marx's Theory of History: A Defense* (Oxford: Oxford UP, 1978); John Roemer, *A General Theory of Exploitation and Class* (Cambridge: Harvard University Press, 1982); Adam Przeworksi, *Capitalism and Social Democracy* (Cambridge: Cambridge University Press, 1985); Jon Elster, *Making Sense of Marx* (Cambridge: Cambridge University Press, 1985).

124. Wright, "What Is Analytical Marxism?" at 13.

125. Ellen Meiksins Wood, "Rational Choice Marxism: Is the Game Worth the Candle," in *Rational Choice Marxism,* ed. Carver and Thomas, at 82.

126. Ibid.

127. Alan Carling, "Rational Choice Marxism," in *Rational Choice Marxism,* ed. Carver and Thomas, at 31. For a current estimation of the significance of Marxism, see "Marx after Communism," *Economist,* 21 December 2002, 18, which reports that "[t]itles in print about Marx outnumber books about Adam Smith by a factor between five and ten."

128. Edward McClennen, *Rational Society* (forthcoming).

129. Edward McClennen, "An Alternative Model of Rational Cooperation," forthcoming in *Justice, Political Liberalism and Utilitarianism: Proceedings of the Caen Conference in Honour of John C. Harsanyi and John Rawls* (Cambridge: Cambridge UP), ms. 27.

130. John Searle, "Rationality and Realism: What Is at Stake?" *Dædalus* 122, no. 4 (fall 1993): 55–84; Edward O. Wilson, Richard Rorty, and Paul R. Gross, "Is Everything Relative? A Debate on the Unity of Knowledge," *Wilson Quarterly* 22, no. 1 (winter 1998): 14–50; Jürgen Habermas, *The Philosophical Discourse of Modernity,* trans. Frederick G. Lawrence (Cambridge: MIT Press, 1987).

131. McClennen, "An Alternative Model of Rational Cooperation," at 27.

132. Binmore, *Just Playing,* at 475.

133. To see how a consistent rational choice position on justice has become pertinent to American jurisprudence, see the work of Richard Posner, who both advocates justice as wealth maximization independent from distributional issues and accepts the consonance between rational choice theory and evolutionary theory. Richard Posner, "Wealth Maximization and Judicial Decision-Making," *International Review of Law and Economics* 4 (1984): 131–35.

134. Binmore, *Just Playing,* at 509.

135. Edward McClennen, "Foundational Explorations for a Normative Theory of Political Economy," *Constitutional Political Economy* 1 (1990): 1.

136. Binmore, *Just Playing,* at 513; see also Richard Dawkins, *The Selfish Gene* (Oxford: Oxford University Press, 1976); John Maynard Smith, *Evolution and the Theory of Games* (Cambridge: Cambridge University Press, 1982).

Epilogue

1. Daniel Bell, *The End of Ideology: On the Exhaustion of Political Ideas in the Fifties* (Cambridge: Harvard University Press, 1960), 238. For a detailed analysis of Bentham's Panopticon as paradigmatic of a new social form of behavior designed to achieve efficiency, see Michel Foucault, *Discipline and Punish: The Birth of the Prison* (New York: Random House, 1977), 135–308.

2. Bell, *The End of Ideology,* at 255.

3. Ibid., 272.

4. George Orwell, *Nineteen Eighty-Four* (New York: Harcourt, Brace and World, 1949).

5. Ibid., 289.

6. Ibid., 31, 167, 232–42.

7. Ibid., 102.

8. Robert P. Abelson, "The Secret Existence of Expressive Behavior," *Critical Review* 9, nos. 1–2 (winter/spring 1995): 31; for research on the Ultimatum game, see Samuel Bowles et al., "In Search of Homo Economicus: Behavioral Experiments in 15 Simple Societies," *American Economic Review* 91, no. 2 (May 2001): 73–78; for the rational choice view of "culture" as a category of analysis in decisionmaking, see James Johnston et al., *Analytic Narratives* (Princeton: Princeton University Press, 1998); Douglass North, "Institutions, Ideology, and Economic Performance," *Cato Journal* 11, no. 3 (1992): 477–88.

BIBLIOGRAPHY

Ableson, Robert P. "The Secret Existence of Expressive Behavior." *Critical Review* 9, nos. 1–2 (winter–spring 1995): 25–36.

"Agency [General Accounting Office] Says McNamara Used 'Rough Judgment' in Setting TFX Award." *Wall Street Journal*, 3 May 1963, 2.

Ahrens, Joachim. *Governance and Economic Development: A Cooperative Institutional Approach*. Cheltenham, England: Edward Elgar, 2002.

Alchon, Guy. *The Invisible Hand of Planning: Capitalism, Social Science, and the State in the 1920s*. Princeton: Princeton University Press, 1985.

Aldrich, John H. "When Is It Rational to Vote?" In *Perspectives on Public Choice: A Handbook*, ed. Dennis C. Mueller, 375–84. Cambridge: Cambridge University Press, 1997.

Alexander, Tom. "McNamara's Expensive Economy Plane." *Fortune*, 1 June 1967.

Alger, Chadwick F. "The External Bureaucracy in the United States Foreign Affairs." *Administration Science Quarterly* (June 1962).

Allais, M. "Le Comportement de l'homme Rationnel Devant le Risque: Critique des Postulats et Axioms de L'ecole Americaine." *Econometrica* 21 (1953): 503–46.

Allen, William R. "Economics, Economists, and Economic Policy: Modern American Experience." *History of Political Economy* 9 (spring 1977): 48–88.

Almond, Gabriel A. "Rational Choice Theory and the Social Sciences." In *A Discipline Divided: Schools and Sects in Political Science*, 117–37. London: Sage Publications, 1990.

Alsop, Joseph. "The New Balance of Power: War and Peace in a Strange World." *Encounter* 10, no. 5 (May 1958): 3–10.

Alsop, Stewart. "How Can We Catch Up?" *Saturday Evening Post*, 14 December 1957, 27.

———. "Our New Strategy: The Alternatives to Total War." *Saturday Evening Post*, 1 December 1962, 13–18.

Alt, James, and Kenneth Shepsle, eds. *Perspectives on Positive Political Economy*. New York: Cambridge University Press, 1990.

Amadae, S. M., and Bruce Bueno de Mesquita. "The Rochester School: The Origins of Positive Political Theory." In *Annual Review of Political Science*, ed. Nelson W. Polsby, 2:269–95. Palo Alto: Annual Reviews, 1999.

Anshen, Melvin. "The Program Budget in Operation." In *Program Budgeting:*

Program Analysis and the Federal Budget, ed. David Novick. Cambridge: Harvard University Press, 1965.

Arrow, Kenneth J. "Behavior under Uncertainty and its Implications for Policy." In *Decision Making: Descriptive, Normative, and Prescriptive Interactions,* ed. David E. Bell, Howard Raiffa, and Amos Tversky, 497–507. Cambridge: Cambridge University Press, 1988.

———. "A Cautious Case for Socialism." *Dissent* (fall 1978): 472–80. "A Difficulty in the Concept of Social Welfare." *Journal of Political Economy* 58 (1950): 328–46.

———. "A Difficulty in the Concept of Social Welfare." In Kenneth J. Arrow, *Social Choice and Justice. Collected Papers of Kenneth J. Arrow.* Oxford: Basil Blackwell, 1984.

———. *General Equilibrium: Collected Papers of Kenneth J. Arrow.* Cambridge: Harvard University Press, 1983.

———. *The Economics of Information: Collected Papers of Kenneth J. Arrow.* Cambridge: Harvard University Press, 1984.

———. "General Equilibrium: Purpose, Analytic Techniques, Collective Choice." *American Economic Review* 64, no. 3 (June 1974): 253–74.

———. "Extended Sympathy and the Possibility of Social Choice." In *Social Choice and Justice: Collected Papers of Kenneth Arrow,* 147–61. Oxford: Basil Blackwell, 1984.

———. *Individual Choice under Certainty and Uncertainty: Collected Papers of Kenneth J. Arrow.* Cambridge: Harvard University Press, 1984.

———. *The Limits of Organization.* New York: Norton, 1974.

———. "Mathematical Models in the Social Sciences." In *The Policy Sciences: Recent Developments in Scope and Method,* ed. Daniel Lerner and Harold D. Lasswell, 129. Stanford: Stanford University Press, 1951.

———. Papers. Rare Book, Manuscript, and Special Collections Library, Duke University, Durham, N.C.

———. "Rational Choice Functions and Orderings." *Economica,* n.s., 26 (May 1959): 121–27.

———. "Rawls's Principle of Just Saving." In *Social Choice and Justice: Collected Papers of Kenneth Arrow,* 133–46. Oxford: Basil Blackwell, 1984.

———. *Social Choice and Individual Values.* New York: Wiley, 1951.

———. *Social Choice and Individual Values,* 2nd ed. New Haven: Yale University Press, 1963.

———. "Social Choice and Individual Values." RAND RM-291. Santa Monica: RAND, 1949.

———. *Social Choice and Justice.* Cambridge: Harvard University Press, Belknap Press, 1983.

———. *Social Choice and Justice: Collected Papers of Kenneth J. Arrow.* Oxford: Basil Blackwell, 1984.

———. "Some Ordinalist-Utilitarian Notes on Rawls's Theory of Justice." In *Social Choice and Justice: Collected Papers of Kenneth J. Arrow,* 96–114. Oxford: Basil Blackwell, 1984.

————. "Values and Collective Decision-Making." In *Philosophy, Politics and Society*, ed. P. Laslett and W. G. Runciman. Oxford: Basil Blackwell, 1967.

Arrow, Kenneth J., ed. *Markets and Welfare*. London: Macmillan, 1991.

Arrow, Kenneth J., and Gerard Debreu. "Existence of an Equilibrium for a Competitive Economy." *Econometrica* 22 (July 1954): 265–90.

Art, Robert J. *The TFX Decision: McNamara and the Military*. Boston: Little, Brown, 1968.

Ascoli, Max. "Thank you, Sputnik!" *Reporter*, 31 October 1957, editorial, 10–12.

Ashmore, Harry S. *Unseasonable Truths: The Life of Robert Maynard Hutchins* Boston: Little, Brown, 1989.

Austen-Smith, David, and Jeffrey Banks. "Elections, Coalitions, and Legislative Outcomes." *American Political Science Review* 82 (1988): 405–22.

————. "Social Choice Theory, Game Theory, and Positive Political Theory." In *Annual Review of Political Science*, ed. Nelson Polsby, 1:259–87. Palo Alto: Annual Reviews, 1998.

————. "Stable Governments and the Allocation of Policy Portfolios." *American Political Science Review* 84 (1990): 891–906.

Axelrod, Robert, and William D. Hamilton. *The Evolution of Cooperation*. New York: Basic Books, 1984.

Baldwin, Hanson W. "The McNamara Monarchy." *Saturday Evening Post*, 9 March 1963, 8–9.

Barber, William J. *From New Era to New Deal. Herbert Hoover, the Economists, and American Economic Policy, 1921–1933*. Cambridge: Cambridge University Press, 1985.

————. "The Spread of Economic Ideas between Academia and Government: A Two-Way Street." In *The Spread of Economic Ideas*, ed. David C. Colander and A. W. Coats. Cambridge: Cambridge University Press, 1989.

Bates, Robert H., et al. *Analytic Narratives*. Princeton: Princeton University Press, 1998.

Bator, Francis M. "The Simple Analytics of Welfare Maximization." *American Economic Review* 47, no. 1 (March 1957): 22–59.

Baumol, William J. "Community Indifference." *Review of Economic Studies* 14, no. 1 (1945–46): 44–48.

————. *Economic Theory and Operations Analysis*, 2nd ed. Englewood Cliffs, N.J.: Prentice Hall, 1965.

Beck, Lewis White. *A Commentary on Kant's Critique of Practical Reason*. Chicago: University of Chicago Press, 1960.

Becker, J. F. "Adam Smith's Theory of Social Science." *Southern Economic Journal* 27 (1961): 13–21.

Beckman, George M. "The Role of Foundations." *Annals of the American Academy of Political and Social Science* 356 (November 1964): 12–22.

Bell, Daniel. *The End of Ideology: On the Exhaustion of Political Ideas in the Fifties*. Cambridge: Harvard University Press, 1960.

Bell, David E., Howard Raiffa, and Amos Tversky, eds. *Decision Making: De-*

scriptive, Normative, and Prescriptive Interactions. Cambridge: Cambridge University Press, 1988.

Bender, Thomas. "Intellectuals, Cities, and Citizenship in the United States: The 1890s and 1990s." In *Cities and Citizenship,* ed. James Holston, 21–41. Durham: Duke University Press, 1999.

——. "Politics, Intellect, and the American University, 1945–1995." *Dædalus; American Academic Culture in Transformation: Fifty Years, Four Disciplines* 126, no. 1 (winter 1997): 1–38.

Bentley, Arthur. *The Process of Government.* Evanston, Ill.: Principia Press, 1949.

Bergson, Abram Burk. "On the Concept of Social Welfare." *Quarterly Journal of Economics* 68 (1954): 233–51.

——. "A Reformulation of Certain Aspects of Welfare Economics." *Quarterly Journal of Economics* 52 (February 1938): 310–34.

Berlin, Isaiah. *Four Essays on Liberty.* London: Oxford University Press, 1969.

Bielefeldt, Heiner. "Autonomy and Republicanism: Immanuel Kant's Philosophy of Freedom." *Political Theory* 25, no. 4 (August 1997): 524–58.

Binmore, Ken. *Game Theory and the Social Contract.* 2 vols. Cambridge: MIT Press, 1994–98.

Black, Duncan. "On the Rationale of Group Decision Making." *Journal of Political Economy* 56 (1948): 123–34.

——. *The Theory of Committees and Elections.* Cambridge: Cambridge University Press, 1958.

——. *The Theory of Committees and Elections.* In *The Theory of Committees and Elections,* 2nd rev. ed., ed. Iain McLean, Alistair McMillan, and Burt L. Monroe, with a foreword by Ronald H. Coase. Amsterdam: Kluwer, 1998.

Black, R. D. Collison. "W. S. Jevons and the Foundation of Modern Economics." *History of Political Economy* 4, no. 2 (fall 1972): 364–78.

Blackett, P. M. S. "Critique of Some Contemporary Defense Thinking." *Encounter* 16, no. 4 (April 1961): 9–17.

Blau, Julian H. "The Existence of Social Welfare Functions." *Econometrica* 25 (1957): 302–13.

Blaug, Mark. *Economic Theory in Retrospect,* 4th ed. Cambridge: Cambridge University Press, 1985.

Blum, William. *Rogue State: A Guide to the World's Only Superpower.* Monroe, Me.: Common Courage Press, 2000.

Bottome, Edgar M. *The Missile Gap: A Study of the Formulation of Military and Political Policy.* Rutherford, N.J.: Farleigh Dickinson University, 1971.

Boulding, Kenneth E. "Samuelson's *Foundations:* The Role of Mathematics in Economics." *Journal of Political Economy* 61 (June 1948): 187–99.

Bowles, Samuel. "In Search of Homo Economicus: Behavior Experiments in 15 Simple Societies." *American Economic Review* 91, no. 2 (May 2001): 73–78.

Brady, Gordon. "Gordon Tullock: His Development as an Unconventional Economist, 1947–1962." In Price Fishback et al., *Public Choice Essays in Honor of a Maverick Scholar: Gordon Tullock,* 1–22. Boston: Kluwer, 2000.

Braybrooke, David. "Farewell to the New Welfare Economics." *Review of Economic Studies* 21 (1954–55): 180–93.

Breton, A. *The Economic Theory of Representative Government*. Chicago: Aldine, 1974.

Brodie, Bernard. "The McNamara Phenomena." *World Politics* 17 (July 1965): 672–87.

———. *Strategy in the Missile Age*. Princeton: Princeton University Press, 1959.

Brodie, Bernard, ed. *The Absolute Weapon: Atomic Power and World Order*. New York: Harcourt, Brace, 1946.

Bryan, Stanley E. "TFX—A Case in Policy Level Decision-Making." *Academy of Management Journal* 7, no. 1 (March 1964): 54–70.

Buchanan, James M. "Better than Plowing." *Banca Nazionale Del Lavoro Quarterly Review* 159 (1986): 370–80.

———. "The Constitution of Economic Policy." *American Economic Review* 77 (June 1987): 243–50.

———. "A Hobbesian Interpretation of the Rawlsian Difference Principle." *Kyklos* 29, no. 1 (1976): 5–25.

———. "Individual Choice in Voting and the Market." *Journal of Political Economy* 62 (1954): 334–43.

———. "An Individualistic Theory of Political Process." In *Varieties of Political Theory*, ed. David Easton, 25–29. Englewood Cliffs, N.J.: Prentice Hall, 1966.

———. James M. Buchanan Collection. Center for Study of Public Choice, Buchanan House, George Mason University, Fairfax, Va.

———. *Liberty, Market and State: Political Economy in the 1980s*. Brighton, England: Edward Elgar, 1986.

———. *The Limits of Liberty: Between Anarchy and Leviathan*. Chicago: University of Chicago Press, 1975.

———. "Positive Economics, Welfare Economics, and Political Economy." *Journal of Law and Economics* 2 (October 1959): 124–38.

———. *Post-Socialist Political Economy*. Lyme, Conn.: Edward Elgar, 1997.

———. *Public Principles of Public Debt: A Defense and Restatement*. Homewood, Ill.: Richard D. Irwin, 1958.

———. "The Pure Theory of Government Finance: A Suggested Approach." *Journal of Political Economy* 57 (December 1949): 496–506.

———. "Social Choice, Democracy, and Free Markets." *Journal of Political Economy* 62 (1954): 114–23.

Buchanan, James M., and Gordon Tullock. *The Calculus of Consent*. Ann Arbor: University of Michigan Press, 1962.

Buchanan, James M., and Nicos E. Devletoglou. *Academia in Anarchy: An Economic Diagnosis*. New York: Basic Books, 1970.

Buchanan, James M., and Richard E. Wagner. *Democracy in Deficit: The Political Legacy of Lord Keynes*. San Diego: Academic Press, 1977.

Buchanan, James M., and R. D. Tollison, eds. *Theory of Public Choice*. Ann Arbor: University of Michigan Press, 1972.

Buchanan, James M., et al. *Reaganomics and After*. London: Institute of Economic Affairs, 1989.

Bundy, McGeorge. *Danger and Survival: Choices about the Bomb in the First Fifty Years.* New York: Random House, 1988.

Bush, Vannevar. *Pieces of Action.* New York: William Morrow, 1970.

Callahan, David. *Dangerous Capabilities: Paul Nitze and the Cold War.* New York: HarperCollins, 1990.

Callon, Michel, ed. *The Laws of the Markets.* Oxford: Blackwell, 1998.

Campbell, R. H., and Andrew S. Skinner, eds. *The Origins and Nature of the Scottish Enlightenment.* Edinburgh: John Donald, 1982.

Campbell, Richmond, and Lanning Sowden, eds. *Paradoxes of Rationality and Cooperation.* Vancouver: University of British Columbia Press, 1985.

Campbell, T. D. *Adam Smith's Science of Morals.* London: Allen and Unwin, 1971.

———. "Scientific Explanation and Ethical Justification in the *Moral Sentiments.* In *Essays on Adam Smith,* ed. Andrew Skinner and Thomas Wilson, 68–82 (Oxford: Clarendon Press, 1975).

Cannan, E. "Adam Smith as an Economist." *Economica* no. 17 (June 1926): 123–34.

Canterbery, Ray E. *The Making of Economics,* 3rd ed. Belmont, Calif.: Wadsworth, 1987.

"Capitalism, Socialism, and Democracy: A Symposium." *Commentary* (April 1978): 29–71.

Carling, Alan. "Rational Choice Marxism." In *Rational Choice Marxism,* ed. Terrell Carver and Paul Thomas, 31–78. London: Macmillan, 1995.

Carver, Terrell, and Paul Thomas, eds. *Rational Choice Marxism.* London: Macmillan, 1995.

Chipman, John. "An Episode in the Early Development of Ordinal Utility Theory: Pareto's Letters to Hermann Laurent." *Cahiers Vilfredo Pareto* 14, no. 37 (1976): 39–64.

Churchman, C. W. "Kant—A Decision Theorist?" *Theory and Decision* 1 (1970–71): 115.

Coats, A. W. "Economic Ideas and Economists in Government: Accomplishments and Frustrations." In *The Spread of Economic Ideas,* ed. David C. Colander and A. W. Coats. Cambridge: Cambridge University Press, 1989.

Coats, A. W., ed. *Economists in Government: An International Comparative Study.* Durham: Duke University Press, 1981.

———. *Economists in International Agencies: An Exploratory Study.* New York: Praeger, 1986.

Cohen, G. A. *Karl Marx's Theory of History: A Defense.* Oxford: Oxford University Press, 1978.

Colander, David C., and Arjo Klamer. "The Making of an Economist." *Journal of Economic Perspectives* 1 (fall 1987): 95–111.

Cole, Alice C., Alfred Goldberg, Samuel A. Tucker, and Rudolph A. Winnacker, eds. *The Department of Defense: Documents on Establishment and Organization, 1944–1978.* Washington, D.C.: Office of the Secretary of Defense, Historical Office, 1978.

Coleman, James S. *The Mathematics of Collective Action*. Chicago: Aldine, 1973.

de Condorcet, M. *Essai sur l'application de l'analyse à la Probabilitè des Décisions Rendues à la Pluralisté des voix*. Paris: 1985.

Cook, Thomas I. "The Methods of Political Science, Chiefly in the United States." In *Contemporary Political Science: A Survey of Methods, Research and Teaching*, 75–90. Paris: UNESCO, 1950.

Cooter, Robert, and Peter Rappoport. "Were the Ordinalists Wrong about Welfare Economics?" *Journal of Economic Literature* 22 (June 1984): 507–30.

Copi, Irving M. "Social Choice and Individual Values." *Ethics* 62 (1952): 220–22.

Cowherd, Raymond G. *Political Economists and the English Poor Laws: A Historical Study of the Influence of Classical Economics on the Formation of Social Welfare Policy*. Athens: Ohio University Press, 1977.

Craig, James R. "Captive Think Tanks Revisited." *Armed Forces Journal International* 113, no. 7 (March 1976): 42–47.

———. "Captive 'Think Tanks'—DoD's $265-Million Hobby Horse?" *Armed Forces Journal International* 113, no. 4 (December 1975): 20–25.

Cropsey, Joseph. "Adam Smith and Political Philosophy." In *The Market and the State*, ed. Andrew Skinner and Thomas Wilson, 132–53. Oxford: Clarendon Press, 1976.

———. "The Invisible Hand: Moral and Political Considerations." In *Adam Smith and Modern Political Economy: Bicentennial Essays on* The Wealth of Nations, ed. Gerald P. O'Driscoll Jr., 165–76. Ames: Iowa State University Press, 1979.

———. *Polity and Economy: An Interpretation of the Principles of Adam Smith*. The Hague: Martinus Nijhoff, 1957.

D., J. F. "Memorandum of a Conversation between the President and the Secretary of State, White House, Washington, D.C., November 7, 1957." *Foreign Relations 1955–1957* 19, Document no. 157.

Dasgupta, Partha, Amartya Sen, and Stephen Marglin. *Guidelines for Project Evaluation*. New York: United Nations, 1972.

Davis, James W. *Politics, Programs, and Budgets*. Englewood Cliffs, N.J.: Prentice Hall, 1969.

Davidson, Donald. "A New Basis for Decision Theory." *Theory and Decision* 18 (1985): 87–98.

Davis, Richard G. "Comment on Arrow and the 'New Welfare Economics.'" *Economic Journal* 68 (1958): 834–35.

Dawkins, Richard. *The Selfish Gene*. New York: Oxford University Press, 1976.

Desai, Megnad. "Social Science Goes to War: Economic Theory and the Pentagon Papers." *Survival* 14 (March–April 1972): 62–67.

Dewey, John. *The Public and Its Problems*. Chicago: Swallow Press, 1988.

Dick, James C. "The Strategic Arms Race, 1957–1961: Who Opened the Missile Gap?" *Journal of Politics* 34 (1972): 1073.

Dickey, Laurence. "Historicizing the 'Adam Smith Problem': Conceptual, Historiographical, and Textual Issues." *Journal of Modern History* 58 (September 1986): 579–609.

Digby, James. *Strategic Thought at RAND, 1948–1963: The Ideas, Their Origins, Their Fates.* RAND NOTE, N-3096-RC (June 1990).

Divine, Robert A. *The Sputnik Challenge: Eisenhower's Response to the Soviet Satellite.* New York: Oxford University Press, 1993.

Dobb, Maurice. "Economic Theory and the Problems of a Socialist Economy." *Economic Journal* 43 (December 1933): 585–598.

———. "Economic Theory and Socialist Economy: A Reply." *Review of Economic Studies* 2 (1943): 144–51.

Donovan, John C. *The Cold Warrior: A Policy-Making Elite.* Lexington, Mass.: D. C. Heath, 1974.

Downie, R. S. Commentary on Thomas Wilson's "Sympathy and Self-Interest." In *The Market and the State: Essays in Honour of Adam Smith,* ed. Thomas Wilson and Andrew Skinner. Oxford: Clarendon Press, 1976.

Downs, Anthony. *An Economic Theory of Democracy.* New York: Harper, 1957.

———. *Inside Democracy.* Boston: Little, Brown, 1967.

———. Review of *The Calculus of Consent. Journal of Political Economy* 72 (February 1964): 87–88.

Dufour, Alfred. "Natural Law and Utility: Pufendorf." In *The Cambridge History of Political Thought 1450–1700,* ed. J. H. Burns, 563–89. Cambridge: Cambridge University Press, 1991.

Easton, David. *The Political System.* New York: Knopf, 1953.

Easton, David, ed. *Varieties of Political Theory.* Englewood Cliffs, N.J.: Prentice Hall, 1966.

Edgeworth, F. Y. *Mathematical Psychics: An Essay on the Application of Mathematics to the Moral Sciences.* London: C. K. Paul, 1881.

Eisenmann, Charles. "On the Matter and Methods of the Political Sciences." In *Contemporary Political Science: A Survey of Methods, Research and Teaching,* 91–131. Paris: Unesco, 1950.

Ekelund Jr., Robert B., and Robert F. Hébert. *A History of Economic Theory and Method,* 3rd ed. New York: McGraw-Hill, 1990.

Ellsberg, Daniel. "Risk, Ambiguity, and the Savage Axioms." *Quarterly Journal of Economics* 75 (1961): 643–69.

———. *Secrets: A Memoir of Vietnam and the Pentagon Papers* (New York: Viking, 2002).

Elster, Jon. *Making Sense of Marx.* Cambridge: Cambridge University Press, 1985.

———. *Sour Grapes: Studies in the Subversion of Rationality.* New York: Cambridge University Press, 1983.

Elster, Jon, ed. *Deliberative Democracy.* Cambridge: Cambridge University Press, 1998.

Emerson, Roger L. "Science and Moral Philosophy in the Scottish Enlightenment." In *Studies in the Philosophy of the Scottish Enlightenment,* ed. M. A. Steward. Oxford: Clarendon Press, 1990.

Entoven, Alain. "Economic Analysis in the Department of Defense." *American Economic Review* 53 (May 1963): 413–23.

———. "Systems Analysis and Decision-Making." *Military Review* 53 (January 1963): 7–17.

Entoven, Alain, and Henry Rowen. "Defense Planning and Organization." In National Bureau of Economic Research, *Public Finances: Needs, Sources, and Utilization*, 365–420. Princeton: Princeton University Press, 1961.

Entoven, Alain, and K. Wayne Smith. *How Much Is Enough?* New York: Harper and Row, 1971.

Farr, James. "Political Science and the State." In *Discipline and History: Political Science in the United States*, ed. James Farr and Raymond Seidelman, 63–80. Ann Arbor: University of Michigan Press, 1993.

Feiwel, George R. "The Potentials and Limits of Economic Analysis: The Contributions of Kenneth J. Arrow." In *Arrow and the Ascent of Modern Economic Theory*, ed. George Feiwel, 1–187. New York: New York University Press, 1987.

Feiwel, George, R., ed. *Arrow and the Foundations of the Theory of Economic Policy*. New York: New York University Press, 1987.

Ferejohn, John A., and Morris P. Fiorina. "The Paradox of Not Voting: A Decision Theoretic Analysis." *American Political Science Review* 68 (1974): 252–36.

Fiorina, Morris P. "Voting Behavior." In *Perspectives on Public Choice: A Handbook*, ed. Dennis C. Mueller, 391–414. Cambridge: Cambridge University Press, 1997.

Fitzgibbons, Athol. *Adam Smith's System of Liberty, Wealth, and Virtue: The Moral and Political Foundations of* The Wealth of Nations. Oxford: Clarendon Press, 1995.

Fleischaker, Samuel. "Values behind the Market: Kant's Response to the *Wealth of Nations*." *History of Political Thought* 17, no. 3 (Autumn 1996): 379–407.

Forbes, Duncan. "Natural Law and the Scottish Enlightenment." In *The Origins and Nature of the Scottish Enlightenment*, ed. R. H. Campbell and A. S. Skinner, 186–204. Edinburgh: John Donald, 1982.

Foucault, Michel. *Discipline and Punish: The Birth of the Prison*. New York: Random House, 1977.

Fraser, L. M. "Notes and Memoranda: The Doctrine of Consumers' Sovereignty." *Economic Journal* 49 (September 1939): 544–48.

Friedman, Jeffrey, ed. "Rational Choice Theory." *Critical Review* 9, nos. 1–2 (winter–spring 1995).

Fry, Michael, ed. *Adam Smith's Legacy: His Place in the Development of Modern Economics*. London: Routledge, 1992.

Fukuyama, Francis. *The End of History and the Last Man*. New York: Harper Business, 1992.

Furner, Mary, and Barry Supple, eds. *The State and Economic Knowledge*. Cambridge: Cambridge University Press, 1990.

Fusfeld, Daniel R. *The Age of the Economist*, 6th ed. London: Scott, Foresman, 1990.

Futrell, Robert F. *Ideas, Concepts, Doctrine: A History of Basic Thinking in the*

United States Air Force, 1907–1964. Maxwell, Ala.: Air Force University, 1975. Reprint, New York: Arno Press, 1980.

Galbraith, James K. "The Exchange of Favors in the Market for Commitments." In David C. Colander and A. W. Coats, eds., *The Spread of Economic Ideas,* 127–40. Cambridge: Cambridge University Press, 1989.

Gale, David. "A Note on Revealed Preference." *Economica,* n.s., 27 (November 1960): 348–54.

Galison, Peter, and Bruce Hevly, eds. *Big Science. The Growth of Large-Scale Research.* Stanford: Stanford University Press, 1992.

Gärdenfors, Peter, and Nils-Eric Sahlin, eds. *Decision, Probability, and Utility: Selected Readings.* Cambridge: Cambridge University Press, 1988.

Gauthier, David. "Constituting Democracy." In *The Idea of Democracy,* ed. David Copp et al., 314–34. Cambridge: Cambridge University Press, 1993.

———. *Morals by Agreement.* Oxford: Clarendon Press, 1986.

Gee, J. M. A. Review of I. C. Wood's "Adam Smith: Critical Assessments." *Scottish Journal of Political Economy* 32, no. 2 (June 1985): 209–18.

Gertzog, Irwin N. Review of *The Calculus of Consent* (1962). *American Political Science Review* 63 (December 1964): 973–74.

Gleason, S. Everett. "Memorandum of Discussion at the 343d Meeting of the National Security Council, Washington, Nov. 7, 1957." *Foreign Relations, 1955–1957* 19: 632.

———. "Memorandum of the Discussion of the 350th Meeting of the NSC [Jan. 6, 1958]." *Foreign Relations, 1958–1960* 3: Document no. 2, 8.

Gleeson, Robert E., and Steven Schlossman. "George Leland Bach and the Rebirth of Graduate Management Education in the United States, 1945–1975." *Magazine of the Graduate Management Admission Council,* spring 1995, 8–46.

Goldstein, J. R. *RAND: The History, Operations and Goals of a Nonprofit Corporation.* RAND P-2236-1 (April 1961).

Goodin, Robert E., Carole Pateman, and Roy Pateman. "Simian Sovereignty." *Political Theory* 25, no. 6 (December 1997): 821–49.

Goodman, Leo A. "Social Choice and Individual Values." *American Sociological Review* 18 (1953): 116–17.

Goodwin, Craufurd, W. "Doing Good and Spreading the Gospel (Economic)." In *The Spread of Economic Ideas,* ed. David C. Colander and A. W. Coats, 157–74. Cambridge: Cambridge University Press, 1989.

Goodwin, Craufurd W., ed. *Energy Policy in Perspective.* Washington, D.C.: Brookings Institute, 1981.

Graaf, Jan de V. *Theoretical Welfare Economics.* Cambridge: Cambridge University Press, 1957.

Grampp, W. D. *Economic Liberalism.* Vol. 2, *The Classical View.* New York: Random House, 1965.

Gray, Colin. *Strategic Studies and Public Policy: The American Experience.* Lexington: University Press of Kentucky, 1982.

Green, Donald P., and Ian Shapiro. *Pathologies of Rational Choice Theory: A Cri-*

tique of Applications in Political Science. New Haven: Yale University Press, 1994.

Green, H. A. John. "Some Logical Relations in Revealed Preference Theory." *Economica,* n.s., 24 (November 1957): 315–23.

Green, Philip. *Deadly Logic: The Theory of Nuclear Deterrence.* Columbus: Ohio State University Press, 1966.

Greider, William. *One World, Ready or Not: The Manic Logic of Global Capitalism.* New York: Simon and Schuster, 1997.

Griswold, Charles L. *Adam Smith and the Virtues of Enlightenment.* Cambridge: Cambridge University Press, 1999.

Gunnell, John G. "American Political Science, Liberalism, and the Invention of Political Theory." *American Political Science Review* 82, no. 1 (March 1988): 71–88.

Haakonssen, Knud. *Natural Law and Moral Philosophy: From Grotius to the Scottish Enlightenment.* Cambridge: Cambridge University Press, 1996.

———. "Natural Law and Moral Realism: The Scottish Synthesis." In *Studies in the Philosophy of the Scottish Enlightenment,* ed. M. A. Stewart, 61–86. Oxford: Clarendon Press, 1990.

———. *The Science of a Legislator: The Natural Jurisprudence of David Hume and Adam Smith.* Cambridge: Cambridge University Press, 1981.

———. "What Might Properly Be Called Natural Jurisprudence?" In *The Origins and Nature of the Scottish Enlightenment,* ed. R. H. Campbell and A. S. Skinner, 205–25. Edinburgh: John Donald, 1982.

Haakonssen, Knud, ed. *Adam Smith.* Sydney: Ashgate Dartmouth, 1998.

Habermas, Jürgen. *Between Facts and Norms.* Cambridge: MIT Press, 1996.

———. *The Philosophical Discourse of Modernity.* Trans. Frederick J. Lawrence. Cambridge: MIT Press, 1987).

———. *The Structural Transformation of the Public Sphere: An Inquiry into a Category of Bourgeois Society,* trans. Thomas Burger. Cambridge: MIT Press, 1989.

———. *The Theory of Communicative Action.* 2 vols. Trans. Thomas McCarthy. Boston: Beacon Press, 1984–87.

Halperin, Morton H. "The Gaither Committee and the Policy Process." *World Politics* 13 (April 1961): 360–84.

Hammond, Paul Y. *Organizing for Defense: The American Military Establishment in the Twentieth Century.* Princeton: Princeton University Press, 1961.

Hampton, Jean. *The Authority of Reason,* ed. Richard Healey. Cambridge: Cambridge University Press, 1998.

———. "The Failure of Expected-Utility Theory as a Theory of Reason." *Economics and Philosophy* 10 (1994): 195–242.

Hands, Wade D. "More Light on Integrability, Symmetry, and Utility as Potential Energy in Mirowski's Critical History." In *Non-natural Social Science: Reflecting on the Enterprise of More Heat than Light,* ed. Neil de Marchi. *History of Political Economy* 25 (ann. supp.). Durham: Duke University Press, 1993.

Hardin, Russell. *Collective Action*. Baltimore: Johns Hopkins University Press, 1982.

———. *Morality within the Limits of Reason*. Chicago: University of Chicago Press, 1988.

———. "Public Choice versus Democracy." In *The Idea of Democracy*, ed. David Copp et al., 157–72. Cambridge: Cambridge University Press, 1993.

Harpham, Edward J., and Richard K. Scotch. "Economic Discourse, Policy Analysis, and the Problem of the Political." In *Handbook of Political Theory and Policy Science*, ed. Edward Bryan Portis and Michael B. Levy, 215–30. New York: Greenwood Press, 1988.

Harsanyi, John C. "Can the Maximin Principle Serve as a Basis for Morality." *American Political Science Review* 69, no. 2 (June 1975): 594–606.

———. "Cardinal Utility in Welfare Economics in the Theory of Risk-Taking." *Journal of Political Economy* 61 (1953): 534–35.

———. "Cardinal Welfare, Individualistic Ethics, and Interpersonal Comparisons of Utility." *Journal of Political Economy* 63 (1955): 309–21.

———. "Welfare Economics of Variable Tests." *Review of Economic Studies* 21 (1953–54): 204–13.

Hart, Gary, "The Big, Lethal Sleep," *New Statesman*, 17 December 2001), 47–48.

Hausman, Daniel M., and Michael S. McPherson. "Economics, Rationality, and Ethics." In *The Philosophy of Economics an Anthology*, 2nd ed., ed. Daniel M. Hausman 252–78. Cambridge: Cambridge University Press, 1993.

Hayek, Friedrich A. von. *The Road to Serfdom*. Chicago: University of Chicago Press, 1944.

Haywood, Oliver. *Military Doctrine of Decision and the von Neumann Theory of Games*. RAND RM-528 (February 1951).

Heims, Steve J. *John von Neumann and Norbert Wiener: From Mathematics to the Technologies of Life and Death*. Cambridge: MIT Press, 1980.

Held, David. *Models of Democracy*, 2nd ed. Stanford: Stanford University Press, 1996 [1987].

Herken, Gregg. *The Counsels of War*. New York: Knopf, 1987.

Herman, Ellen. *The Romance of American Psychology, 1940–1970*. Berkeley: University of California Press, 1995.

Herndon, James F., and Joseph L. Bernd, eds. *Mathematical Applications in Political Science*. Vol. 6. Charlottesville: University of Virginia Press, 1972.

Hersh, Seymour M. *The Dark Side of Camelot*. Boston: Little, Brown, 1997.

Hertzberg, Hendrik. "Comment: Tuesday, and After." *New Yorker*, 24 September 2001, 27.

Herzog, Arthur. *The War-Peace Establishment*. New York: Harper and Row, 1963.

Hicks, J. R. "The Foundations of Welfare Economics." *Economic Journal* 49 (December 1939): 696–712.

Hildreth, Clifford. "Alternative Conditions for Social Orderings." *Econometrica* 21, no. 1 (January 1953): 81–94.

————. *The Cowles Commission in Chicago, 1939–1955*, 2. New York: Springer Verlag, 1986.

Hilgard, Ernest R., and Daniel Lerner. "The Person: Subject and Object of Science and Policy." In Daniel Lerner and Harold D. Lasswell, eds., *The Policy Sciences: Recent Developments in Scope and Method*, 16–43. Stanford: Stanford University Press, 1951.

Hirschman, Albert O. *The Passions and the Interests: Political Arguments for Capitalism before Its Triumph*. Princeton: Princeton University Press, 1977.

Hitch, Charles J. *Decision-Making for Defense*. Berkeley: University of California Press, 1966.

Hitch, Charles J., and Roland N. McKean. *The Economics of Defense in the Nuclear Age*. Cambridge: Harvard University Press, 1963 [1960].

Hobbes, Thomas. *Leviathan*, ed. Richard Tuck. Cambridge: Cambridge University Press, 1991.

Hobsbawn, Eric. "Democracy Can Be Bad for You." *New Statesman*, 5 March 2001, 26.

Hollinger, David H. "The Defense of Democracy and Robert K. Merton's Formulation of Scientific Ethos." In *Science, Jews, and Secular Culture: Studies in Mid-Twentieth-Century American Intellectual History*, 80–96. Princeton: Princeton University Press, 1996.

————. "Science as a Weapon in *Kulturekämpfe* in the United States during and after World War II." In *Science, Jews, and Secular Culture: Studies in Mid-Twentieth-Century American Intellectual History*, 155–74. Princeton: Princeton University Press, 1996.

————. *Science, Jews, and Secular Culture: Studies in Mid-Twentieth-Century American Intellectual History*. Princeton: Princeton University Press, 1996.

Hont, Istvan, and Michael Ignatieff. "Needs and Justice in the *Wealth of Nations*: An Introductory Essay." In *Wealth and Virtue: The Shaping of Political Economy in the Scottish Enlightenment*, ed. Istvan Hont and Michael Ignatieff, 1–44. Cambridge: Cambridge University Press, 1983.

Hooks, Gregory. *Forging the Military-Industrial Complex: World War II's Battle of the Potomac*. Urbana: University of Illinois Press, 1991.

————. "The Rise of the Pentagon and U.S. State Building: The Defense Program as Industrial Policy." *American Journal of Sociology* 96 (1990): 358–404.

Horkheimer, Max, and Theodore W. Adorno. *Dialectic of Enlightenment*, trans. John Cumming. New York: Continuum, 1989.

Hounshell, David. "The Cold War, RAND, and the Generation of Knowledge, 1946–1962." *Historical Studies in the Physical and Biological Sciences* 27, no. 2 (1997): 237–67.

Houthakker, H. S. "Revealed Preference and the Utility Function." *Economica*, n.s., 17 (May 1950): 159–74.

Hume, David. *A Treatise of Human Nature*, ed. Selby-Bigge, rev. P. H. Nidditch. Oxford: Oxford University Press, 1888.

Hunt, E. K. *History of Economic Thought: A Critical Perspective*. Belmont, Calif.: Wadsworth, 1979.

Huntington, Samuel P. *The Common Defense.* New York: Columbia University Press, 1961.

Hutchison, Terence. *Before Adam Smith: The Emergence of Political Economy, 1662–1776.* Oxford: Basil Blackwell, 1988.

Ingrao, Bruna, and Giorgio Israel. *The Invisible Hand: Economic Equilibrium in the History of Science,* trans. Ian McGilvray. Cambridge: MIT Press, 1990.

Isaacson, Walter, and Evan Thomas. *The Wise Men: Six Friends and the World They Made: Acheson, Bohlen, Harriman, Kennan, Lovett, McCloy.* New York: Simon and Schuster, 1986.

Jackman, Simon. "Liberalism, Public Opinion and their Critics." In *The Flight from Science and Reason,* ed. Paul R. Gross et al. Baltimore: Johns Hopkins University Press, 1996.

Jackson, Henry M. *The National Security Council: Jackson Subcommittee Papers on Policy Making at the Presidential Level.* New York: Praeger, 1965.

Jann, Werner. "From Policy Analysis to Political Management? An Outside Look at Public-policy Training in the United States." In *Social Sciences and Modern States,* ed. Peter Wagner et al., 110–30. Cambridge: Cambridge University Press, 1991.

Janos, Andrew C. *Politics and Paradigms: Changing Theories of Change in Social Science.* Stanford: Stanford University Press, 1986.

Jardini, David Raymond. "Out of the Blue Yonder: The RAND Corporation's Diversification into Social Welfare Research, 1946–1968." Ph.D. diss., Carnegie Mellon University, May 1996.

Jevons, William Stanley. "Brief Account of a General Mathematical Theory of Political Economy." *Journal of the Royal Statistical Society* 29 (June 1886): 282–87.

———. *The Theory of Political Economy,* 4th ed. London: Macmillan, 1931 [1911]. Reprint, ed. R. D. Collison Black. Baltimore: Penguin, 1970.

Johnson, James. "How Not to Criticize Rational Choice Theory: Pathologies of Common Sense." *Philosophy of the Social Sciences* 26, no. 1 (March 1996): 77–91.

Jones, Greta. *Science, Politics, and the Cold War.* London: Routledge, 1988.

Kahn, Herman. *On Thermonuclear War.* Princeton: Princeton University Press, 1960.

———. *Thinking about the Unthinkable.* New York: Avon, 1962.

Kahn, Herman, and I. Mann. *Techniques of Systems Analysis.* RM-1829-1-PR. Santa Monica: RAND, 1957.

Kaldor, N. "Welfare Propositions of Economics and Interpersonal Comparisons of Utility." *Economic Journal* 49 (September 1939): 549–52.

Kant, Immanuel. *Groundwork of the Metaphysic of Morals,* trans. H. J. Paton. New York: Harper and Row, 1964.

———. *The Metaphysical Elements of Justice,* trans. John Ladd. Indianapolis: Bobbs-Merrill, 1965.

Kaplan, Fred. *The Wizards of Armageddon.* New York: Simon and Schuster, 1983.

Katzenbach Jr., Edward L. "Ideas: A New Defense Industry." *Reporter* 2 (March 1961): 17–21.

Kaufmann, William W. *The McNamara Strategy.* New York: Harper and Row, 1964.

Kaysen, Carl. "A Revolution in Economic Theory?" *Review of Economic Studies* 14, no. 1 (1946–47): 1–15.

Kelly, Jerry S. *Arrow's Impossibility Theorems.* New York: Academic Press, 1978.

Kemp, Murray C. "Arrow's General Possibility Theorem." *Review of Economic Studies* 21 (1953–54): 240–43.

Kemp, Murray, and Yew-Kwang Ng. "Arrow's Independence Condition and the Bergson-Samuelson Tradition." In *Arrow and the Foundations of the Theory of Economic Policy,* ed. George R. Feiwel, 223–42. New York: New York University Press, 1987.

Kennedy, John F. *The Strategy of Peace,* ed. Allan Nevins. New York: Harper, 1960.

Klausner, Samuel Z., and Victor M. Lidz, eds. *The Nationalization of the Social Sciences.* Philadelphia: University of Pennsylvania Press, 1986.

Kloppenberg, James T. *The Virtues of Liberalism.* Oxford: Oxford University Press, 1998.

Knight, Frank H. *The Dilemma of Liberalism.* Ann Arbor: Edward Brothers, 1933.

———. "Economics and Human Action." In *The Philosophy of Economics,* ed. Daniel M. Hausman. Cambridge: Cambridge University Press, 1984.

———. *On the History and Method of Economics.* Chicago: University of Chicago Press, 1956.

Kolakowski, Leszek. *The Alienation of Reason,* trans. Norton Guterman. New York: Doubleday/Anchor, 1969.

Kolowski, Peter. *Staat und Gesellschaft bei Kant.* Tübingen: Mohr, 1985.

Komer, Ambassador R. W. "Defense Forum." *Armed Forces Journal International* 113, no. 6 (February 1976): 5.

Kraft, Joseph. "McNamara and His Enemies." *Harper's Magazine,* August 1961, 41–48.

———. "RAND: Arsenal for Ideas." *Harper's Magazine,* July 1960, 69–76.

———. "The War Thinkers." *Esquire,* September 1962, 102.

Kuhn, Thomas. *The Structure of Scientific Revolutions.* Chicago: University of Chicago Press, 1962.

Lagemann, Ellen Condliffe. *The Politics of Knowledge: The Carnegie Corporation, Philanthropy, and Public Policy.* Middletown, Conn.: Wesleyan University Press, 1989.

Lalman, David, Joe Oppenheimer, and Piotr Swistak. "Formal Rational Choice Theory: A Cumulative Science of Politics." In *Political Science: The State of the Discipline,* 2nd ed., ed. Ada W. Finifter, 77–104. Washington, D.C.: American Political Science Association, 1993.

Landreth, Harry, and David C. Colander. *History of Economic Theory,* 2nd ed. Boston: Houghton Mifflin, 1989.

Lane, Melissa. *Plato's Progeny: How Plato and Socrates still Captivate the Modern Mind.* London: Duckworth, 2001.

Lange, Oscar. *Economic Theory of Socialism.* Minneapolis: University of Minnesota Press, 1938.

———. "The Foundations of Welfare Economics." *Econometrica* 10, no. 3–4 (July–October 1942): 215–28.

———. "The Scope and Method of Economics." *Review of Economic Studies* 13, no. 1 (1945–46): 19–32.

Lange, Oscar, and Fred M. Taylor. *On the Economic Theory of Socialism.* New York: McGraw Hill, 1964.

Lawrence, David. "Coming Down to Earth." *U.S. News and World Report,* 18 October 1957.

Leites, Nathan. *Operational Code of the Polit Bureau.* New York: McGraw Hill, 1951.

Lehmann, Nicholas. "Paper Tiger: Daniel Ellsberg's War." *New Yorker,* 4 November 2002, 96–99.

Leonard, Robert J. "Chalk and Cheese: Mirowski Meets Douglas and Bloor." In *Non-natural Social Science: Reflecting on the Enterprise of More Heat than Light,* ed. Neil de Marchi, 259–70. *History of Political Economy* 25 (ann. supp.). Durham: Duke University Press, 1993.

———. "Creating a Context for Game Theory." In *Toward a History of Game Theory,* ed. E. Roy Weintraub, 29–76. Durham: Duke University Press, 1992.

Lerner, A. P. "Economic Theory and Socialist Economy." *Review of Economic Studies* 2 (1943): 51–61.

———. *Economics of Control: Principles of Welfare Economics.* New York: Macmillan, 1944.

———. "A Rejoinder." *Review of Economic Studies* 2 (1943): 152–54.

Lerner, Daniel, and Harold Lasswell, eds. *The Policy Sciences: Recent Developments in Scope and Method.* Stanford: Stanford University Press, 1951.

Leslie, Stuart W. *The Cold War and American Science: The Military-Industrial-Academic Complex at M.I.T. and Stanford.* New York: Columbia University Press, 1993.

Levine, Alan J. *The Missile and Space Race.* London: Praeger, 1994.

Lindblom, Charles E. "Political Science in the 1940s and 1950s." *Dædalus: American Academic Culture in Transformation: Fifty Years, Four Disciplines* 126, no. 1 (winter 1997): 225–52.

Lippman, Walter. *The Phantom Public.* New York: Harcourt Brace, 1925.

Lipset, Martin, ed. *Politics and the Social Sciences.* New York: Oxford University Press, 1969.

Little, I. M. D. *A Critique of Welfare Economics.* Oxford: Clarendon Press, 1957.

———. "Social Choice and Individual Values." *Journal of Political Economy* 60 (1952): 422–32.

Locke, John. *Second Treatise on Government,* ed. C. B. Macpherson. Indianapolis: Hackett, 1980.

Lohmann, Susanne. "The Poverty of Green and Shapiro." *Critical Review* 9, no. 1–2 (winter–spring 1995): 127–54.

Loomes, G., and Robert Sugden. "Regret Theory: An Alternative Theory of Rational Choice under Uncertainty." *Economic Journal* 92 (1982): 805–24.

Lowi, Theodore J. "The State in Political Science: How We Become What We Study." *American Political Science Review* 86, no. 1 (March 1992): 1–7.

Lubell, Samuel. "Sputnik and American Public Opinion." *Columbia University Forum* 1 (winter 1957): 15–21.

Luce, R. Duncan, and Howard Raiffa. *Games and Decisions: Introduction and Critical Survey*. New York: Wiley, 1957.

MacCormick, Neil. "Adam Smith on Law." In *Adam Smith*, ed. Knud Haakonssen, 189–209. Sydney: Ashgate Dartmouth, 1998.

———. "Law and Enlightenment." In *The Origins and Nature of the Scottish Enlightenment*, ed. R. H. Campbell and A. S. Skinner, 150–66. Edinburgh: John Donald, 1982.

Machiavelli, Niccolo. *The Prince*, ed. Quentin Skinner and Russell Price. Cambridge: Cambridge University Press, 1988.

Machlup, Fritz. "Capitalism and its Future Appraised by Two Liberal Economists." *American Economic Review* 33 (1943): 301–20.

MacIntyre, Alasdair. *After Virtue*, 2nd ed. Notre Dame: University of Notre Dame Press, 1984.

MacPherson, C. B. *Democratic Theory: Essays in Retrieval*. Oxford: Clarendon Press, 1973.

Maloney, John. *Marshall, Orthodoxy, and the Professionalisation of Economics*. Cambridge: Cambridge University Press, 1985.

Manne, Henry G. *An Intellectual History of the School of Law, George Mason University*. Arlington, Va.: Law and Economics Center, George Mason University School of Law, 1993.

———. Review of *The Calculus of Consent* (1962). *George Washington Law Review* 31 (June 1963): 1065–71.

Marchi, Neil de, ed. *Non-Natural Social Science: Reflecting on the Enterprise of More Heat Than Light. History of Political Economy* 25 (ann. supp.). Durham: Duke University Press, 1993.

Marwell, Gerald, and Ruth Ames. "Economists Free Ride. Does Anyone Else? Experiments on the Provision of Public Goods. IV." *Journal of Public Economics* 15, no. 3 (June 1981): 295–310.

"Marx after Communism." *Economist*, 21 December 2002, 18.

Mas-Colell, Andreu, Michael D. Whinston, and Jerry R. Green. *Microeconomic Theory*. New York: Oxford University Press, 1995.

May, R. J. Review of *The Calculus of Consent* (1962). *Australian Quarterly* (December 1963): 111–13.

McClennen, E. F. "An Alternative Model of Rational Cooperation." In *Justice, Political Liberalism and Utilitarianism: Proceedings of the Caen Conference in Honour of John C. Harsanyi and John Rawls*. Cambridge: Cambridge University Press, forthcoming.

———. "Constitutional Choice: Rawls vs. Harsanyi." In *Philosophy in Economics*, ed. J. C. Pitt, 93–109. Dordrecht: Reidel, 1981.

————. "Foundational Explorations for a Normative Theory of Political Economy." *Constitutional Political Economy* 1 (1990): 67–99.

————. *Rationality and Dynamic Choice: Foundational Explorations.* Cambridge: Press Syndicate of the University of Cambridge, 1990.

————. "Sure-Thing Doubts." In *Decision, Probability, and Utility: Selected Readings,* ed. Peter Gärdenfors and Nils-Eric Sahlin, 245–69. Cambridge: Cambridge University Press, 1988.

McDougal, Walter A. *Heavens and the Earth.* New York: Basic Books, 1985.

McGinnis, Robert. Review of *The Calculus of Consent* (1962). *Annals of the American Academy of Political and Social Science* 346 (March 1963): 188.

McKean, Roland. *Efficiency in Government through Systems Analysis: With an Emphasis on Water Resources Development.* New York: Riley, 1958.

McKean, Roland N., and Melvin Anshen. "Limitations, Risks, and Problems." In *Program Budgeting: Program Analysis and the Federal Budget,* ed. David Novick, 285–307. Cambridge: Harvard University Press, 1965.

McKelvey, Richard D., and Peter C. Ordeshook. "A General Theory of the Calculus of Voting." In *Mathematical Applications in Political Science,* vol. 6, ed. James F. Herndon and Joseph L. Bernd. Charlottesville: University of Virginia Press, 1972.

McLean, Iain, Alistair McMillan, and Burt L. Monroe, eds. *The Theory of Committees and Elections,* 2nd rev. ed., with foreword by Ronald H. Coase. Amsterdam: Kluwer, 1998.

McNamara, Robert S. "In Retrospect: The Tragedy and Lessons of Vietnam." Interview by Brian Lamb, 23 April 1995. Booknotes Transcript, C-SPAN. Available at www.cspan.org or www.booknotes.org.

Meade, James E. Review of *The Calculus of Consent* (1962). *Economic Journal* 73 (March 1963): 101–4.

Medema, Steven G. "'Related Disciplines': The Professionalization of Public Choice Analysis." Unpublished paper presented at a history of economics conference, Duke University, Durham, N.C., spring 1999.

————. "'Related Disciplines': The Professionalization of Public Choice Analysis." *History of Political Economy Annual Supplement* 32 (2000): 289–323.

Melman, Seymore. *The Defense Economy: Conversion of Industries and Occupations to Civilian Needs.* New York: Praeger, 1970.

————. *Our Depleted Society.* New York: Rinehart and Winston, 1965.

————. *Pentagon Capitalism: The Political Economy of War.* New York: McGraw Hill, 1970.

————. *The Permanent War Economy: American Capitalism in Decline.* New York: Simon and Schuster, 1974.

Mendelson, Everett, Merritt Roe Smith, and Peter Weingart, eds. *Science, Technology and the Military.* 2 vols. Dordrecht: Kluwer Academic Publishers, 1988.

Merriam, Charles E. "Political Science in the United States." In *Contemporary*

Political Science: A Survey of Methods, Research and Teaching, 233–48. Paris: Unesco, 1950.

Merton, Robert K. "A Note on Science and Democracy." *Journal of Legal and Political Sociology* 1 (1942): 116.

Milgate, Murray, and Shannon C. Stimson. "The Figure of Smith: Dugald Stewart and the Propagation of Smithian Economics." *European Journal of the History of Economic Thought* 3, no. 2 (summer 1996): 225–53.

Mill, J. S. *On Liberty*. New York: Penguin Books, 1984.

Miller, Gary J. "The Impact of Economics on Contemporary Political Science." *Journal of Economy Literature* 35 (September 1997): 1173–1204.

Miller, L., et al. "Operations Research and Policy Analysis at RAND, 1968–1988." RAND N-2937-RC (April 1989).

Mini, Piero V. *Philosophy and Economics: The Origins and Development of Economic Theory*. Gainesville: University Presses of Florida, 1974.

Mirowski, Philip. *Machine Dreams: Economics Becomes a Cyborg Science*. Cambridge: Cambridge University Press, 2002.

———. *More Heat Than Light: Economics as Social Physics, Physics as Nature's Economics*. Cambridge: Cambridge University Press, 1989.

Mirowski, Philip, and Wade Hands. "A Budget of Paradoxes: The Postwar Stabilization of American Neoclassical Price Theory." Paper presented to the conference "Transformation of American Postwar Economics," Duke University, Durham, N.C., April 1997.

Mishan, E. J. *Cost-Benefit Analysis: An Introduction*. New York: Praeger, 1971.

———. *Welfare Economics: An Assessment*. Amsterdam: North-Holland Publishing, 1969.

———. *Welfare Economics: Ten Introductory Essays*, 2nd ed. New York: Random House, 1964.

Mitchell, William C. "The Shape of Political Theory to Come: From Political Sociology to Political Economy." In *Politics and the Social Sciences*, ed. Seymour Martin Lipset, 101–36. New York: Oxford University Press, 1969.

———. "Virginia, Rochester, and Bloomington: Twenty-Five Years of Public Choice and Political Science." *Public Choice* 56 (1982): 101–19.

Mizuta, Hiroshi, and Chuhei Sugiyama, eds. *Adam Smith: International Perspectives*. New York: St. Martin's Press, 1993.

Mo, Terry. "On the Scientific Status of Rational Choice Theory." *American Journal of Political Science* 23, no. 1 (February 1979): 215–41.

Mok, Ka Ho. "Impact of Globalization: A Study of Quality Assurance Systems of Higher Education in Hong Kong and Singapore." *Comparative Education Review* 44, no. 2 (May 2000): 148–74.

Mongin, Phillippe. "Value Judgements and Value Neutrality in Economics: A Perspective from Today." *Centre for Philosophy of Natural and Social Science*, Discussion Paper Series 60102 (December 2001): 18–28.

Monroe, Kristen Renwick, ed. *Contemporary Political Theory*. Berkeley: University of California Press, 1997.

———. *The Economic Approach to Politics: A Critical Reassessment.* New York: HarperCollins, 1991.

Moore, Arnold B. "Setting the Record Straight about CNA." *Armed Forces Journal International* 113, no. 5 (January 1976): 26–27.

Moos, S. "Laissez-Faire, Planning and Ethics." *Economic Journal* 55 (April 1945): 17–27.

Morgan, Mary. *The History of Econometric Ideas.* Cambridge: Cambridge University Press, 1990.

Mueller, Dennis C. "Public Choice: A Survey." *Journal of Economic Literature* 14, no. 2 (June 1976): 395–433.

———. *Public Choice II.* New York: Cambridge University Press, 1989.

Mueller, Dennis C., ed. *Perspectives on Public Choice: A Handbook.* Cambridge: Cambridge University Press, 1997.

Murphy, C. J. V. "The Education of a Defense Secretary." *Fortune*, May 1962, 102.

Murphy, James Bernard. "Rational Choice Theory as Social Physics." *Critical Review* 9, no. 1–2 (winter–spring 1995): 155–74.

Muzzio, Douglas, and Gerald De Maoi. "Formal theory and Prospects of Policy Science." In *Handbook of Political Theory and Policy Science*, ed. Edward Bryan Portis and Michael B. Levy, 127–45. New York: Greenwood Press, 1988.

Myint, Hla. *Theories of Welfare Economics.* Cambridge: Harvard University Press, 1948.

Nasar, Sylvia. *A Beautiful Mind: A Biography of John Forbes Nash, Jr., Winner of the Nobel Prize in Economics.* New York: Simon and Schuster, 1998.

Nelson, Robert H. "The Economics Profession and the Making of Public Policy." *Journal of Economic Literature* 25 (March 1987): 49–91.

von Neumann, John. *The Computer and the Brain.* New Haven: Yale University Press, 1958.

von Neumann, John, and Oskar Morgenstern. *Theory of Games and Economic Behavior.* Princeton: Princeton University Press, 1944.

Newlon, Daniel H. "The Role of the NSF in the Spread of Economic Ideas." In *The Spread of Economic Ideas*, ed. D. C. Colander and A. W. Coats, 195–228. Cambridge: Cambridge University Press, 1989.

Nichols Jr., James H., and Colin Wright. *From Political Economy to Economics and Back?* San Francisco: ICS Press, 1990.

Niehans, Jürg. *A History of Economic Theory: Classic Contributions, 1720–1980.* Baltimore: Johns Hopkins University Press, 1990.

Niskanen, William A. *Bureaucracy and Representative Government.* New York: Aldine-Atherton, 1971.

North, Douglass. "Institutions, Ideology, and Economic Performance." *Cato Journal* 11, no. 3 (1992): 477–88.

———. *Structure and Change in Economic History.* New York: Norton, 1981.

Novick, David, "Beginning of Military Cost Analysis 1952–1961." Talk presented at Science Applications, Inc., Los Angeles, 9 January 1979.

Nozick, Robert. *Anarchy, State, and Utopia.* Oxford: Basil Blackwell, 1974.
———. *The Nature of Rationality.* Princeton: Princeton University Press, 1993.
Okin, Susan Moller. "Reason and Feeling in Thinking about Justice." *Ethics* 99 (January 1989): 240–49.
Olson Jr., Mancur. *The Logic of Collective Action.* Cambridge: Harvard University Press, 1965.
———. "The Plan and Purpose of a Social Report." *Public Interest* 15 (Spring 1969): 85–97.
———. "The Relationship between Economics and the Other Social Sciences: The Province of a 'Social Report.'" In *Politics and the Social Sciences,* ed. Seymour Martin Lipset, 137–62. New York: Oxford University Press, 1969.
———. Review of *The Calculus of Consent* (1962). *American Economic Review* 52 (December 1962): 1217–18.
Olson Jr., Mancur, and Christopher K. Clague. "Dissent in Economics: The Convergence of Extremes." *Social Research* 38, no. 4 (winter 1971): 751–76.
Oncken, August. *Adam Smith and Immanuel Kant. Der Einklang und das Wechselverhältnis ihrer Lehren über Sitte, Staat und Wirtschaft, 1, Abt. Thik und Politik.* Leipzig, 1877.
Ordeshook, Peter C. "Engineering or Science: What is the Study of Politics?" *Critical Review* 9, no. 1–2 (winter–spring 1995): 175–88.
Orlands, Harold. "Academic Social Scientists and the Presidency." *Minerva* 24, nos. 2–3 (summer–autumn 1986): 172–204.
Orwell, George. *Nineteen Eighty-Four.* New York: Harcourt, Brace and Word, 1949.
Ostrom, Vincent. *The Intellectual Crisis in American Public Administration,* rev. ed. Tuscaloosa: University of Alabama Press, 1974.
P., C. M. Review of *The Calculus of Consent* (1962). *Ethics* 75 (October 1963): 65–68.
Palmer, Gregory. *The McNamara Strategy and the Vietnam War: Program Budgeting in the Pentagon, 1960–1968.* Westport, Conn.: Greenwood Press, 1978.
Pareto, Vilfredo. *Manual of Political Economy,* ed. A. S. Schwier and A. N. Page, trans. A. S. Schwier. New York: Augustus M. Kelley, 1971.
———. "On the Economic Principle." *International Economic Papers* 3 (1953): 180–96.
Parry, Albert. "Why Should We Have Been Surprised?" *Reporter,* 31 October 1957.
Pattanaik, Prasanta K. "Some Paradoxes of Preference Aggregation." In *Perspectives on Public Choice: A Handbook,* ed. Dennis C. Mueller, 215–21. Cambridge: Cambridge University Press, 1997.
Pattanaik, Prasanta K., and Kotaro Suzumura. "Rights, Welfarism and Social Choice." *American Economic Review* 84, no. 2 (May 1994): 435–39.
Paul, Ellen Frankel. *Moral Revolution and Economic Science: The Demise of*

Laissez-faire in Nineteenth-Century British Political Economy. London: Greenwood Press, 1979.

"Pentagon Considers Boosting Civilian Role in Procuring Weapons." *Wall Street Journal,* 19 March 1963, 1.

The Pentagon Papers. By Neil Sheehan, Hedrick Smith, E. W. Kenworthy, and Fox Butterfield. New York: Bantam Books, 1971.

The Pentagon Papers: The Defense Department History of United States Decisionmaking on Vietnam. 5 vols. Boston: Beacon Press, 1971–72.

Persky, Joseph. "The Ethology of *Homo Economicus.*" *Journal of Economic Perspectives* 9, no. 2 (spring 1995): 221–31.

Pigou, A. C. *The Economics of Welfare,* 4th ed. London: Macmillan, 1952.

"Planning-Programming-Budgeting: Initial Memorandum." Prepared by the Subcommittee on National Security and International Operations, Committee on Government Operations, U.S. Senate, 1967, 3, bound in *Planning Programming Budgeting.* Subcommittee on National Security and International Operations, Committee on Government Operations U.S. Senate, 91st Cong. Washington, D.C.: Government Printing Office, 1970.

Pocock, J. G. A. "Authority and Property: The Question of Liberal Origins." In *Virtue Commerce and History: Essays on Political Thought and History, Chiefly in the Eighteenth Century,* 51–72. Cambridge: Cambridge University Press, 1985.

——. "Cambridge Paradigms and Scotch Philosophers: A Study of the Relations between the Civic Humanist and the Civil Jurisprudential Interpretation of Eighteenth-Century Social Thought." In *Wealth and Virtue,* ed. Istvan Hont and Michael Ignatieff, 235–52. Cambridge: Cambridge University Press, 1983.

——. *The Machiavellian Moment: Florentine Political Thought and the Atlantic Republican Tradition.* Princeton: Princeton University Press, 1975.

——. *Political Language and Time: Essays on Political Thought and History.* Chicago: University of Chicago Press, 1960.

——. *Virtue, Commerce, and History: Essays on Political Thought and History, Chiefly in the Eighteenth Century.* Cambridge: Cambridge University Press, 1985.

Pocock, J. G. A., ed. *The Varieties of British Political Thought, 1500–1800.* Cambridge: Cambridge University Press, 1993.

Popkin, Samuel L. *The Rational Peasant: The Political Economy of Rural Society in Vietnam.* Berkeley: University of California Press, 1979.

Popper, Karl R. *The Open Society and Its Enemies.* 2 vols. London: George Routledge, 1945.

Porter, Theodore M. "Interpreting the Triumph of Mathematical Economics." In *Non-natural Social Science: Reflecting on the Enterprise of More Heat Than Light,* ed. Neil de Marchi. *History of Political Economy* 25 (ann. supp.). Durham: Duke University Press, 1993.

——. "Objectivity as Standardization: The Rhetoric of Impersonality in Measurement, Statistics, and Cost-Benefit Analysis." *Annals of Scholarship* 9 (1992): 19–59.

———. "Quantification and the Accounting Ideal in Science." *Social Studies of Science* 22 (1992): 633–51.

———. *Trust in Numbers: The Pursuit of Objectivity in Science and Public Life.* Princeton: Princeton University Press, 1995.

Portis, Edward Bryan, and Michael B. Levy, eds. *Handbook of Political Theory and Policy Science.* New York: Greenwood Press, 1988.

Posner, Richard. "Wealth Maximization and Judicial Decision-Making." *International Review of Law and Economics* 4 (1984): 131–35.

Poundstone, William. *Prisoner's Dilemma: John von Neumann, Game Theory, and the Puzzle of the Bomb.* New York: Doubleday, 1992.

Prados, John. *The Soviet Estimate: U.S. Intelligence Analysis and Russian Military Strength.* New York: Dial Press, 1982.

"Preparing for Terror." *Economist,* 30 November 2002, 11.

Pressman, Steven, and Gale Summerfield. "The Economic Contributions of Amartya Sen." *Review of Political Economy* 12, no. 1 (2000): 89–113.

Przeworski, Adam. *Capitalism and Social Democracy.* Cambridge: Cambridge University Press, 1985.

Quade, Edward S. *Analysis for Military Decisions.* Chicago: Rand McNally, 1964.

Rawls, John. "Concepts of Distributional Equity: Some Reasons for the Maximin Criterion." *American Economic Association* 64 (May 1974): 141–46.

———. "Constitutional Liberty and the Concept of Justice" (1963). In *John Rawls: Collected Papers,* ed. Samuel Freeman, 73–95. Cambridge: Harvard University Press, 1999.

———. "Justice as Fairness" (1958). In *John Rawls: Collected Papers,* ed. Samuel Freeman, 47–72. Cambridge: Harvard University Press, 1999.

———. "Justice as Fairness: Political Not Metaphysical." *Philosophy and Public Affairs* 14, no. 3 (summer 1985): 223–51.

———. "Kantian Constructivism in Moral Theory" (1980). In *John Rawls: Collected Papers,* ed. Samuel Freeman, 303–58. Cambridge: Harvard University Press, 1999.

———. "Some Reasons for the Maximin Criterion" (1974). In *John Rawls: Collected Papers,* ed. Samuel Freeman, 225–31. Cambridge: Harvard University Press, 1999.

———. *A Theory of Justice.* Cambridge: Harvard University Press, 1971.

Reder, Melvin Warren. *Studies in the Theory of Welfare Economics.* New York: Columbia University Press, 1947.

Redford, Emmette S. "Reflections on a Discipline." *American Political Science Review* 54, no. 4 (December 1961): 755–79.

Reisman, David. *The Political Economy of James Buchanan.* London: Macmillan, 1990.

Report for the Study of the Ford Foundation on Policy and Program. Detroit: Ford Foundation, 1949.

Reyerson, James. "Games People Play: Rational Choice with a Human Face." *Linguafranca* 9, no. 6 (December–January 2002): 60–71.

Ricci, David M. *The Tragedy of Political Science: Politics, Scholarship and Democracy.* New Haven: Yale University Press, 1984.

Rider, Robin. "Operations Research and Game Theory: Early Connections." In *Toward a History of Game Theory*, ed. E. Roy Weintraub, 225–40. *History of Political Economy* 24 (ann. supp.). Durham: Duke University Press, 1992.

Riker, William H. *The Art of Political Manipulation.* New Haven: Yale University Press, 1986.

———. "Causes of Events." *Journal of Philosophy* 56 (1959): 281–92.

———. *Democracy in the United States.* New York: Macmillan, 1953.

———. "Events and Situations." *Journal of Philosophy* 54 (1957): 57–70.

———. "The Future of a Science of Politics." *American Behavioral Scientist* 21 (1997): 11–38.

———. *Liberalism against Populism: A Confrontation between the Theory of Democracy and Social Choice.* San Francisco: Freeman, 1982.

———. "The Paradox of Voting and Congressional Rules for Voting on Amendments." *American Political Science Review* 52 (1958): 349–66.

———. Review of *The Calculus of Consent* (1962). *Midwest Journal of Political Science* 6 (November 1962): 408–11.

———. *The Strategy of Rhetoric: Campaigning for the American Constitution.* New Haven: Yale University Press, 1996.

———. "A Test of the Adequacy of the Power Index." *Behavioral Science* 4 (1959): 120–31.

———. *The Theory of Political Coalitions.* New York: Yale University Press, 1963.

———. "The Two-Party System and Duverger's law: An Essay on the History of Political Science." *American Political Science Review* 82 (1982): 753–66.

———. William H. Riker Papers. Department of Rare Books and Special Collections, University of Rochester, Rochester, N.Y.

Riker, William H., ed. *Agenda Formation.* Ann Arbor: University of Michigan Press, 1993.

Riker, William H., and Peter C. Ordeshook. *An Introduction to Positive Political Theory: A Synthesis and Exposition of Current Trends in Political Theory based on Axiomatic and Deductive Reasoning.* Englewood Cliffs, N.J.: Prentice Hall, 1973.

———. "A Theory of the Calculus of Voting." *American Political Science Review* 67 (1968): 753–66.

Riker, William H., and Ronald Schaps. "Disharmony in Federal Government." *Behavioral Science* 2 (1957): 276–90.

Robbins, Lionel C. *Economic Planning and International Order.* London: Macmillan, 1937.

———. *An Essay on the Nature and Significance of Economic Science.* London: Macmillan, 1932.

———. *An Essay on the Nature and Significance of Economic Science,* 2nd ed. London: Macmillan, 1935.

Roberts, Chalmers M. "Gaither Report Said to Picture U.S. in Grave Danger."

Washington Post and Times Herald, 20 December 1957, reprinted in the *Congressional Quarterly Weekly Report* 15, no. 52 (December 1957): 1328–30.

Rockefeller Brothers Fund. *International Security: The Military Aspect.* January 1958.

Rockefeller Panel Report. *Prospect for America.* Garden City, N.Y.: Doubleday, 1961.

Roemer, John. *A General Theory of Exploitation and Class.* Cambridge: Harvard University Press, 1982.

Roll, Eric. *A History of Economic Thought,* 4th ed. Homewood, Ill.: Richard D. Irwin, 1974.

Roman, Peter J. *Eisenhower and the Missile Gap.* Ithaca: Cornell University Press, 1995.

Roos, J. P. *Welfare Theory and Social Policy: A Study in Policy Science.* Helsinki: Societas Scientiarum Fennica, 1973.

Rosen, Allen D. *Kant's Theory of Justice.* Ithaca: Cornell University Press, 1993.

Ross, Dorothy. *The Origins of American Social Science.* Cambridge: Cambridge University Press, 1991.

Ross, Ian. "Adam Smith (1723–90): A Biographical Sketch." In *Adam Smith: International Perspectives,* ed. Hiroshi Mizuta and Chuhei Sugiyama, 1–25. New York: St. Martin's Press, 1993.

———. *The Life of Adam Smith.* Oxford: Clarendon Press, 1995.

Rothenberg, Jerome. "Conditions for a Social Welfare Function." *Journal of Political Economy* 61, no. 5 (October 1953): 389–405.

Rothschild, Emma. *Economic Sentiments: Adam Smith, Condorcet, and the Enlightenment.* Harvard: Harvard University Press, 2001.

Rothschild, K. W. "The Meaning of Rationality: A Note on Professor Lange's Article." *Review of Economic Studies* 14, no. 1 (1945–46): 50–52.

Rousseau, Jean-Jacques. *The Social Contract,* trans. Maurice Cranston. Harmondsworth, England: Penguin, 1968.

Rowen, Henry. *National Security and the American Economy in the 1960's.* Study Paper No. 18, Joint Economic Committee, 86th Cong., 2d Sess. Washington, D.C.: Government Printing Office, 1960.

Rowley, Charles K. Introduction to *Public Choice Theory,* ed. Charles K. Rowley, 1:xiv–xvi. Brookfield, Vt.: Edward Elgar, 1993.

———. *The Right to Justice.* Cheltenham: Edward Elgar, 1992.

Rowley, Charles K., ed. *Social Choice Theory.* 3 vols. Hants, England: Edward Elgar, 1993.

Rowley, Charles K., and Alan T. Peacock. *Welfare Economics: A Liberal Restatement.* London: Martin Robertson, 1975.

Rowley, Charles K., and M. Vachris. *Why Democracy in the U.S. May Not Produce Efficient Results.* Fairfax, Va.: Center for the Study of Public Choice, George Mason University, 1990.

Russell, Bertrand. *Introduction to Mathematical Philosophy,* 2nd ed. London: Allen and Unwin, 1920.

Samuelson, Paul A. *Foundations of Economic Analysis.* Cambridge: Harvard University Press, 1948.

Sandel, Michael J. Introduction to *Liberalism and Its Critics,* ed. Michael J. Sandel. Oxford: Blackwell, 1984.

———. *Liberalism and the Limits of Justice.* Cambridge: Cambridge University Press, 1982.

Satz, Debra, and John Ferejohn. "Rational Choice and Social Theory." *Journal of Philosophy* 91, no. 2 (1994): 71–87.

Savage, Leonard J. "The Sure-Thing Principle" (1961). In *Decision, Probability, and Utility: Selected Readings,* ed. Peter Gärdenfors and Nils-Eric Sahlin, 245–69. Cambridge: Cambridge University Press, 1988.

Schabas, Margaret. *A World Ruled by Number: William Stanley Jevons and the Rise of Mathematical Economics.* Princeton: Princeton University Press, 1990.

Schelling, Thomas. *Strategy of Conflict.* Cambridge: Cambridge University Press, 1960.

Schick, Frederic. "Dutch Bookies and Money Pumps." *Journal of Philosophy* 83, no. 2 (February 1986): 112–19.

Schilling, Warner R., Paul Y. Hammond, and Glenn H. Snyder. *Strategy, Politics and Defense Budgets.* New York: Columbia University Press, 1962.

Schlesinger, James R. *The Political Economy of National Security: A Study of the Economic Aspects of the Contemporary Power Struggle.* New York: Praeger, 1960.

Schnepp, Gerald J. "Social Choice and Individual Values." *American Catholic Sociological Review* 12 (1952): 243.

Schochet, Gordon J. "Why Should History Matter? Political Theory and the History of Discourse." In *The Varieties of British Political Thought, 1500–1800,* ed. J. G. A. Pocock, 321–57. Cambridge: Cambridge University Press, 1993.

Schofield, Norman. "Rational Choice and Political Economy." *Critical Review* 9, nos. 1–2 (winter–spring 1995): 189–90.

Schotter, Andrew. "Oskar Morgenstern's Contribution to the Development of the Theory of Games." In *Toward a History of Game Theory,* ed. E. Roy Weintraub, 15–28. Durham: Duke University Press, 1992.

Schumpeter, Joseph A. *Capitalism, Socialism, and Democracy.* London: Allen and Unwin, 1943.

———. *History of Economic Analysis,* ed. Elizabeth Boody Schumpeter. New York: Oxford University Press, 1954.

Seabright, Paul. "Social Choice and Social Theories." *Philosophy and Public Affairs* 18, no. 4 (fall 1989): 365–87.

Searle, John. "Rationality and Realism: What Is at Stake?" *Dædalus* 122, no. 4 (fall 1993): 55–84.

"Secretary of Defense McNamara: 'We Can Afford Whatever Is Necessary.'" *Armed Forces Management,* 12 November 1965, 35–37.

"Secretary's Authority Reaches Peak." *Missiles and Rockets* 12 (March 1993): 74–75.

Seidelman, Raymond. *Disenchanted Realists: Political Science and the American Crisis, 1884–1984.* Albany: State University of New York Press, 1985.

Seidler, Michael J. "Pufendorf, Sociality and the Modern State." *History of Political Thought* 17, no. 3 (1996): 354–78.

Sen, Amartya. "Choice Functions and Revealed Preference." *Review of Economic Studies* 38 (1971): 304–17.

———. *Collective Choice and Social Welfare.* San Francisco: Holden-Day, 1970.

———. "The Impossibility of a Paretian Liberal." *Journal of Political Economy* 78, no. 1 (1970): 152–57.

———. "Internal Consistency of Choice." *Econometrica* 61, no. 3 (May 1993): 495–521.

———. "Liberty and Social Choice." *Journal of Philosophy* 80, no. 1 (January 1983): 4–28.

———. "Liberty, Unanimity and Rights." *Economica,* n.s., 43 (August 1976): 217–45.

———. "Maurice Dobb." In *The New Palgrave: A Dictionary of Economics,* ed. J. Eatwell, M. Milgate, and P. Newman, 2:910–12. London: Macmillan, 1987.

———. "Maximization and the Act of Choice." *Econometrica* 65, no. 4 (July 1997): 745–79.

———. "Minimal Liberty." *Economica,* n.s., 59 (May 1992): 139–59.

———. *On Ethics and Economics.* Oxford: Basil Blackwell, 1987.

———. "Rationality and Social Choice." *The American Economic Review* 85, no. 1 (March 1995): 1–24.

———. "Rational Behaviour." In *The New Palgrave: A Dictionary of Economics,* ed. J. Eatwell, M. Milgate and P. Newman, 4:68–76. London: Macmillan, 1987.

———. "Rational Fools: A Critique of the Behavioral Foundation of Economic Theory." In *Choice Welfare and Measurement,* 84–106. Oxford: Basil Blackwell, 1982.

———. *"Social Choice and Justice:* A Review Article." *Journal of Economic Literature* 23 (December 1985): 1764–76.

Shapiro, Ian. *Political Criticism.* Berkeley: University of California Press, 1990.

Shapley, Deborah. *Promise and Power: The Life and Times of Robert McNamara.* Boston: Little, Brown, 1993.

Shapley, Harlow. "Satellite Hysteria." *Nation,* 26 October 1957.

Shapley, L. S., and M. Shubik. "A Method of Evaluating the Distribution of Power in a Committee System." *American Political Science Review* 54 (1954): 787–92.

"Sharp Military Civilian Conflict in Pentagon Being Pointed Up by Study of TFX Award." *Wall Street Journal,* 14 March 1963, 4.

Shepherd, Christine, M. "Newtonianism in Scottish Universities in the Seventeenth Century." In *The Origins and Nature of the Scottish Enlightenment,* ed. R. H. Campbell and A. S. Skinner, 65–85. Edinburgh: John Donald, 1982.

Shepsle, Kenneth. *The Giant Jigsaw Puzzle.* Chicago: University of Chicago Press, 1978.

Shepsle, Kenneth, and Barry Weingast. "Structure-Induced Equilibrium and Legislative Choice." *Public Choice* 37, no. 3 (1981): 503–20.

Sherry, Michael. *In the Shadow of War: The United States since the 1930s.* New Haven: Yale University Press, 1995.

Simon, Herbert. "Two Heads Are Better Than One: The Collaboration between AI and OR." *Interfaces* 17 (July 1987): 8–15.

Simons, Henry C. *Economic Policy for a Free Society.* Chicago: University of Chicago Press, 1948.

Simpson, Christopher, ed. *Universities and Empire: Money and Politics in the Social Science during the Cold War.* New York: New Press, 1998.

Skinner, Andrew S. "Adam Smith: Philosophy and Science." *Scottish Journal of Political Economy* 19 (1972): 307–19.

———. *A System of Social Science: Papers Relating to Adam Smith,* 2nd ed. Oxford: Clarendon Press, 1996.

Skinner, Andrew S., and Thomas Wilson, eds. *Essays on Adam Smith.* Oxford: Clarendon Press, 1975.

Smith, Adam. *An Inquiry into the Nature and Causes of the Wealth of Nations.* 2 vols. Ed. R. H. Campbell and A. S. Skinner. Indianapolis: Liberty Fund, 1976.

———. *Lectures on Jurisprudence,* ed. R. L. Meek, D. D. Raphael, and P. G. Stein. Indianapolis: Liberty Classics, 1978.

———. *Lectures on Rhetoric and Belles Lettres,* ed. J. C. Bryce. Oxford: Oxford University Press, 1983.

———. "The Principles Which Lead and Direct Philosophical Enquiries; Illustrated by the History of Astronomy." In *Essays on Philosophical Subjects,* ed. W. P. D. Wightman and J. C. Bryce. Indianapolis: Liberty Classics, 1982.

———. *The Theory of Moral Sentiments,* ed. D. D. Raphael and A. L. Macfie. Indianapolis: Liberty Fund, 1982.

Smith, Bruce L. R. *The RAND Corporation.* Cambridge: Harvard University Press, 1966.

Smith, James A. "Think Tanks and the Politics of Ideas." In *The Spread of Economic Ideas,* ed. D. C. Colander and A. W. Coats, 175–94. Cambridge: Cambridge University Press, 1989.

Smith, John Maynard. *Evolution and the Theory of Games.* Cambridge: Cambridge University Press, 1976.

———. *Mathematical Ideas in Biology.* London: Cambridge University Press, 1968.

Smith, Mark C. *Social Science in the Crucible: The American Debate over Objectivity and Purpose, 1918–1941.* Durham: Duke University Press, 1994.

Smith, Richard Austin. "The $7-Billion Contract That Changed the Rules." Parts I and II. *Fortune,* March–April 1963.

Smith, Rogers M. "The Arms of Liberalism." In *Liberalism and American Constitutional Law.* Cambridge: Harvard University Press, 1985.

———. "If Politics Matters: Implications for New Institutionalism." *Studies in American Political Development* 6 (1992): 1–36.

———. "Still Blowing in the Wind: The American Quest for a Democratic, Scientific Political Science." *Dædalus; American Academic Culture in Transformation: Fifty Years, Four Disciplines* 126, no. 1 (winter 1997): 253–88.

Smithies, Arthur. "Economic Welfare and Policy." In *Economics and Public Policy*. Washington, D.C.: Brookings Institute, 1955.

Snead, David L. *The Gaither Committee, Eisenhower, and the Cold War*. Columbus: Ohio State University Press, 1999.

"Social Sciences: Expanded Role Urged for Defense Department." *Science*, 21 April 1967.

Solberg, Winton U., and Robert W. Tomilson. "Academic McCarthyism and Keynesian Economics: The Bowen Controversy at the University of Illinois." *History of Political Economy* 29, no. 1 (spring 1997): 55–82.

Solow, Robert M. "How Did Economics Get That Way and What Way Did It Get?" *Dædalus; American Academic Culture in Transformation: Fifty Years, Four Disciplines* 126, no. 1 (winter 1997): 39–58.

Somers, Harold M. "Social Choice and Individual Values." *Journal of Political Economy* 60 (1952): 170–71.

Somit, Albert, and Joseph Tanenhaus. *The Development of Political Science: From Burgess to Behavioralism*. Boston: Allyn and Bacon, 1967.

Spengler, J. "Adam Smith and Society's Decision-makers." In *Essays on Adam Smith*, ed. A. S. Skinner and T. Wilson, 390–414. Oxford: Clarendon Press, 1975.

Spiegel, Henry W. "Adam Smith's Heavenly City." In *Adam Smith and Modern Political Economy: Bicentennial Essays on* The Wealth of Nations. Ames: Iowa State University Press, 1979.

Spinoza, Benedict. *A Treatise on Politics*, trans. William Maccall. London: Holyoake, 1854.

Stein, Herbert. "The Washington Economics Industry." *American Economic Review* 76, no. 2 (May 1986): 1–9.

Steuart, Sir James. *An Inquiry into the Principles of Political Oeconomy*. 2 vols. Ed. A. S. Skinner. Edinburgh: Oliver and Boyd, 1966.

Steward, Dugald. "Account of the Life and Writings of Adam Smith, LL.D." In *Adam Smith, Essays on Philosophical Subjects*, ed. W. P. D. Wightman and J. C. Bryce. Oxford: Clarendon Press, 1980.

Stewart, Mark. "Army R & D Should Pay Off—But Hasn't." *Armed Forces Journal International* 112 (August 1975): 24–26.

Stigler, G. J. "The Development of Utility Theory." Parts I and II. *Journal of Political Economy* 58 (1950): 307–27, 373–96.

Stiglitz, Joseph. *Globalization and Its Discontents*. New York: Norton, 2002.

Stimson, Shannon C. "Economic Liberalism." Unpublished manuscript, 1996.

Stockfisch, J. A. *The Intellectual Foundations of Systems Analysis*. Santa Monica: RAND, 1987.

Stokey, Edith, and Richard Zeckhauser. *A Primer for Policy Analysis*. New York: Norton, 1978.

Strotz, Robert H. "How Income Ought to be Distributed: A Paradox in Distributive Ethics." *Journal of Political Economy* 66 (June 1958): 189–205.

Sugden, Robert. "Rational Choice: A Survey of Contributions from Economics and Philosophy." *Economic Journal* 101 (July 1991): 751–85.

———. "Social choice and Individual Liberty." In *Contemporary Economic Analysis,* ed. M. J. Artis and A. R. Robay, 243–71. London: Croon Helm, 1983.

Sugden, Robert, and Alan Williams. *The Principles of Practical Cost-Benefit Analysis*. Oxford: Oxford University Press, 1978.

Surányi-Unger, Theo. "Individual and Collective Wants." *Journal of Political Economy* 61, no. 1 (February 1948): 1–22.

"Sustaining Hope: Is the World Bank Turning Marxist?" *Economist*, 24 August 2002, 56.

Sutton, Francis X. "The Ford Foundation: The Early Years." *Dædalus* 116 (winter 1987): 41–49.

Suzumura, Kotaro. "Alternative Approaches to Libertarian Rights." In *Markets and Welfare*, ed. Kenneth J. Arrow, 215–42. London: Macmillan, 1991.

———. *Rational choice, Collective Decisions and Social Welfare*. Cambridge: Cambridge University Press, 1983.

Tarascio, Vincent J. "Vilfredo Pareto and Marginalism." *History of Political Economy* 4, no. 2 (fall 1972): 406–25.

Taylor, Charles. *Human Agency and Language*. Cambridge: Cambridge University Press.

Taylor, General Maxwell. *The Uncertain Trumpet*. New York: Harper, 1960.

Taylor, Overton H. *A History of Economic Thought: Social Ideals and Economic Theories From Quesnay to Keynes*. New York: McGraw-Hill, 1960.

Teichgraeber III, Richard. "Rethinking *Das Adam Smith Problem*." *Journal of British Studies* 20 (1981): 106–23.

Thomson, Herbert F. "Adam Smith's Philosophy of Science." *Quarterly Journal of Economics* 79 (1965): 212–33.

Thweatt, William O., ed. *Classical Political Economy: A Survey of Recent Literature*. Boston: Kluwer Academic Press, 1988.

de Tocqueville, Alexis. *Democracy in America*. New York: Vintage Books, 1990.

Tollison, R. D. "Public Choice and Legislation." *Virginia Law Review* 74 (1988): 339–71.

Trachtenberg, Marc. "Strategic Thought in America, 1952–1966." In *Writings on Strategy, 1961–1964, and Retrospectives*. New York: Garland, 1988.

Trotsky, L. D. *Soviet Economy in Danger*. New York: Pioneer Publishers, 1933.

Tuck, Richard. "The Imperfect History of Perfect Competition." Centre for History and Economics, Kings College, Cambridge University (April 1999).

Tullock, Gordon. *The Economics of Special Privilege and Rent-Seeking*. Boston: Kluwer Academic Press, 1980.

————. "Origins of Public Choice." In *The Makers of Modern Economics*, ed. Arnold Heertje, 3:122–40. Brookfield, Vt: Edward Elgar, 1997.

————. *The Politics of Bureaucracy*. Washington, D.C.: Public Affairs Press, 1965.

Tully, James, ed. *Meaning and Context: Quentin Skinner and his Critics*. Princeton: Princeton University Press, 1988.

Tversky, Amos, and Daniel Kahneman. "Rational Choice and the Framing of Decision." In *Decision Making, Descriptive, Normative, and Prescriptive Interactions*, ed. David E. Bell, Howard Raiffa, and Amos Tversky, 167–92. Cambridge: Cambridge University Press, 1998.

U.S. Senate, Permanent Subcommittee on Government Operations. *The TFX Contract Investigation: Hearings*. 88th Cong., 1st Sess., vols. 2 and 3, Parts 1–10. 1963.

Ulmer, Stanley S. "The Role of 'Costs' in Political Choice: A Review of James H. Buchanan and Gordon Tullock, *The Calculus of Consent*." *Conflict Resolution* 7, no. 2 (1963): 171–76.

UNESCO. *Contemporary Political Science: A Survey of Methods, Research and Teaching*. Paris: UNESCO, 1950.

Veblen, T. B. "Why Is Economics Not an Evolutionary Science. In *The Portable Veblen*, ed. M. Lerner, 215–40. New York: Viking Press, 1948.

Viner, Jacob. "The Intellectual History of Laissez Faire." *Journal of Law and Economics* 3 (1960): 45–69.

————. *The Role of Providence in the Social Order*. Philadelphia: American Philosophical Society, 1972.

Vines, Kenneth. Review of *The Calculus of Consent* (1962). *Journal of Politics* 25 (February 1963): 160–61.

Wagner, R. E. "The Calculus of Consent: A Wicksellian Retrospective." *Public Choice* 56 (1988): 153–66.

Wallis, W. Allen. "The Statistical Research Group, 1942–1945." *Journal of the American Statistical Association* 75, no. 370 (June 1980): 320–30.

Walras, Léon. *Elements of Pure Economics or The Theory of Social Wealth*, trans. William Jaffé. London: Allen and Unwin, 1954.

Wang, Jessica. *American Science in an Age of Anxiety: Scientists, Anticommunism and the Cold War*. Chapel Hill: University of North Carolina Press, 1999.

Ward, Benjamin. Review of *The Calculus of Consent* (1962). *Southern Economic Journal* 29, no. 4 (1963): 351–53.

Waszek, Norbert. "Adam Smith in Germany, 1776–1832." In *Adam Smith: International Perspectives*, ed. Hiroshi Mizuta and Chuhei Sugiyama, 163–80. New York: St. Martin's Press, 1993.

Weber, Max. *The Protestant Ethic and the Spirit of Capitalism*. London: Allen and Unwin, 1971.

————. "Science as a Vocation." In *From Max Weber*, ed. H. H. Gerth and C. W. Miles, 129–56. New York: Oxford University Press, 1972.

Weingast, Barry R. "The Political Foundations of Democracy and the Rule of Law." *American Political Science Review* 91, no. 2 (June 1997): 245–63.

Weingast, Barry R., and N. J. Moran. "Bureaucratic Discretion or Congressional Control." *Journal of Political Economy* 91 (1983): 765–800.
West, Edwin G. *Adam Smith and Modern Economics: From Market Behaviour to Public Choice.* Brookfield, Vt: Edward Elgar, 1990.
———. *Adam Smith: The Man and His Works.* Indianapolis: Liberty Press, 1976.
———. "Developments in the Literature of Adam Smith: An Evaluative Survey." In *Classical Political Economy: A Survey of Recent Literature,* ed. William O. Thweatt, 13–44. Norwell, Mass.: Kluwer, 1988.
Westbrook, Robert B. *John Dewey and American Democracy.* Ithaca: Cornell University Press, 1991.
White, General Thomas D. "Strategy and the Defense Intellectuals." *Saturday Evening Post,* 4 May 1963.
White, Michael. "Why Are There No Demand and Supply Curves in Jevons." *History of Political Economy* 21, no. 3 (1989): 425–56.
Wicksell, Knut. *Finanztheoretische Untersuchunger.* Jena: Gustav Fisher, 1896.
Wightman, W. P. D. "Adam Smith and the History of Ideas." In *Essays on Adam Smith,* ed. A. S. Skinner and T. Wilson, 44–67. Oxford: Clarendon Press, 1975.
Wildavsky, Aaron. "Planning-Programming-Budgeting: Rescuing Policy Analysis from PPBS." *Public Administration Review* 29, no. 2 (March–April 1969). Reprinted for the use by the Subcommittee on National Security and International Operations, 91st Cong. Washington, D.C.: Government Printing Office, 1969, 3–18.
———. "The Political Economy of Efficiency: Cost–Benefit Anaylsis, Systems Analysis, and Program and Budgeting." *Public Administration Review* 26, no. 4 (December 1966). Reprinted in *Planning Programming Budgeting,* Inquiry of the Subcommittee on National Security and International Operations, U.S. Senate. Washington, D.C.: Government Printing office, 1970, 614–36.
Wilde, D. J., and C. S. Beighter. *Foundations of Optimization.* Englewood Cliffs, N.J.: Prentice Hall, 1967.
Williams, John. *Hunting the Tiger (and Other Aspects of the Active Life).* Santa Monica: RAND, 1954.
Wilson, Edward O., Richard Rorty, and Paul R. Gross. "Is Everything Relative? A Debate on the Unity of Knowledge." *Wilson Quarterly* 22, no. 1 (1998): 14–50.
Wilson, Thomas, and Andrew S. Skinner, ed. *The Market and the State: Essays in Honour of Adam Smith.* Oxford: Clarendon Press, 1976.
Winch, Donald. "Adam Smith and the Liberal Tradition" (1988). In *Adam Smith,* ed. Knud Haakonssen, 359–77. Sydney: Ashgate Dartmouth, 1998.
———. "Adam Smith: Scottish Moral Philosopher as Political Economist." *Historical Journal* 35 (1991): 91–113.
———. *Adam Smith's Politics: An Essay in Historiographic Revision.* Cambridge: Cambridge University Press, 1978.
———. "Developments in the Literature on Adam Smith: An Evaluative Survey:

Comment." In *Classical Political Economy: A Survey of Recent Literature,* ed. William O. Thweatt, 45–52. Norwell, Mass.: Kluwer, 1988.

———. *Economics and Policy: A Historical Study.* London: Hodder and Stroughton, 1969.

———. *Riches and Poverty: An Intellectual History of Political Economy in Britain, 1750–1834.* Cambridge: Cambridge University Press, 1996.

Wise, David, and Thomas D. Ross. *The Invisible Government.* New York: Random House, 1964.

Wittgenstein, Ludwig. *On Certainty,* ed. G. E. M. Anscombe and G. H. von Wright. New York: Harper and Row, 1969.

———. *Philosophical Investigations,* 2nd ed. Trans. G. E. M. Anscombe. Oxford: Blackwell, 1953.

Wohlstetter, Albert. "The Delicate Balance of Terror." *Foreign Affairs* 37, no. 2 (January 1959): 211–34.

———. "Nuclear Sharing: NATO and the N+1 Country." *Foreign Affairs* 39, no. 3 (April 1961): 355–86.

Wohlstetter, Albert, F. S. Hoffman, R. J. Lutz, and H. S. Rowen. *Selection and Use of Strategic Air Bases.* Santa Monica: RAND, 1954.

Wood, Ellen Meiksins. "Rational Choice Marxism: Is the Game Worth the Candle." In *Rational Choice Marxism,* ed. Terrell Carver and Paul Thomas, 79–135. London: Macmillan, 1995.

Wright, Erik Olin. "What Is Analytical Marxism." In *Rational Choice Marxism,* ed. Terrell Carver and Paul Thomas, 11–30. London: Macmillan, 1995.

Wriglesworth, John. *Libertarian Conflict in Social Choice.* Cambridge: Cambridge University Press, 1994.

Zuckerman, Mortimer B. "Sheep, Wolves, and Reality." *U.S. News and World Report,* 16 December 2002, 59–60.

INDEX

Adorno, Theodor, 254

Air Force: Gaither Report emphasizing agenda of, 49; RAND having access to, 32; RAND systems analyses for, 40–46; satellite system proposal of, 33; and TFX fighter program, 65–67

Alchon, Guy, 31

Aldrich, John H., 187, 327n. 23

Allais, Maurice, 247

Almond, Gabriel, 12

Alsop, Stuart, 54

altruism: Arrow's impossibility theorem and, 110; Buchanan and Tullock on, 141; evolutionary biology on, 8

American Economics Association, 221

Anderson, Admiral, 65

Arendt, Hannah, 254

Arnold, Henry "Hap," 32

Arrow, Kenneth J.: "Behavior under Uncertainty and its Implications for Policy," 86; Buchanan and Tullock influenced by, 136–37; Cold War context of, 16, 125–26, 194; as Cold War defense intellectual, 85; on consumer demand function, 233; contributions to economics, 85–86, 170; at Cowles Commission, 85, 103, 123, 125; and criteria problem, 245; on decision theory in policy analysis, 245–46; democratic values supported by, 255; "A Difficulty in the Concept of Social Welfare," 124; and Enlightenment values, 88, 157, 195; "Extended Sympathy and the Possibility of Social Choice," 270; and Hicks's *Value and Capital*, 100, 124; on marginalism and rational choice theory, 230; Marxism opposed by, 19, 85, 90,

180; on maximization and rationality, 228; Nobel Prize for, 86, 116, 125; on Pareto optimality, 240, 241; and Popper, 21; professional trajectory of, 85; on prototypical preference profiles, 132; and RAND Corporation, 12, 76, 78, 85, 103, 125; rational choice as defined by, 100; "rational choice" coined by, 127; "Rational Choice Functions and Orderings," 233; and Rawls, 14, 251, 258, 270; and Riker, 79, 162; at seminar on rationality and justice, 258; social choice theory of, 12, 83; on socialism, 175, 183–84; top secret security clearance of, 85; on utilitarianism in economics, 340n. 27. See also *Social Choice and Individual Values*

Arrow's impossibility theorem, 102–16; in Arrow's Nobel prize announcement, 86; Cold War context of, 102–3, 112, 125–26; consequences of, 83–84; and democratic theory, 104, 111, 116, 117, 128, 131, 175; five conditions of, 111–16, 245–46; Harsanyi and, 260–61; on independence of irrelevant alternatives, 112, 115; individualism as premise in, 107, 111, 114, 122, 131; initial formulation in RAND report, 85, 103, 124; and marginalist economics, 83, 108–9, 110, 111, 132; on markets, 83, 106, 117, 119, 128, 131, 175; and moral relativism, 114, 116; and Pareto optimality, 241; policy analysis and, 245, 247–48; rationality in, 104, 108–10, 111, 116, 119, 122, 127, 132; reviewers on, 117–18; Riker and, 162, 172–73; and Sen's Paretian Liberal

Arrow's impossibility theorem (*continued*)
Paradox, 273–74, 275; as theoretically
anticipated, 84, 103–4, 122; three-person proof, 105–6; two-person, two
commodity case, 104–5; universality
assumed in, 106; welfare economics
and, 83, 87, 104–5, 106, 107–8, 111,
112, 113, 115–16, 117–22, 128; what
is unprecedented in, 122
artificial intelligence, 7
Augenstein, Bruno, 60

Barlow, Edward, 39, 40, 43, 302n. 34
Baumol, William J., 101
Bedeaux, Charles, 292
behavioral sciences. *See* social and behav-
ioral sciences
behaviorist approach in political science,
160, 161, 255
"Behavior under Uncertainty and its Impli-
cations for Policy" (Arrow), 86
Bell, Daniel, 291, 292
Bender, Thomas, 159, 160
beneficence, 215, 216, 281
Bentham, Jeremy, 259, 291–92
Bentley, Arthur, 177
Bergson, Abram, 103, 118, 119, 317n. 106
Berlin, Isaiah, 171–72, 173, 174
"Berlin's Division of Liberty" (MacPher-
son), 174
betrayal, 294–95
B-52 Stratofortress, 42
Binmore, Ken: commitment to rational
self-interest, 14, 277; on fairness, 286;
Game Theory and the Social Contract,
284–86; on individualism, 277; *Just
Playing*, 284, 285; on markets, 288; on
Marxism, 286; on maximin principle,
285–86; *Playing Fair*, 284; on rational
choice liberalism as antidote to communism and fascism, 289; and Rawls, 284,
285; Whiggish reformism of, 284, 285,
286
Bissell, Richard M., 52
Black, Duncan: on Arrow's use of "rationality," 127; Buchanan and Tullock
influenced by, 136–37; on democratic
decisionmaking and Arrow's impossibility theorem, 132; on mathematical
and literary language in economics,

126; "On the Rationale of Group Deci-
sion Making," 11, 123, 125; as outside
context of American national security,
78, 125; priority dispute with Arrow,
87, 122–28; in Public Choice Society,
12; RAND request for papers of, 125;
Riker and, 161; *The Theory of Committees and Elections*, 124, 125
Blackett, P. M. S., 311n. 187, 312n. 189
Blaug, Mark, 222
Bohemian Grove, 39
Bottome, Edgar M., 307n. 117
Bradley, Mark E., 65
Brecht, Arnold, 254
British Association for the Advancement of
Science, 221
Buchanan, James M.: Cold War context of,
16, 194; on corruption of economics,
202; on democratic decisionmaking as
due process, 338n. 113; democratic values supported by, 255; early writings
of, 135–36; end of partnership with
Tullock, 153; and Enlightenment values, 157, 195; on general equilibrium
economics, 149, 202; Hayek compared
with, 19; on individual liberty versus
social welfare, 276; on individuals as
ends in themselves, 152; on Keynesianism, 144, 194; on legal frameworks for
markets, 193; on mainstream American
economics, 144; on markets and collective decisions, 117; Marxism opposed
by, 143, 180; meets Tullock, 136; Nobel prize for, 152–53; on normative
consensus, 151–52; Olson on New Left
and, 144, 181, 185; and Popper, 21;
"Positive Economics, Welfare Economics, and Political Economy," 319n. 11;
Post-Socialist Political Economy, 133;
principle of self-interested action extended to politics by, 203–4; in Public
Choice Society, 12, 134, 145; on public
choice theory as interdisciplinary, 148;
public choice theory of, 12, 133–55;
Public Finance in Democratic Process,
146; *Public Principles of Public Debt:
A Defense and Restatement*, 136; "The
Pure Theory of Government Finance,"
135; and RAND Corporation, 12, 76,
78, 145; and Rawls, 149, 150–51, 258,

259; resigns from University of Virginia, 145, 321n. 37; and Adam Smith, 139, 141–42, 155, 194, 195, 198–205, 208, 211–12; "socialism is dead," 133, 153, 154; on the status quo, 152, 282. See also *Calculus of Consent, The*
budget constraints: Arrow's work contrasted with, 83, 109; in equimarginal principle, 225; in marginalist economics, 234, 246. *See also* constrained maximization
Bureau of the Budget, 73–74
Burke, Arleigh A., 55
Bush, George W., 1
Bush, Vannevar, 55

Calculus of Consent, The (Buchanan and Tullock): as canonical work of rational choice theory, 11–12, 78, 176; on constitutional design, 137–43, 199; in contractarian tradition, 138, 142; as drawing line between moral philosophy and political science, 140–41; Enlightenment insights in, 139; and Madison and the Founding Fathers, 138–39; on majority rule, 137, 140, 142, 143, 173; on normative judgments as derivable from objective analysis, 141, 142, 144–45; Public Choice Society discussions of, 146; reviews of, 137, 319n. 16; Riker's *The Theory of Political Coalitions* compared with, 167
California, University of, Berkeley, 74
Cannan, E., 197
"Can the Maximin Principle Serve as a Basis for Morality" (Harsanyi), 267
capitalism (free-market economics): balance between social justice and economic freedom in, 16; the capitalist spirit, 97, 99, 111; Gauthier on, 282–83; and Lange's postulate of rationality, 97, 98; rational choice theory linking democracy with, 4, 182–84; Riker on democracy and, 174; Schumpeter on survival of, 15, 16–17; self-interest associated with, 198; word dropping out of postwar social theory, 159. *See also* capitalist democracy; markets
Capitalism, Socialism, and Democracy (Schumpeter), 16, 182, 183

capitalist democracy: Arrow on social choice in, 83; Arrow's impossibility theorem and, 83, 85, 112, 116, 117, 122, 128, 130; Bush on, 1; concerns for persistence of, 2, 88–89, 134; and Enlightenment values, 88; rational choice liberalism providing conceptual foundation of, 2–4, 12–13, 15–16, 22–23, 159, 176–89, 296; as triumphant, 2, 84–85
case study approach in political science, 160, 161
categorical imperative, 19, 113
CED (Committee for Economic Development), 55–56, 62, 63
Center for the Advanced Study of the Behavioral Sciences (Stanford University), 78–79, 163
Center for the Study of Public Choice (Virginia Polytechnic Institute), 145
character: as contrasted with preferences as the defining features of an individual, 218
Chicago school of economic theory, 135
choice. *See* consumer choice; rational choice liberalism
Churchill, Winston, 33
citizenship: Arrow's conception of citizen sovereignty, 4, 107–8, 111, 112, 113, 114, 116, 131–32, 188, 241; Buchanan and Tullock on citizens' sovereignty, 140; changing language of sovereignty and, 4, 188; in classic republicanism, 256–57
civic humanist tradition, 257
Clague, Christopher K., 181
class conflict, 178
classic republicanism, 256–57
Coase, Ronald, 123
Cold War: Arrow's impossibility theorem and, 102–3, 112, 125–26; game theory in decisionmaking in, 7, 76; as ideological struggle, 1–2; as internal U.S. struggle, 30; the national security state in, 27–80; RAND Corporation in, 9–10, 30, 251–52; rational choice theory's role in, 2–4, 12–13, 15–16, 22–23, 154, 155, 158–60, 194, 251–52; and Adam Smith's espousal of freedom, 194–95; Western triumph in, 1, 84–85
Coleman, James, 8, 145

TFX fighter program, 65–67, 68, 309n. 151
Theory of Committees and Elections, The (Black), 124, 125
Theory of Games and Economic Behavior, The (von Neumann and Morgenstern), 6–7, 11, 76, 103, 117, 176, 228
Theory of Justice, A (Rawls), 258–73; and Harsanyi's utilitarianism, 258–70; as pivotal point in political theory, 14, 258, 290; rational choice theory and, 14, 149
Theory of Moral Sentiments (Smith): on aggregate outcomes as unintended consequences, 206, 208; competing traditions in, 198; naturalistic mode of explanation of, 205; on prudence, 215, 217, 218; on self-love, 214; sympathy and self-interest in, 195
Theory of Political Coalitions, The (Riker), 164–67; as canonical work of rational choice theory, 12, 164, 176; Downs influencing, 162, 165, 176; realism of, 166–67; written at Center for the Advanced Study of the Behavioral Sciences, 79, 163
Theory of Political Economy, The (Jevons), 224, 225
Thomas Jefferson Center for Studies in Political Economy and Social Philosophy, 136, 138, 320n. 22
Thünen, Johann Heinrich von, 223
Tillman, Betty, 145
time-motion studies, 244, 292
Tocqueville, Alexis de, 3
trade unions, 179–80
transitivity: in Arrow's impossibility theorem, 83, 104, 108, 110, 111, 113, 116, 119, 124; and Condorcet voting paradox, 103, 105, 119; in expected utility theory, 247; Houthakker's semi-transitivity, 232, 334n. 44; and means–end rationality, 292; motivations of requirement of, 239–40; in rational choice definition of rationality, 229, 296
Trinkl, Frank, 60
Trotsky, Leon, 94
trust, 294–95

Tuck, Richard, 178–79, 186
Tullock, Gordon: denied tenure at University of Virginia, 145, 321n. 37; end of partnership with Buchanan, 153; and Enlightenment values, 157; Marxism opposed by, 143, 180; meets Buchanan, 136; in Public Choice Society, 12, 134, 145; public choice theory of, 12, 133–55; Rawls contrasted with, 150–51; and Rawls's "Justice and the Theory of Constitutional Choice," 149. See also *Calculus of Consent, The*
Tversky, Amos, 8, 247
Tyler, Ralph W., 55

Ultimatum game, 296
United Kingdom, 173, 183
universalism: Dewey and Merton on, 88, 129, 130, 157; of economics for Arrow, 84, 86, 87, 90–96, 97, 100, 106, 116; of social science, 290
Urban Management Program (Stanford University), 75
utilitarianism: Arrow's impossibility theorem and, 84, 111, 113, 115, 116; basic principle of, 259; Buchanan on, 202; of Hardin, 279; least action principle in, 292; Rawls opposing, 258–70; Sen's Paretian Liberal Paradox and, 280
utility: the criteria problem, 42, 145, 244–45, 247; diminishing marginal, 225; interpersonal comparisons of, 100–102, 104–5, 115–16, 260–61; Jevons's principle of equimarginal, 223–29; value determined by, 230. *See also* expected utility theory; maximization; preferences
U-2 intelligence-gathering flights, 51–52, 57, 303n. 64

value, 221, 223, 224
Value and Capital (Hicks), 100, 124
Veblen, Thorstein, 99
veil of ignorance, 150–51, 262–63, 264, 265, 266
Vietnam War, 72, 75
Ville, J., 230, 233, 234
Virginia, University of, 136, 138, 145